REMEMBERING
OUR RELATIONS

CANADIAN HISTORY AND ENVIRONMENT SERIES

SERIES EDITOR: Alan MacEachern
ISSN 1925-3702 (Print) ISSN 1925-3710 (Online)

The Canadian History & Environment series brings together scholars from across the academy and beyond to explore the relationships between people and nature in Canada's past.

Alan MacEachern, Founding Director
NiCHE: Network in Canadian History & Environment
Nouvelle initiative canadienne en histoire de l'environnement
http://niche-canada.org

No. 1 · *A Century of Parks Canada, 1911–2011*
Edited by Claire Elizabeth Campbell

No. 2 · *Historical GIS Research in Canada*
Edited by Jennifer Bonnell and Marcel Fortin

No. 3 · *Mining and Communities in Northern Canada: History, Politics, and Memory*
Edited by Arn Keeling and John Sandlos

No. 4 · *Canadian Countercultures and the Environment*
Edited by Colin M. Coates

No. 5 · *Moving Natures: Mobility and the Environment in Canadian History*
Edited by Ben Bradley, Jay Young, and Colin M. Coates

No. 6 · *Border Flows: A Century of the Canadian-American Water Relationship*
Edited by Lynne Heasley and Daniel Macfarlane

No. 7 · *Ice Blink: Navigating Northern Environmental History*
Edited by Stephen Bocking and Brad Martin

No. 8 · *Animal Metropolis: Histories of Human-Animal Relations in Urban Canada*
Edited by Joanna Dean, Darcy Ingram, and Christabelle Sethna

No. 9 · *Environmental Activism on the Ground: Small Green and Indigenous Organizing*
Edited by Jonathan Clapperton and Liza Piper

No. 10 · *The First Century of the International Joint Commission*
Edited by Daniel Macfarlane and Murray Clamen

No. 11 · *Traces of the Animal Past: Methodological Challenges in Animal History*
Edited by Jennifer Bonnell and Sean Kheraj

No. 12 · *Remembering Our Relations: Dënesųłıné Oral Histories of Wood Buffalo National Park*
Athabasca Chipewyan First Nation with Sabina Trimble and Peter Fortna

Dënesųłiné Oral Histories of Wood Buffalo National Park

REMEMBERING OUR RELATIONS

ATHABASCA CHIPEWYAN FIRST NATION
WITH SABINA TRIMBLE AND PETER FORTNA

Canadian History and Environment Series
ISSN 1925-3702 (Print) ISSN 1925-3710 (Online)

© 2023 Athabasca Chipewyan First Nation

University of Calgary Press
2500 University Drive NW
Calgary, Alberta
Canada T2N 1N4
press.ucalgary.ca

All rights reserved.

This book is available in an Open Access digital format published under a CC-BY-NCND 4.0 Creative Commons license. The publisher should be contacted for any commercial use which falls outside the terms of that license.

LIBRARY AND ARCHIVES CANADA CATALOGUING IN PUBLICATION

Title: Remembering our relations : Dënesųłıné oral histories of Wood Buffalo National Park / Athabasca Chipewyan First Nation with Sabina Trimble and Peter Fortna.
Names: Trimble, Sabina, author. | Fortna, Peter, author. | Athabasca Chipewyan First Nation, author.
Series: Canadian history and environment series ; 12.
Description: Series statement: Canadian history and environment series ; no. 12 | Includes bibliographical references and index.wIdentifiers: Canadiana (print) 20230565670 | Canadiana (ebook) 20230566111 | ISBN 9781773854120 (hardcover) | ISBN 9781773854113 (softcover) | ISBN 9781773854137 (open access PDF) | ISBN 9781773854144 (PDF) | ISBN 9781773854151 (EPUB)
Subjects: LCSH: Wood Buffalo National Park (Alta. and N.W.T.)—History. | CSH: Dënesųłıné—Wood Buffalo National Park Region (Alta. and N.W.T.)—History. | CSH: Dënesųłıné—Wood Buffalo National Park Region (Alta. and N.W.T.)—Biography. | LCGFT: Oral histories. | LCGFT: Biographies.
Classification: LCC E99.C59 R46 2023 | DDC 971.23/2004972—dc23

The University of Calgary Press acknowledges the support of the Government of Alberta through the Alberta Media Fund for our publications. We acknowledge the financial support of the Government of Canada. We acknowledge the financial support of the Canada Council for the Arts for our publishing program.

This project was funded in part by the Government of Alberta.

This book has been published with the help of a grant from the Federation for the Humanities and Social Sciences, through the Awards to Scholarly Publications Program, using funds provided by the Social Sciences and Humanities Research Council of Canada.

  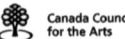

Copyediting by Rhonda Kronyk
Cover image: Leonard G. Flett, Wood Bison in Watercolour.
Cover design, page design, and typesetting by Melina Cusano

Contents

List of Figures	vii
Abbreviations	ix
Acknowledgements	xi
Foreword by Chief Allan Adam	xv
Preface by Elder Alice Rigney	xix
ACFN Elders' Declaration on Rights to Land Use (8 July 2010)	xxi
Community Member Biographies	xxiii
INTRODUCTION: nuhenálé noréltth'er	1
CHAPTER 1: nuhenéné hoghóídi	37
Oral History	51
CHAPTER 2: t'ahú tsąba nálye nį yati nedhé hólį, eyi bek'éch'á ejere néné hólį	67
Oral History	73
CHAPTER 3: t'ahú ejeré néné hólį ú t'ahú nuhghą nįh łą hílchú	89
Oral History	113
CHAPTER 4: 1944 k'e nánį denesųłiné ʔená bets'į nųłtsa k'eyághe ts'én nílya	127
Oral History	132
CHAPTER 5: edeghą k'óíldé íle ajá ú nuhenéné thú bek'e náidé	145
Oral History	161
CHAPTER 6: t'ąt'ú náidé nuhghą hílchú łąt'e kúlí ąłų dene k'ezí náidé	179
Oral History	192

CHAPTER 7: t'a nuhél nódher sí nuhenéné bazį́ chu t'ąt'ú nuheba horená duhų́, eyi beghą dene héł hoílni ... 201

    Oral History ... 214

CONCLUSION: t'ąt'ú erihtł'ís hólį eyi bet'á dene néné chu tu ghą k'óílde ha dúé ... 235

APPENDIX 1: Building a Community-Directed Work of Oral History ... 247

APPENDIX 2: List of Oral History Interviews from 2020–2021 ... 259

APPENDIX 3: Digital Copies of Archival Documents ... 261

Notes ... 265

Bibliography ... 293

Index ... 303

List of Figures

Figure 0.1: ACFN Elders discuss the report draft and book project at the ACFN 2022 Elders' Meeting, Fort Chipewyan. Photo by Peter Fortna, June 2022. — 4

Figure 0.2: Map of Park Boundaries. Map produced by Emily Boak, Willow Springs Strategic Solutions, 2021. — 7

Figure 0.3: Map of lands taken up within ACFN's core homelands in what is now Alberta. Map produced by Michael Robson, Willow Springs Strategic Solutions, 17 July 2023. — 20

Figure 0.4: View of Lake Athabasca from Fort Chipewyan. Photo by Peter Fortna, 2018. — 29

Figure 1.1: *Hudson's Bay Company post, Fort Chipewyan, Alberta, 1919.* Source: CU1108601, Courtesy of Libraries and Cultural Resources Digital Collections, University of Calgary. — 41

Figure 1.2: Map of settlements at House Lake & Peace Point. Map produced by Emily Boak, Willow Springs Strategic Solutions, 2021. — 44

Figure 1.3: *A Dene encampment at Fort Chipewyan, ca. pre-1921.* Source: CU1108812, Courtesy of Libraries and Cultural Resources Digital Collections, University of Calgary. — 45

Figure 1.4: Map of places of cultural importance taken up by the Wood Buffalo National Park. Map produced by Emily Boak and Michael Robson, Willow Springs Strategic Solutions, 2023. — 46

Figure 1.5: *Ester Adam (née Piché), Drying Fish. Trap-line, Ft. Chipewyan, Summer 1952.* Source - Provincial Archives of Alberta, A17153 — 61

Figure 2.1: Map of Treaty 8. Map produced by Emily Boak, Willow Springs Strategic Solutions, 2021. — 69

Figure 2.2: ACFN Members gather for Treaty Days, Fort Chipewyan in June 2018. Photo by Peter Fortna. — 70

Figure 3.1: Map of the original Park Boundaries. 1922. LAC RG85 Vol. 1390, File 406-13. — 90

Figure 3.2: F.H. Kitto's map of proposed boundaries for a bison preserve. F.H. Kitto to J.B. Harkin, 12 January 1921. LAC RG85, Vol. 1390, File 406-13. — 96

Figure 3.3: *Buffalo scow unloading at Peace River, 1925.* Source: Provincial Archives of Alberta, A4723.   100

Figure 3.4: *First shipment of 200 Wainwright Bison arrives, 1925.* Source: CU1103322, Courtesy of Libraries and Cultural Resources Digital Collections, University of Calgary.   100

Figure 3.5: *Buffalo calves unloaded and heading west at Peace Point along 7 miles timber cut to open lands, 1925.* Source: Provincial Archives of Alberta, A4727.   101

Figure 3.6: Summary of Warden Dempsey's report re: *Buffalo - Map showing location of Buffalo that have left the Park up to 6th Jan. 26. April 1926.* RG85-D-1-A, Vol 1391, File 406-13.   102

Figure 3.7: Map of permitting zones A, B, and C established to differentiate among access rights for harvesting after the 1926 expansion. Map produced by Emily Boak, Willow Springs Strategic Solutions, 2021.   105

Figure 5.1: *Camp for police dogs and Wood Buffalo park warden's dogs, 1952.* Source: A17163, Provincial Archives of Alberta.   157

Figure 5.2: Map of Warden Dempsey's Patrol, including sites checked. Attachment to a memo from Hume to Rowatt, 28 March, 1933. RG85-D-1-A, Vol. 152, File 420-2.   158

Figure 6.1: Photo of Chief Jonas Laviolette, Ft. Chipewyan. 1948-1954, Source - Provincial Archives of Alberta A17118.   181

Figure 6.2: Photo of ACFN's Flag, Fort Chipewyan. Photo by Peter Fortna, at ACFN Elders' Meeting June 2022.   183

Figure 6.3: Map of ACFN IR201 Reserves. Map produced by Emily Boak, Willow Springs Strategic Solutions, 2021.   185

Figure 6.4: Map of the boundaries of the preserve set by 1935 Order-in-Council 298-35. Map Produced by Emily Boak, Willow Springs Strategic Solutions, 2021.   189

Figure 6.5: A Round Dance at ACFN's Treaty Days, 2018. Fort Chipewyan. Photo by Peter Fortna.   190

Abbreviations

ACFN	Athabasca Chipewyan First Nation
AER	Alberta Energy Regulator
CBC	Canadian Broadcasting Corporation
CIRNAC	Crown-Indigenous Relations and Northern Affairs Canada
CFS	Children & Family Services
CMC	Committee for Cooperative Management [of Wood Buffalo National Park]
CPAWS	Canadian Parks and Wilderness Society
CRP	Conservation through Reconciliation Partnership
DIA	Department of Indian Affairs
DIAND	Department of Indian and Northern Affairs
ECCC	Environment & Climate Change Canada
HBC	Hudson's Bay Company
ILI	Indigenous Leadership Initiative
IPCA	Indigenous Protected and Conserved Areas
ISC	Indigenous Services Canada
IUCN	International Union for Conservation of Nature and Natural Resources
LAC	Library and Archives Canada
LARP	Lower Athabasca Regional Plan
MCFN	Mikisew Cree Fist Nation
NWC	North West Company
NWT	Northwest Territories
OUV	Outstanding Universal Value
PAA	Provincial Archives of Alberta
RCMP	Royal Canadian Mounted Police

RFMA	Registered Fur Management Area
TARR	Treaty and Aboriginal Rights Research
TLU	Traditional Land Use Study
UNESCO	United Nations Educational, Scientific and Cultural Organization
WBNP	Wood Buffalo National Park
WHC	World Heritage Committee
WSSS	Willow Springs Strategic Solutions
WWII	World War Two

Acknowledgements

The experiences of the relatives and Ancestors of the Dënesųłıné and of the living and deceased members of Athabasca Chipewyan First Nation (ACFN), are the heartbeat of *Remembering our Relations*. This book happened because grandparents, great-grandparents, and great-great-grandparents passed down, from generation to generation, their oral histories and testimony about what happened in the history of Wood Buffalo National Park. We wish first and foremost to honour their sharing, bear witness to their suffering, and recall and lift up their strength, resistance, and love. The book starts and finishes with their words and memories. We are deeply grateful to the many who shared their stories and passed on their belief in justice and healing.

A work like this one depends on the knowledge, time, and care of so many people. This book is dedicated to the late ACFN Elders Alec Bruno and Pat Marcel, who worked tirelessly throughout their lives and leadership to draw attention to the history of the Wood Buffalo National Park (WBNP). Their efforts to expose the violence of WBNP and lift up the voices of Dene people who experienced that violence were catalysts for this research project. Chief Allan Adam's Foreword to *Remembering Our Relations* pays tribute to his grandmother Helene Piche-Bruno and her son (Chief Allan's father), the late Alec Bruno. A Preface from Elder Alice Rigney, a sister of Elder Pat Marcel and granddaughter of Ester Piche. Chief Allan and Elder Alice have provided an eloquent tribute that is far more meaningful than our own attempts to describe the importance of Pat's and Alec's work could ever be.

Many ACFN members and staff played central roles in the production of this book and in the research that preceded it. As will be described later in the book, the work began with a research project starting in 2019, which resulted in a report released in 2021, titled *A History of Wood Buffalo National Park's Relations with the Dënesųłıné*. The intention of the report research was to document the history of the Park and its harmful intergenerational impacts on ACFN, in order to inform negotiations for a formal federal apology and reparations. Athabasca Chipewyan First Nation established a community steering committee before the research for the original 2021 report began. Members of this committee played invaluable roles throughout all stages of this work and put a lot of time and energy into the research report and the book. Committee members were involved, for example, in planning and conceiving the project and work early on, working out to navigate the research process throughout the COVID-19 pandemic, overseeing the work, engaging with the larger community regularly, reviewing and revising drafts, and developing the manuscript and in so many other ways. The committee developed the research plan and questions that guided the work starting in 2019 and made sure the project proceeded with the community's goals, concerns, and intentions at its heart. The late Pat Marcel, Brian Fung, Rose Ross, Jay Telegdi, Lisa Tssessaze, Olivia Villebrun, Leslie Wiltzen, staff at Counsel Public Affairs, Inc., and Larry Innes at Olthuis Kleer Townshend Law, worked tirelessly since the research report project began in 2019. At the time, Elder Pat Marcel was the lead and chair of the committee and lead negotiator with the Government of Canada. His passing in late 2020 was a heartbreaking loss for all of us as well as for the wider community. Elder Pat's nephew Leslie Wiltzen took over Pat's roles thereafter. We are thankful for both Elder Pat's and Leslie's guidance and leadership.

Lisa Tssessaze's suggestion that we do something beyond the original report to honour and centre the voices of the Elders and their oral histories led to the idea for this book. Lisa, Jay Telegdi, and Rose Ross have also been leaders throughout the process. Their immense commitments of time, creativity, and work must be highlighted. They ensured that the work proceeded on the community's terms and timeline, and under their guidance. Lisa, Jay, and Rose organized and led meetings; facilitated ongoing communications with ACFN members and Elders, Chief and Council, and the wider community; ensured protocol was correctly upheld throughout the process; wrote and edited biographies; reviewed and revised drafts of the original report and manuscript chapters; obtained permissions from every person who shared oral testimony or from next-of-kin for those who since have passed; provided critical feedback; and asked important questions. The list goes on. Thank you so much for everything.

The project team are thankful as well to ACFN leadership, including both the Elders' Council and Chief and Council, whose contributions and feedback kept the project alive. Engaged as he has been with many so other important issues outside of the WBNP research project, Chief Allan Adam graciously shared time, knowledge, energy, and stories.

We are grateful to Elders Alice Rigney, Edouard Trippe de Roche and Keltie Paul for reviewing the manuscript as the members of the ACFN Elders' review panel in early 2022 while it simultaneously underwent University of Calgary (UCalgary) Press' academic peer review. Alice, Ed, and Keltie shared so much valuable feedback — not only during this review, but throughout the life of the project. Ed and Keltie also provided us with one of the first reviews of the original report. We are grateful as well to other ACFN members and Elders who reviewed sections of the manuscript and provided revisions to their interview transcriptions and excerpts, including Jimmy Deranger, Kristi Deranger, Dora Flett, Garry Flett, Lorraine Hoffman, Hazel Mercredi, Julie Mercredi, and Leslie Wiltzen. Many ACFN Elders also shared feedback on project updates at several Elders' Gatherings in Fort Chipewyan.

Thank you also to Josh Holden and ACFN Elder Cecilia Adam who wrote the Dënesųłıné chapter titles for this book. They also provided important instruction on the Dene language and spellings for this book. We are grateful for the work of ACFN member Angela Marcel, who scheduled interviews and meetings with Elders and members in early 2021 for the original report. Thank you also to ACFN Elder Leonard Flett for sharing his stunning watercolour for the cover design of this book, which was the winning submission for ACFN's book cover image contest that took place in 2022.

Heartfelt thanks to Tara Joly, who while working for Willow Springs Strategic Solutions (Willow Springs) became the lead researcher on this project when Willow Springs became involved in 2019. Alongside Sabina Trimble and Peter Fortna, several members of the Willow Springs team worked on various parts of this book. We are grateful to Emily Boak and Michael Robson for producing the GIS maps. Thanks so much to Julia Schwindt for proofreading and assisting in many other capacities to pull everything together at the end. Thank you to Jasmine Trimble for the transcriptions of many of the interviews that took place between 2020 and 2021.

We are so grateful for the detailed and thoughtful feedback from two anonymous reviewers, and from Alan MacEachern, the editor for the Canadian History & Environment Series at the University of Calgary (UCalgary) Press. Our team has been incredibly lucky to work with copyeditor Rhonda Kronyk, who is a member of Tsay Keh Dene First Nation, a founding member of the Indigenous Editors Association, and a member of the Indigenous Editors'

Circle. Rhonda's exceptional work as an editor on the manuscript, sensitive approach to the oral history sections, and strong commitment to centering the community's voices and intentions cannot be overstated. We are so thankful for the energy, time, and thoughtfulness she brought to the work. Thank you!

Thank you also to Helen Hajnoczky at UCalgary Press, who believed in this project. Your graciousness, encouragement, and patience throughout the publication process kept us going! We're so lucky to have worked with you. Deep thanks as well to Brian Scrivener, Alison Cobra, and Melina Cusano at UCalgary Press, who facilitated the project with their energy.

The prior work of several academic researchers provided a critical foundation, especially for the introductory sections of each chapter. We discuss the literature that has influenced us in the Introduction, but we also wanted to take some space here to highlight the important contributions of Patricia McCormack, John Sandlos, Ave Dersch, Theresa Ferguson, Henry Lewis, and Tara Joly to our understandings of the history of Wood Buffalo National Park and the surrounding region. Their work helped us to focus our own and assisted with navigating the expansive, often overwhelming, archive of information that has been recorded and collected in the 100 years of this national park's history. A quick glance at the endnotes will make evident the importance of their intellectual groundwork. We are thankful as well to historian John Wall from Parks Canada, staff at Library and Archives Canada and the Provincial Archives of Alberta, and ACFN staff who manage the community's record collection for their facilitation and helpful assistance as we gathered archive sources. LAC staff also digitized thousands of pages of archival material for us when public health restrictions barred us from physically going to the archives.

Finally, and most importantly, we wish to honour the work and contributions of every ACFN member and Elder, both living and passed, as well as their Dene, nehiyaw, and Métis kin and neighbours. Your oral histories and testimony are the foundation of this story and form the core of every chapter of the book. One paragraph of acknowledgement seems so insufficient — but here it is. Thank you for sharing with us, for advancing this work, for making this book happen. You are the reason *Remembering Our Relations* (and the research that preceded it) exist, and the reason for any good that comes of it. We hope that that this book does justice to what you have shared.

To everyone, mahsi cho.

Foreword

By Chief Allan Adam

I remember one of the first times my Granny Helene Piché (née Adam) told me about what the creation of Wood Buffalo National Park did to her and her family. My Granny was a strong woman, but she had buried that story and carried it inside so the family wouldn't have to carry it. It wasn't until much later that I learned the truth from her and from my father, the late Alec Bruno.

She told me the story when we were eating moose, a moose which I had hunted in the Park. When I told her where I got the moose, she just pushed her plate away and said she wouldn't eat it. My Granny then shared her story. She was a fluent Dënesųłiné speaker, and told the story mostly in Dene, so I only understood parts of it. What I did understand was that her family was from Birch River in the Park, and that at some point they were kicked out and she wasn't allowed back. I asked my father Alec Bruno later about what had happened. I said, "Dad, what is this about Granny being kicked out of the Park?" And then he told me everything.

I had always wondered why my family had been poor, and why my Granny had moved around so much. You see, she had grown up at Birch River, but when she was young she married a man and they moved to Fort Chipewyan. Several years later he died during one of the epidemics. When she tried to come home to grieve and get the support of her family, she was not allowed. The Park had taken over the land. My father elaborated; he told me that when Granny tried to go home with her kids, the Park wardens threatened her and said she had to leave. He said that Granny's house had been burned down by the wardens when she first left the Park with her new husband. Her home in the Park was gone.

After her attempt to return home was cruelly denied, she bounced around and relocated many times, trying to find a new home. But her true home was on the Birch River, and without it she was in a way homeless for the rest of her life. When she married my grandfather, her second husband, they took care of each other, and things got a little better, but it was still hard, because her house still wasn't her home. The wardens' threats stayed with her and had consequences that lasted a long time. Of the seventeen children she had, just four survived because of the harsh life they were forced to live. This was the reason she couldn't eat the moose - it reminded her of the home the government took away.

My father and I have told this story in this book. It's a painful story that a lot of the families in our community share. The oral histories and the words of our grandparents and parents, of our relatives and ancestors, are being shared here so the world might know what happened. Wood Buffalo National Park was the heart of the Dene homelands, and when it was removed, Dene people suffered. Before it was taken away, people lived on the land and water. It provided everything they needed, with abundant wildlife. It's one of the richest places in the world in terms of wildlife, resources, land and water. My Granny, and so many others, lost all that, and were left homeless, with only memories of what used to be. The Park's rules meant that she could never go home, and so she kept that suffering inside, shielding her kids and grandkids from the pain. Yet, despite all her efforts, as well as those of her generation, the pain moved through generations.

The people today suffer the memories and trauma of this, a trauma that when combined with residential schools, hydrodams and oil sands pollution, casts a very long and dark shadow. For too long people have kept these traumas inside, not wanting to share them for fear of burdening others, but as we move down this road for future change we are learning that healing is only possible once we shed light and tell present and future generations what happened.

That's why ACFN has been doing this work and created this book. That's why we've been telling the stories and calling on the government to acknowledge what it did. My Granny sharing her story, and my Father passing it on and pressing for change, are part of why the work began. I'm thankful to the many people who agreed to share their stories. It is good and strong medicine that will heal our Nation. I think that is why my Granny shared her story with me, so that I can understand what happened; and so that we all can understand what happened and that we can grow and be a strong in our home once again.

As we learn and understand these stories, we can grow and reclaim ourselves and our Nation. We are the original stewards of this land from time immemorial. We are the proud Dënesųłıné; the K'ai Tailé Dene. We're sharing this story because it will help to heal us, and through healing we will be prepared to take back our rightful place in our home.

I hope that you'll hear these stories and listen. We are sharing it because the Dene people of ACFN want our relatives to be remembered and we believe that there can be a better future for all of us.

Preface

Elder Alice Rigney

I wasn't aware that my granny, Ester Piché, who was born in 1897, lived at House Lake (Birch River).[1] In fact I didn't know about this place at all. You see, I was raised in the Holy Angels Residential School in Fort Chipewyan, Alberta, from the age of five. During those years I lost all contact with my family and history. I didn't ask [my family], as the topic of where my grandparents lived was never discussed. I couldn't talk to my parents in my Dene language, as this was taken away in the Mission.[2] I never asked about where, how, or who was my lineage.

It was my older brother Pat who awoke this awareness of my granny and the conditions in Wood Buffalo National Park. She was forced to leave her home and family, leaving everything behind. She was Dene and did not want to become a Cree member. She left with other families and relocated to the Delta.[3]

This move must have been difficult, but my granny was a strong Dene woman and hardships were not new to her. She endured, and I remember her as a strong, resilient woman. But my years knowing her were too short. What the Wood Buffalo National Park did was cruel and unforgiving, and this continued for more than one hundred years—I honour my brother Pat for bringing this issue to us. My brother's determination to undo this wrong is now in the open and I, along with ACFN, am forever grateful for him. He was a "force to be reckoned with." I am proud to call him my brother and opening the door to spaces where reconciliation can take place.

ACFN Elders' Declaration on Rights to Land Use (8 July 2010)

This is our Dënesųłıné territory, our Traditional Lands. We have occupied these lands for the last 10,000 years and maybe longer. Our traditions go on and we have the right to continue our traditional way of life. We agreed only to share our lands and we still consider these lands ours. Clearly, we have been here longer than anybody. Governments must recognize that we still have the right to use these lands.

Our Rights to use the lands and water on Traditional Lands have never been extinguished. The Traditional Lands, and our rights to use of the lands, are central to our Dene culture, identity, and well-being. They are essential to the well-being of our future generations and their ability to sustain our culture in a changing world.

The meaningful practice of our Treaty Rights depends on having sufficient lands and resources to exercise those rights. Sufficient refers to not only quantity but quality, including what is required to fulfill our cultural and spiritual needs.

Our parents and grandparents have told us that Treaty 8, signed by our Chief Laviolette in 1899, is an intergovernmental agreement that, in return for sharing our Traditional Lands, upholds our inherent Dene rights to land use and livelihood. In our experience, Alberta is not upholding their end of the treaty and is sacrificing our rights to industrial development. We have never been properly consulted and the federal and provincial governments have never accommodated our rights or compensated us for infringements.

ACFN has had enough with having our land destroyed, no one is dealing with it; neither at the federal nor the provincial Crown levels. Yet you come to us for approval of new projects. It is time for governments to stop cheating us of our rights to land use and livelihood, culture, and identity without proper consultation, mitigation, and compensation.

As the Elders of our community, we demand that our ability to practice our constitutionally protected Treaty Rights and traditional uses is sustained within our Traditional Lands for future generations. We demand that our rights are protected in the LARP[1] and any other initiatives proposed by governments.

The lands from Firebag north, including Birch Mountain on the west side of river, must be protected. Richardson Backcountry is not to be given away—not to any government.

Everything we do here, we do to protect our rights to land use, livelihood, and culture.

Community Member Biographies

CHIEF ALLAN ADAM

Chief Adam was born in 1966 in Edmonton, Alberta. He has been in an ACFN leadership role since 2004 and was elected Chief in 2008. Chief Adam has testified in joint review panels for several industrial applications and at numerous federal standing committees and has provided strong leadership for his Nation during challenging times. The intergenerational impact of WBNP displacement has motivated Chief Adam's goal to correct historical injustices to Dënesųłıné members.

HORACE ADAM

Horace was born in High Channel, Saskatchewan in 1941. He attended the Gold Fields school in 1949 and then went to school in Uranium City, Saskatchewan from 1952 to 1957. Horace worked for the Department of Natural Resources in Forestry as a patrol man for eleven years in Uranium City. He drove a taxi for sixteen years and worked for Acden (an ACFN owned Corporation). Horace enjoys people and treating people well. He loves to smile and make people happy.

ALEC BRUNO

Alec was born along the shores of Jackfish Lake, Alberta on 8 March 1936. His mother, Helene Bruno, lived on the land that eventually became Wood Buffalo National Park. She was kicked out of her home when she was only twenty-two and lost everything. Alec attended residential school for sixteen years. He fished, trapped, and hunted around the Old Fort, Alberta area. He grew up in Old Fort and reluctantly relocated to Fort Chipewyan in 1966. He had two sons, Allan (Chief Adam) and James Adam.

FRANCOIS BRUNO
Francois was born in Fort Chipewyan on 18 February 1909. Old Fort was his home primarily, but he, his family, and his extended family moved to fish, hunt, harvest, and trap. He and his wife Helene had sixteen children (some from his wife's previous marriage); four of the children grew up to be adults. The family moved to Fort Chipewyan in 1966. In 1975 they began to raise their grandchildren.

HELENE (PICHE) BRUNO
Helene Bruno was born in the House Lake settlement near the Birch River, Alberta on 14 August 1900. She married her first husband at fifteen or sixteen, and they were together to until his death in 1929. After the buffalo park was expanded, she was told to leave her home at House Lake and that if she wanted to move back, she would have to join the Mikisew Cree First Nation. She married Francois Bruno in the 1930s. They lived in Big Point, Old Fort, and Jackfish Lake and moved to Fort Chipewyan in 1966. In 1975 they began to raise their grandchildren.

RENE BRUNO
Rene August Bruno was born in Jackfish, Alberta on 21 February 1934. Rene attended Holy Angels Residential School in Fort Chipewyan. He speaks fluent Dënesųłiné, Cree, and English. He was a Band Councillor from 1996 to 2003. Rene married Mary Mercredi and had seven children. He has many grandchildren and one great-great-granddaughter. Rene enjoys traditional food, living out on the land, boat rides, and teaching his grandchildren how to trap.

JIM DERANGER

Jim is the son of Isadore and Therese Deranger. He has a political science degree and worked for ACFN as a band administrator in 1980s. As a business contractor, he assisted the Dënesųłıné, building their economic development plans in Northern Saskatchewan. Today Jim lives in Fort Chipewyan and is Co-chair of the ACFN Elders Council.

FREDOLINE DJESKELNI DERANGER

Fredoline is the son of Isadore and Therese Deranger. He has a civil engineering degree and worked most of his life on oilsands sites. Fred is passionate about reading and learning each and every day. Today Fred is researching old stories and the history of the Dënesųłıné and brings forward the ancient teachings from the Elders.

DORA FLETT

Dora is one of the eldest daughters born to Isadore and Therese Deranger. She is knowledgeable in the Dënesųłıné language, heritage, and practices. Dora lived off the land for many years and holds wisdom in the herbal medicines that are used for healing. She is the matriarch of five generations and is a proud ACFN member.

ELIZA MARIE FLETT

Eliza was born 31 December 1927 at the Birch River settlement in Wood Buffalo National Park. She married Raphael Flett in the 1930s. Eliza prepared moose hides and fish nets, beaded, and made clothing for her family. She lived a traditional life off the land until her family was removed from the Park. From there they moved to Old Fort, then to Jackfish Reserve, and finally to Fort Chipewyan in 1972. Eliza spoke only Dene and a bit of Cree, and she was able to in write in syllabics. She raised her family with tradition and love.

ELIZABETH FLETT

Elizabeth Flett (née Simpson) was born in 1922 at Peace Point. She was the daughter of Isidore Simpson and Corrone Benoit who were among the Dene families transferred to the Cree Band in 1944. After attending Holy Angels Residential School, Elizabeth married a non-Status man, Duncan Flett, in 1943. Under the *Indian Act*, she lost her Status and left the Park. After *Bill C-31* was passed in 1985, changing the *Indian Act* provision that stripped Indigenous women of their Status for marrying non-Status men, Elizabeth applied to regain her Status. Indian Affairs reinstated her as a member of Athabasca Chipewyan First Nation rather than to Mikisew Cree First Nation, of which both her parents and eleven siblings were now members. Because of this, Elizabeth and her thirteen ACFN children were refused access to her family home at Peace Point in Wood Buffalo National Park. Elizabeth was fluent in Dënesųłıné, Cree, French and English. It was amazing to listen to her switching from one language to another during conversations with different groups of people. She loved the bush life and was often referenced as Gramma Bush by her family.

GARRY FLETT

Garry was born in Peace River, Alberta but grew up in Fort Smith, Northwest Territories. He attended school in Fort Smith and Yellowknife, Northwest Territories. Garry then entered an apprenticeship as a heavy-duty mechanic and did his training in Edmonton and Calgary. In 1979, he moved to Fort McMurray and started a career with Syncrude Canada Ltd. where he remained for thirty years prior to retirement. Garry was asked by the Chief and Council of ACFN to lead their business group in 2009 and continues as the Chief Executive Officer of Acden today. Garry enjoys fall hunting and getting out on the land as much as he can but mostly enjoys time with family and friends.

JOHN FLETT
John was born in 1960 at Fort McMurray and raised in Fort Chipewyan, Point Brule, and Poplar Point. John spent lots of time on the land at his family's cabins in Cluff lake, Douglas River, and at Sandy Lake in Saskatchewan N22. John is humble and still enjoys his time out on the land. He was a heavy equipment operator at Syncrude, and prior to that he was a labourer at the Cluff Lake mine. Currently, he's enjoying retirement and regularly visits the family cabin in the Delta.

LEONARD FLETT
Leonard is an ACFN Elder who speaks fluent Dënesųłıné and is an active land user. His parents are Liza and Raphael Flett. Leonard was born at Jackfish Lake and spent ten years in residential school. He is active in industry advisory committees where he raises concerns on the changes he has seen on our lands. Leonard is also a member of the Elders Advisory Council.

SCOTT FLETT
Scott was born and raised in Fort Chipewyan. He worked for the Alberta Environment field office in Fort Chipewyan collecting samples. Scott also served on the ACFN Council from 2011 to 2015. Today he spends most of his time at his cabin on the Fletcher Channel, at the southern end of Lake Athabasca. Scott enjoys traveling and spending time with his grandchildren and is an active member of the ACFN Elders Council and sits on various committees.

FRED "JUMBO" FRASER
Fredrick R. Fraser, better known as "Jumbo," was born and raised in Fort Chipewyan. Jumbo was a modest and kind man who was always willing to share his Traditional Knowledge of the land and wildlife with younger generations. Jumbo saw dramatic differences in the land, wildlife, and water level throughout his years. He witnessed the last migration of tens of thousands of caribou as they passed in front of his home—the migration lasted for two weeks. Jumbo also witnessed the

water level drop after the Bennett Dam was built, and the resulting shift in waterfowl migration routes away from Fort Chipewyan. Jumbo wasn't shy to voice his concerns to the government and industry. Jumbo, a champion dog musher, entrepreneur, Métis president, justice of the peace, marriage commissioner, volunteer fire fighter/fire chief, and storyteller, also worked for the Wood Buffalo National Park and in water management with Regional Municipality of Wood Buffalo Municipal Affairs. Jumbo remained active until his death in 2022.

LESLIE LAVIOLETTE

Leslie is an ACFN Elder and an active land user. He is also an ACFN trapline holder. Leslie is very familiar with ACFN traditional lands and has seen changes over time. He is passionate about ACFN rights and culture and has testified in a number of hearings for ACFN and attends ongoing meetings regarding the protection of caribou. Leslie believes that all members need to be out on the land, especially our young people and Elders.

BIG JOHN MARCEL

Big John was born in Fort Chipewyan in 1943 and grew up in Jackfish. He attended Holy Angels Residential School for ten years. Big John worked as a bus driver for Bishop Piche School and Northland School for ten years. He moved to Fort McMurray in the 1970s and worked as a heavy equipment operator. He was a trapper when he was younger and used a dog team. Big John enjoys life even though it is tough to get around as he gets older.

FRANK MARCEL

Frank was an ACFN Elder and active land user. He was born at Jackfish Lake and attended residential school for several years. At the ACFN quarterly annual Elder meetings, Frank raised concerns on the changes he has seen on our lands. Frank enjoyed being out on the land and sharing his Traditional Knowledge with the youth.

JOHN H. MARCEL
John is an ACFN Elder and active land user. John was born on ACFN traditional territory to Madeline and Ben Marcel. He spent several years in residential school. John enjoys the outdoors and being out on the land.

PAT MARCEL
Elder Pat Marcel, former ACFN Chief (1987–1990), was a respected leader and champion for upholding ACFN's Treaty Rights. Pat taught us about our Treaty, how important it was, and that ACFN needed to have these Rights recognized and upheld. He was a youth mentor and the lead on numerous special projects and committees, sharing traditional science. Pat was also the former chair of the Dënesųłıné Elders Committee.

CHARLIE MERCREDI
Charlie Mercredi was born and raised in Old Fort. He is one of twelve children born to Antoine and Victoria Mercredi. He spent most of his life living off the land to support his two children, Hazel and Charles, with his wife Georgina. Charlie taught his children to be humble, work hard, not be lazy, work during the day and relax at night, and never depend on anyone—if you want to do something just do it.

MARIE JOSEPHINE MERCREDI
Josephine was born in 1913 and lived a long life as a traditional Elder who raised her children on the land. She spoke Dënesųłıné, French, and English and carried and shared the ancient stories passed down to her. She is featured in ACFN's book, *Footprints on the Land*. Josephine gathered medicines and her Dene style beadwork was adored by all. She had an abundance of love that she shared with her sixteen children. Josephine is often remembered singing t'asunde wasika, a traditional Dené hymn.

VICTORINE MERCREDI

Victorine was born in Old Fort in 1916. She was a traditional Elder who raised her children out on the land. She had twelve children, one being former Chief Tony Mercredi. Victorine served on the ACFN council for ten years. She spoke Dënesųłıné and shared old stories, including the history of our Treaty and was instrumental in helping her people. She was well known for her traditional sewing and beadwork and her knowledge with our Traditional medicines. Victorine is most remembered practicing midwifery out on the land in Old Fort, Jackfish, Flour Bay, and throughout ACFN traditional territory.

ESTER PICHE NÉE ADAM

Ester was born in 1897 in Fond du Lac, Saskatchewan. Her first marriage was to Jonas Platcote and her second was to Louie Piche. Her children are Marie Madeline Marcel, Eliza Piche and Pierre Piche. She lived in the Peace-Athabasca Delta at House Lake and along Birch River. Esther was forced from her homeland when Wood Buffalo National Park was formed. She moved to Moose Point at the southeastern edge of Lake Athabasca, then to Poplar Point on the Athabasca River, and finally settled at Jackfish Reserve. She spoke Dënesųłıné, told stories, and loved to cuddle her grandchildren. She was a tall, elegant lady and a perfectionist who trapped and maintained her home with her children. She lived traditionally on the lands until 1974.

ERNIE "JOE" RATFAT

Joe was born in the bush around Fort Chipewyan. He currently lives in British Columbia and enjoys traveling and spends his time working with feather fans, running Sweat Lodges, and conducting ceremonies. His goal is to help heal our young people. Joe has Traditional Knowledge, some of which he has passed down in this book. Joe is a Mikisew Cree First Nation member, but in his heart he is Dene. He speaks Dënesųłıné and his parents are Dene.

ALICE RIGNEY

Alice was born in a tent by the Big Dock in Fort Chipewyan. She attended Holy Angels Residential School, Grandin College in Fort Smith, Northwest Territories, and went to school in Edmonton. Alice worked as a social worker and in the community school teaching Dënesųłiné. Alice enjoys sharing her culture by teaching the Dënesųłiné language to community members. She loves gardening and living on the land.

DONNA MERCREDI SHORTMAN

Donna was born and raised in Fort Smith, Northwest Territories. She has three children, thirteen grandchildren, and three great grandchildren. She is an active land-user and enjoys spending time at her cabin on the Athabasca River. Donna is currently working as the manager of the Kahkiyow Keykanow Elders Care Centre in Fort Chipewyan. She is blessed to raise her grandchildren and comes from a strong line of Dene women and men. Donna is a proud Dene and ACFN member.

LORI-ANN STEVENS

Lori-Ann is the daughter of John and Beverly Tourangeau. She received her Bachelor of Social Work degree from the University of Calgary and currently works as ACFN's social worker and development manager. When she is not working, Lori enjoys spending time with her five children, gardening, and taking her two dogs for walks.

BEVERLY TOURANGEAU

Beverly worked at Nunee Health in Fort Chipewyan as an Indian Residential School worker and at Paspew House, also in Fort Chipewyan, as a Director. Her pastime comforts are beading, sewing, and creating beautiful garments for her family and friends. You can always find Bev in her garden sharing her wisdom about growing food. She has three children and eleven grandchildren. Beverly resides in Fort Chipewyan.

EDOUARD TRIPPE DE ROCHE & KELTIE PAUL

Edouard and Keltie have been married for thirty-five years. Both lived in Fort McMurray, Alberta for over twenty years and now reside in North Battleford, Saskatchewan. Edouard has Traditional Knowledge and stories shared from past generations; Keltie is a long-time social science researcher and an anthropologist. Both Edouard and Keltie have provided key information to the development of this book. Edouard and Keltie are keen on seeing how the historical injustices against our Dene people could be corrected with reconciliation.

LESLIE WILTZEN

Leslie is an ACFN member and resides in Fort Smith, Northwest Territories. He regularly visits his cabin in WBNP and is a strong advocate for ACFN members coming back to their traditional lands in the Park. Leslie is employed as the regional superintendent for the South Slave Department of Lands with the Government of Northwest Territories.

*Dedicated to the memory of
the late Elders Pat Marcel and Alec Bruno*

Introduction: nuhenálé noréltth'er

So when the [white] people came to talk to [my Ancestors], they were saying the buffalo was declining down south and they wanted land for the buffalo. And they could use that land for a number of years, and First Nations people in that region, in the area, on the land, could just go on doing what they want to do. But after they got the land, things changed, yeah? They developed policies saying that 'you can't do this, you can't do that.' And the Elders were trying to tell the officials that it's not what the first official had said.

And then after that, they came back after with their document saying that you have to leave. Or you had to be with Cree Band, they said—all the people that were in those little settlements, those little camps . . . they were ACFN. Then what happened after that? They burnt their houses down, and they were never compensated for that. Also, [the AFCN people] felt that there was an injustice because they said they were going to not do this, not do this and they turned around and did it. And they were kind of upset with that and nobody talked about it because no one was translating.

And now they're saying, some of our Elders are saying that, that land is ours, you should just give it to us. There's no need for us to negotiate it. We let them use it for X number of years, and the use has expired. Now give it back to us.

—Jimmy Deranger

In December 2022, just a few days before the one-hundredth anniversary of the establishment of Wood Buffalo National Park (WBNP), the Canadian Parks and Wilderness Society (CPAWS) issued a public statement indicating that it would rename one of its most prestigious awards: the Harkin Award, meant to acknowledge individuals "who have demonstrated a significant contribution throughout their lifetime through words and deeds to the conservation of Canada's parks and wilderness." The award was named after J.B. Harkin, who was the Commissioner of the Dominion Parks Branch from 1911–1936, and who is sometimes remembered as the "father" of national parks in Canada. Athabasca Chipewyan First Nation (ACFN) is a Dene community whose homelands were divided and taken up for the establishment and subsequent expansion of Wood Buffalo National Park in the 1920s. Explicitly wishing to challenge celebratory discourse around national parks and wildlife sanctuaries in Canada, the Nation urged CPAWS to rename the award because of Harkin's role in the expulsions and exclusions of Dene peoples and the violations of Treaty 8 that followed the establishment of the Park. As ACFN Chief Allan Adam stated, the community feels that it is critical to shift the way the public thinks not only of figures like J.B. Harkin but also of "the entire history of Canada's National Parks." CPAWS agreed to change the name of the award before the end of 2023.[1]

Public discourse around national parks and other such protective spaces tend to uncritically celebrate them as symbols of Canadian national history and identity and as important triumphs of twentieth-century environmentalism. Yet, as ACFN's work toward the renaming of the Harkin Award suggests, Indigenous experiences with national parks challenge the celebratory narratives. The oral history that opens this chapter—shared by ACFN Elder Jimmy Deranger in Spring 2021—highlights the exclusions and injustice at in the heart of WBNP history as it is remembered by Dënesųłiné[2] people. Jimmy's words suggest that, for the Dënesųłiné who had resided in the area since time immemorial, WBNP was an instrument of colonialism in their homelands. The Park boundaries, policies, and management throughout the twentieth century played central roles in what Andrew Woolford and Jeff Benvenuto characterize as colonialism's "very basic relation of dispossession, elimination and replacement" in northern Alberta.[3] In Dene historical memory and experience, the Park has been an important part of systemic efforts by colonial states to remove Indigenous Peoples, ways of life and societies from the land, and to deny of Indigenous connections and claims to place, in order to replace them with settlers.⁴ Dene people who had lived, travelled, and thrived along the Athabasca River, Birch River, Peace River, Slave River, and Gull River, and on the shores of other bodies of water within what became WBNP boundaries, saw their homes and harvesting areas taken up by the Park. Their families and communities were divided by Park boundaries, and their movements and ways of life were restricted by settler land and wildlife management policies, including strict and evolving harvesting laws governing Indigenous lives and movements throughout the twentieth century. The Dënesųłıné title of this introductory chapter, roughly translating to "it happened in front of us," points to the importance of telling the history of the Park as the Dene ancestors of ACFN members experienced and witnessed it—getting the story right.

The renaming of the CPAWS award was just a small part of a much larger campaign for justice in which ACFN has been engaged for many years. Starting in April 2022, the Nation initiated negotiations with the government of Canada to obtain a formal, national apology and compensation for the harm inflicted on the community and their Dënesųłıné ancestors since the establishment of WBNP. ACFN hired Willow Springs Strategic Solutions (WSSS) to undertake a collaborative research project to document the historical events and communicate the Park's widespread, intergenerational impacts. This work resulted in *A History of Wood Buffalo National Park's Relations with the Dënesųłıné: Final Report*, which ACFN shared with community members, government officials and policymakers, media, and the general public in summer 2021.⁵ After formal discussions with the government began, Elders and community members who had been involved in the project expressed the wish that the story be shared in other ways that would reflect and honour the community's experiences and oral histories. As ACFN member Donna Mercredi emphasized, "It should be told. It should be out there in the open. People should know."

That is how we got here, to this book. A key difference between the original report and this book has to do with intentions: although the report centred ACFN oral histories, it was written primarily with the goal of informing negotiations with settler governments. This book came together primarily to highlight and honour the oral history and testimony of the community. The goal of the chapters that follow is to present a narrative of the Park's history that takes seriously the experiences, knowledge, and oral histories of the Dënesųłıné peoples whose lives it dramatically altered after it was established

Fig. 0.1 ACFN Elders discuss a draft of *A History of Wood Buffalo National Park's Relations with the Dënesųłıné* report and this book at the ACFN 2022 Elders' Meeting, Fort Chipewyan. Photo by Peter Fortna, June 2022.

in 1922. We see this as a community-directed work of research for justice, for land back, and for community empowerment that will challenge attempted colonial erasures of Dënesųłıné voices and knowledge. Jimmy's opening history—and the oral histories and testimony shared by many ACFN members and Elders in this book—present important challenges to attempted erasures characteristic of the history of national parks in Dene homelands and across Canada.

"Long ago there was no border": Building a park in Dënesųłıné Homelands

Wood Buffalo National Park extends over nearly 45,000 square-kilometres of northern boreal plains and forest, encompassing vast wetlands, grasslands, and salt plains, the Caribou and Birch Mountains and several key river systems in the region. It crosses the borders of the province of Alberta and the Northwest Territories. The Slave and Athabasca Rivers form its easternmost boundary, and the Park also houses the Peace-Athabasca Delta, the world's largest inland boreal delta and its second largest freshwater delta, where the Peace and Athabasca Rivers meet with the Slave River and Lake Athabasca. This delta encompasses over 320,000 hectares containing eleven major habitat sites, freshwater lakes, and smaller river channels, and sustaining at least 215 species of waterbirds, eighteen species of fish, forty-four species of mammals, and thousands of species of insects and invertebrates.[6] With most of the Peace-Athabasca Delta contained within its boundaries, WBNP houses ecosystems and plant and animal life that are exceptionally diverse. As its name suggests, the primary concern of its original creators was to preserve North America's last remaining herd of wood bison, but its intentions and purposes have shifted over time. The Park earned UNESCO World Heritage Site status in 1983 as the home of the only breeding habitat in the world for endangered whooping cranes and "great concentrations of migratory wildlife" including many species of birds, elk, bison, and moose.

The Park is also located in the heart of the traditional territories and homelands of at least eleven Dene, Métis, and Cree communities who have inhabited the region for generations and whose lands and waterways were taken up for the creation of the Park despite their clearly voiced dissent;[7] ACFN is one of these eleven groups. The Park is located in the heart of Dënesųłıné homelands, where Dene oral histories and archaeological records tell us the people have resided, travelled and seasonally harvested, settled, built homes, and thrived for thousands of years.[8] Elders and members stress that the environment taken up by the Park sustains Dënesųłıné identity, knowledge, language, and culture, and maintains cultural, spiritual, mental, and physical health. People's widespread movements on the land and water keep them closely connected to kin across vast distances. The Park also encompasses places of relatively recent significance to ACFN, such as two centuries-old settlement sites at House Lake/Birch River, where some of the ancestors of ACFN lived and seasonally until the 1920s and 1930s. There are gravesites and harvesting areas at Lake Mamawi, Moose Island, Lake Dene, and along the Birch Mountains and another centuries-old settlement at Peace Point, (which ACFN's Ancestors once shared with their nearest neighbour, now known as Mikisew Cree First Nation). Dene people moved freely in these territories, and their homelands were not defined by strict and artificial boundaries that curtailed their movements until after Treaty 8—but more so after the establishment of the Park in 1922.[9] As ACFN Elder Dora Flett explained, "I never heard of anybody going hungry. Long ago, there was no border. You could go anywhere you want. Nobody said, 'you're there, you're there, you're there.' You're just free going. There was no border." After the 1922 establishment and then 1926 expansion of the Park, this all changed. As ACFN members wrote in 2003, the Park became a central part of the processes whereby "an originally healthy and relatively affluent society . . . has been colonized and disenfranchised and has been losing traditional lands."[10]

The Park was first established with the intention to preserve the last remaining wood bison herd. In a 1912 letter to Parks Commissioner J.B. Harkin, one of its early champions, a Parks Branch official named Maxwell Graham, characterized the need to establish protective boundaries for the wood bison as being in "the interest of the entire people of this Dominion, and to some extent that of the entire civilized world."[11] Ten years later, in December 1922, an Order-in-Council established the boundaries of the Park to encircle roughly 27,000 square-kilometres of Indigenous lands and waters on both sides of the Alberta/NWT border, and the federal Department of the Interior (Northern Affairs Branch) was granted administrative authority. Indigenous Peoples who had taken Treaty, including members of the Cree Band (today, Mikisew Cree First Nation [MCFN]) and some members of the Chipewyan Band (now ACFN), were permitted to live and harvest in the Park.

The Park was expanded south of the Peace River to take up a total of 45,000 square kilometres in 1926. This annex, which met with significant opposition from Indigenous land users in the region, immediately followed the 1925 importation of 6,673 plains bison from Buffalo National Park (which had been established in 1909) in Wainwright, Alberta. Soon after arriving, the imported plains bison migrated outside of the boundaries of the original Wood Buffalo Park to feed near Lake Claire, close to a Dene settlement where ancestors of ACFN had lived and harvested for many generations. The Park's administrators annexed these lands to expand the Park and provide state protection for the migrated plains bison. After the annex, a strict permitting system regulated access and land use in the expanded Park, including for those Indigenous Peoples whose rights were protected under Treaty 8. While treaty harvesters had been permitted to remain in the original Park boundaries from 1922–1926, only those living or actively harvesting within the expanded boundaries in 1926 could apply for permits to continue harvesting there or even to visit family in the Park. The Dene community was effectively split between those with and without access to the Park. Thus, after

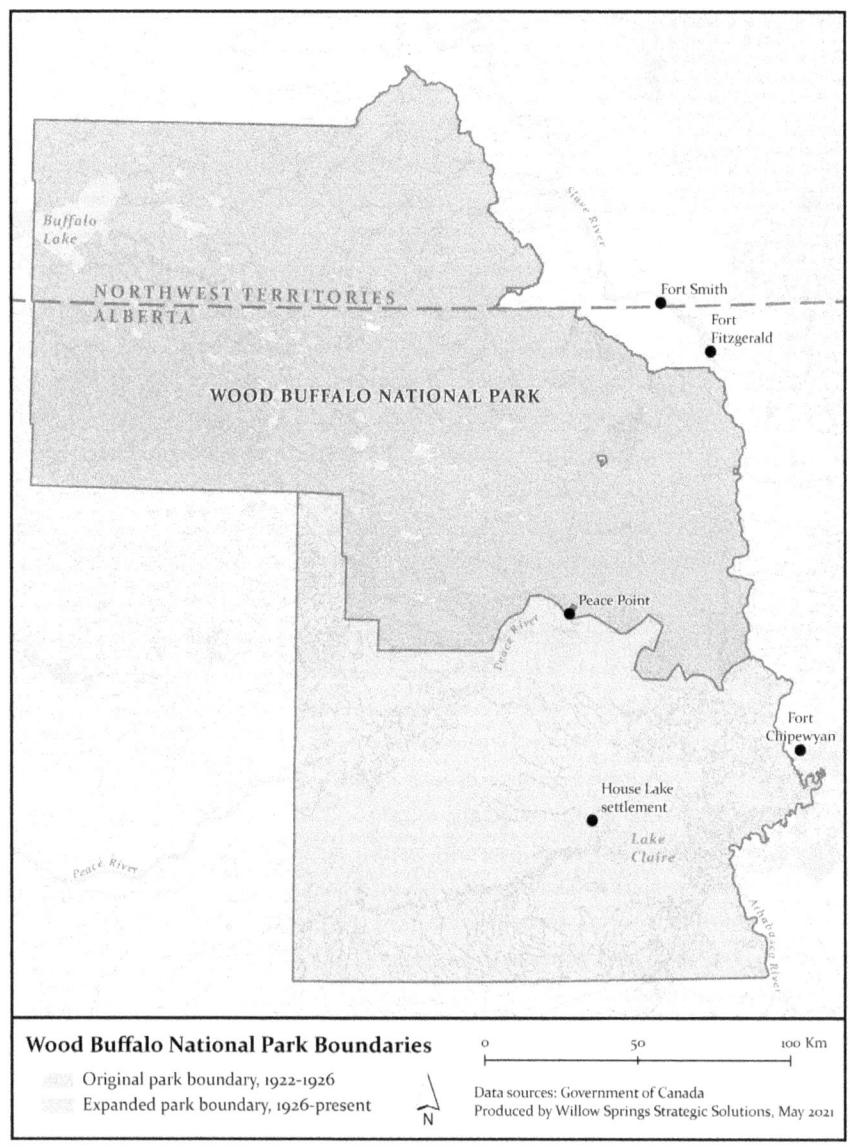

Fig. 0.2 Map of Wood Buffalo National Park Boundaries. Map produced by Emily Boak, Willow Springs Strategic Solutions, 2021.

this expansion many Dene families who had resided and harvested primarily south of the Peace River saw their rights and access to their homelands eroded and restricted.

After 1926, an increasingly strict suite of harvesting laws sought to control Indigenous lives and relation to land throughout the Park and province, and a growing warden system enforced the new laws. Working with the Royal Canadian Mounted Police (RCMP), wardens and their supervisors could revoke Indigenous individuals' permits to hunt, trap, and travel the land and had the power to fine and jail land users should they be found breaking the rules. In 1944, local Indian agent Jack Stewart transferred half the Chipewyan Band population still living in WBNP to the treaty annuity payment list[12] of the Cree Band, who had for the most part been granted permits to remain in the Park. This essentially split the Chipewyan Band in half and transferred many families to the Cree Band. This process is described in Chapter 4. Numerous Dënesųłıné residents and families were denied access to the Park or evicted from their homes after this transfer; if they refused to transfer bands, they had to abandon their land-use areas and homes in the Park. According to the oral histories, those who sought to return home later were not allowed to return; in some cases, wardens burned down former residents' cabins. As a direct result of these restrictions and displacements, and within the wider context of other drastic transformations in their lands throughout the twentieth century, Dene people denied access to the Park faced severe hardship and sometimes starvation, especially from the 1930s–1980s. Colonial officials usually ignored or dismissed persistent attempts by Dënesųłıné residents and leaders to assert rights, challenge unjust and contradictory policy, and attain some form of protection from the changes they faced. The oral histories and testimony shared in this book about what Dene people have suffered across the generations are a direct result of WBNP's history.

Wood Buffalo National Park's cooperative management efforts since the 1980s, which position Indigenous communities as partners in the management of the Park, continue to sideline Dene concerns and perspectives. As some ACFN members suggest, government officials make decisions that affect Dene harvesters, which has "fostered a climate of distrust and cynicism."[13] Historical distrust and a structure that tends to relegate Indigenous leaders to a secondary consulting or advisory position (rather than to meaningful decision-making positions) has limited the potential of new management efforts and left Dënesųłıné participants feeling sidelined and dismissed, as has been the case in the administration of WBNP since its creation. Scholarly critiques of national parks have also demonstrated the challenges related to Parks Canada's co-management and attempts at consultation with Indigenous Peoples in recent decades across the country.[14] As J.W. Johnston and Courtney Mason point out, co-management schemes in national parks in Canada do not shift the balance of power—decision-making authority rests with Parks Canada, and while Indigenous concerns and priorities may be highlighted or considered, Indigenous communities are not the final decision-makers.[15] In many ways, therefore, ACFN's oral histories suggest WBNP's policy has played a key role in the history of colonial violence and elimination perpetrated against the Dënesųłiné peoples whose lands and waterways WBNP takes up. In effect, the Park became an instrument of colonial power in Dënesųłiné homelands after 1922.

Situating Our Story of Wood Buffalo National Park

Academic Discussions of Parks and Protected Nature Areas

One important area of influence for this book comes from the vast scholarship of national parks and other protected areas in Canada and around the world, especially their violent relations with Indigenous Peoples. From Canada's most famous national parks like Banff and Jasper in the Rocky Mountains, to smaller provincial parks like Desolation Sound on the southwest coast of British Columbia, the common story is that parks and their administrations often violently displaced, excluded, and impoverished Indigenous Peoples, with long-term, intergenerational impacts.[16] In line with much of this literature, we see national parks as instruments of colonialism. As Maano Ramutsindela writes, national parks across the world have been central to the enforcement of "colonial rules of behaviour."[17] Deeply racialized and gendered assumptions about Indigenous land use were driving forces in histories of protected nature spaces. Youdelis et. al. argue that parks officials have often "vilified" Indigenous lifeways, and resident peoples were subsequently "violently evicted or coercively displaced" from protected areas.[18] In turn, expulsions and restrictions were typically accompanied by high levels of surveillance and strict punishment to control Indigenous movements and restrict their ways of life. In the creation of protected areas in Canada and across the British empire, Indigenous residents were rarely—if ever—included in decision-making processes, and their knowledge was usually ignored, dismissed, or discredited. Meanwhile, "nearly unbridled development and extractivism" taking place adjacent to protected areas are deemed acceptable by settler states and industry—amplifying existing pressure on Indigenous lands and evicted communities created by expulsions in the first place.[19]

In these ways, Indigenous Peoples globally have experienced protected nature areas as instruments of colonial dispossession and violence. Parks have been central to Canadian colonialism not only because many expelled Indigenous families and criminalized their ways of life, but also because they contributed to what Patrick Wolfe describes as colonial elimination: the forcible removal of Indigenous Peoples' presence, their connections and claims to the land, and the attempted dissolution of Indigenous societies, to make way for and justify settler dominance.[20] Woolford and Benvenuto write that the genocidal force of Canadian settler colonial policies has varied across time and across regions, but that even in this unevenness, at the heart of Canadian colonialism has always been "the very basic relation of dispossession, elimination and replacement."[21] Parks have been part of the genocidal colonial processes that, as these scholars describe it, aim to destroy in order to replace.[22]

Historians have analysed the intersecting and sometimes contradictory intentions and ideologies driving the establishment of protected nature areas, such as the desire to create and preserve an aesthetic of "pristine" and human-free wilderness,[23] wildlife and game conservation,[24] and tourism and other economic development and resource management activities,[25] all of which were aimed at the advancement of settler control over land and natural resources. Often, the expulsions of Indigenous Peoples for the creation of national or provincial parks went together with policies of assimilation and elimination. As some historians point out, in the context of more southerly parks like Banff and Jasper, the expulsion of Indigenous Peoples from their homelands and the restrictions on their ways of life for the establishment and management of national parks, directly reinforced Indian Affairs' assimilationist policies. Indian Affairs officials hoped Park expulsions would force Indigenous Peoples to take up a sedentary and agricultural existence on reserves.[26] In many ways, then, protected areas and the policies that govern them have led to profound and long-lasting impacts for Indigenous communities, lives, and homelands.[27] Ramutsindela describes park intentions and outcomes as "a complex entanglement" of national identity-building, colonial power expansion, and competition over natural resources and land. He explicitly connects this complex entanglement to colonial genocide and elimination, which he calls "a broader process of extermination."[28] In this book, oral histories explicitly connect Park policy, alienations of Dene people from their homelands and kin, and the wider regime of colonial land and resource management with critical discussions of colonial elimination in Canada.[29] Dene oral histories of Wood Buffalo National Park suggest that the experiences of the Dene people with the Park shared commonalities with the experiences of Indigenous Peoples in the histories of other national parks, as described across this vast historiography. However, WBNP's history is unique in a number of ways.

The preservation of a pristine wilderness, a prevalent theme among historians of national parks in the 1990s and early 2000s, such as American environment historian William Cronon, was not the driving force for Wood Buffalo National Park for most of its history.[30] But preservation ideologies did play a role, especially in the Park's early years. Chapter 3 shows how early champions of a sanctuary for the wood bison employed explicitly preservationist language, paired with intentions to erase Indigenous Peoples from the land. Parks officials claimed that the only way to preserve the bison would be to establish a vast sanctuary where all harvesting would be prohibited. Even in the face of strong opposition from Indian Affairs, the vision of elimination was pursued. After the original Park had been created via with the rule that local treaty harvesters could continue hunting, fishing, and trapping within the Park boundaries, O.S. Finnie, then Director of the Northwest Territories and Yukon Branch of the Department of the Interior, hoped to find "some means by which all Indians may be kept out of the area" since he felt their presence stopped it from being a true "sanctuary."[31] Proponents of elimination like Finnie and Maxwell Graham, a Parks Branch official and strong early proponent of the creation of the bison sanctuary, felt that the preservation of bison was in the interests of the advancement of "civilization," which, they implied, did not include the ways of life and presence of Indigenous Peoples. As Valaderes writes, "Canada's national parks are . . . a symbolic landscape used for identity formation whereby natural and cultural elements are inscribed with literal and symbolic value that result in an exclusion of communities and in some instances, a denial of access and subsistence rights in these landscapes held as a natural resource by the Canadian state" or by the Dominion or indeed by all of the so-called "civilized world."[32]

Some historians of Canadian national parks, such as Ted Binnema and Melanie Niemi, demonstrate how, in many cases across Canada, Indigenous

Peoples were expelled from their territories (which were subsequently turned into parks) to appease sports hunting and conservation societies, to establish a tourism industry in the area, and to alienate people from their lands and ways of life in order to subject them to assimilationist policies and institutions.[33] While some of the policies and intentions at the heart of these southerly parks were distinctive from Wood Buffalo, there are striking similarities as well, especially visible in the discourse of public officials, the outcomes of the establishment of parks for Indigenous Peoples and, ultimately, Indigenous Peoples' experiences with park policies and their outcomes. One central impetus for the creation of national parks in Canada, according to Binnema and Niemi, was game conservation—largely influenced in more southern parks by the strong lobbying voice of sports hunters and conservation societies. Conservation policy was typically intent on protecting game populations and habitats, not necessarily for their intrinsic value or for the sake of a pristine wilderness aesthetic, but rather to ensure they survived in the interest of sport hunting or to fulfill other economic needs in the future. Writing on Jasper National Park, Ian MacLaren says that those who "espoused the doctrine of conservation" usually demonized Indigenous harvesting practices. They "insisted on a distinction between subsistence and sport hunting; that distinction symbolized nothing less than the gulf between uncivilized and civilized humans that newcomers were anxious to mark."[34] As was the case in Wood Buffalo National Park, where false assumptions about Indigenous overharvesting played a role in eliminations of Indigenous Peoples from the land, this kind of rhetoric was rarely backed up with solid evidence, MacLaren argues.

In his history of Riding Mountain National Park in Manitoba, John Sandlos writes that, like with other national parks, a "complex array of local and state-driven priorities" underwrote the forcible expulsion of Keeseekoowenin Ojibway Nation members from their homes for the creation of the Park. He describes this as "one of the most egregious incidents of coercive conservation in Canadian history."[35] In 1936, members of this community were forcibly expelled from their homes at Clear Lake, on one of their reserves, Indian Reserve 61A, which the Parks Branch expropriated for the expansion of Riding Mountain National Park. The Keeseekoowenin people's harvesting and ways of life were subsequently criminalized. At Riding Mountain, "the constant and very real threat of fines and expulsion from the park area reinforced the fact that the Keeseekoowenin Ojibway were now regarded as an alien presence on the landscape they regarded as home."[36] Similar processes took place in Kluane National Park in the southwest part of the Yukon, where officials kept Southern Tutchone families out of their territories and policed their land-use and movements throughout the twentieth century. Tutchone residents were denied access to the region that became the Park, where they had lived and harvested for generations. This, David Neufeld writes, devastated their livelihoods and local economies.[37] Furthermore, in the establishment and management of Kluane National Park, the state "denied, not only the validity, but even the existence of the long tradition of deep local contextual knowledge shaping Southern Tutchone values, land use practices and their relationships with the newcomers."[38] Indeed, as Binemma and Niemi argue, "those responsible for removing peoples from parks have often been highly trained people who assumed that their knowledge and oversight were far more valuable than that of local people whose knowledge—accumulated over many generations—and constant presence on the land rendered them highly attuned to subtle changes in the environment."[39] In these ways, conservation policies in and around Parks ultimately have "had the effect of marginalizing local customary uses of wildlife, and in that sense [were] part of . . . colonization," as Tina Loo argues.[40]

Conservation ideology also often paired with an interest in developing a tourism economy. Valaderes describes conservationism as often "buttressed by broader commercial interests."[41] As Sandlos argues, the "pragmatic grab" for Indigenous land at Clear Lake was a necessary precursor to the development of the region for "a projected horde of visitors" who Parks officials imagined might turn the area into "a genteel tourist resort for middle- and upper-class whites."[42] Ultimately, Indigenous Peoples were "written out" of the land to make space for a "civilized" pleasuring ground. Animals protected by this Park were "redefined" as a recreational resource rather than "a source of sustenance."[43] Similarly, MacLaren writes of the transformation of Indigenous territories in what is now Jasper National Park into a so-called "cultured wilderness"—a protected nature area for the enjoyment of primarily white, upper-middle-class tourist families. It also became a thoroughfare for sports hunters. MacLaren writes, "the well-heeled began to make Jasper the departure point for their hunts farther up the eastern slopes," where hunting was not prohibited.[44] But, as he argues, the "establishment of playgrounds entailed the removal of native families who had suddenly become 'squatters.'"[45] Meanwhile, settler development was encouraged. For example, in Rocky Mountains Park (now Banff National Park), town centres were established explicitly to *draw* settler visitors to the area, including permanent settler residents.

In the southerly parks, these processes were closely tied to the "civilizing" agenda of Indian Affairs. For example, as Binemma and Niemi write in the context of Banff, Indian Affairs officials considered the restriction of the Stoney Nakoda people's harvesting rights to be a "blessing in disguise" because it would force people into a sedentary and agricultural existence.[46] Jason Johnston and Courtney Mason write similarly that exclusions foregrounding Jasper National Park's creation supported "colonial processes of assimilation that were occurring across Canada" including "the forced removals of Indigenous Peoples onto reserves for First Nations, and onto Crown Lands for Métis people."[47] These forced removals, along with the theft of generations of Indigenous children from their families to forcibly move them into residential schools, worked together to sever Indigenous Peoples and families from each other, from homelands, and from their ways of life, languages, and cultures. As such, the creation of parks and expulsions of Indigenous Peoples were driven by colonial powers vying for control over land, waters, and natural resources while also explicitly working to eliminate Indigenous Peoples and ways of life as threats to settler normalcy and dominance.

There are a number of important similarities between Dene histories of WBNP and what the wider literature discusses. Like in other national parks, the vilification of Dene ways of life played a critical role in the development of Wood Buffalo National Park's policies and boundaries in the first half of the twentieth century. Theresa A. Ferguson writes that throughout the Park's history, settler officials developed a "literary tradition" that perpetuated an image of Indigenous Peoples as "non-conservers." This was a narrative that both ignored deeply rooted Dene knowledge and stewardship of the environment and claimed that non-Indigenous knowledge and wildlife management were superior. In turn, this narrative reinforced Park policy—including exclusions and restrictions of Indigenous ways of life throughout the Park's history.[48] As in other Parks, forced displacements, evictions, and the criminalization of Indigenous ways of life are central issues that emerge in Dene oral histories. Furthermore, histories of national parks that attend to oral histories reveal striking similarities between the experiences of Indigenous Peoples in other Park histories and the Dene experiences discussed in this book. Sandlos indicates that the archival documents contain little evidence of what occurred on the day wardens expelled Keeseekoowenin people from their homes at Clear

Lake. However, local oral histories clearly indicate that on that traumatic day wardens and RCMP forced people out with little time to gather their belongings and subsequently burnt down their homes.[49] These living memories are similar to what Dene oral histories tell us about expulsions from the Birch River settlements and subsequent burning of cabins by wardens—events about which archive sources are conspicuously silent. Similarly, Roberta Nakoochee writes that Tutchone Elders told her their families experienced aggressive intimidation tactics by wardens in Kluane Game Sanctuary (now Kluane National Park and Reserve)—something that, again, the Dene oral histories point to repeatedly in Chapter 5 but that archival sources tend to be silent on.[50]

There are some important differences between Wood Buffalo National Park and other national parks in Canada. Unlike in many of the other Canadian parks and sanctuaries, sports hunting and tourism were not central priorities for Wood Buffalo Park in its early years—although occasionally officials did mention the tourism potential of a sanctuary with the world's only known surviving herd of wood bison. Furthermore, unlike what happened in the southern parks, Indian Affairs strongly opposed the total expulsion of Indigenous Peoples for the creation of Wood Buffalo Park because sedentary agriculturalism was not a feasible alternative to subsistence hunting in the northern boreal climates of the region. So, whereas Indian Affairs generally agreed to the demands of Parks officials to displace Indigenous families and outlaw Indigenous harvesting practices in Banff, Jasper, and elsewhere, Wood Buffalo Park in 1922 became the first National Park to allow some Indigenous harvesting within its boundaries (but Métis hunters and trappers were excluded). Patricia McCormack has written extensively about Wood Buffalo National Park, describing its history as "conditioned by external political and economic considerations" that drove policy shifts in the management of bison (and, in turn, of people), which were usually reactive and often contradictory.[51] Because the Park was not intended to draw tourism or sports hunting, and because Parks officials were forced to allow Indigenous Peoples to live and continue harvesting within Park boundaries, some administrators did not consider it a "real" national park in its early years. Still, both Parks and Indian Affairs officials were keen to increase the state's oversight and control of Indigenous harvesting and ways of life, and (like in other Parks around Canada) the Park's boundaries, policies, and permitting system played important roles here. The intentions for the Park tended to shift over the twentieth century to align more with state interests in wildlife and game management, control over local land-use, and resource development.

In the end, as the oral histories shared in this book demonstrate, regardless of the intentions of Parks officials, the outcomes of this Park ultimately were displacement and the increased state management of Indigenous lives. In her 2010 book, McCormack argues that the Park was instrumental to larger processes—especially in the twentieth century—whereby Indigenous Peoples and "their way of life, their knowledge, and their Treaty Rights would be dismissed by those with power over them."[52] John Sandlos similarly argues that within one generation of signing Treaty 8, this Park became key to "the assertion of state power over a wildlife population that had been under the local control of Native hunters for generations."[53] Tara Joly's sensitive analysis of bison management in WBNP centres on the experiences of the Métis community in Fort McMurray. She describes the wood bison in the Park as "entangled in a complex web of government-defined harvesting rights and species protections, which come up against legal orders and territorial authority."[54] Bison management in the Park was directly tied to the erosion of Indigenous sovereignty and authority over lands, waters and life, while colonial officials re-wrote bison as "productive units" rather than as "autonomous, spiritual actors in a shared environment" as they are understood under Métis legal orders.[55] Park policy, she concludes, played a critical role in the disruption of Indigenous governance and relations to bison.

The conclusions of these authors align with what we hear in the Dene oral histories: WBNP was in many ways a key instrument of colonial elimination and violence in northern Alberta. The intentions and ideologies shaping this park and its governing policies were a "complex entanglement"—they were never static, but shifted over time and were often contradictory and reactive; that is, they responded to the changing priorities of the provincial and federal governments. The Park ultimately became a key space where shifting (and at times conflicting) state goals of wildlife preservation, game conservation, and natural resource management were inextricable from state attempts to control, restrict, and erase Indigenous lives and ways of life—with specific and long-term implications for the Dene people of the region.

Literature on colonialism in Northern Alberta: "It was all part of it"

ACFN's oral histories tell us that the history of the Park cannot be understood without reference to the wider context of colonialism in the North. For this reason, another important influence for some parts of this book comes from studies of colonialism and resource extraction in the Canadian North—which, as some historians argue, are distinct from histories of colonialism in southern parts of Western Canada.[56] These distinctions are important for understanding the history of this Park as an instrument of colonial elimination in Northern Alberta.

McCormack demonstrates in her 2010 history of Fort Chipewyan that prior to the early twentieth century, direct colonial encounters (i.e. person-to-person) in what is now Northern Alberta were relatively scarce and centred around Roman Catholic missions and Hudson's Bay Company trading posts.[57] For nearly 150 years prior to the Park's establishment, the Indigenous Peoples of the region, including the Dene people, were deeply engaged in the northern fur trade—on which relations with non-Indigenous newcomers were primarily based. McCormack sees the Park and the surrounding game management system that took hold after 1922 to be central to the processes whereby colonial power took hold in the North – significantly shifting the nature of those relations. Whereas Indigenous Peoples retained their sovereignty, ways of life and mobility before 1922, after the Park's creation federal agents were "now empowered to introduce the full weight of the Canadian legal and political systems" in Dene territories.[58] Over time, the colonial state's "theoretical sovereignty" in the North "became real sovereignty... and an edifice of internal colonization was constructed."[59] Control over resource management and extractive industries took hold as the central focus of the colonial regime in what became northern Alberta.[60] In time, Indigenous People's rights, ways of life, and concerns "were largely disregarded when they clashed with initiatives intended to 'develop' the North."[61]

In time, what some scholars describe as "extreme extraction" became a key characteristic of twentieth-century colonial history in Northern Alberta.[62] Historian Allan Greer positions intensive resource extraction as a distinctive manifestation of colonialism in twentieth and twenty-first century Canadian history and "the predominant form of intrusion into Indigenous spaces in recent decades."[63] Drawing on Patrick Wolfe's definition of settler colonialism as elimination, Westman, Gross and Joly write that settler colonialism and extreme extraction are deeply interrelated processes that work together to transform Indigenous homelands and sever Indigenous connections to kin and place in the North. They argue that "settler colonialism seeks to erase multiple stories of and claims to the land, specifically those rooted in Indigenous legal orders, with the colonial goal of perpetual access to and use of the land: creating settler home on Indigenous land." [64] Further, they argue that extractive processes are distinct from, but entangled with, the eliminationist tendencies of settler colonialism. They conclude that "extractivism in northern Alberta represents part of the broader agenda of settler colonialism: acquiring territory, eliminating (or containing) Indigenous presence, and controlling land and resources. In short, extreme extraction can be a product of and an agent of these settler colonial relations."[65]

Zoe Todd also writes in the same collection that "the ebbs and flows of settler colonial resource economies stretch so much farther than the actual site of extraction" citing the example of oilsands activities over the past several decades, which transformed the environment around her family's cabin (at Baptiste Lake, roughly 300 kilometres south of major sites of bitumen extraction in the Athabasca oil sands region) as oil booms brought an influx of settlers building houses and busts, in turn, led them to desert the developments.[66] Like settler colonialism, extractive colonialism "tend[s] to erase local knowledges and understandings of relationships to non-human beings" and attempts to remove particular place-based relations from the land and water.[67] As Joly argues elsewhere, in the colonial extraction dynamic, "land use" becomes a settler colonial category whereby the "Athabasca region is represented as no longer Indigenous, but exclusively an extractive territory, in which Indigenous sovereignties are rendered invisible" so that land can be rewritten in terms of its extractive value. Such erasures and rewritings ignore treaty obligations and dramatically alter Indigenous People's ability to relate to their homes and homelands.[68] Some critics go so far as equating extreme extraction with genocide; Huseman and Short write that the elimination and extractivism in oil- and other resource-rich areas as part of a process of "slow industrial genocide" being committed against Indigenous Peoples in places like northern Alberta.[69]

In their discussions about the Park, Dene oral histories often refer to industrial projects, activities, and corporations at work in their homelands, with which ACFN members are intimately familiar. WBNP is located directly north of the Northern Alberta oil sands, where extreme extractive activity across Indigenous territories has placed immense pressure on Indigenous lands, waterways, and communities—including through the extraction of bitumen and oil deposits, sand, gravel and other minerals (such as uranium) as well as through commercial fishing, and the harvesting of timber and pulp. As a central component of Alberta's energy economy and a focal point of its extractive activities, the oil sands industry is also one of the world's largest sources of energy and of fossil fuel revenue. It is understood to be one of the greatest contributors to global climate change and, according to both Western science and Indigenous Peoples' lived experiences, to environmental degradation in the region. Oil sands extraction refers to the extraction of a type of oil called bitumen, which is mixed with large deposits of sand, clay, and water through various techniques that are both energy- and water-intensive. The largest oil sands patch that is shallow enough to be mined is in the Athabasca region, north of Fort McMurray—upstream of the Park and ACFN's homelands. Canada initiated oil production in the Athabasca oil sands region in the 1960s, and it became a significant commercial endeavour for the province in the decades that followed, according to Hereward Longley.[70] Through a series of Treaty infringements and twentieth-century federal and provincial land-use policies that have privileged extraction over Indigenous rights and ways of life, Indigenous Peoples across the region, have lost access and connection to their homelands as a direct result of the oil sands industry.[71] Alongside other parts of the Alberta energy sector, as well as the many other extractive industries in the region, Westman et. al. tell us that oil sands have "complex synergistic and cumulative environmental and socioeconomic impacts . . . that are not well understood," as well as profound cultural impacts that are understood even less.[72]

Impact assessments commissioned by settler states and Indigenous governments—including some by ACFN and neighbouring Indigenous communities— have demonstrated the extensive change resulting from extractive activities in Indigenous territories.[73] The ACFN Elders' "Declaration of Rights to Land Use," included in the frontmatter to this book, give voice to this reality. As Elders wrote in 2010, "Alberta is not upholding their end of the treaty and is sacrificing our rights to industrial development. We have never been properly consulted and the federal and provincial governments have never accommodated our rights or compensated us for infringements. . . . It is time for governments to stop cheating us of our rights to land use

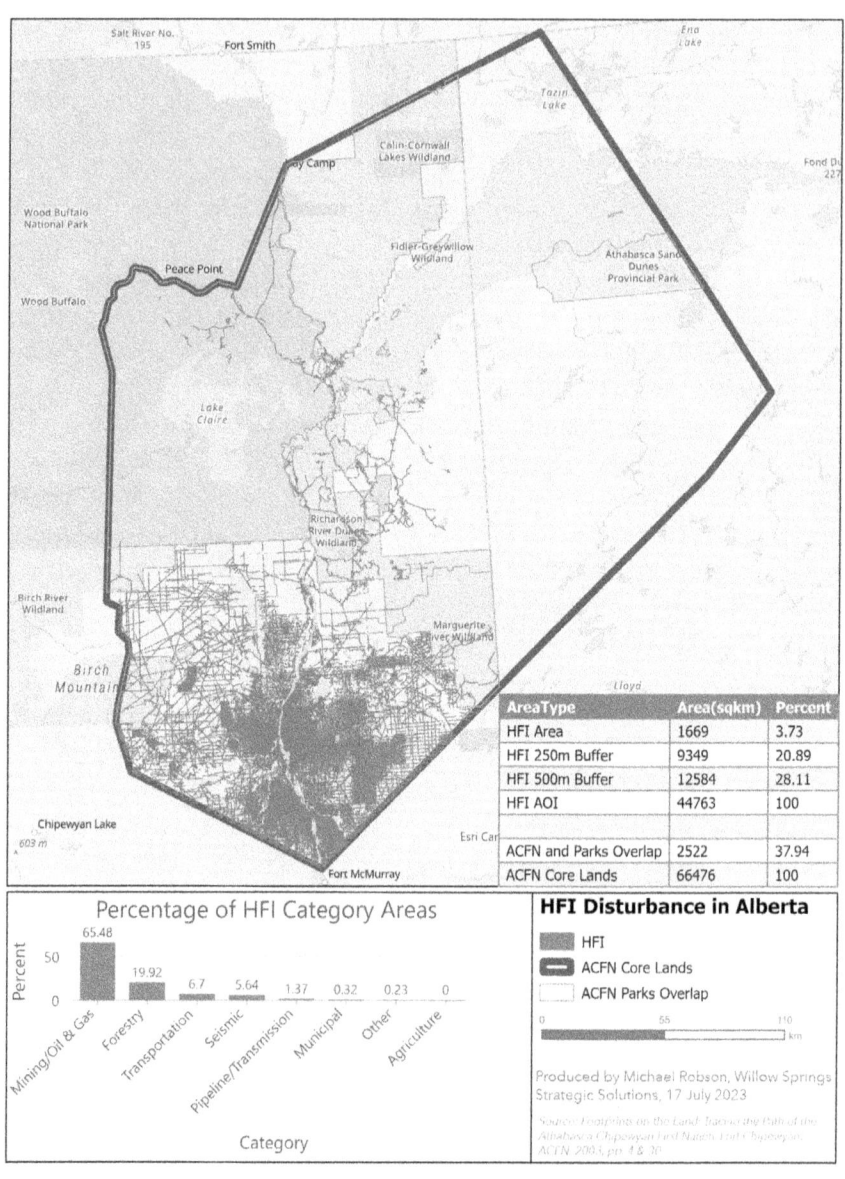

Fig. 0.3 Human footprint inventory map depicting some of the lands taken up within ACFN's core homelands in Alberta.

and livelihood, culture, and identity." Extreme extraction has proceeded despite, and indeed at the expense of, ACFN's Treaty and Indigenous Rights, health and well-being, connections to homelands, and ways of life. "ACFN has had enough with having our land destroyed; no one is dealing with it," the Declaration continues.[74] Oral histories and testimony shared in this book likewise typically position intensive and widespread extractive activities as critical in the landscape of colonial elimination and environmental destruction in Dene homelands.

Figure 0.3 shows Human Footprint Inventory (HFI) data from the Province of Alberta that is overlaid on a portion of ACFN's homelands. HFI is a digital representation of human-generated disturbances (e.g., agriculture, forestry, oil sands extraction) on the land. The portion of ACFN's homelands depicted in this map does not reflect the full extent of Dënesųłıné territories and homelands, but rather a portion that is described as the "Core Lands" in ACFN's 2003 publication *Footprints on the Land*. The HFI data demonstrates what percentage of those Core Lands (not including waterways and shores) has been disturbed or taken up for various human uses, including for protected parks. The data also shows a percentage of lands taken up with two buffer scenarios, one of 250 metres and one of 500 metres. While the data is helpful for understanding some of the colonial shifts in ACFN's homelands, the map should not be taken as a total picture of all change in Dene territories, since it does not and really cannot depict the complexity and far-reaching nature of the impacts of extreme extraction, especially in the upstream oil sands region. Indeed, the downstream impacts of extraction taking place far south of the ACFN Core Lands depicted here do not show on the map. The quantification of "human disturbance" in a percentage as shown on by HFI map also cannot clearly get at the interruption of continuity across Dene homelands. That is, it does not meaningfully display just how "cut up" the lands and waters are by Park boundaries, oil and gas sector mining, forestry, settlement and other industries. It also cannot depict the far-reaching and complex social and cultural impacts of various human activities in Dene homelands: the correlation between being unable to travel and harvest in a continuous and uninterrupted area of homelands and the interruption of intergenerational knowledge and language transmission. The map cannot represent impacts of the industries it includes (or of the intensive extractive activity upstream of the area displayed) on the health and abundance of fish, birds, mammals, and trees, or the quality of air and water. Many ACFN oral histories and testimony shared in this book, especially those in Chapter 7, shed light on some of these complex impacts. The HFI map is not included here to suggest that colonial dispossessions can be quantified or understood as a percentage of disturbed versus undisturbed lands. Rather, it depicts in a limited way a part of the combined extent of colonial dispossessions and eliminations taking place in Dene homelands for the purposes of resource extraction and other industries, and for protected parks.

The unique history of colonialism and extreme extraction in Dene territories in Northern Alberta is part of the backdrop for the harms and intergenerational trauma that Wood Buffalo National Park's formation and management inflicted. The physical displacements and separations of Dënesųłıné families due to Park policies occurred within a wider historical context of drastic changes that Dene people in Northern Alberta were already facing by the 1920s. Oral histories and written archives alike shed light on the devastation of multiple influenza and smallpox epidemics in the 1920s and of the Residential School System on families and the community. The profound implications of an influx of settlers throughout the twentieth century, the growth of resource extraction starting in the 1950s and 1960s, the destruction of the Peace-Athabasca Delta and the many habitats it sustains (especially of fur-bearing animals) after the construction of the W.A.C. Bennett Dam in 1967, and the increasing power of the Canadian state over Northern Alberta are discussed at greater length in Chapter 7. These have all been important outcomes of the increasing power and surveillance of colonial governments and officials over Dene homelands and ways of life. The painful and long-term impacts of Park evictions and permitting regulations, put in place in 1926 to control and restrict Dene movements and harvesting in the expanded Park, as well as a strict system of harvesting laws, have combined with the ecologically harmful activities described above to erode Dënesųłıné connections to and sovereignty over the land and water.

Honouring oral histories

Dene oral history and testimony are the heart of this book, so we drew inspiration from the approaches of other Indigenous-led and collaborative works of oral history as *Remembering Our Relations* came together. Indigenous Elders, Knowledge Holders, and communities have done important work, sometimes in collaboration with academics, to gather and share oral histories and traditions and to tell their own stories on their own terms, for the benefit of the community.⁷⁵ These works demonstrate the critical importance of oral histories for understanding communities' experiences and perspectives on the past. We agree with Greg Younging who argues that oral traditions, knowledge, and oral histories are legitimate forms of knowledge that can stand on their own without comparison to written knowledges. They must be understood, contextualized, and analysed on the terms of those who share them.⁷⁶ Oral traditions are "complex, multi-layered, sophisticated, and richly textured," literary scholar Daniel Heath Justice explains.⁷⁷

Yet Dene Elders tell us that oral history and knowledge have too often not been taken seriously—treated instead as secondary or supplementary to other, primarily Western-produced, forms of knowledge. ACFN Elder Jimmy Deranger recounted an experience he had in the 1970s when interviewing Elder Johnny Piche for the Treaty and Aboriginal Rights Research program (TARR) in Treaty 8 territory. When Jimmy's co-interviewer Thomas Piche began the conversation, Johnny Piche expressed frustration about the tendency to privilege the written word. Jimmy recalls:

> He told us his name was Thomas Piche. That this paper he has is really, really important. With all the words written all over it. The Elder [Johnny Piche] couldn't read and write, right? So, he was telling him that on a paper. [Thomas] was looking at me, then he was looking at Johnny, so [Johnny] turned to me and he was flipping that paper around, like looking at the words. Flipping it around and looking at the words and flipping through the pages, where you can't read what was written.
>
> And he said to me in the Dene language, "I don't understand," he said, "How this paper's important. You know about the land" he said. "Because it's only paper. Look outside, the land is still there," he said. I don't see how these papers can say that land is important when the land has been there for a long, long time. And he said that: "I don't understand it. I don't really know why there's all these little black things all over the papers," he said. And it was the words on the paper, right? He said, "I don't understand," he said. The only thing I understand how important this paper is, if I took it in the bush and made fire with it. That's what he said.

Johnny Piche's frustration with the assumed dominance of paper was important, suggesting that it has coincided with denials and exclusions of oral knowledge and refusals of Dene ways of knowing, understanding and living on the land. Indeed, the chapters that follow discuss some of the ways that, as McCormack explains, "Aboriginal knowledge, which was extensive and richly detailed, was mostly ignored, overridden by assumptions" throughout the history of the Park.[78] These exclusions became central means and justifications for the violence colonial governments, institutions, industries and settlers committed against Indigenous Peoples and homelands in the hundred years following the Park's establishment. It is our belief that by taking oral history seriously in this book, we can challenge dominant interpretations of Canadian National Park history that have excluded Indigenous knowledge and voices. As historian Winona Wheeler points out, the best ways to refuse and challenge such colonial erasures often "can be found within the community itself."[79]

The oral history sections of each chapter are drawn from several places. First, most of the thirty ACFN, MCFN and Métis Elders and community members who were interviewed for the original 2021 research report wished to include some of their testimony in this book. The project team worked with them to ensure that their voices and stories were included on their terms. Elders and other ACFN members reviewed their testimony and, if they wished, revised their interview transcriptions or the sections of the manuscript where their words appeared. In several cases, those who wished to do so selected, reviewed, edited, and situated excerpts from their interviews in the book manuscript where they felt it made most sense to include them. *Remembering Our Relations* also relies heavily on transcriptions from past interviews in research previously conducted by, with, or for the Nation. With permissions from next-of-kin and other relatives, the book incorporates much oral testimony shared by Elders in 1974 for the Treaty and Aboriginal Rights (TARR) program, at the time a branch of the Indian Association of Alberta. Under this important research initiative, TARR employed local researchers to record Indigenous oral histories of Treaty 8, and of surrounding and subsequent historical events, including the creation of the Park. Along with several co-researchers, ACFN member Jimmy Deranger interviewed numerous ACFN (at the time called the Chipewyan Band) members, Métis people and, MCFN (at the time, the Cree Band) members – who, prior to the 1944 membership transfer, would have identified as Dene, even though they were enrolled as Cree Band members because of the transfer. During their discussions, Elders shared extensively about the treaty, reserve-making and Wood Buffalo National Park, as well as many other related subjects. Their testimony is central to this book.[80]

Several other oral histories included in *Remembering Our Relations* were more recently recorded. In February 2010, ACFN Elder Rene Bruno, whose grandfather Alexandre Laviolette was a Dene Chief and original signatory of Treaty 8, and whose mother was present at the 1899 signing of Treaty 8, shared his oral history of the Treaty with Nicole Nicholls, who worked for the ACFN Industry Relations Corporation. This oral history was passed to Rene by his mother. An extensive excerpt of the transcription opens the oral history section of Chapter 2. Rene's oral history was in Dënesųłıné, so ACFN Elder Arsene Bernaille translated it to English. Another recording comes from Elder Pat Marcel in 2013. Working with Arlene Seegerts, he recorded his family's oral history of a 1935 Order-in-Council that was intended to protect Treaty Rights of those Dene people who had been denied access to the Park; this history is quoted throughout the book and then at length in Chapter 7 and in the Conclusion. Additionally, several excerpts included below come from Elder interviews for ACFN's Dene Laws research project in 2015, in which the Nation's lawyers worked with Dene Knowledge Holders and Elders to discern and record Dene traditional laws and legal systems. Finally, four ACFN Elders recorded responses to a written questionnaire about the history of Wood Buffalo National Park before the research for this project began. The date of this questionnaire is not indicated, but some members recall that it happened around 2008. Their responses provide critical perspectives and context to the oral testimony included in each chapter.

Our goal was to stay close to the words shared in original interviews, with little editorial interference beyond those interferences that are inevitable in the transcription process (e.g. the loss of intonation, gestures, facial expressions, pauses, and emotional inflection). When agreed on by the community steering committee and Elder reviewers, minor edits were made for clarity. For example, although the original interview transcriptions are "true" to the recordings and include all "false starts" to sentences, "ums" and "uhs", crosstalk, interruptions and interjections, these are not included in the excerpts in this book. In addition, where a speaker's intended meaning or emphasis would be more clearly understood if a reader had the full transcription or could listen to interview to hear the tone, pauses, or emotional context, we have sometimes provided additional context. Sometimes, we do this through the inclusion of an explanatory word in square brackets. At other times, we add a brief statement in italics before the excerpt to provide contextual details that might not be clear without reading the full interview transcript. Occasionally we also include context in a footnote.

The reader will also note that some chapters contain more oral testimony than others, and that some of the oral narratives are extensive, spanning two or more pages, while others are very brief, no more than a few sentences long. This is because we wished to reflect the great diversity of voices and perspectives—and ways of communicating—that came across during interviews. For example, members and Elders sometimes spoke at length about a topic while weaving in their knowledge about related subjects. Some passages are included in one chapter but not in another where the theme of their interwoven discussions could fit. We felt it was more important to maintain the original flow of the discussion rather than to break things up in order to fit them into our thematic chapter structures (unless specifically requested by the interviewee during review of the manuscript). Elders and members do not disentangle their knowledge of Park history, or their family histories, from the wider context of Treaty 8 and colonization in Northern Alberta, or from their experiences with the long-term intergenerational impacts of Park history. We chose not to 'disentangle' discussions that cover a lot of ground (unless, as described below, a significant amount of time and dialogue had occurred in between thoughts)—because to separate them would be a type of disservice to the community's oral knowledge. We did on a rare occasion edit to address the passage of time in a conversation. For example, during an interview a speaker might have answered a question, proceeded to answering further questions, and then returned to the original question much later, emphasizing different points and details they had not previously discussed, which may have been prompted by the progression of the conversation over time. In these cases, we sometimes retain the original dialogical context to reflect the generativity of the conversations and of oral knowledge. These excerpts include responses or follow-up questions from the interviewer. At other times, however, we use ellipses to demonstrate that significant time has elapsed between related comments on a subject and that other, sometimes lengthy, discussions have taken place between them. We also use ellipses to remove sensitive or personal testimony or that includes references that could make it possible to identify a speaker who wished to remain anonymous.

On anonymity, almost one-quarter of the individuals who shared testimony for the report and this book requested to remain anonymous, including many of the women who shared knowledge for this project. Looking at the biographies of contributing members, which only include those individuals who wished to have their identities shared in the book, one might be inclined to conclude that it was mostly men who shared oral histories for this project. The number of women and men who shared their stories was comparable, but many women Elders who shared their testimony requested anonymity. Several explained that they desired anonymity because they felt fearful of repercussions of sharing their stories—whether potential retaliations from the Park or impacts on their relations with family, friends, neighbours, or others who might take issue with their memory of the events. During reviews of the transcriptions, report, and book manuscript, interviewees could review their anonymity preferences and update them if they wished to do so. Several Elders who had requested anonymity in the original report decided to include their names in the book after reviewing and revising their oral history excerpts and sections of the manuscript draft.

Elimination policies in Canada have shifted how the community is able to share stories from one generation to the next, as is the case for many other Indigenous communities. The very limited number of Dene language passages in this book—the majority of the oral histories were recorded and transcribed into English—is testament to the harmful intergenerational impacts of the Park's exclusions as well as other forms of colonial violence, especially in residential schools. ACFN Elder Alice Rigney, who is one of the community's few remaining fluent Dene speakers explained, "The language is pretty-well gone. You know, mostly everybody speaks English." She and other Elders from ACFN are working hard to revitalize the language. Alice teaches Dene classes to the Elders and does much of the Nation's transcription and translation work. "To me," she said, "the Dene language is so important that I'm going to be teaching it." For this book, the Elders determined that it was important to include audio recordings of Dene language passages with English translations wherever possible to honour the Elders who told their stories in their own language, and to demonstrate how some things cannot be communicated the same way in English. Several digital audio recordings of oral histories in the Dene language are available online. We have also included some excerpts that were recorded in English in some of the chapters.[81]

Centering Dënesųłıné Experiences and Understandings

A central goal of *Remembering Our Relations* is to present a narrative and interpretations of the Park's history that take seriously the experiences, knowledge, and oral histories of the Dënesųłıné peoples whose lives it dramatically altered after it was established in their homelands. Oral histories about the Park, passed down through the generations in this community, point to several key themes. In ACFN historical memory, early Park management oversaw colonial refusals of Dene knowledge and rights, as well as forcible removals of Dene people and ways of life from the land. Combined with restrictive conservation regulations and other colonial policies and processes, such refusals and removals resulted in traumatic intergenerational harm. Dispossession also coincided with the omissions from written records that are exposed when we center Dene oral historical interpretations. Examples include the oral history cited numerous times by Elders, but omitted from written records, of officials' promises that the Park would only be temporary and that Dene people would get the land back after a period of time.

Each chapter of this book touches on some of these themes and is divided into two parts. First, a summary of the chapter theme provides context, with reference to the oral histories, archival records, and secondary literature. Next, each chapter contains excerpts of oral history and testimony from the dozens of interviews that took place between 1974 and 2021. The community steering committee also felt it was important to include copies of some of the archival documents that were key to this history, so links to digital reproductions of some of these written sources are included in Appendix 3. By bringing together a wide range of oral historical, archival, and secondary sources, we build out several broad themes and conclusions based on the community's own critical interpretations of the history of Wood Buffalo National Park.

Dënesųłıné homelands and ways of life

The first crucial theme that emerged from this work is that Dene oral histories highlight the importance of Dënesųłıné relations to, and knowledge of, the land, air, and water and the human and non-human, sentient and non-sentient life they support. Chapter 1, nuhenéné hoghóídi, relies heavily on oral knowledge to provide this critical context to the history of the Park, discussing the community's deep and longstanding relations to the territories that it took up after 1922. Dene peoples have always upheld the traditions, teachings,

Fig 0.4 View of Lake Athabasca from Fort Chipewyan. Photo by Peter Fortna, 2018.

practices and relations necessary to ensure respectful stewardship of the territories and the protection of their Indigenous and Treaty Rights. Their respectful practices across a vast and rich landscape ensure people live healthy lives and maintain social connections and kinship networks throughout the territory from one generation to the next. Like other protected nature areas in Canada and worldwide, WBNP's history was characterized by officials who dismissed local people's knowledge, lives, needs, and concerns. As Ferguson writes, the dominant "literary tradition" in government thinking perpetuated a harmful and inaccurate image of Indigenous Peoples as irresponsible, and thus justified non-Indigenous power over the land, water and animals.[82] ACFN Elder Alice Rigney agrees: "There's this concept that the white people think different than the land users," so non-Indigenous conceptions and land management policies overrode Dënesųłıné people's longstanding relations to, and understandings of, the land and water.

Wood Buffalo National Park and Treaty 8

Oral histories also locate the Park firmly in the context of Treaty 8. This is the core focus of Chapter 2. For generations, Dënesųłıné Elders have articulated the view that WBNP's creation, expansion, and management were violations of Dënesųłıné rights to use and occupy their territories. These rights have existed since time immemorial and were enshrined in treaty when the Chipewyan Band signed Treaty 8 at Fort Chipewyan in 1899. Parks officials claimed that the land taken for WBNP had been ceded and surrendered in 1899, so the Nation no longer had rights to use the land in the Park. They also consistently re-framed Dënesųłıné rights as privileges that were granted by the state. Typically, the Park administration conceded to granting access to Dene people only because of pushback from Indian Affairs officials, missionaries, and Indian Agents, who feared that displaced families would be forced to rely heavily on federal social assistance—a fear that eventually materialized as a direct outcome of twentieth-century Park policy. Some community members have concluded, therefore, that Crown commissioners did not negotiate Treaty 8 in good faith but used it as an intentional means of cheating the local people out of their lands and resources. As ACFN Elder Victorine Mercredi succinctly said in 1998, "They broke their word long ago."[83]

"They weren't aware of WBNP being created"

Dene oral histories tell us that community members did not consent to the creation, expansion, or management of the Park in their territories, and that many people did not even know about it. Chapters 3, 4, and 5 argue that Parks and Indian Affairs officials proceeded to make decisions and changes with limited or no dialogue with the local people most affected. And indeed, archival and oral evidence shows that some Dene leaders actively opposed the Park and that the Park's administration consistently overlooked or dismissed Dene opposition and concerns. Elder Alec Bruno summarized, "The Elders said they weren't aware of WBNP being created . . . no government officials ever came to them for consultation or input from the trappers and hunters of the region. So this proves that they, the government, didn't intend to share this with our people. Trappers and hunters weren't given any say in the formation of WBNP."[84] Other Elders have suggested that, if Dënesųłıné leaders were consulted about the Park in the early days, they were led to believe that their lands would only be loaned temporarily for the bison sanctuary. Much oral testimony suggests that Parks officials promised residents and land-users that the land transferred to the Park would be returned after a limited time—in some oral histories, after no more than 15 years, and in others after 99.

Oral histories express other important counter-narratives to what is contained in the written records. For example, if relying solely on the written records, a reader might be led to conclude that the 1944 membership transfer from what was then called the Chipewyan Band to the Cree Band took place without much impact on the community.[85] The oral histories shared in Chapter 4 challenge this assumption, suggesting that the transfer occurred without the consent or knowledge of many community members and resulted in serious harm to individuals, families, and the community that is still felt today. Government records and warden reports are also relatively sparse in details related to specific forcible removals of Dënesųłıné families from Birch River, or elsewhere in the Park, or to intimidation tactics used by wardens. Whereas Elders and members relate family histories of forcible evictions, warden reports and park memoranda tend to refer to permit refusals and revocations that resulted in exclusions from the Park rather than eviction. Yet, when read alongside textual archives, oral histories clearly demonstrate that, whether by eviction or permit restrictions or both, Dene residents and land-users were often arbitrarily excluded from their territories, homes, and harvesting areas.

WBNP, colonial eliminationism and Dene resistance

Elders and members have also emphasized the violent nature and harmful outcomes of the Park's and province's conservation and land management regime. Chapter 5 presents testimony about Dene people's relationships with wardens and the restrictive game and land-management laws controlling their movements and relations to the land throughout the twentieth century. Elders and members emphasize that Park policy prioritized preserving and conserving animals over Indigenous lives and was steeped in racialized rhetoric about Indigenous land use common to the time. As the late Elder Alec Bruno explained in a statement that is included at length in Chapter 3, "As I see it the government had eradicated our people from their homeland just to be replaced by bison."[86] Bruno's point about eradication is important. It helps us to understand the Park as an instrument of colonial elimination, which Patrick Wolfe has famously described as "the organizing principle of settler-colonial society"—ultimately, the striving for "the dissolution of native societies."[87] Dene oral histories tell us that the Park not only advanced other colonial processes of dispossession and elimination in Northern Alberta taking the forms of residential schools, epidemics and extreme extraction, but also was in itself eliminationist. In the early years of the Park, officials were explicit about their desire to eliminate Indigenous Peoples and ways of living from what became the Park area. Later, permitting laws and other state land and resource management policies also played key roles in attempts at colonial elimination.

Throughout the chapters that follow, we discuss how alienations from kin, land and water, and erosions of Dene ways of life in the history of this Park, were "inherently destructive to Indigenous collectivities" and thus should be defined as colonial attempts at elimination.[88] Members and Elders draw causal lines between the Park and wide-ranging and intergenerational impacts on Dënesųłıné individuals, families, and community. Relying heavily on community testimony, Chapters 6 and 7 focus on these impacts and Dënesųłıné people's resistance and healing. Virtually all ACFN members who shared testimony for this book described in detail direct and cumulative impacts, past and present. The direct impacts of the Park were compounded and intensified in the wider environment of colonial elimination in Dene territories. Elder Edouard Trippe de Roche expresses this view succinctly: "We've been in prison since they set foot in America."

But Elders and community members also emphasize that throughout this history, Dënesųłıné people have also resisted and refused the violence of the Park in creative and diverse ways. As Elder Alice Rigney said when she reviewed the first draft of the book, "we are very resilient people. We are still here and will still be here." At times, Dene leaders made efforts to convince officials to revise government policy, using Park policies to fight against them. At other times, they openly protested Park policies and exclusions, and asserted their concerns through various means about the harmful impacts of Park exclusions. Dene Elders and members continue to assert their Treaty Rights and maintain their ways of life in the face of colonial violence. Furthermore, as many Elders indicated during interviews, Dënesųłıné people shared with one another in times of need. This principle has helped members of the community survive the drastic changes of the twentieth century and harms wrought by the Park and other colonial systems. ACFN's survival, Chief Allan Adam concluded, "is because of determination and hard work . . . The memory embedded in the heart gives us the determination to fight for who we are today." In Chapter 6, we discuss some of the ways that Dene people refused and resisted colonial violence as it played out in the history of the Park.

Remembering for the future

Finally, ACFN members perceive Parks Canada's more recent attempts to address relations with Indigenous Peoples through co-management and reconciliation to be too little, too late. The concluding chapter discusses more recent changes to the management of the Park and Parks Canada's attempts to reframe its relationships with Indigenous Peoples. To many members, such attempts to rectify the relationship, rarely designed or approached on communities' own terms, are inadequate and disingenuous—more conciliatory talk than transformative action. Dënesųłıné people living outside the Park still find themselves on the periphery of discussions and co-management schemes. Yet Elders and members express the view that Parks Canada and the Canadian public can play a role in making transformative change. This is why the community has pursued this justice-oriented research initiative. By uplifting and amplifying local knowledge and experiences, the community believes that words can lead to action: reparative and compensatory action that is defined by Elders, members, and leadership—on their terms and in their timeframe.

"I want everything to come out in the open"

Chief Allan Adam told us in February 2021, "We just want them to know—sure, Wood Buffalo National Park wants to open up to the world . . . and brag about the beauty and the richness and the scenery and everything. But before they do that, we just want everybody to know the story that happened to us." The "them" Chief Adam is likely referring to is UNESCO, which designated Wood Buffalo National Park a World Heritage Site in 1983, describing it then as "the most important protected area within the Canadian Taiga biogeographical province."[89] In 2015, 2017, 2019, and 2021, the UNESCO World Heritage Committee requested that Canada develop an action plan for WBNP due to concerns that the impacts of oil sands and hydro-electrical development threatened the health and integrity and the Park's Outstanding Universal Value, including the Peace-Athabasca Delta. UNESCO has exhorted Canada to address its "lack of engagement with First Nations and Métis in monitoring activities," recommended "clear and coherent policy and guidance" toward "genuine partnership" with rights-holding Indigenous communities and noted with concern "insufficient consideration of traditional ecological knowledge" as threats to the Park's World Heritage Site designation.[90] A 2017 UNESCO Mission Report on the Park highlighted significant changes to the Peace-Athabasca Delta in recent decades, resulting in "multiple, major and complex challenges, stressors and threats at very different scales" especially to Indigenous Peoples who call it home.[91] Nevertheless, to the best of ACFN's knowledge the history of violence and displacement on which the Park is based has not been explicitly addressed in UNESCO communications.

By explicitly centering Dene oral histories, this book aims to challenge colonial erasures and eliminations, bringing local and essential perspectives to bear on the wider critiques of Canada's National Parks system, and questioning the celebratory language often surrounding National Parks in the wider public discourse. Some of the testimony included in this book centres on personal experience and perspectives, while much draws on oral Traditions and histories that have been passed down through generations. Every word is critical to telling the community's story on the community's terms. Dënesųłıné members, Elders, and leaders remind us that this process of amplifying their histories is key for healing and the well-being of future generations. Explaining how he lives with the legacy of his granny Helene Piche's traumatic experience with the Park, Chief Allan Adam demonstrates the present and future significance of sharing the community's oral histories:

> Now ACFN is coming back in there, you got people pushing back against us because they don't want us there, because they've lived too comfortably not knowing the history about what happened. And if they know the history I don't think it would be so forceful in regards to how we were treated and how we're still being treated today. You know, I feel for my granny. She was the one that took it hard the most, you know, she was the one that lost everything. But she had heart and determination, probably didn't even realize that her grandson would be Chief of the Nation one day and how this would come back to haunt me, you know, and make me fight. That's what gives me heart. That [is why I] never give up—a grown man should cry. Chiefs should have to cry. It's through tears that the trail will never be broken again. That's what has to heal.

And my granny left [passed away] in 1992. Everything that my granny told me when she was at home, probably about 60 to 70 percent of that information she gave me, I follow that and keep that dearly as a Chief. That's what makes me who I am. Everything that she taught me—everything; everything she told me, the stories, I've sat down with her listen to her about what she had to go through to make us who we are today. And you know what, I don't want that shame to continue to happen. I want everything to come out in the open and let's move on. Because that [shame] is what's tearing this community apart.

As Chief Adam suggests, and as the many oral histories in this book demonstrate, the voices of those who came before touch the lives and experiences of the people to this day. This book is one way that ACFN wishes to honour and amplify the voices and lives of the past, present, and future. Doing so not only fills gaps in the history of the Park, challenging erasures from narratives about WBNP and the wider history of Canadian National Parks. It is also crucial to the journey for healing and justice Dënesųłıné peoples have pursued for the past century.

1

nuhenéné hoghóídi

The story of Wood Buffalo National Park and its impacts on the lives of Dënesųłıné people requires an introduction to the community's deep and longstanding relations to the lands and waterways taken up by the Park and the region. The Dene title for this chapter, meaning "we watch over/protect our land," indicates the importance of these relations and of Dene stewardship over the land and water. In many of the oral histories shared in this book, Elders and members focus on the importance of the land and water and the life they support to the lives of the Dene people. Elder Jimmy Deranger's testimony powerfully communicated the extent and significance of the area that Dënesųłıné people consider their homeland and territories, and the deep connection the Dene have always had to it:

> So that land is a huge, huge land, and it was Dënesųłıné land. And the Dënesųłıné people then, wherever they were, when people died, that's where they buried them, on the land... the Elders were saying that the land was made with Dene blood. And so, we asked how? They said, "wherever the Dene were traveling, wherever they died, they buried the people, and that blood went back into the land." That's how the Dene land is recognized today. Because it was made by Dene blood wherever the blood went back into the land, all over the land. And [the Elders] were saying that the Dene people, the caribou, and the wolf are one person. And that's how the Dene people recognize themselves today in Dene lands. That's why they have a strong attachment to the land.

For the Dënesųłıné, the importance of the land, water, air, and the sentient and non-sentient relatives they sustain is not defined strictly economically, and their many ways of relating to and understanding the physical world are interconnected and must be understood holistically. The colonial natural resource management system imposed in the twentieth century stressed Dene relations to the land and water, divided the environment into categories to be controlled, and dismissed and ignored Dene ways of knowing and being in their territory. Everything ties together in Dene worldviews: Elders and community members discussed the holistic importance of the lands, waters, and all living beings. Free and unimpeded access to homelands sustains people's health and well-being; supports livelihoods and local economies; provides physical, cultural, social and spiritual nourishment; underlies Dene law and governance; sustains widespread social and kinship relations; ensures the intergenerational transmission of knowledge, language and history; and safeguards cultural continuity. So, the creation, expansion and management of Wood Buffalo National Park had complex and long-term impacts on the Dënesųłıné peoples who had, prior to the Park's existence, lived and moved freely in their homelands since time immemorial. In this chapter, Elders and members share their memories and their families' oral histories describing Dënesųłıné relations to their extensive territories, as well as the ways these relations have changed over time.

The Dene people of the Athabasca River, Birch River, Peace River, Slave River and Gull River[1]

The many names of the ancestors of ACFN shed light on the extent and significance of the lands and waterways the community has considered their homelands since time immemorial.[2] The name Etthen eldeli Dene indicates the vastness of Dene territories, which historically was defined by the migratory patterns of caribou herds. K'ái Tailé Dene translates roughly to the "real people of the land of the willows," referring to the low, woody shrub vegetation that grows throughout much of the Peace-Athabasca Delta, demonstrates the importance of this environment to Dene identities and lives.[3] The language of Treaty 8 clearly indicates that the Dënesųłıné lived, traveled, and depended on the lands in range of all the rivers in the region: commissioners referred in writing to "The Chipewyan Indians of Athabasca River, Birch River, Peace River, Slave River and Gull River."

The oral history and testimony shared in this chapter tells how Dënesųłıné people lived, moved, harvested, and thrived far and wide. In 1974, one Fort Chipewyan Elder explained:

> The people had trapped, hunted and fished around Lake Clair[e] and Mamawi as far back into the interior to the Birch Mountains.

> The people who lived at Little Rapids had also trapped, hunted and fished around Lake Claire into the interior as far back to the Birch Mountain and Birch River. We lived at Jackfish Creek. We hunted, trapped and fish up to the Caribou Mountains. From Peace Point, we trapped and hunted to the Caribou Mountains.[4]

Mikisew Cree First Nation (MCFN) Elder Mary "Cookie" Simpson, whose family resided at Peace Point for decades before they were forcibly transferred in 1944 to the Cree Band (Chapter 4), explained that when she was in residential school, children used to introduce each other by the names of places where they lived. She recalled Dene students saying they came from Gull River and Peace River. "They had homesteads all over the bush," she said. One Elder explained to ACFN member and social worker Lori Stevens that the people traveled toward the Peace River along the Embarras River, following the Peace and Slave Rivers to trap beaver. "They all had that portion for where they would hunt beavers and whatnot. . . . they used to go before the Park was created in the 1920s . . . that was all the area . . . everybody went there.» Oral histories and ethnohistorical studies tell us that that Dene homelands were not defined by boundaries until after the negotiation of Treaty 8 in 1899 and the establishment of the Park in 1922.[5]

"We are the land because the land is us"[6]

Oral histories and testimony tell us that the identities and lives of the Dene people are inextricable from their relations to their homelands. As Elder Alice Rigney eloquently explained, "we are the land because the land is us—that's how we think of it. We are part of it." She continues, "Water is life, and Mother Nature is who looks after us, but we have to look after her. And in between that, that's where the work and the trust is needed." Alice's words tell us that Dënesųłiné relations to the land, water, and the life they support have always been marked by movement, active and responsible stewardship, trust, and reciprocity. Historically, Dene people traveled for much of the year in small groups for subsistence purposes and settled seasonally at other times of the year, usually near waterways like the Peace and Birch Rivers and Lakes such as Lake Claire, Lake Mamawi, and House Lake. ACFN member Scott Flett explained that people's widespread movements on the land and water also kept them closely connected to kin, lands, and resources across vast distances, noting that the land is "all Dene." He expands, "They just moved around, eh—they didn't stay in one area. They probably went to . . . places where they could spend the winters and stuff like where there's food you know, there's fish, abundance of the wildlife, you know. They moved around, eh? Like they're all relatives, right?" Trails that ethnographer Laura Peterson and Dene and Cree Elders uncovered in WBNP in 2018 demonstrate that the area that became the Park was part of an extensive network of paths, harvesting grounds, and homelands that supported the seasonal subsistence movements and the kinship networks on which the people depended.[7]

Dene relations to the land and water have always been diverse and adaptive. Members and Elders described berry-picking, medicinal and other plant harvesting, hunting, trapping, fishing, and gardening as critical subsistence practices that have upheld families and the community throughout the centuries. The Dene people historically harvested caribou and other large game like moose and bison, as well as migratory birds and smaller mammals like rabbits and fur-bearing animals like beaver, mink, and muskrat. Beginning in the late-eighteenth and into the mid-twentieth centuries, trapping fur-bearing animals became both a way of life and a living for Dene people. Elder Big John Marcel said that trapping was for him both subsistence and income. From his own experience he recalled: "this area was my bank, eh. When I was young, whenever I was broke, I would hitch up my dogs and I'd go to our reserve and I'd set traps and I'd killed a couple hundred rats. You know, and I'd come back in town and I'd sell it, I'd sell it to buy the stuff that I need. And it was my bank for me." Elder Jimmy Deranger similarly explained, "When you fly to Fort Chip, look down there. That's our bank. When you look on the land that you're flying into Fort Chip, you look all around, as long as your eye can see. That's our bank. Your bank is Bank of Montreal." Dene people have also always picked berries, fished on the small lakes, and traded along the rivers. These ways of relating to lands and waters have not only sustained people's lives but also have kept the community connected across the territories. Many of the oral testimonies in this chapter also suggests that maintaining connections to the land has been key to the intergenerational transmission of knowledge. It upholds Dënesųłıné ways of living, being, and knowing. For example, Elder Alice Rigney said that her grandmother, Ester Piché, was happy and healthy living near Lake Claire, picking berries and medicines, drying fish, and sharing knowledge with her children: "she made her medicines and passed all this knowledge on. And some of that knowledge is passed on to me."

Fig. 1.1 *Hudson's Bay Company post, Fort Chipewyan, Alberta, 1919*, Libraries and Cultural Resources Digital Collections, University of Calgary, CU1108601.

As Alice's oral history suggests, the lands and waters are like a pharmacy, where people go to gather medicines—sustaining Dene people's mental, spiritual, emotional, and physical health and well-being. Elders' testimony indicates that Dene people harvested salt from the salt flats, gathered birch, and also harvested the medicinal, spiritual, and cultural resources the Delta and surrounding area sustains. Scott Flett explained that the people "had certain areas to get their medicines and stuff, eh. Rat Roots and lavender tea and stuff like that is harvested." Elder Ed Trippe de Roche and Keltie Paul also described the environment as a place to heal: a "hospital," a "retreat," a "spa," and somewhere to "get away from it all," and reflect on life. Elders told researcher Laura Peterson in 2018 that they survived the violence and trauma of residential schools by getting out to the land when they returned home.[8] Edouard Trippe de Roche recalled that when he was a child in residential school, summers spent on the land were a retreat, a time to heal and reconnect: "everybody wanted to get out [of residential school]," he said, "we wanted to go back to the land, you know . . . This was, the life we all wanted, and we were taken away from it. That's the retreat we'd get after ten months in the residential school."

Reliant on the land and waterways as they always have been, Dene people have practiced responsible stewardship. Elder Pat Marcel wrote that they "always had the responsibility of living in balance with the natural environment."[9] Elders think of the land and water as living and sentient, and of their relations to the land and water not just as "land use" but as kinship. Healthy relations with non-human kin are reciprocal and respectful. The Dënesųłıné engaged in controlled burning, for example, and studied the migration and breeding patterns of game and fowl to determine appropriate harvesting seasons. Until they were outlawed under the settler land management regime in the twentieth century, Dene controlled burning practices and other such relations of care are "part of a holistic system of ecosystem stewardship" which exemplifies how, as Cardinal-Christianson et. al. put it, the Indigenous Peoples of this region have always "understood that humans were not the only agents of change in the boreal forest."[10] Ethnographic research that Henry Lewis and Theresa Ferguson did with Indigenous harvesters in northern Alberta in the 1970s and 1980s demonstrated that Indigenous Peoples of the northern boreal forest, including the Dënesųłıné, deeply understood the "systemic, relational effects of burning . . . [and were] well aware of the highly variable ecological relationships . . . resulting from [both] natural and man-made fires."[11] These seasonal patterns and respectful practices across a vast and rich landscape have ensured that Indigenous Peoples lived healthy lives and maintained social connections and kinship networks throughout the territory from one generation to the next.

Intertwined with these stewardship practices of actively and respectfully tending the environment are Dene laws of sharing. Elders emphasized that Dene people take care of each other and of strangers in times of need by living in respectful relation to the land and water and sharing what they have. ACFN member Leslie Laviolette explained, "You know, the sharing part is: we take what we need, and if we have too much, we go give our Elders that taught us all these tools." As Dene laws state, sharing "is an umbrella law; under it sit all the other laws. It was of absolute importance that people share what they had long ago for survival. Share all the big game you kill. Share fish if you catch more than you need for yourself and there are others who don't have any." Helping flows from this: "Help others cut their wood and other heavy work. Help sick people who are in need; get them firewood if they need it. Visit them and give them food. When you lose someone in death, share your sorrows with the relatives who are also affected by the loss. Help out widows as much as possible and take care of orphaned children."[12] Dene laws depend on sharing, helping, and living in loving relation with the land and water, and with all human and non-human kin. Under Dene law, living in good relations with the land and water is closely interconnected with living in reciprocal and caring relationships with community and kin.

Dene places taken up by the Park

Oral histories and archaeological evidence point to many places of importance to the Dënesųłıné within what are now the boundaries of the Park. Most frequently in their oral histories, Elders described Dene settlements along the Birch River (near Lake Claire), and at Peace Point on the Peace River, where Dene families resided and harvested for centuries and eventually built permanent settlements in the eighteenth century. As the fur trade grew, Dene seasonal movements shifted to align with a growing emphasis on fur trapping, and to eventually make use of seasonal wage labour opportunities such as commercial fisheries or sawmills. People began to settle more permanently and in larger groups to be closer to the trading centres, including the Hudson's Bay Company Posts in Fort Chipewyan and Fort McMurray and the other economic and social opportunities that were arising. For example, oral histories tell us that Dene people lived and harvested near Lake Claire for generations, and it is likely that the settlements expanded in the late 1700s and early 1800s after the Northwest Company built a wintering fur trade post at the mouth of the Birch River. Some Elders indicated that the growing power of the colonial wildlife and resource management system also pushed people to settle more permanently in or near the towns and posts. In the oral testimony shared in this chapter, Elders vividly recall some of those settlements, or what their parents and grandparents told them about it. Their relatives were born there, harvested there, married there, and were buried there.

Dënesųłıné families shared space at Peace Point with the local Mikisew Cree community (which became MCFN) before the forced membership transfer of 1944. Members of the Simpson family, who are of Dënesųłıné heritage, described Isidore Simpson's homestead at Peace Point. The family built a two-storey home there in the 1920s before they (excepting one

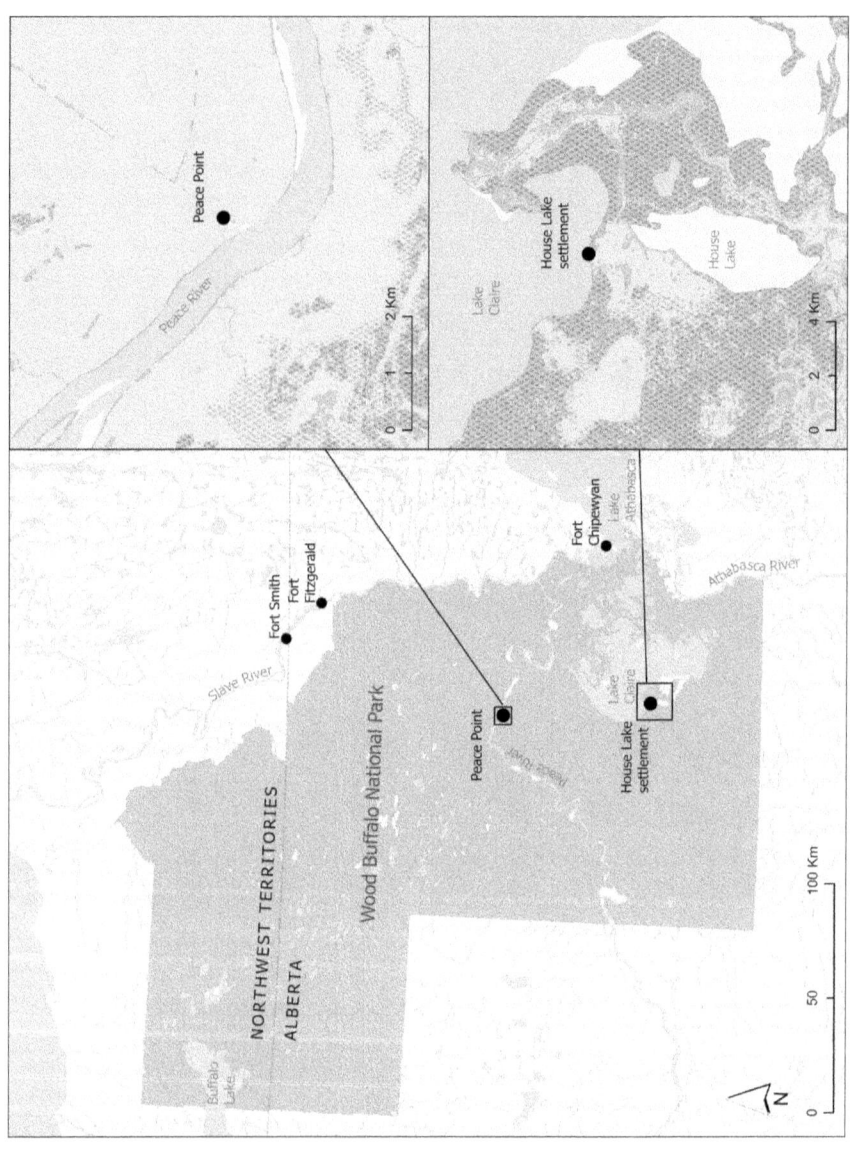

Fig. 1.2 Map of settlements at House Lake and Peace Point. Map produced by Emily Boak, Willow Springs Strategic Solutions, 2021.

Fig. 1.3 *A Dene encampment at Fort Chipewyan, pre-1921*, Libraries and Cultural Resources Digital Collections, University of Calgary, CU1108812.

daughter, Elizabeth Flett [née Simpson]) were transferred to the Cree Band. One Simpson family member stated that Dënesųłıné people lived throughout Peace Point (along with a few Cree Band members) and had homesteads all the way up the trail to Fort Chipewyan. ACFN Elder Dora Flett recalled that her mother lived at Peace Point but was forced to move to Old Fort after the 1926 Park annex; some of her relatives even moved as far away as Saskatchewan. Dene people also established settlements, lived, traveled, harvested, and tended the land throughout other parts of what became the Park, including at Moose Island (sometimes called Carlson's Landing), Egg Lake, Lake Mamawi and Dene Lake, and at other places along the Athabasca, Birch, Gull, Peace, and Slave Rivers, along the Caribou Mountains, and as far south as the Birch Mountains, about 80 kilometres from the southeast corner of the Park. Fort McMurray Elder Ray Ladouceur explained, "Oh, they were all over back there, eh? Gull River, up the Peace River, you know. They did well for themselves, them Dene in those days, eh? Surviving on the land." He continues, "Lake Claire, Lake Mamawi, they'd fish in those areas . . . like way down the bay and all over, you know. Sweetgrass . . . it was good. It was survival, you know."

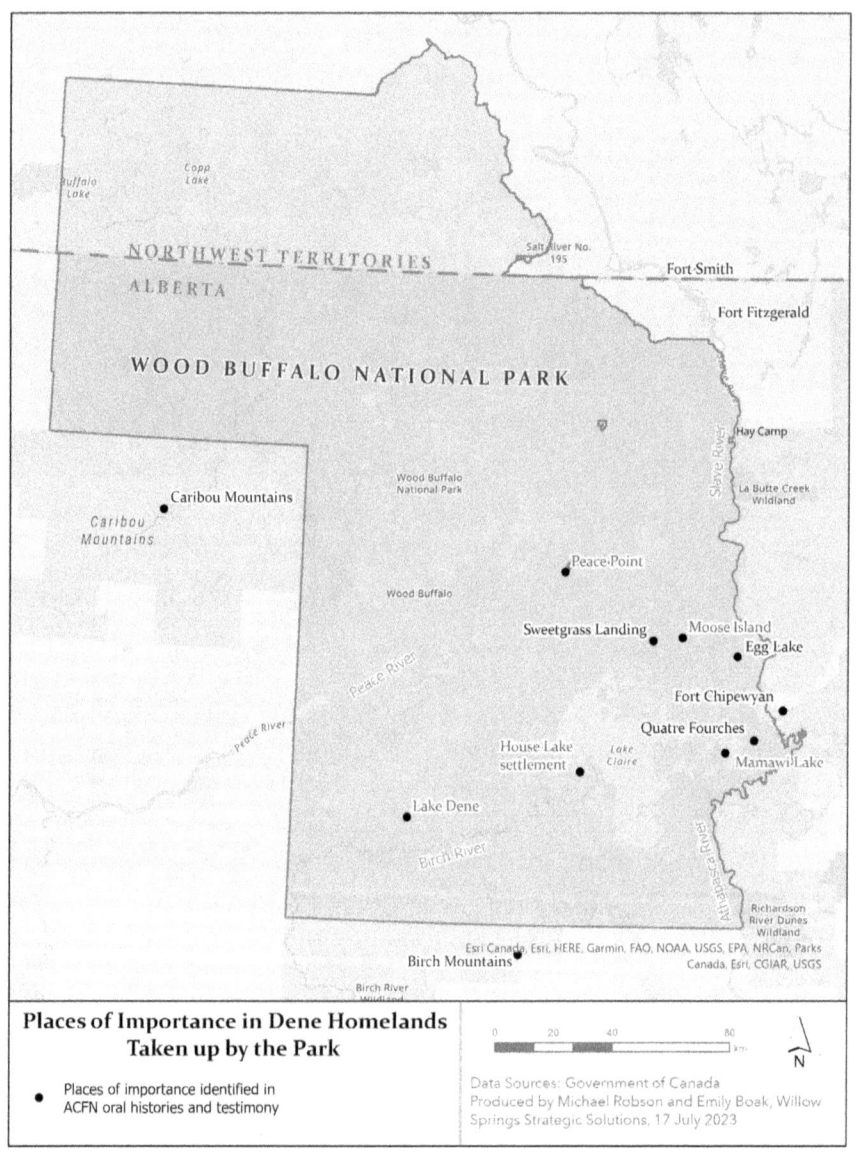

Fig. 1.4 Map of places of cultural importance taken up by the Wood Buffalo National Park. Map produced by Emily Boak and Michael Robson, Willow Springs Strategic Solutions, 2023.

Two Dënesųłıné settlement sites were also built southwest of the Birch River Delta, between Lake Claire and House Lake, and along the southern shore of Lake Claire. In 2011, archaeological studies demonstrated that Dene people had settled in two places: "one near Spruce Point on Lake Claire and the other along an intermittent creek close to the north shore of House Lake."[13] The area was rich and abundant: "The House Lake settlements at Birch River are located in an area containing variable and plentiful resources, such as water-fowl, fish, abundant fur bearing animals and large mammals."[14] People built cabins and houses (which were later burned down by park officials) and grew gardens at these settlements. Culturally modified trees, depressions, foundations, refuse pits, and trails are all markers of longstanding Dene presence there.[15] Materials uncovered at the sites included things residents would have used daily, such as lanterns, wash tubs, kitchen wares, tools, gramophones, and other household items.[16] Dene people lived and harvested at these settlements until they were evicted from the Park. Oral histories and some archival sources also indicate that people were living and harvesting there well into the 1930s. For example, Supervising Park Warden M.J. Dempsey wrote in 1930 that there were Dene people still living and working in the Birch River area at that time: "there are frames for drying meat at many places and camping places are numerous." He also noted signs of beaver, as well as the tracks of moose, deer, bear, fox, mink, and skunk and signs of hawks. The warden recommended increased surveillance because of the presence of Dene people who strongly opposed the possibility of more wardens at their settlements and rich harvesting areas.[17] Some of the oral histories shared in this book relate family stories about the settlements at Birch River. Even though life was hard sometimes, people thrived and lived with joy at their settlements and surrounding homelands.

Some Elders also point to Dene graves and cemeteries throughout and beyond the boundaries of the Park. Leslie Laviolette mentions Dene sites at Moose Island (near Peace Point), and Elder Fredoline Deranger/Djeskelni points to "another small settlement at the Dene Lake, which is west of Birch River, its higher elevation, maybe fifteen, or maybe twenty miles. It's a small lake, but . . . there's settlements, there's graves all over, there's even tombstones all over the place too."[18] As Djeskelni's oral testimony implies, graves and cemeteries help keep the Dene people connected to their homelands. The Regional Municipality of Wood Buffalo (RMWB) undertook an archaeological survey of marked and unmarked gravesites throughout RMWB in 2010.

Twenty-one gravesites were identified within the boundaries of the Park.[19] Oral testimony confirms that many of these, including graves located at Lake Claire, along the Birch and Peace Rivers, at Moose Island, Lake Mamawi, and Quatre Fourches are Dene sites. The gravesites are evidence of the widespread and longstanding Dënesųłıné presence in and beyond the lands and waterways that became part of the Park. They also commemorate the devastating history of epidemics and residential schools that ravaged Dene communities in the twentieth century.

Colonial changes and shifting relations to the land

Elder Josephine Mercredi lamented in 1998 that people were suffering because they no longer lived freely from the land. "It would be better to live like old times," she said, "to live off the lake—the land. The children used to listen to you. We used to all pray before bed. If things were the same, my children might have been still alive, better off."[20] ACFN Elder Rene Bruno explained in 2010 that, living off the land as they had always done, people had been healthy, happy and self-sufficient.

> Everything was good then—the water, the land. Now everything is polluted. Lots of muskrat in the past—people had lots of money all year round from the winter trapping. Didn't spend money foolishly. They weren't lazy, they worked hard . . .
>
> Years ago, the people lived off the land. They knew everything, how to survive. No one can do things the way people used to do things. Nowadays, people go to the university, but they don't know anything about the bush life. Long ago, people knew everything, they worked hard.[21]

The changes to the way of life Josephine and Rene pointed to were combined outcomes of the many colonial processes, institutions, and policies taking shape after the signing of Treaty 8, and especially after the establishment of the Park in 1922.

As some Elders emphasized during their interviews, residential schools were central to the changes to Dene ways of life, connections to place, and sense of identity. Because children were forced into residential schools, they were unable to spend as much time on the land; for several generations, the connections to the land and intergenerational transfer of knowledge was severed. Devastating epidemics in the 1920s and 1930s also affected these connections. The decline of the fur trade, the catastrophic effects of the W.A.C. Bennett Dam, and the combined effects of extreme extraction in Dene territories have also had significant impacts on the ways that the Dene people relate to the land and water and all life they support. The colonial conservation regime throughout the twentieth century resulted in what Cardinal-Christianson et. al. described as "cultural severance . . . an act, intentional or not, that functionally disrupts relationships between people and the land" by repressing and criminalizing Dene ways of life and stewardship practices.[22] As discussed in greater detail in Chapter 7, the convergence of these colonial shifts combined with Park exclusions and policies and the 1944 transfer to the Cree First Nation to radically transform Dene people's connections to their homelands and knowledge. The way of life and prosperity of the Dënesųłıné people was further interrupted twenty-three years after Treaty 8 was signed, when the Park was created. Yet, even through great change, the Elders maintain that the Dënesųłıné people have always been resourceful and adaptive while maintaining their deep-rooted relations to the land. As Alice Rigney said, "we are very resilient people. We are still here and will still be here."[23] Despite devastating changes and colonial attempts at eliminating the way of life in Dene territories, people continued to live as they had always done—though, as the chapters that follow will show, their lives were restricted significantly by the Park and wildlife management regulations.

Conclusion

Living seasonally on the land, moving freely throughout a vast and rich territory, adapting to change over time, and sharing and taking care of the land and each other, the Dënesųłıné were affluent, healthy, and happy until the Park was created in 1922.[24] Marie Josephine Mercredi explained in 1998, "I barely remember how happy the people used to be, enjoying our livelihood. The babies did not cry. [We] would all get together in one place and tell stories, jokes and have a great time, everyone was happy."[25]

Wood Buffalo National Park takes up a substantive area in the massive homelands of the Dënesųłıné. Its boundaries and harvesting rules have impeded Dene people's ways of life, interrupted relations to the land, water, and stewardship practices, and eroded Dene sovereignty. In addition, evictions from settlements within the Park have had a significant impact on the community. Some Dënesųłıné families residing along the Birch River, at the

House Lake and Peace Point settlements, and harvesting elsewhere in the Park, lost access to their family homes, gravesites, spiritual and cultural sites, gardens, and harvesting areas. As Elder Alice Rigney emphasized when reviewing a draft of this book, the Dene people of the Peace-Athabasca Delta region lived a vibrant, healthy, and mobile lifestyle prior to colonization and the Park's establishment.

The oral histories and testimony shared in this chapter reflect on Dënesųłıné relations to the land, water and sentient and non-sentient relatives, as well as the ways in which these relations have shifted over time. ACFN members and Elders tell about seasonality and stewardship, people's movements throughout the wider territory, harvesting practices, kinship connections, Dene laws, and senses of belonging and identity. The oral history and testimony shared here underline the importance of maintaining strong and fluid connections to Dene homelands and ways life. They also help us understand the profound implications of Wood Buffalo National Park on those connections, which have been undermined and interrupted through the Park's creation, expansion, and management.

ORAL HISTORY

Alec Bruno and Charlie Mercredi (2015)

During this interview for ACFN's Dene Laws Project, Charlie Mercredi shared his oral history in Dene. In the written transcription that follows, Alec Bruno translates Charlie Mercredi's message. A digital audio recording of Charlie Mercredi's oral history in Dene is available online.[26]

SCAN TO LISTEN

Alec: What Charlie is saying is we, the three of us here, we live off the land and because when you live out on the land and not in town here, you do things for yourself, everything. You learned to hunt, fish, and anything for your way of life out on the land. You don't have much time to have fun. Not too much. The only time we shared our time together was in the evening. One place we sit and, you know have fun, tell jokes and stuff. That's the only time. In the daytime we were doing something.

What he is saying is that because we've done it that way, we knew how to survive out on the land. Today kids are not like that because they live in town, and they don't go out on to the land too often. Last fall there was a couple of boys who went boating and they were lost for two or three days I think, and we had to go looking for them, and all this time they just ran out of gas. They didn't take enough gas, I guess. They had to go look for them and brought them back. Stuff like that. Nothing like that ever happened to us when we were out on the land. We knew where we had to go. That's the difference today and fifty years ago. This is what we found. So, his [Charlie Mercredi's] story, when you hear his story, it will be pretty well all the same. I trapped in a different area than him. Rene trapped in a different area than him, but at the end of the day it's all the same thing. Over and over, we hunt, we trap, we fish, and you know, we did everything that you have to do on the land.

So with that, when I first started trapping with my dad, I was fifteen, and when we got out on the land, on the trap line, he said 'one day, my son, you have to watch everything I do. If you're not sure, ask me any question but not too many questions. If you watch me, you will learn, and you won't have to talk too much.' That's the way he taught me, and the first thing you do when you're on the land, he said, everything you see around you—trees, lakes, rivers, ice, snow—whatever is there, you have to use it all to survive out here on the land and you have to respect it. The first thing you do is respect the land. Take care of the land and the land will take care of you. This is the way he put it to me. I always followed that. Always remembered his words when I started travelling by myself. And when I had my two boys, I started taking them out. I took them out of school and to the lake. It's about 100 kilometers away from here, in the middle of the winter. It wasn't easy for them but they both did well, and I didn't take them both at the same time. Only one boy at a time. They learned lots from that. I taught them what my dad taught me. How to hunt, how to trap and also, I told them about respect for the land and also respect the animals that you are hunting. It's just that the way life that was meant for you was to use the land, animals, everything, and you have to respect everything. Always thank it. My dad used to say when you kill a moose or a caribou, always thank the land for providing you with this animal. You killed it, he offered his life to feed you. That's why you killed it.

And that's how it is for everything for life out on the land, and you always watch everything you do, even when you're travelling. You hit a lake you've never been on before, or you were there last winter, this winter could be thin ice or something, you run out there and check the ice and make sure it's safe before you cross, same with the river. Everything you do, you have to think before you do it. Especially cutting wood. You cut wood with an ax. We didn't have power back then, all we had is an ax and if you didn't take care of that ax, you could chop yourself and hurt yourself pretty bad. And if you were that many miles back, then by yourself, it's not easy. When we had dog teams it was different. Dog team would take you home. Skidoo—no. Skidoo is fast but if you break down that far back and you have no parts what are you gonna do? You're going to have to walk. And if you got sick or cut yourself, what you going to do? You know, things like that, you have to learn before you do it so it doesn't happen. Those are the things that my dad taught me.

And the best thing, I always remember, always look after the land with respect and everything should be good for you and that's the law of the land. That I learned from him. Today, Western science, don't understand our laws and they don't record it, but I think we should be listened to by you guys and learn where we are coming from and where we would like to take this story to one day down the road. That's what I want from this interview thing . . . That way everybody will understand the Dene law. Dene law is not so much in words. All you could say is Dene law is to live off the land and take care of the land and take care of yourself and respect the animals and everything, other than that what more can I tell you?

Alec Bruno

During an interview for the 2015 Dene Laws project, Elders Alec Bruno and Rene Bruno discussed living off the land and Dene ways of life in the Dene language. A digital audio recording of their conversation in Dene is available online.[27]

SCAN TO LISTEN

Another story my mom used to tell me: Long ago, this was before the white man came to this world, everybody used to live on the land, summer and winter. And there was one old man who used to live with his people and told the people before he died, 'we're lucky, everything is good on the land right now. Lots of caribous, moose, fish, and all these things, you know.' But he said—I could see he was the kind of person who foresees the future—he told people, 'I see,' he said, 'down the road, many years from now, the food that we eat off the land, that same food will kill us.'

And that's what's happening now. See how these people can predict things like that, foresee things. We never had that kind of knowledge cause already things were changing. How did they know these things? I don't know. I used to ask my dad about it, and he said well, that's the way people were long ago, they lived off the land, they lived on the land, they're out there hunting the animals and they are living with the animals, that's what they are. That's how we address Dene people, they are living just like animals themselves, living on the land. You never see white people or nothing, never got food by the store. Just eat meat, fish, whatever. Yeah, that was a long time ago and then when the Creator started coming in and started creating food and everything, everything changed. Totally everything changed, then the guns came along and everything.

Long ago, they just used arrows and spears to kill. See how tough life was? But they were happy because they had a lot of animals to eat. For them, they know how to eat. Today, now, [if] you have to go into the bush to kill a moose with a spear—you'll never eat. That's the difference I think, the way I understand the people back then, years ago, and today. What changed the people was the Western science.

Fredoline Deranger/Djeskelni (19 March 2021)

There was a settlement in Birch River and there was also another small settlement at the Dene Lake, which is west of Birch River. It's higher elevation, maybe fifteen, or maybe twenty miles. It's a small lake, but if you Google it, it will come up as Dene on that lake. And there's settlements, there's graves all over, there's even tombstones all over the place too.

We were all over. I talked to an Elder about Quatre Fourches when he was just a little guy. He said he went there to look after dogs after breakup, in June, I think. And he said it was only Dënesųłıné there, nobody else. Dënesųłıné came from the north, south, east, and west. They all came to the Delta. And they spend the summer in the Delta hunting, visiting, and preparing for the winter . . . I'm interested in the Dene names who were living there. Not living there but who were there because the Dene did not live anywhere – they lived on the whole land. They traveled and lived on the land from season to season.

Jimmy Deranger (24 March 2021).

During his interview, Jimmy Deranger shared the following oral history in Dene and then translated it into English. A digital audio recording of this oral history in Dene, with the English translation (which is transcribed below), is available online.[28]

When the land was there 15,000 years ago, there was the Barrenland Dene who was using the land right at the tree line. And they would go to the Northwest Territories, into the tundra. And then they would go back in the tree line—that's where they lived. That's where they were. And then they went further south. There was Dene that lived in the bush. They were the Dene [of] the Bush. And that's where they lived. And then there was other Dene that lived around the lakes, way up in the Northwest Territories and also Lake Athabasca and around Hatchet Lake [Saskatchewan] and Haylong Lake and Head Lake. All the Dënesųłıné that lived around those big lakes. And then there were Great River Dene people. Like the Slave River, Athabasca River, Fond du Lac River, Stony Rapids River, those are big rivers that the Dene used to live around at those shores, at those lakes too. And then there's Birch Mountain Dene who live around the Birch Mountain area. So, there were five groups of Dene people living in these areas and then on the land which was northern BC, Alberta, northern Alberta and northern Manitoba. And then there's southern Inuit which was, some years ago, was Northwest Territories but now it's Inuit. Then Northwest Territories, some in Northwest Territories.

So that land is a huge, huge land, and it was Dënesųłıné land. And the Dënesųłıné people then, wherever they were, when people died, that's where they buried them, on the land. There's graves all over that land. And others at that time was saying even to this very day, to quite recent like in the late 1990s, the Elders were saying that the land was made with Dene blood. And so, we asked how? They said, wherever the Dene were travelling, wherever they died, they buried the people, and that blood went back into the land. That's how the Dene land is recognized today. Because it was made by Dene blood. Wherever the blood went back into the land, all over the land. And they were saying that the people, the caribou, and the wolf are one—are one person. And that's how the Dene people recognize themselves today in Dene lands. That's why they have a strong attachment to the land. There's so many things I heard in the Dene language, I'll probably be the last person that ever heard it . . .

And even though there were five groups of Dene people, the ones that [were] really up north – Barrenland Dene and Bush Dene, and the Great Lakes Dene, and the Great Rivers Dene, and the Birch Mountain Dene, they travelled. They always did meet each other, somewhere on Dene lands to exchange information about how they are living, about hunting, trapping, and where their food is and where other people have met other people. So, there was always interaction between them over the centuries. They always have been there. The only person that were new were the traders that came into the region, to Hudson Bay. And then the Hudson Bay traders just allowed us to be on our land as owners of the land. They recognized that we were the owners of the land. And then the missionaries came after. And then geologists came after. And then the settlers came after. Each group had a different view of land. But the Dene people always had their same view.

Dora Flett (19 March 2021)

I never heard of anyone going hungry. Long ago, there was no border. You could go anywhere you want. Nobody says, "you're there, you're there, you're there." You're just free going, no border, nothing.

My dad made a sleigh out of birch trees. You would get a big piece of birch, about five inches, a big piece. Take three like that that are two inches, and then he put them in the water for one week so he could bend it. The head of the sleigh, to bend it. They made everything their own.

It was good; we lived off the land long ago. Nobody really had a house, they lived in a tent. Some of them lived in a tent all year round. They had dog teams in the winter. In the summer we could go by boat all over, but in the winter, we used dog teams. We could kill moose and make dry meat, or we could catch fish and make dry fish. There was no fridge in the bush.

Scott Flett (17 March 2021)

That whole area was like, they signed a treaty, like I said—Birch River, Gull River, south of Lake Claire also. The whole side of the south of Lake Athabasca and Lake Claire and stuff, that was all Dene territory, eh. It's all Dene.

Well, they were kind of nomads back in the day, yeah? They just moved around, they didn't stay in one area. They probably went to places where they could spend the winters and stuff. Like where there's food you know, there's fish, abundance of the wildlife. They moved around, eh? Like they're all relatives, right?

Yeah, there were [seasonal] cycles. Like this is the fur hub, used to be the fur hub of the country. This Fort Chip, all the rats, muskrats, just everything comes out to here, pretty plentiful. That's why probably Fort Chipewyan was established because of the fur trade. But, yeah, like I said, I think [19]74 there was a big flood in the spring and then [19]78 I think it was a couple of times it flooded in certain areas. But last year the whole thing flooded and now we have to start over cause everything all flooded so, all those little surviving things, the cycle for say, the little mice and stuff. A lot of animals will depend on mice to eat. Foxes and martens and all this, wolves. So those are gone. Yeah, the Delta here is even migratory birds like in the springtime, man, used to fly, lots used to fly through here in the Spring and that's when people harvested most of all their birds for the summer and for the whole winter, eh? Geese and stuff. And then last year was the, the flyways are changing. Their migratory routes are changing. I don't know where they're going, I think somebody said they're going more up Lake Athabasca, and they're probably coming in from Saskatchewan, coming up that way. So, they're coming through Alberta and a lot of people said it's the oil sands, all the smog from the oil sands and stuff. They're not flying through; they're going around it.

There's lots [of ACFN Ancestors and relatives] buried in and around the Park. I think there's a cemetery at the Moose [Island] or something over there, too, with Dene people. They found a gravesite, like graveyard. Yeah, there was a lot of people, Dene people's thing in that area and stuff. And there was lots of people, they moved around here and there all over the place, but a lot of people stayed right there. Back in the day there was no TV or communication. Maybe they had a radio back in the day but there was nothing to inform about.

Ray Ladouceur (18 March 2021)

Oh, they were all over back there, eh? The Gull River, up the Peace River, you know, they did well for themselves, them Dene in those days, eh? Surviving on the land. And there were some in our part of the country, in Old Fort, there's Dene. You go [to] Old Fort and then Jackfish [is a] Dene place, and there's Dene there. They survived, you know. . . .

I can't kick on the life of the past you know, there was a little hardship, but we survived. Especially, they'd help one another, the Dene and the Crees there, and the Métis, you know. They helped one another. Nobody goes hungry. If somebody goes by, somebody who's got no meat, they fed him. That I've seen myself. One time there's an old man there and hardly any food. My dad and I were going out hunting inland, I was sixteen years old. I camped there. On the way back, I brought him one caribou. One caribou, one dog team. Holy man, was he ever happy. He had meat now, you know. Yeah, that's the way we did. We helped one another. You don't go by a place with people going hungry, you give them meat. People used to be happy, some of those old Dene, because we always helped one another. Going hungry? Somebody'd feed us. Especially the Elders. They used to be real good hunters. Now, when they're old they couldn't hunt, they couldn't do nothing for themselves. There's people out there helping one another, the Dene helped those Elders. Go hunt for them, cut wood for them—for survival. And those people used to be a hell of a good hunters, but as you get old what are you going to do?

Leslie Laviolette (22 March 2021)

We just took what we needed. And if we got more, well, we'd pass it on to our Elders. That guided us in our day, how to hunt, and gotta feed back to other people. You know, the sharing part is we take what we need, and if we have too much, we go give [to] our Elders that taught us all these tools.

Big John Marcel (18 March 2021)

JM: Well, as far as I know, it was all in that area because there used to be lots of muskrats and stuff at that time in that area, so everybody was trapping rats.

When I was younger and when we were living in Jackfish Lake, we did a lot of trapping. When I was young, this area was my bank. When I was young, whenever I was broke, I would hitch up my dogs and I'd go to our reserve and I'd set traps and I killed a couple hundred rats and I come back in town and sell it to buy the stuff that I need, and it was my bank for me. That's the way I always had it. You know, I was young, that was my bank for me.

ST: So did you catch a lot?

JM: Oh, yeah. Well, we used to go out when they had open season and the best season at that time was in May. We usually go out in May, and we don't come back till open water eh, back to Chip.

ST: Did you go hunting, as well?

JM: Well, of course! You know that's how we did [it] a long time ago.

ST: Yeah.

JM: Well, yeah, we hunt all the time. Either we'll get some moose, or we get some birds when they first come in. You know, that was our lives.

ST: So, what about when they made all the rules about hunting, did that change things when they made the park?

JM: Well, in the parks it sure did, but our area, we trapped there at all times. That was our area. You know, used to be all, mostly all, the families that lived around the area. They had their own trapline, and you know everybody helped each other.

Marie Josephine Mercredi (1998)

It would be better to live like old times, live off the lake—the land. The children used to listen to you. We used to all pray before bed. If things were the same, my children might have been still alive, better off.

We used to live pretty good. People used to travel out on the land. The babies were carried on the back of women, in a papoose. They would make warm blankets to wrap the baby in when they traveled. You could hear the babies breathing. Babies must have been tough. The people were nomadic, where they went to camp, they would scrape snow to set up camps, teepees. They would stand the baby against a tree and pitch tents; some were hung in a tree off a branch. The babies were good. They were so quiet; they would sit and watch the people set up camp.

I barely remember how happy the people used to be, enjoying our livelihood. The babies did not cry. They would all get together in one place and tell stories, jokes and have a great time. Everyone was very happy.

Traders would come from Fort McMurray to bring supplies; mail was brought by dog team or horses. Dog team and horses traveled the same pace; this same method was probably used between Edmonton and Fort McMurray. A dance would be held along the Athabasca River, wherever the traders stopped to camp when they hauled freight, between Fort McMurray and Fort Chipewyan.

Victorine Mercredi (1998)

The land was their land, nobody was chief—they lived the way they wanted. There was no such thing as chiefs. Men were equal. Usually, a woman was chosen to be the leader of a group that traveled together. The one picked usually was most knowledgeable about the land. The group would combine their food and eat together. If someone did not have something they shared. People helped one another.

Keltie Paul (25 November 2020)

But where the people used to live and hunt, on the Peace River side, it was mostly the Cree who were in there but there were Chipewyan coming in and out. And before the park, there weren't registered traplines. So, they'd come in and choose a trap line or hook up with some distant relative, or if they saw smoke from a cabin, they knew that they couldn't trap in that area, so they'd move on to another area. So, often down there, there was a mixture of people coming in and out because there was really a global economy that they were involved in, basically the Hudson's Bay Company.

And the area that we're looking at is really a shopping cart for pharmaceuticals. It is also the most extensive, outside of the northwest coast, biodiverse area in Canada. It had geese, and moose, and woodland caribou, barren caribou, you name it, it's in there. So, this was a place that people had access to quite a bit of food. There was always bison to hunt, snowshoe hare was a particularly large part of the diet.

And the cultural and spiritual significance of the land—that was their land. That was their ancestral land. That was the land they were born on. And you and I know what it's like to be born on something, born on a farm or born into a community. That's what it means to us. You can imagine what it would have meant to people who were actually living off the land, who saw spirits into all kinds of things like the water, the mighty Peace [River], the Athabasca [River]. And to have things happen like that, and being kicked out of their own land, it's akin to what happened with the Israelis and the Palestinians quite frankly, and I think that's disgusting. So, they really uprooted an entire culture and took them from everything. Landscape is important to people. It's important to you and me. When people go through a tornado, they come out and the landscape is gone, they go into shock. They just wander around the community, just shocking. And that's what it means to all people, is the landscape matters, the fish matter, the frog matters, everything matters because that's what we are familiar with. We love that. We're so connected too, and if someone comes and steals that from us, then I mean, that's going to shock us for generations and generations because they've stolen. They've stolen, really, paradise. They've stolen Eden from those people who had been there, I don't know, long, long, long, long, long, long ago—eons.

And the pharmaceuticals—I don't know if you know, but there's a massive study of pharmaceuticals that were used at that time in the North. It's huge. And it's a really great thing. And I mean, those were things that were the comfort of the people. The things that would comfort the sore throat, to fix the body, fix the hematoma. My mother-in-law, Edouard's mother,[29] was an expert in that. I used to follow her around whenever she went to get stuff because Edouard has all sorts of colitis, so she needed things to fix him when he was in the hospital. And, I mean, the way that she moved through the forest, through the muskeg, to everything, to bang, bang, bang, bang, bang, bang, picking up all of these things that would be able to make him better, to cure him. I mean, can you imagine if you were kicked out and didn't have any pharmacy? That's outrageous.

Alice Rigney (16 March 2021)

In this passage, Alice discusses her granny, Ester Piche, who was born, raised, and married at one of the Birch River settlements. Her family was forced to relocate after the 1944 band membership transfer (see Chapter 4). Alice's memories of her granny are about time spent at Jackfish Lake.

Fig. 1.5 *Ester Adam (née Piché), Drying Fish, Trap-line, Ft. Chipewyan, summer 1952.* Provincial Archives of Alberta, A17153.

If I was to put myself in my granny's shoes, she had to make clothes for her children. She used rabbit skin to make jackets and caribou hides to make clothing, moose hides for moccasins, because you couldn't go buy these things. So, she utilized the land wherever she was. . . .

Yeah, you know, my granny died when I was still a young woman and I never really got to—she used to tell me stories when I was little. And she spoke only Dene, and I understood but I didn't speak it, so I lost her stories. But she probably was telling me stories about how strong she was because she only had two daughters and my mom from a first marriage. And then her husband died, and she remarried and had another daughter and her husband died. And so, she raised her daughters and trapped, and there's talk about [how] she was a midwife. She was fairly tall, and she was the matriarch. I mean if you slouched over, she would make you sit up straight .

She was always busy. She loved, in the summertime, when I stayed with her. She would have a little tent set up. And in the morning, she'd make a little fire outside and sit by the fire and make her tea and would have tea and bannock for breakfast. And she made dry fish. She made my mum and my aunt very skillful sewers, and she was a good provider. There's stories of mum saying that they used to go pick cranberries in the fall time till the berries were just about frozen. But granny would take them out and build a fire and warm her hands, and just pick because that was the food. We didn't have a store like now to go and get what we need. And so, she used her medicines and made her medicines, and passed all this knowledge on, and some of that knowledge is passed on to me.

You know, regardless of whether you're Cree or Dene or wherever you live, you utilize the natural resources to sustain you for the year. So, you'd pick your medicines towards fall, you know, all your berries, and then you'd have a garden—because my parents always gardened, and I'm sure my granny was like that too. And, in those days after she left House [Lake] and she moved to Old Fort, to Poplar Point, the caribou still needs to come into this area from Northern Saskatchewan. And she would be able to harvest, my mom and my aunt would harvest the caribou and my granny would cut it all up, and there's all this sharing and then tanning the hides or drying it for rugs and, yes, she was a busy woman.

Every year they had a big, huge garden and my dad was an awesome hunter, and fisherman, and trapper. Him too, he never had any formal education, but he knew the land like the back of his hand. And his stories, you know, and then my oldest son followed. My dad and my brothers taught him how to become a land user, a trapper, and hunter. And so that tradition still continues.

Lori Stevens (25 May 2021)

I did have an Elder actually, she came to visit me, and she was talking about how at the Embarras River and then going up towards the Peace, they [the Dene] all had that portion for where they would hunt beavers and whatnot. And, when they were pushed out, that's why everybody went to Jackfish. That was her interpretation of it. So, she definitely did tell me that they used to go before the Park was created in the 1920s, that was all the area. It wasn't just one specific Nation was allowed to hunt there, everybody went there and more specifically for the beavers because the Dene people did eat a lot of it. So yeah, she said mostly Embarras, that area, like Lake Claire, like that. But she said up towards, following the Peace and the Slave. . . .

I know they used the waterways in the winter. There's history of when the fur trade first started that they would guide the fur traders and they knew the whole area. My Papa Isidore, it's my great-grandfather Isidore Voyageur. He was a kind of like—not a scout but a guide. He was a guide for Uranium City[30] and all that area on the other side, to the Park. But he also did work on this, he guided people. So, I would say that because of my family's histories, and his as a guide, he would take them. And we had family in Fort Fitzgerald, the

Dene people there—our families are all connected, but kind of split up now because of the Park.

Edouard Trippe de Roche (25 November 2020)

ET: My mum and dad used to trap, and my grandparents used to trap in Wood Buffalo Park. I heard stories of them traveling in the park, trapping in the park in the spring and winter seasons. And I also have siblings buried there, at a graveyard in the Park.

ST: Oh, do you know when your grandparents were trapping in there?

ET: Well way before 1930 cause my mum and dad married 1930. And my mother was probably a young teenage girl then when they were going up to Peace River. And she's talking about my grandfather having an outboard motor, three horse. And they had a big boat for going through the rapids somewhere up there.

ST: So, if they were trapping in there before the 1930s, were they kicked out afterward at any point, or did they have permits later on?

ET: They never had permits. Because they were—I really don't know—because my mom said—they must have lived in a park at some point or another because I know of two siblings buried in what is now called Moose Island. And so, in order for two people, two of my siblings to die, they don't die in just one day. So, they must've lived there for a little while. . . .

When I was in residential school, they took me from Fort McMurray all the way to Fort Chip. And then eventually, we moved. My mom and dad moved to Fort Chip, so they'd be closer to us. Anyways, being in residential school, all the kids that I grew up with in residential school, June was the longest month of the year cause everybody wanted to get out of the mission. We called it the mission. We wanted to go back to the land. We'd go, when we left Chip [where Holy Angels Residential School was located], we used to go to Jackfish Lake to the reserve. We lived there all summer in a tent, and we'd make dried foods, make dry meat in the bush, go for a swim in the swamp. You know, doing stuff like that. And, I don't know, well, Fort Chip was a ghost town in the summer. Because everybody was in the bush. It didn't matter where you went—to the Park or to the reserve. Anywhere as long as it's in the bush. Pickin' berries. Eating fish. No store-bought meat, you know. This was the life we all wanted, and we were taken away from it. That's the retreat we'd get after ten months in the residential school.

Leslie Wiltzen (21 January 2021)

I mean you can go to the store and buy a turkey. You could go out and get ten turkeys and have a deep-freeze full of turkeys where you could eat turkey once a month. Right now, you know that our geese, our turkeys, our ducks are your chickens. That's the equivalent. The superstore. We don't have the big supermarkets. You look at Fort Chip where prices of food is, they were outrageous up to the point where the Northern Market was put in place. I mean, you look at meat, it's expensive. So, you have to supplement that somehow to make a living, to feed a family. I mean, if you have a large family, imagine what one pound of hamburger does for you. Not very much. So, to be able to supplement that, those resources. And the Aboriginal people have always, always supplemented their resources by depending on what's on the land. Not abusing it—but depending on what's on the land, whether it be a small grouse, a rabbit, or duck, a goose, moose, deer, whatever it might be, they supplemented their diets with traditional foods.

Anonymous Fort Chipewyan Elder (1974)

Since we are the original inhabitants of the land, we have the Aboriginal rights to the land. The land was inhabited by Chipewyans and Crees. The Indians did not go beyond the imaginative boundaries. They trapped, hunted, and fished in the area that they were quite familiar with.

Yes, they lived at the Catfish camping site. They had lived in two other areas also, Little Rapids and Sweetgrass, which is in the Wood Buffalo National Park before the Park was even there. As a young man, I had hunted ducks and fished for a living. Then there were no buffaloes and white men. Where at the present time Snowbird lives along in a southwesterly direction from the community of Fort Chipewyan approximately 35 miles.

The people had trapped, hunted, and fished around Lake Claire and Mamawi as far back into the interior to the Birch Mountains. The people who lived at Little Rapids had also trapped, hunted, and fished around Lake Claire back into the interior as far back to the Birch Mountain and Birch River.

We lived at Jackfish Creek. We hunted, trapped and fished up to the Caribou Mountains. Also from Peace Point, we trapped and hunted to the Caribou Mountains.

Some of the people living around Peace Point and Jackfish Creek had trapped and hunted and fished in a northerly direction as far as Fort Smith.

The people from Fort Smith had also hunted, trapped and fished in a southerly direction. The two groups had at times met each other in the wilderness. I must also mention the fact that the people from Fort Smith had also trapped and hunted in a westerly direction as far as Caribou Mountains.

What I have told you was mentioned to me by my father. Other than that, we considered as important, I can't think of any. But how I raised my children was by means of trapping, hunting, and fishing. My youngest boy is now nineteen years old. I have raised him by means of hunting, trapping, and fishing till he was eleven years of age. There was no welfare at that time. I had raised my family by means of trapping, hunting, and fishing. Many families have also raised their family the same way I did.

Therefore, the land that we inhabit is rightfully ours. It doesn't belong to the buffalo, and it doesn't belong to the white people since we are the original inhabitants of the land. We have the Aboriginal rights of the land to claim as ours. It belongs to both the Cree tribe and the Chipewyan tribe.

Anonymous ACFN Elder (2015)

Well, my Elders, what they usually do, they go easy on the land. They don't play around on the land, with the animals or anything. They don't want to damage the land. I know some old-timers said to us they stayed there for winter, where they were, or where they lived in the spring, they put something [there]. They paid the land, they put something there, whatever they have. Or wherever they go, the first time they've been there, they see a lake or something, first time before they go in there, they pay them too. They don't have anything, they pray to the water, the river or the lakes. Even the animals and—when you skin them, you don't just—what do you call it—you hang it up, you don't just throw it over there. You hang it up. You don't throw around, even the bones. Most bones like the caribou, you don't play around with. You don't play around with the land.

2

t'ahú tsąba nályé nį yati nedhé hólį, eyi bek'éch'á ejere néné hólį

Dënesųłıné oral traditions locate the history of Wood Buffalo National Park firmly in the context of Treaty 8. For generations, Elders and Knowledge Holders have argued that the Park always has been a violation of Dënesųłıné rights to live in, relate to, and steward their territories as they have always done—rights that are enshrined in Treaty 8. The Dënesųłıné title for this chapter encapsulates this perspective. According to Elder Cecilia Adam, it means: "When the treaty was made, a great law was made. Against that [in contradiction] the Park was created."

In July 1899, leaders representing the Dënesųłıné peoples of the Athabasca River, Birch River, Gull River, Peace River, and Slave River met at Fort Chipewyan with Treaty commissioners representing the British Crown to negotiate and sign an adhesion to Treaty 8. Elders' accounts of the event point to both oral and written agreements made in good faith during several days of negotiations. According to the oral histories, Dene leaders understood Treaty 8 as an agreement to peacefully share their lands and waterways with the Crown in exchange for various protections and necessities, including reserve lands, annuities, uniforms, schools and teachers, tools and equipment for agricultural activity where possible, and, most importantly, the uninterrupted "right to pursue their usual vocations of hunting, trapping and fishing throughout the tract surrendered."[1] Crown commissioners noted in their reports on the events that they had assured local leaders these rights would remain unimpeded as long as the grass grew, the sun shone and the rivers flowed.[2] As Elder Louis Boucher told the Indian Association of Alberta's TARR team in 1974:

> The commissioner representing the Queen who was here to make the treaty payment picked up a blade of grass and said, "in the future, this will never be taken away from you. Don't have

any wrong ideas about it. You will always have it. As long as the sun walks and the rivers flow. The way you are making a living in the bush will never be restricted."³

Elder Jimmy Deranger explained the importance of this promise to protect the rights of the Dënesųłıné in perpetuity:

> Whose land is it? Nobody's [i.e. not settlers']. Ours, ours. It's always been ours. Now the natural grass is still growing, the water at Lake Athabasca and the rivers are still flowing. And the sun is still shining. And that's our land. And the Dënesųłıné people and Mikisew people, the Métis people are still using the land as they did before contact and during contact, and to this very day. And will continue to use it. They had used it for 15,000 years, and they will continue to use it for another 15,000 years.

The *Declaration of Rights to Land Use* that ACFN Elders released in 2010 clearly articulates Dene interpretations of the Treaty: "Our parents and grandparents have told us that Treaty 8, signed by our Chief Laviolette in 1899, is an intergovernmental agreement that, in return for sharing our Traditional Lands, upholds our inherent Dene rights to land use and livelihood." Further, "The meaningful practice of our Treaty Rights depends on having sufficient lands and resources to exercise those rights. Sufficient refers to not only quantity but quality, including what is required to fulfill our cultural and spiritual needs."⁴ In 2010, ACFN Elder Rene Bruno recorded an oral history of the signing of Treaty 8 at Fort Chipewyan in 1899—His testimony is in the Oral History section of this chapter. Rene's grandfather, Chief Laviolette, was a signatory—and his mother, who was present at the signing of the Treaty, told him the oral history of what happened there. He explained that it took days to negotiate and sign the agreement because "the Chief gave the commissioner a rough time," making sure commissioners knew the area was Dënesųłıné territory—"that's why we say we own this land" he said. In signing the Treaty, Dene leaders agreed that "they were going to share it [the territory]; that's what they told them. That's the kind of agreement that was made. As long as the sun is shining, river is flowing, and grass is growing." Yet, despite this promise, Rene concluded, "they [the government] are breaking it now. That is what's happening."⁵ As the oral histories shared in this section demonstrate, the Park's creation and expansion, and its management throughout

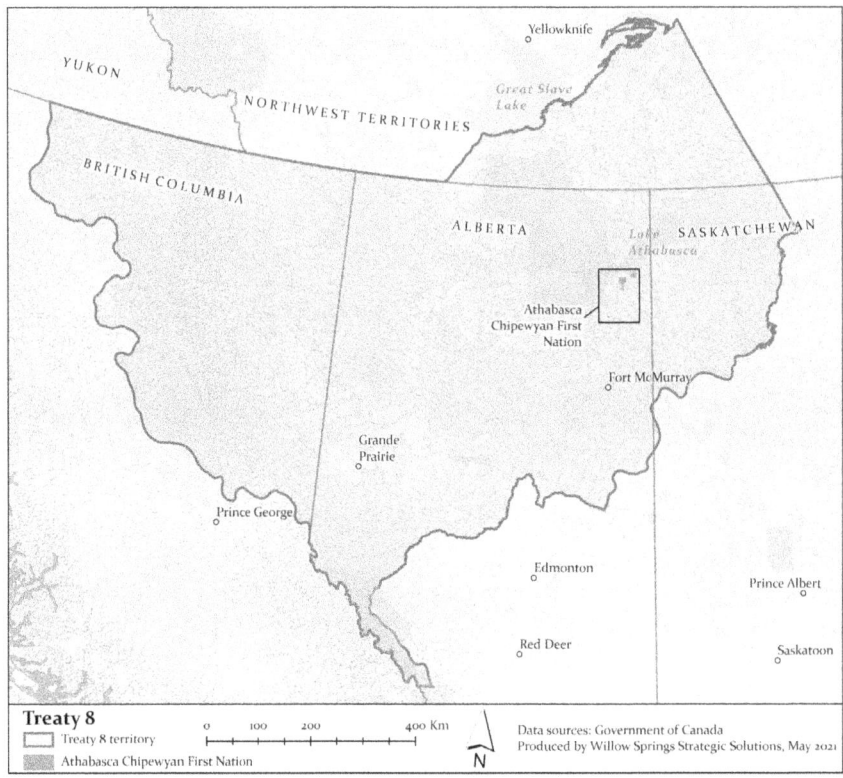

Fig. 2.1 Map of Treaty 8. Map produced by Emily Boak, Willow Springs Strategic Solutions, 2021.

the twentieth century, were among the many violations of treaty that he and the *Elders Declaration* point to.

Oral histories indicate that most of the Crown's oral promises were broken and forgotten in the decades that followed. Furthermore, several terms and promises made orally at the time of the commission were later revoked or altered in the written Treaty document. In his extensive history of Treaties 8 and 11, historian René Fumoleau writes that the precedent for these violations occurred immediately upon signing. He explains how Pierre Mercredi, an interpreter for Treaty 8 who was present at Fort Chipewyan in 1899, recalled that initially there were two versions of the Treaty. The original version, which he witnessed and interpreted in Fort Chipewyan in 1899

Fig. 2.2 ACFN members gather for Treaty Days, Fort Chipewyan, June 2018. Photo by Peter Fortna.

for Dënesųłıné leaders, contained the provision that Dene people would maintain their rights to reside, harvest, and move across the land forever. He maintained that a second version of the Treaty was sent to leaders later on; it contained the additional terms stating that the Dënesųłıné rights to "pursue their usual vocation" was restricted.

> That they shall have right to pursue their usual vocations of hunting, trapping and fishing throughout the tract surrendered as heretofore described, subject to such regulations as may from time to time be made by the Government of the country, acting under the authority of Her Majesty, and saving and excepting such tracts as may be required or taken up from time to time for settlement, mining, lumbering, trading or other purposes.[6]

Mercredi maintained that this clause had been added after the fact: "When the copy came back, that second clause (that they shall promise to obey whatever hunting regulations the dominion government shall set) was in it. It was not there before." He continued, "I have no doubt the new regulation breaks that old Treaty. It makes me feel bad altogether because it makes lies of the words I spoke then for Queen Victoria." Mercredi concluded, "The old Chief came to me and told me that I had spoken the words for Queen Victoria and they were lies. He said that if she had come and said those words herself, then, and broken them, she would have been an awful liar."[7] According to oral histories, the language in the written document eventually made it possible for government officials to take up Dënesųłıné Treaty Lands as they saw fit. In this way, Parks officials sometimes justified the taking up of lands for the Park, the imposition of a suite of strict game regulations throughout the twentieth century, and the evictions and displacements of Dënesųłıné people. Thus, the history of the Park has been interpreted by the community as a history of broken treaty promises and of violations of Dënesųłıné Treaty and Hereditary Rights.

Because of the violations of the Treaty that have characterized the history of the Park, some community members have concluded that Crown commissioners did not undertake the Treaty in good faith, but rather, the Treaty was an intentional means of cheating the local people out of their lands and resources. Chief Jonas Laviolette wrote in 1928, "I would like my brother Indian on the outside to know how the Treaty is being cheated with us . . . I want everyone to know that the White man has gone back on us, with his bargain with us . . . we are getting so tired of asking all the time and no one takes a bit of notice of us . . . I treat my dogs better than we are being treated."[8] Elder Alice Rigney recalled her brother, the late Elder Pat Marcel, telling her, that "they signed the treaty saying, 'we'll take care of you,' when all they wanted to do was exploit all our resources. When you think about it, that's what the Treaty was." Alice believes that Park was part of a long process of treaty violations and an attempt to subordinate or erase Indigenous Peoples who had signed treaty and agreed to peacefully share their lands and waters. "They [the treaty commissioners] must have been real smooth talkers," she stated. "When [the Dene leaders signed that document, everything changed—but not to our advantage. We're a sovereign nation because we signed a Treaty with the Queen of England but we're way at the bottom, beneath the federal government." The creation of the Park in Dene territories, and the accompanying wildlife management policies restricting Dene lives, have in many ways taken priority over the obligations the Crown has to the Dene people.

Furthermore, the Dënesųłıné have consistently argued that the Treaty should have been accounted for throughout the history of the Park, whenever decisions were being made about it or harvesting policy was being generated or revised. Some express the view that the creation of reserves should have preceded the establishment of the Park, in order to protect Dënesųłıné rights, lives, and ways of life before Dene homelands were annexed for bison preservation. Whether the Crown commissioners signed Treaty 8 in good faith or not, a common interpretation emerges through the oral histories across the generations: the terms and promises of Treaty 8, especially the promise to protect Dene people's rights to move, live, and harvest throughout their territories as they had always done, were violated through the creation, expansion, and management of Wood Buffalo National Park. As Elder Victorine Mercredi succinctly said in 1998, "They broke their word long ago."[9]

The oral histories shared in this chapter elaborate on this perspective, suggesting that the creation, expansion and management of the Park fit into a wider historical pattern of Treaty promises broken by colonial governments managing land-use in Dënesųłıné territories and across Alberta and western Canada. Oral testimony, therefore, demonstrates that WBNP became a key player in the history of colonial elimination in Dene territories and northern Alberta. Dene Elders, however, have never forgotten the original terms and intentions of the Treaty and continue to publicly voice these interpretations, challenging the infringements and violations that the Park, along with many other colonial policies, processes, and institutions, represented.

ORAL HISTORY

Alec Bruno (2015)

Just after Treaty was signed, white people, the government, the federal government, when they signed the Treaty, they promised the First Nations a lot of things. Now a hundred-and-something years later, all those promises that they had given, they are taking away from us slowly. And the people are still saying 'how come?' They promised us these things. We never asked them. The thing about, the way I understand Treaty 8 signing is the government, the federal government promised the people, we'll share the land, and the people said, 'we're not giving you this land away, we're not giving you this land, we'll share it with you.' So the government says 'ok, we'll do that but we'll give you all this, you can have this, anything you want, you don't have to pay for anything.' Now it's all changing and lot of medication that was promised to us we have to buy, you know. And school, we have to pay for, well right now the government pays but how long is that going to go on for?

You know, the law of the land is how you look at it, how you understand it and if you as an individual person, trapping out on the land, you make your own laws. You don't make them, you just live by it, that's how I look at it, you know.

Francois Bruno (1974)

The chiefs took the treaty money under the conditions that our way of life will not be curtailed by any regulations that may prevent us from living our lifestyle. The commissioner had clearly stated that no curtailment of any regulations to prevent you from the natural way of life that you now lived. It doesn't seem to be so now. There are regulations preventing us from living off the land.

Rene Bruno (2010)

ACFN Elder Rene Bruno, whose grandfather Alexandre Laviolette was a Dene Chief and original signatory of Treaty 8, shared his oral history of the Treaty in February 2010 with Nicole Nicholls (an ACFN member and staff member at ACFN Industry Relations Corporation). This oral history was related to Rene by his mother, who was present at the signing of Treaty 8. He spoke in Dënesųłıné, and Elder Arsene Bernaille translated it to English.

At the time they signed the Treaty, the missionaries were already here for fifty years. Lots of people already knew how to read and write. When the missionaries came, they taught everyone how to read and write in syllabics—they [the Old People] were pretty good [at it].They knew that the Treaty was coming way before the Treaty was signed. All the people gathered here at Ft. Chip when it was time to sign it . . . there was a nice gathering place, high ground, a beautiful place. That's where they signed the Treaty. When they signed the Treaty, the water was really high, all the way up to here. It was 1899 in June.

The commissioner was here. It took them four days before [Dene leaders] signed the Treaty because it took them a long time. Scared they would go to jail or something like that. The Commissioner said Queen Victoria sent him to sign the Treaty with the Native people. When [my] Grandfather was going to sign the Treaty, he said everything had to be written down—not just talked about before it was signed. The commissioner's name was Conroy. His Grandfather knew how to write in syllabics—that's how he signed his name. . . .

His Grandfather was the Chief—he was the hereditary Chief: when you die, one of your family takes over. When Alexandre Laviolette died, Jonas Laviolette took over. They had the signed treaty in a box with a padlock on it, just like you keep a pipe in.

When his Grandfather died, his wife gave the document—the box with the padlock—to Jonas Laviolette [Alexandre Laviolette's brother]. Rene's mom could read and write and used to help the Chief and write letters. Mary-Anne was her name.

When they signed the Treaty, the Government made a lot of promises to the Native people, but nothing has been done. A lot has been broken—like paying tax, paying for medicine. It should not have happened like that. [My] grandfather told the Government "I don't want you to take away the land. As long as the sun is rising here, the river flowing, the lake is here, and the grass is growing, nothing will change." That's the kind of treaty they made.

The Commissioner said: "Queen Victoria has sent me, I didn't come by myself." When they signed the Treaty, the Commissioner told them, "you live off this land—the fish, the fur-bearing animal, the timber. You don't have to pay anything in that because this is your land. Plus, you don't have to pay land tax because this is your land." The Commissioner told them, "we'll share this land between you and me. We'll never take away the land, we'll share. We could share the land". The Commissioner gave them uniform—"as long as you use this uniform you'll have power, just like government. As long as you have the uniform, you'll be just like the government of this land."

My mom [Mary-Anne] told me everything about this. My mom had all the documents and was looking after it.

What I told you here, it's all true because my mom told him everything that happened in the past. It's not by hearing [second-hand]. My mom was a big girl already, she was there when they signed the Treaty, so she was there when they did those things.

It took them four days before they signed it. The Chief gave the Commissioner a rough time. You see the land as far as you can see, you live on that land, it's your land. That's why we say this is Dënesųłıné territory, why we say we own this land. Because the Commissioner said we would share the land because that's the deal that was made. Treaty is a powerful thing and oil companies don't know nothing about it.

There was only one Nation here at one time—only Dene people. His grandfather came here for Christmas, took seven days to get here from the south. Some trappers come from east from Saskatchewan. Some from NWT.

The Commissioner pointed to the east, the north and south and said 'you control all that land.' That's why we say we own all the resources.

In 1938, the federal government had a meeting behind closed doors and signed an agreement with the provincial government to look after the resources. That's why the provincial government says they own the land and resources. But where's ours? Where's our land? They were going to share it, that's what they told them. That's the kind of agreement that was made. As long as the sun shining, river flowing, and grass growing. They are breaking it now. That is what's happening. . . .

When they signed the Treaty, the way the Government made the promise, the government told them, "I'll promise you cows and plow, we'll give you a ration for food and all the tools for garden" but they've never seen that yet today. Over 200 years now. That's what those Native people are fighting for now.

They promised ammunition, [fishing] net—to make a living with. They put a stop to it. Years ago, people didn't need welfare, it only started thirty to forty years ago. People used to live off the bush—they didn't need welfare.

Years ago, the people never lived on welfare. They used to trap all year round, all winter. They never ran short of money. Everything was good then—the water, the land. Now everything is polluted. Lots of muskrat in the past—people had lots of money all year round from the winter trapping. Didn't spend money foolishly. They weren't lazy, they worked hard.

Rene says he never even came close to what people used to trap. They used to work hard and there was lots of money.

Years ago, the people lived off the land. They knew everything, how to survive. No one can do things the way people used to do things. Nowadays, people go to the university, but they don't know anything about the bush life. Long ago, people knew everything, they worked hard.

The treaty was made here in 1899. We never knew the price of land nor did our Elders. We didn't have any schools then. Once when I was going around with my dad, but now I was able to think for myself, we heard about money. The Queen was sending us money. It was Queen Victoria. She was going to care for us like we were her children.

This was what the commissioner said when the first treaty payment was made at Fort McMurray. Some were not going to accept it. My uncles, they were five in the family, my father was the sixth one. One uncle was in the bush when that business of treaty was taken. My father was encouraging his younger brothers to take the treaty money. He said the understanding was that there would be no end to the money, and I recall vividly that we were paid $15.00 including the children.

The following year they already reduced the amount to $5.00. Long ago our land was very nice. There was no drinking. Very seldom did we see a white man. Nothing was restricted and the Indians made a good living in the bush. Then when I was a young man, I worked on the barges.[10] The money wasn't that good. It was $1.00 per day. But everything was cheaper at the time, not like today. But we were happy about it because we were young. . . .

Within this area, not one person saw the signing of the Treaty. That is the Elders who are still here. I'm probably the only one. The promises the Queen made to us, many of the people have lost. The commissioner representing the Queen who was here to make the treaty payment picked up a blade of grass and said, "In the future, this will never be taken away from you. Don't have any wrong ideas about it. You will always have it. As long as the sun walks and the rivers flow. The way you are making a living in the bush will never be restricted." That was told to us by the Queen from overseas, Queen Victoria. But now the white man is so dishonest. We have lost many things. This is the information I've been told about when I've made my visits to the outside. About the reserve allotment. I was in the Camsell Hospital [in Edmonton] with a councillor from Slave Lake. He said, "Your uncle had forty square miles of reserve, as it was written down." He [the councillor Rene spoke to in Edmonton] eventually became a Chief. He was selected by my father. His name was Don Boucher. That was what took place at the Treaty. Everybody shook hands. It was written that the Queen sent the money and she would care for us as if we were her children. The message was, 'too many Indians are starving to death in the bush. I don't want that to happen again. That is why I'm sending you money.' This was the message brought by the commissioner. That is when we received $15.00 per head.

From then on everything went well. There was no drinking, everybody was making a good living. People were trapping and making money. I was young, too. I also trapped. Finally, I arrived here at Fort Chipewyan. It is during this time that things weren't going good for me. There were councillors, but it wasn't like today where they attend meetings away from here on the outside. Usually at treaty time there was a meeting, and I too would listen in. Only the Chief and Council would talk, and we would listen. They would ask to be given ammunition for hunting, when it would be open for muskrats, when the hunting would end. These are the only things they discussed with the agent. This is what I observed when I sat in the meetings. He [the Indian Agent] also told us we couldn't kill game of the female species. Also, the ducks, we couldn't kill them during the summer. They would be cared for by the Park officials—that was their work. This still is in effect here in our area. We can't kill ducks, only when it is open season when they are flying. This is the information I can give you. I still have a bit of memory at my old age and still do well for myself.

Fredoline Deranger/Djeskelni (19 March 2021)

So, to put it in a nutshell, everything began to change with the Treaty. England, France, Netherlands, and all those people were already eyeing the land from Europe. I guess the treaty was used to further their insight into our territory. Wood Buffalo is not what we expected from the newcomers, because before Wood Buffalo, the Dënesųłıné, from day one, looked after all the Europeans when they came into Canada. They had poor clothing, no roads, no machines at that time. So the Dënesųłıné went ahead and clothed them and fed them and looked after them for over 200 years. So that's a common knowledge amongst the Dënesųłıné people of our country.

Jimmy Deranger (24 March 2021)

It's got to start with the preamble. That there was five First Nations, five Dënesųłıné people—principles, you know? The principles of the preamble that the land was given to us by the Creator for our use, for generations, for generations, for generations. Number two, there are five Dënesųłıné groups. Barrenland Dënesųłıné, Great Lake Dënesųłıné, Great River Dënesųłıné, Bush Dënesųłıné and Birch Mountain Dënesųłıné. Three, that all over Dënesųłıné land, as the Dënesųłıné died, they buried them. And the blood went back into the land, and they recognized that through the blood, after they were buried, that it was made by Dënesųłıné blood. And that's [what] shaped the relationship to the land. Four, in Treaty 8, where it says that when the land is going to open up, that they need to consent with the 'said Indians.' And we're the 'said Indians.' Is it one sided? Or is it supposed to be together? And then, there's still in Treaty, when they regulate [i.e. impose regulations on Indigenous land-use] from time to time, the regulations had to be [made with] the consent of the said Indians. It's those principles. It applied then, it applies now, and it ties into the future. It's Dënesųłıné land. It's our homeland.

Before that, they were free. We just want to be free. That's what the motto was at the time, you could say motto but, it's a principle, eh? We just want to be free. It's right in Treaty 8, we just want to be left alone. We just want to be free. We just want to be free on our lands. We just want to be free on our traditional lands.

I mean, it's our land. Whose land is it? Nobody's. Ours, ours. It's always been ours. Now the natural grass is still growing, the water at Lake Athabasca and the rivers are still flowing. And the sun is still shining. And that's our land. And the Dënesųłıné people and Mikisew people, the Métis people are still using the land as they did before contact and during contact, and to this very day. And will continue to use it. They had used it for 15,000 years, and they will continue to use it for another 15,000 years.

Felix Gibot (1974)

The same promises were reiterated. The Indian said, 'You now have worked on me for two days, and now on the third day, I will talk to you. What you are saying is that the promises are being made in good faith. My people will now be cared for by the government. But I will tell you one thing. I don't want my people to be sent away from our land. I want them to stay here at Fort Chipewyan. It is large enough that there is room for everybody.'

The commissioner told him that this land which now belongs to you, that is the land you can keep. None will be restricted to you. You can make your living the way it suits you best. The Chief said, 'Yes.' That is when they put the coat on him and he was officially made Chief. He indicated that since he was now the Chief, he didn't want the commissioners to say no to anything he said or requested. 'When you make promises to me and I say yes, I have given you my word to last forever. If I agree to anything again, that is my final word and I expect the same from you. The promise you have made I want that fulfilled.'

Margaret and Daniel Marcel (1998)

In this oral history recorded in 1998, Margaret and Daniel Marcel discuss some of the ways the Treaty has not been honoured. They also discuss the devastating impacts of the W.A.C. Bennett Dam and extractive activities on the waters and animals of the region—impacts that are infringements on rights to harvest that were supposed to be protected under Treaty 8.

Only $5.00, always $5.00, was a lot of money in them days when things were cheaper. One good thing is we get free medical.

Today, they tell us if we don't move back to our reserve we will have to pay for our own medical and taxes in Fort Chipewyan. If we move back to the reserve everything will be paid for like taxes and utilities. We are paying our own taxes now; the Treaties are not being honored. The Cree have their own land, reserve, and we have to go to their reserve to purchase tax exempt gas and tobacco . . . The people used to pay $10.00 a year for the trap line, now they pay $80.00 per year. We are also taxed for fuel. The Chipewyan were told that being Treaty meant these things would be provided all their lives, as long as the rivers flow, the mountains stand, etc.

The traps they used all their lives have changed as well for muskrats, marten, and minks. There are different traps now, bigger ones. The traps today are too powerful and destroy the furs. They are only useful as a bear trap. These traps are dangerous, if a person gets caught, they would get really hurt—it could break their limbs. They caught a marten once and it died, which is unusual because they are very tough and hard to kill.

Daniel says he used to go to Old Fort Bay to hunt for meat: moose, geese, ducks in the spring when they came in from the south, and when they went back south, they stopped there again. The geese now do not stop in Old Fort because it dried out, there is no food for them to stop and eat. Likewise, as a result of flooding and oil spills, there are no muskrats either. The meat is spoiled when we do trap animals, because of oil spills. When they find muskrat's den, they find oil in their homes and the rats are sick. They have bleeding noses.

Marie Josephine Mercredi (1998)

Alexandre Laviolette signed the Treaty, but I did not understand the Treaty. Nothing was said in front of me—I was only told about the signing of the Treaty. The Queen's representatives (the red coats) came in full dress, they had guns and shells strapped around them. A week before the signing of the Treaty, [the people] made Alexandre the Chief. He was a smart man. Alexandre thought the men in red with the guns were there to slaughter them. This is what he told the People, he also told the People, the day before the Treaty was to be signed, that he was still not in agreement and did not want the Treaty. The next day they all met outside. The RCMP removed the shells and guns from their attire as Alexandre told them and money was passed out over a few days to the Cree and Chipewyan.

Victorine (Victoria) Mercredi had told [me] that they talked for one week, questioning all the things that would have an effect on them. The people were to receive $15.00 each and the chiefs $25.00 or more. They were told they were to be paid later. When money was sent in they took back $10.00 and were given $5.00 each. They were told the $10.00 they held back was to be saved for the future. They have never seen that money that was to be kept for them.

After the signing of treaty and allotment of money, the government gave a buffalo or two for everyone to share, to cook for the dance, everyone cooked. Everyone was happy and danced for one week. They got a lot of help for store-bought goods to use to cook the feast. People helped themselves to prepare for the feast. The people with both Chipewyan and Métis blood would be considered treaty. Métis with no Chipewyan blood were put separate.

Victorine Mercredi (1998)

They gave $12.00 to families, the whole family with kids included. That was changed to $15.00 per person and $7.00 was put into a bank, into a trust for us. This is what my] father told [me]. The chief asked what they wanted from us. The commissioner promised that they would not break any promises, that they would not take even a strand of grass. They were made to believe they were friends forever. A handshake sealed the promise: 'whatever is needed will be provided like the treaty says, we will never bother you for your land.' There was a three-day meeting. Three days later the treaty was signed. They said the land will never be taken away. For as long as the river flows, and the mountains stand, their word will never be broken.

They broke their word a long time ago. There were two cows given. One for the Cree and one for the Chipewyan. The bands celebrated and made a feast with the cows, a roast. At that time, they were given rations for one year: tobacco, blankets, and dry goods....

The government is selling land to other people. We no longer own the land. The Indians believed that they were partners after the Treaty. The Treaty is no longer honoured.

Alice Rigney (17 March 2021)

My late brother Pat [Marcel] was a spokesman for them [ACFN]. He was a chief negotiator for the ACFN industry and whatnot. And he always used the treaty as a weapon because we, the First Nations, signed a Treaty with the Queen, the Crown.

And here when you think about it, we have the Crown and then the feds and then the provincial and then the municipality and then the First Nation. So we're way down there when we signed a Treaty with the Crown. And, I mean, that treaty promised us that they would take care of us and whatnot, why did we need taking care of? We survived thousands of years before they came. And, my brother [Pat] used to say that they signed the Treaty saying, 'we'll take care of you,' when all they wanted to do was exploit all our resources. When you think about it, that's what the Treaty was. I mean, it was a real cruel way to trick the people and trying to assimilate them into the white society.

Magloire Vermillion (13 February 1974)

Yes, they told me the way the Treaty was signed. My mother and grandmother had told me. It was then that I had first heard of the way the Treaty was signed. The commissioners had pitched a tent at Hudson's Bay Point. That's the site where the actual negotiations had taken place. The commissioner at the time had told us people, 'As long as those islands are there, and the river flows and the sun shines, you people can retain your way of life from hunting, trapping, and fishing. Our government will not make restrictions that will keep you from your traditional lifestyle. It is for your own good that the agreed terms of the agreement will be respected by our government.'

It was on the terms agreed upon, of having the people retain our lifestyle, from hunting, trapping and fishing, that no curtailment of any kind will restrict us from this way of life. It was then the people accepted the Treaty money along with the provisions of the Treaty which were flour, shots, powder, bacon.

We, at the time, didn't know of the real intention of the government, that in later years we were going to have restrictions that would prevent us from our way of life. We had also thought that everything (hunting, trapping, and fishing) will be respected for our own goodwill. As years passed, the government has since imposed upon their agreed terms of restriction that has prevented us from trapping, hunting and fishing. Regulations that we thought would bever be imposed.

In fear of further impositions to the terms of the Treaty, Pierre Mercredi, the Chipewyan interpreter, had warned the people that probably sometime in the future, there would be further curtailment preventing us from our rights to trap, hunt, and fish.

The people at this time were still using the breechcloth and living in teepees. When the Treaty was signed, it was then introduced to the people that such a garment known as pants existed. It was then the people had first worn pants. Before that, it was breechcloth. My grandfather, whose name was Cree Bear, used to use his breechcloth till his death.

Even since the Treaty was signed, we were slowly being restricted with game regulations, preventing us from trapping, hunting, and fishing. There were no such people as Park wardens.

There were some people less fortunate than us who were in need of some sort of assistance to help them because of this situation. There were also some buffaloes around then. They were not as good. Shortly after this, they [the government] have them [the buffalo] brought in from the prairies and along with these buffaloes came the Park wardens.

We were not as free to hunt and trap as we were used to because of these regulations that were made. We were not allowed to hunt snow geese and also were not allowed to use snares to snare our game. It's not legal to use, although we had used this type of method to trap our game. We were then not allowed to trap or hunt beyond these regulations they called a season. If we did, we will then be brought before the law.

'Yes, it's your right to hunt, trap in all seasons,' was what they [the commissioners] had said to us, free to hunt ducks any time or the year.

Leslie Wiltzen (21 January 2021)

When you look at Treaty 8, when it was signed, again I go back to Treaty, our document that was signed in 1899 by Chief Laviolette, it clearly states that "the Chipewyan Indians of the Athabasca river, Chipewyan of the Birch River, the Chipewyan Indians of the Peace River, the Chipewyan Indians of the Slave River and the Chipewyan Indians of Gull River." Now, all those rivers that I just named to you, in 1899, we were told we'd be able to hunt, carry our traditional activities, right? So every one, other than the Athabasca River, runs its boundary on the Wood Buffalo National Park—from twenty-seventh baseline all the way down to Fletcher Channel, up to Embarras. And then from there to Fletcher, and it changes. So when the Treaty was signed, that was all assigned there, saying that was ACFN traditional territory.

Then all of a sudden, speed it up to 1926, we were told to leave. Now we're going to be excluded of all those areas that we signed treaty to in 1899. Now tell me if that's breaking Treaty. Is that right? Was that what was negotiated in the Treaty? That after 10 years of Treaty, the federal government should be able to come and tell us "you have to leave, you're no longer allowed in this part of the country." No, the Treaty was broken.

And that's been clearly stated time and time again in oral history. You know, we go back to 1926, and here we are in 2021 and we're still talking about the broken promises that the federal government put upon the people of the Chipewyan Nation, and what they forced them to endure in the process. I mean, not only the immediate suffering, the starvation and the hunger and the lack of food and the forced to swallow your dignity and ask for handouts. But also, when you go back, you start going through all that time in history where our people weren't allowed to try to practice their traditional history in their traditional territory, up to even you know, when I go back to the 80s, sneaking around in the park hoping not to get caught [by Park wardens]. So, I mean, that had decades and decades and decades and decades. Finally, we have a century of hardship that has occurred because of broken treaty, because of a broken treaty.

Anonymous Fort Chipewyan Elder (6 February 1974)

The Treaty commissioners had set up a tent, along with the R.C.M.P. The question of surrendering the land to them was the main question, but along with this question was the Treaty money and scrip. 'We will give you all the provisions free, forever.' All those who want to take the Treaty money could take the money as they wished, and all those that wanted the scrip could also take the scrip as they wished.

Many of the Indians took the Treaty. It was before I was born, but I am telling you of what I was told. There are other resources and people who may know of how they heard of how the Treaty was signed, like Jack Wylie, the father of Horace Wylie and Victor Mercredi.

They were talking for three days, one day for the Crees and one day for the Chipewyans. The final day was when they actually signed the Treaty with the agreements for us Indians, that all rights pertaining to our way of life will never be curtailed by any laws.

The headmen [political leaders and Treaty negotiators] for the Indians of both tribes were Janos Martin [the leader of the Cree Band], Alexander Laviolette, Julian Ratfat, and my grandfather who was one of the councillors, Incz Sepp [Laviolette, Ratfat and Sepp were leaders representing the Chipewyan Band]. It was then they started giving the treaty money to the Indians on the final day they met each other, the commissioner and the chiefs, with all the money on the table. It was then the commissioner pointed to the sun, the river and the hills looking west, that you can see from the Hudson Bay Point, about where the mission and school are today, that we will never have any laws that will prevent you from your way of life, like hunting, fishing, trapping. But today, long after the Treaty was signed, many of the words of the commissioner are not fulfilled today, since there are laws curtailing our way of life when there shouldn't be any.

In the past, before the treaty was signed, our way of life was not restricted by any laws. We never had thought there would be a day that there would be restrictions preventing our way of life.

And after these agreements were reached by both parties, they then had a Pow Wow, with a feast of two cows which were given to the party by the Roman Catholic Church for this occasion.

It should be written in the Treaty, when it was signed. Now where is this treaty? Maybe the Fathers [priests] have it. They [the government] really are not concerned about our welfare. They never were. They had only seemed to be concerned about the money they used to get from our furs. The government, I don't think, knew about what was agreed on by our forefathers.

It has been a long time since the Treaty was signed. It never occurred to us that we would be curtailed with the regulations interfering with our way of life. The wild game that we hunted and trapped we thought in those days will always be our way of life, without restrictions of any kind. It was then the provision was given us—bacon, shots for our guns.

Yes, it was written on moosehide by the commissioners, that our way of life will remain as so.

At first, we were given $12.00, then they took $7.00 back for the provisions we get today. You know, our grandfathers never told us much about how the Treaty was signed. The only time they mentioned the Treaty was when it interfered with our way of life. We were always living in the bush. I think I have told you enough of all that I can remember, from what [my] grandfather told me.

Anonymous Fort McKay/Fort Chipewyan Elder (7 February 1974)

I was born in Fort McKay.

Traditionally, our people, young and old, when our people mentioned to them what concerned them as an important matter, they listened because it was a matter of importance. That is what I was taught to do is listen and when my father talked to us about the Treaty, I listened attentively to my father. 'When I first heard about the Treaty, it was from my father,' [my father] told me. The people who were white were the commissioners who came to make the Treaty with us. At that time, we didn't have an official headman of any kind since we were always not in a group, we attended to our own privileges of support for our families [i.e. people lived and travelled in smaller groups not requiring headmen and chiefs]. Yet we were able to choose from the people gathered before the actual negotiations, a man with considerable understanding of the concepts of negotiations. He was called Jonas Martin, an Elder. So the people had chosen him to represent us since we were convinced that he could negotiate our demands.

The commissioner was explaining the terms of the Treaty, if we wanted to take the Treaty money, to the Elder.

Martin said, 'If we take this Treaty money, you will perhaps eventually take away our land from us, since you are using the Treaty money as a gimmick.'

Commissioner said, 'No, we will not take your land in exchange for the Treaty money. It was the Queen who has given you this money because she had heard from informative sources that you people were desperately struggling to survive from the land with considerable hardships. She heard that the people of this region were starving. That is the real reason why she has sent this money, so you can make a living. [Your] life will not be interfered with by any outside sources that will prevent you from going about your daily activities, fishing, trapping, and hunting for a living. No restrictions of any kind will interfere with your way of life. You can trap, fish and hunt in any area you wish. You are free to go about your lifestyles.' Martin said, 'If we take this Treaty money, perhaps this money that you are so desperately trying to give us, keep us from our present lifestyle. Perhaps from this money, as a gimmick, will prevent us from trapping, fishing, and hunting. Perhaps we will not be as free to do as we wish.'

Commissioner: 'No, that's not the reason. Even if you take this money, your lifestyle will not be curtailed by any regulations. As long as the sun shines and the river flows, we will not make regulations that will restrict you from trapping, fishing, and hunting, as long as those elements that I have described are functioning, forever you are free to do as you wish. Even the migration of many white people into this country, they will not even take a blade of grass from you. They will not even chop a branch from your land.'

Martin: 'The terms that you have described to us, that there will be no restrictions of any kind to our lifestyles, no curtailment to prevent us from trapping, hunting and fishing, as you say, as long as the sun shines and the river flows and forever. Then we will take the Treaty money.'

After the Treaty was signed, there was a big Pow Wow.

After the First World War we Indians started migrating into the settlement of Fort Chipewyan. Many young Indians were placed in the mission that was run by the Roman Catholic Church. I was one of those young people. I was probably 12 years old then when my father took me out of the mission, when I was able to understand and reason for myself. It was then my father had told me of the way the Treaty was signed, and I have told you all I can recollect concerning the way the Treaty was signed.

It was shortly after this that we [the Nation] decided to take a reserve for means of trapping, fishing, and hunting. My father was then a councillor with Chief Cowie [a Cree Band Chief]. When the Treaty was made, as I told you, there was to be a migration of white people into the area. There will be probably many remembering that this is why we decided to take a reserve for our means of trapping, fishing, and hunting.

It was also said in the agreed terms, that we can set aside a reserve for trapping, hunting and fishing which pertains to our way of living. The area that we choose as land will not be bounded by miles and acres. We are free to take the territory according to our demands of taking, since we are close to nature, and the wildlife that roam the land have no established boundaries. Our forefathers were told by the commissioner to take land as large as they wish.

It was on these terms when my father was councillor with Chief Cowie....

First Treaty was made in Fort McKay. My father was there when the Treaty was made. My father told me about it and also other old people. Although I was young, I listened to them talking about the Treaty. At the time when they paid the first Treaty, my father was a young man. One day the government officials were sent by the Queen to Fort McKay. There was a man by the name of Orphan (Ts'ineke) who was chosen by the Chipewyans to speak on their behalf. The government people told the Chipewyans that they brought them some money. So Ts'ineke did not know whether it was good or not, so he told the people, 'maybe if we take this money we might have trouble and we won't be free to hunt, trap, and fish as we like.' But the government men told them the Queen sent you this money because there were too many people starving to death, so we don't want this to happen again. But anyway, ever since we can remember, we went hunting, trapping, and fishing anywhere and no one stopped us. Maybe this will interfere with our rights, but they said, 'A long as the sun shines and the river flows, these promises would never be broken.' Only after he was sure that they made these promises, he agreed to sign his X on the papers. But before he signed the paper, the government men told him, 'In a short while there will be a lot of white men on this land, so before they come, choose the best places that you want to preserve for yourself to live on.' This land will be preserved for you. They did not mention how many acres or miles. They just told them to choose themselves some land. So only then did he sign his name. So that's how they signed the Treaty. Kawee was the Chief at the time. The place where they called Peace Point was where a few of our people went to look at the land they wanted to choose. After a meeting with government officials my father chose a piece of land and claimed it. This piece of land was twenty miles long and four miles wide. With this land he claimed two lakes that he took so they would have fish for food. After he took the two lakes, it would have been ten miles wide. So the government broke his [its] promise and told them they were taking too much land, so to this day, they don't have a reserve.

I believe that the only thing the government bought was the land surface, timber and grass. As far as I am concerned, I still believe that I own the game, fish, birds, and also the gas, oil, minerals, etc. underground.

For only $5.00 a year, I don't think he [the government] should own everything.

At that time when we made the Treaty, the government promised to give us a game warden to protect game for us. And also, the government promised us a policeman to protect us from trouble.

There were no borders on our land, as far as hunting game, fishing, etc. was concerned. We could go to Saskatchewan or any place to hunt and no one stopped us. Now things are changing against the promises of our Treaty.

3

t'ahú ejeré néné hólį ú t'ahú nuhghą nįh łą hílchú

In the early 2000s, the late Elder Alec Bruno described Wood Buffalo National Park as a violation of Treaty 8. He stated, "our people were promised that as long as the sun rose, river flows, and the grass grows, the people will never be interfered with as to where they lived and maintained their way of life traditionally. Their land will never be taken away from them. Yet twenty-some years later our people were told to leave their respective area and relocate elsewhere."[1] Dene histories of Wood Buffalo National Park, like Alec Bruno's, consistently return to this important interpretation. The title of this chapter, t'ahú ejeré néné hólį ú t'ahú nuhghą nįh łą hílchú, translates to "when the Park was created, and when a lot of land was taken from us," emphasizing the profound loss of access to Dene homelands that accompanied the creation of the Park. In interviews from the 1970s to the present, Elders have consistently indicated that the Park was both established in 1922 and expanded in 1926 without the knowledge or consent of most of the Indigenous residents in the area who would be most affected by it. Rather, oral histories suggest that the few Dene leaders who were told about the Park were led to believe that the existence of a bison sanctuary in Dene lands would only be temporary—that Dene lands were being loaned to the government for the protection of bison. Additionally, the restrictions subsequently imposed on Dene lives and lifeways through a permitting system, harvesting laws, and forced relocations and exclusions of Dene families and harvesters from their homes and harvesting places in the Park, represented a violation of Treaty 8. Finally, these restrictions resulted in widespread and intergenerational harm to Dene families, harvesters and community.

This chapter focuses on the establishment of Wood Buffalo Park in 1922 and the subsequent expansion of its boundaries in 1926, after the importation of nearly 7,000 plains bison to the Park starting in 1925. Drawing together the

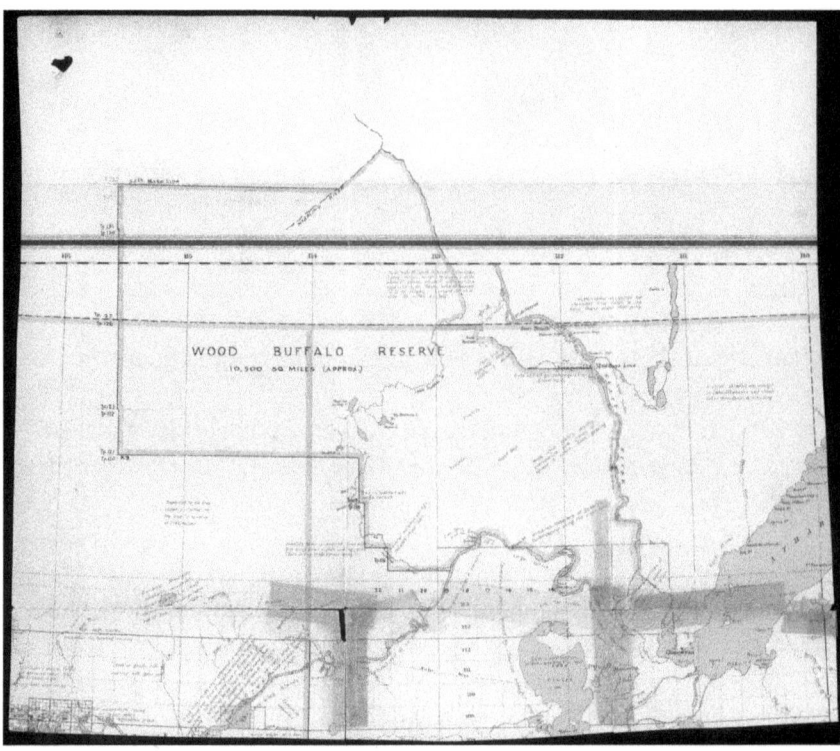

Fig. 3.1 Map of the original Wood Buffalo Park boundaries, 1922. LAC RG85, vol. 1390, file 406-13.

oral histories and the expansive archival record from the early decades of the Park, it becomes apparent that the intentions and management of the Park shifted over time, often reactively as issues emerged. Prior to 1922, officials positioned the preservation of wood bison as essential to the Dominion and Empire—and to "the entire civilized world" as Maxwell Graham put it in a letter to Parks Commissioner J.B. Harkin in 1912.[2] They contended that the presence and ways of life of Indigenous Peoples were a threat to the wood bison's preservation, implying that Indigenous Peoples and ways of life did not belong to the so-called "civilized world" and were therefore unwanted. As was the case elsewhere in the British Empire's growing network of parks and game sanctuaries, such implications justified the forcible displacement of Indigenous Peoples who lived and harvested throughout the Peace-Athabasca

Delta, and of non-Indigenous peoples for the first four years of the Park's existence. Through this kind of discourse and subsequent displacements and restrictions on Indigenous ways of life, the Park and policies governing it explicitly became tools of colonial elimination in the region, with long-term implications for the relatives of ACFN.

The intentions and policies governing the Park also shifted over time, often reactively. Dene resistance and interventions by the Indian Affairs Branch prevented the total displacement of all Indigenous Peoples within the Park in the early years. When the herd of plains bison in the boundaries of Buffalo National Park in Wainwright, Alberta became too large to manage, from 1925–28 officials moved some of them north to Wood Buffalo Park, despite widespread opposition from local Indigenous residents and the global scientific community. The newly imported plains bison migrated out of the 1922 boundaries of Wood Buffalo Park immediately afterward. In turn, officials expanded those boundaries south of the Peace River, into Dene homelands in the Peace-Athabasca Delta. They then established a permitting system to regulate the movement and activities of residents and harvesters throughout the Park. The Park also became a means to shore up state control over the northern fur economy. Seven years before the Park was established, Parks Commissioner J.B. Harkin suggested that a bison sanctuary could serve as a sanctuary for fur-bearers and a designated area to provide sport and recreation opportunities for those living nearby.[3] In the early decades, then, Park policy was intent on taking up lands to preserve wood bison and to manage wildlife resources; in turn officials could restrict Indigenous lives and lifeways that stood in the way of state control. Ultimately, the restrictions imposed on human access and movement throughout the Park, resulted in the displacement of Dene people from their homes and harvesting areas. This was especially the case after the 1926 Park expansion and subsequent establishment of a strict permitting system regulating movement and activity in the Park. While officials' intentions vacillated from preservation to conservation to resource management, their goals were inextricable from state attempts to control, restrict, and eliminate Indigenous lives and lifeways as the power of the colonial state over lands, waters, and natural resources shifted north.

Dene oral histories articulate the community's perspective that while the original establishment of the Park posed challenges, the 1926 expansion of Wood Buffalo Park had more severe and wider spread impacts. Following the 1926 annex of Dënesųłıné lands to expand the Park south of the Peace River, the strict new permitting regulations increased state control over Dene lives, movements, and land-use. Permit revocations or denials, coupled with expulsions of Dene people from their homes and harvesting areas, led in turn to hunger and economic hardship, as people struggled to procure enough food, supplies or money to subsist. As Elder Horace Adam and other ACFN members hold, this was a clear violation of treaty that resulted in harm for Dene families. He states, "after the Treaty was signed and the federal government took over the National Park . . . the Indigenous Peoples didn't get access. So the Park was stolen." Colonial policies of displacement and control in Dene territories were then enforced and strengthened through the expansion of the Park's warden system, discussed further in Chapter 5. Imposed restrictions ensured that many Dene people stayed out of the Park out of fear of violent repercussions. "Even today," states one ACFN Elder, "I will not go to the Park. I wouldn't even think of going to the Park . . . in all our family, nobody goes to the Parks. Nobody."

"Steps cannot be taken too soon": Early plans for a bison sanctuary

The idea to establish a bison sanctuary was first proposed as early as 1911 as a solution to what some officials perceived as the urgent need to preserve the last-known remaining wood bison herd in North America. At this time, bison hunting (including by Indigenous harvesters) had been prohibited under the 1894 *Unorganized Territories Preservation Act*. But this ban was set to last only until 1912. Foreseeing that state control over wood bison protection would soon come to end, and concerned that the population was still endangered, officials from the Department of the Interior—especially Maxwell Graham, Parks Branch, Animal Division; O.S. Finnie, Director, Northwest Territories and Yukon Branch; and F.H. Kitto, Natural Resources Intelligence Branch—sought to establish more permanent protections through the creation of a sanctuary or national park covering the entire wood bison range from the Caribou Mountains to the Slave River. One Parks Branch memorandum emphasized that "it seems very desirable that some action be taken as soon as possible to afford additional protection to the wood buffalo" and that "there is grave danger" facing the bison because of the 1912 conclusion of the ban on bison hunting.[4]

Claims about the urgent need to preserve species like the wood bison of this region and to manage and conserve other species went hand-in-hand with a widely held view that wolves and human hunters were a "menace," and that a sanctuary where all hunting was prohibited and wolves were culled was the best means of protecting species of interest.[5] Officials considered Indigenous harvesters in particular to be a threat. In a 1912 letter to Parks Commissioner J.B. Harkin, heavily laden with preservation rhetoric of the time, Maxwell Graham recommended that a park that would remove the presence of local Indigenous Peoples to preserve bison be established north of the Peace River. "The only way to continue in abundance and in individual vigour any species of game, is to establish proper sanctuaries," where "no hunting or trapping . . . should be allowed," according to Graham.[6] He claimed this was in the interest of the Dominion and Empire: "The interest of the entire people of this Dominion, and to some extent that of the entire civilized world, is centred on the continued existence of the forms of animal life."[7] Like in the context of other Parks across Canada, discourses about preservation were usually mixed with racist rhetoric about Indigenous harvesters, and this was often used to justify the creation of park boundaries that excluded and evicted Indigenous residents.[8] Elimination of Indigenous Peoples was a key focus of the early agendas of Park proponents. Graham's concerns for the interests of the "entire people" of the Dominion and of the so-called "civilized world" necessarily implied the exclusion, and, indeed, the elimination of the concerns and ways of life of the people who had lived in the region since time immemorial. In these ways, as Valaderes writes, like other Parks, the wood bison range, imagined as a sanctuary, became "a symbolic landscape used for identity formation" that necessitated first "a denial of access and subsistence rights" and the severance of Indigenous People's connections to lands, waters, and ways of life.[9]

Racist assumptions about Indigenous People's ways of life were, of course, unfounded. Deeply embedded responsible stewardship practices have always been at the heart of Dënesųłıné legal systems and social worlds. ACFN Elder Pat Marcel's oral history explains that "the Dënesųłıné have always had the responsibility of living in balance with the natural environment."[10] McCormack writes that the decline of wood bison in the late nineteenth century was more likely the outcome of devastating natural disasters and overhunting by settlers for the supplying meat to fur traders of the North West Company and Hudson's Bay Company in the 1880s—rather than the "low hunting pressures" that Indigenous Peoples placed on the species.[11] Reports by Dominion surveyors and researchers in the region also suggested that local Indigenous hunters were widely obeying the game laws and not killing wood bison in the early twentieth century.[12] In park warden reports and Indian Affairs records from the 1920s and 1930s, wardens and Indian Agents suggested that this remained the case in later years as well.[13] Wardens' diaries from the 1920s to the 1930s also contained frequent references about Dene residents reporting to the wardens if they had come across a deceased bison, maybe to assist with the information gathering that wardens had to do in early decades of the Park, or maybe to avoid accusations that they had something to do with the death.[14] Thus, although the game laws represented an imposition of colonial restrictions on Dene ways of life and an infringement of the Treaty—as Dene oral histories emphasize—people generally abided by them. Nonetheless, some administrators were "willing to exaggerate the dangers facing the bison population" as Sandlos writes, especially the threat they perceived Indigenous harvesting posed.[15] These exaggerations fed what Teresa Ferguson calls the dominant "literary tradition" in the history of the Park, which established and perpetuated inaccurate images of Indigenous Peoples as "non-conservers" and underpinned shifts in control over lands, waters and wildlife into the hands of the colonial state.[16] Racialized rhetoric worked alongside urgent appeals to preserve the species, justifying the creation of a Park and the imposition of increasingly strict game regulations over time.

In 1916, following several months of research and land surveys, Maxwell Graham drafted and forwarded to the Superintendent of Indian Affairs an Order-in-Council, outlining detailed plans to establish a Dominion Park of roughly 23,300 square kilometres.[17] But Graham and his peers' goals of creating a sanctuary devoid of all human activity faced strong opposition from Indigenous residents, Indian agents, and missionaries working in the area, discussed later in this chapter. This ultimately delayed the process and resulted in a more moderate arrangement in the initial years. At first, Indian Affairs Superintendent General Arthur Meighen stated that he "would be very glad to cooperate in any way" with the Parks Branch.[18] However, several other ministers vehemently opposed the bison sanctuary fearing it would interfere with local Indigenous People's subsistence practices, which would in turn lead to hunger and increased reliance on social assistance. Imposing park boundaries over such a large area, some critics suggested, could only worsen existing hunger and hardship: unlike southern parks such as Banff or Jasper, displaced Indigenous residents in the Delta would not be able to engage in an agricultural way of life to survive on if their subsistence practices were interrupted by a park. Indian Affairs wished to avoid the potential financial consequences they might face as a result. Meighen shifted his position on the bison sanctuary, agreeing with his colleagues that it would be undesirable for social assistance to "take the place of that ability to help themselves which Indians alone can exercise if they are in the environment of wildlife."[19] Frustrated by this disapproval, Graham argued that time lost was precious. He urged that "steps cannot be taken too soon to ensure the successful carrying out of the carefully prepared plans made by this Branch for the preservation of the beneficent animal life." He also claimed that only "a few" people regularly hunted in the area, and that these people did not "possess any special rights entitling them by Treaty to hunt through that territory," contrary to the provisions of Treaty 8.[20] Despite Graham's urgent appeals, the plans for the sanctuary were put on hold during the First World War after Parks Commissioner James Harkin concluded for various reasons—not the least being Indian Affairs' opposition—"the matter must stand."[21] A hiatus on park planning took place from 1916–1920.

Park Planning Resumed

In 1920 the discussion resumed. F.H. Kitto, from the Natural Resources, Intelligence Branch of the Department of the Interior, who had spent two weeks in the bison range for a natural resource survey earlier that year, raised the suggestion once more to create a bison sanctuary to solidify state control over the wood bison.[22] On the wood bison range, he wrote: "I would strongly urge that a prompt settlement of the question of ownership be made with the Alberta authorities, and that this area be made a national park, in order that these buffalo, the last remaining herd roaming in a free state, be preserved."[23] Kitto reiterated the earlier views of Park champions that the sanctuary could have multiple purposes. Within the limits he proposed, Kitto noted "many species of valuable fur-bearing animals, large game and many birds" and suggested to J.B. Harkin that a breeding ground or sanctuary for those species would bring additional value if the bison sanctuary were established.[24]

The Advisory Board on Wildlife Protection passed a resolution calling for the creation of a park in June 1920.[25] Two summers later, Graham accompanied Dominion land surveyor Fred Siebert on an investigation to gather more information and determine the boundaries of a proposed sanctuary.[26]

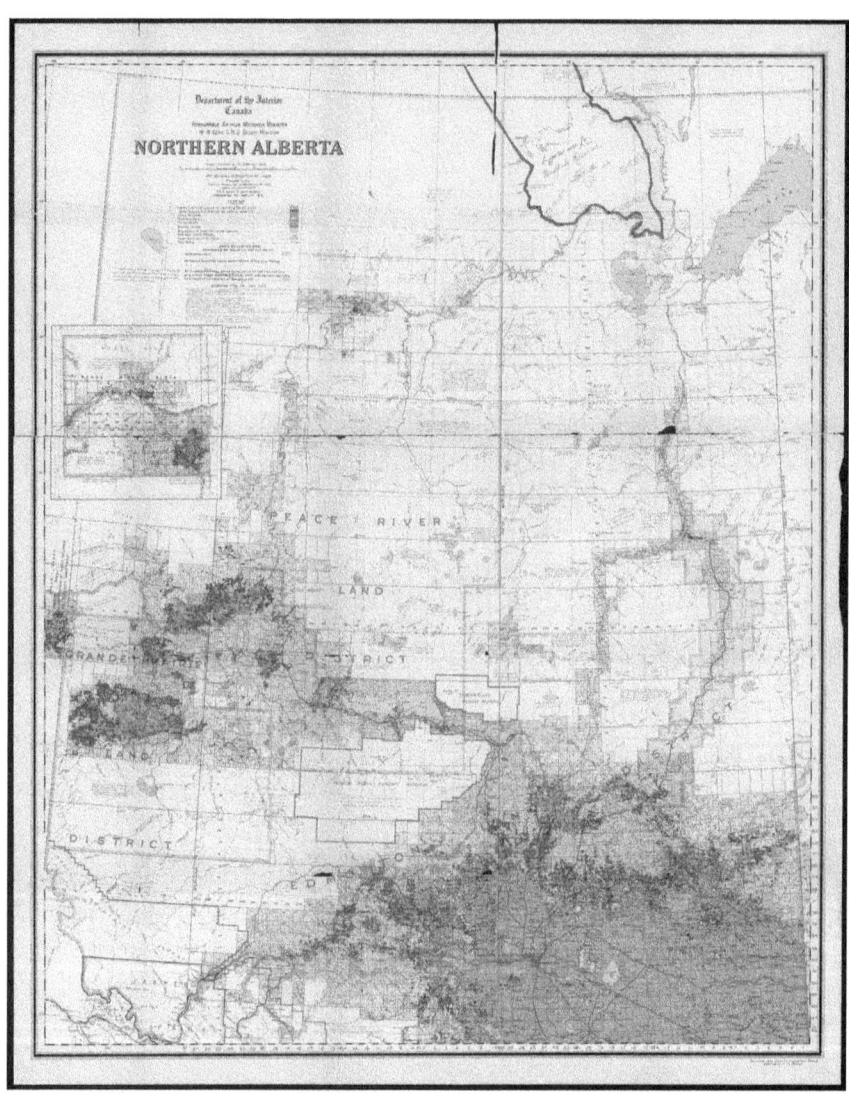

Fig. 3.2 F.H. Kitto's map of proposed boundaries for a bison preserve. F.H. Kitto to Harkin, 12 January 1921, LAC RG85, vol. 1390, file 406-13.

The Department of the Interior committed to providing the surveyors with "'every possible facility' for carrying out a thorough investigation."[27] Seibert and Graham mapped out the potential boundaries based on their observations of herds on both sides of the boundary between Alberta and the Northwest Territories. Throughout the autumn of 1922, Graham continued to advance his view that a prohibition on trapping and hunting in the area was urgently required in order to protect the bison herd, and that he considered the situation to be "acute," fearing that trappers scared bison away from their winter habitats.[28] Following Graham and Seibert's final report, Order-in-Council P.C. 2498 established Wood Buffalo Park in December 1922. The Park boundaries, encompassing 27,000 square kilometres on both sides of the Alberta/NWT border, were made official, and the Department of the Interior was granted administrative authority over the new park.

Officials conceived the new Park as a multi-purpose sanctuary, not only necessary for the preservation of bison, but also useful for the conservation of other game and the management of the fur-based economy. A 1912 memorandum penned by J.B. Harkin suggested that the bison sanctuary space could also serve as a "natural fur-breeding sanctuary as it abounds with fur-bearing animals of all kinds and through the probable overflow, provide food and sport for the surrounding district."[29] Tourism was another opportunity some officials imagined for the Park. In 1923, Maxwell Graham wrote that, although the potential for tourism in Wood Buffalo Park was not as great as in the southerly national parks, he hoped that "with proper publicity being given to the presence of the buffalo in the park, the fact that these buffalo are today the only wild ones left in the world, the further fact of their being fairer specimens than any others of their species, and the further fact that transportation facilities by water from Waterways to Peace Point will enable anyone to step off the boat into the park, will draw many tourists."[30] As historians have shown of other parks in Canada, the boundaries of Wood Buffalo National Park were imagined as necessary not just to preserve wood bison, but also to control Indigenous lives and to increase the profitability of the land, water, and wildlife for the Dominion.[31]

Ongoing opposition from Indian Affairs limited restrictions on Indigenous harvesting in the Park. Park planners eventually came to a compromise. Whereas no harvesting was allowed in any other national park per the *Dominion Parks Act*, Wood Buffalo National Park became the first in Dominion history to allow some Indigenous land use via a special clause added to the Order-in-Council. Harvesters with Treaty Status could continue to live, travel, and harvest in the Park, as long as they abided by game laws and did not kill bison. All other harvesters were excluded. As Finnie later wrote to Graham, "If we had not allowed the Treaty Indians to hunt and trap in the Park there would have developed such strong opposition to the creation of the park that we would not have been able to secure it at all."[32] But pressured as they were by Indian Affairs, Parks administrators never referred to Indigenous Peoples' access to the Park as a Treaty Right. Rather, in both policy and discourse, Indigenous Peoples' rights were often framed as privileges, granted by the government on grounds of compassion rather than as Treaty obligation. Graham claimed that "the game and the forests belong to the nation and not to the individual and the use of them by the individual is limited to such privileges as may be accorded him by law."[33] He wrote to Finnie in 1923, "a great concession is made in granting hunting and trapping privileges to Treaty Indians in a special game sanctuary," and in 1924, he noted that the Branch considered the granting of these "privileges" as an "ethical consideration" rather than an obligation.[34] This attitude persisted throughout the twentieth century. Federal fur supervisor R.I. Eklund wrote in 1955, for example, "The fact that Wood Buffalo Park is a National Park as is Elk Island, Banff and Jasper, it is my humble opinion that hunting, trapping or fishing by any person, whether Treaty Indian or not, is a privilege and not a right."[35] The main reason Dënesųłıné people could maintain access to the Park under Order-in-Council P.C. 2498 in the first few years of its existence was because of cost-savings for the Indian Affairs Branch—officials wanted to prevent an increase in the need to distribute more federal social assistance.

Ultimately, the Park became an instrument in the expansion of colonial control in Dene homelands in the twentieth century. Dene leaders had signed the Treaty in 1899 under the impression that their lives and movements on the land would never be restricted. After the Park was created, however, they perceived that treaty promises would not be upheld forever and that the Park would likely restrict them in the future. Indeed, although Dene families could remain within the original park boundaries initially, new restrictions and expanded Park boundaries imposed after 1926 denied many access to their homelands and harvesting grounds, as Dënesųłıné leaders had suspected. As Elder Jimmy Deranger explained, "after they got the land, things changed... they developed policies saying that 'you can't do this, you can't do that.'" The establishment of the Park in 1922 thus marked the start of a history of broken Treaty promises, creating serious hardship for the Dënesųłiné residents that the Park dispossessed.

The 1926 annex: "it will never be a sanctuary"

Though Finnie, Graham, and Kitto had achieved their victory by establishing the bison sanctuary with limited human use in 1922, they continued to pursue the total elimination of Indigenous residents and harvesters from the Park in the years that followed. Finnie wished to find "some means by which all Indians may be kept out of this area," arguing that "[a]s long as they are permitted to enter it will never be a sanctuary" and "we will be in constant suspense regarding fires and the killing of buffalo, and the wild life of course will seriously suffer."[36] Graham and Finnie were both unhappy with their earlier compromise with Indian Affairs. "The fact remains," Finnie reiterated in December 1925, "that so long as anybody is allowed to shoot, or otherwise disturb the game in the Park, it will lose its effectiveness as a sanctuary."[37] He hoped an arrangement could be made with Indian Affairs to "buy off these Indians" in order to keep them out of the Park since he felt there was no way to know "whether they are killing buffalo or not."[38] Yet Finnie's elimination goal faced continued disapproval from Indian Affairs agents and his superiors. Deputy Superintendent General Duncan Campbell Scott, for example, responded to one of Finnie's proposals to expand the Park in 1925 stating, "it is my view both official and personal that the vital interests of the Indians should be paramount and should have precedence even over the protection of wildlife."[39] District agent John McDougal agreed. He felt that, even though "every unbiased person in the North country will agree" bison protection was important and local harvesters could be "a nuisance and a menace," eviction would result in severe hardship for families who had been harvesting in the region for many generations.[40]

Because of ongoing opposition, the plan to eliminate Indigenous Peoples from the Park was largely unsuccessful. However, further displacements of Dene people from their homelands and restrictions on their lives were yet to come. The importation of several thousand young plains bison from the Buffalo National Park in Wainwright, Alberta, to Wood Buffalo Park was the catalyst for these displacements. Plans to import plains bison started in 1923, when Deputy Minister W.W. Cory suggested to Parks Commissioner Harkin that "it would be a good idea to transfer some of the healthy young stock to the Wood Bison Reserve administered by the Northwest Territories Branch."[41]

Fig. 3.3 *Buffalo scow unloading at Peace River, 1925.* Provincial Archives of Alberta, A4723.

Fig. 3.4 *First shipment of 200 Wainwright Bison arrives in Wood Buffalo National Park, 1925.* Libraries and Cultural Resources Digital Collections, University of Calgary, CU1103322.

Fig. 3.5 *Buffalo calves unloaded and being moved west at Peace Point along a seven-mile long timber cut to open lands, 1925.* Provincial Archives of Alberta, A4727.

This was largely a response to the rapid growth of the Wainwright herd, which was now escaping the southern park boundaries and destroying nearby pastureland. Despite widespread concerns that the tuberculosis-infected herd would mix with and infect the northern Alberta wood bison, Park officials pursued the scheme with vigour. They ignored the warnings of Dominion zoologists and members of the global scientific community, who repeatedly, and at times vehemently, expressed opposition in the media, directly to the Department of the Interior, and even to Prime Minister Mackenzie King.[42] Between 1925 and 1928, 6,673 plains bison were shipped by rail and barge to the Park and released on the west side of the Slave River.[43] As predicted, the imported plains bison mixed with the wood bison and introduced tuberculosis and brucellosis, a problem Parks Canada still manages to this day. Furthermore, the plains bison began migrating out of the Park boundaries almost immediately, and wardens reported gradual but continuous southward migrations for months.[44] Many moved to the Lake Claire area and other Dene homelands to feed there.

Administrators were suddenly faced with the problem of protecting the bison that had migrated. They decided to enlarge the Park by annexing the

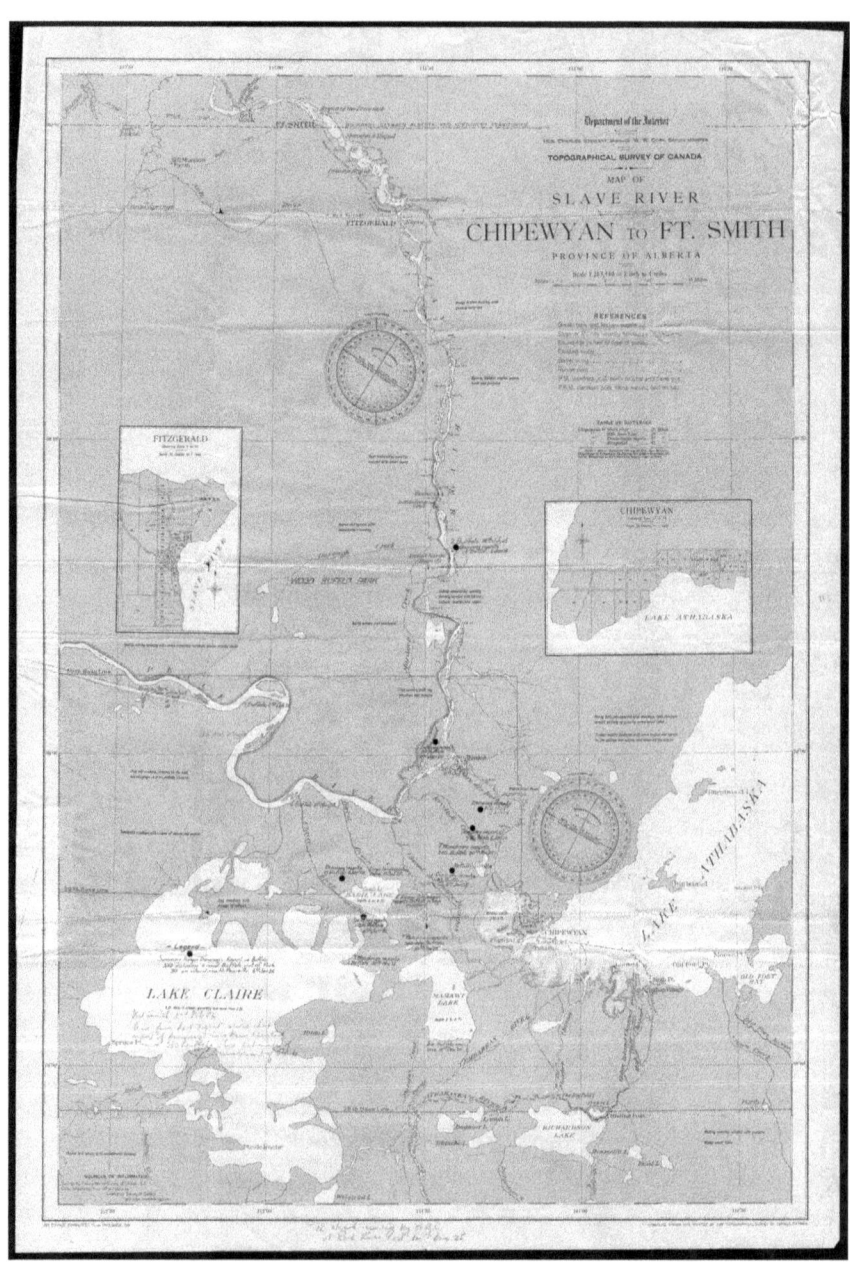

Fig. 3.6 Summary of Warden Dempsey's report *Buffalo—Map showing location of Buffalo that have left the Park up to 6th Jan. 26*, April 1926, LAC RG85-D-1-A, vol 1391, file 406-13.

lands that made up the new bison range, primarily south of the Peace River, where many Dënesųłıné families lived, harvested, and moved since time immemorial. Finnie wrote to McDougal in February 1926, instructing him to map out potential boundaries of the expanded Park and to ensure that they were "liberal" enough to respond to future migrations of the bison "farther afield." McDougal knew the plan would spur strong opposition. He replied that Parks administrators "must expect strong opposition from the residents of Chipewyan . . . since the area would include the main rat breeding grounds and the best duck, goose, and wavey shooting in Canada." Dempsey also feared that expanding the Park or creating an adjacent sanctuary to the south would "create a hardship" for local families if they were deprived of the ability to harvest there.[45] Though Finnie communicated this concern, Cory believed that those who might be affected by an expanded Park could harvest to the east of the Athabasca River—ignoring not only the implications of forcing people to move away from their homes and established harvesting areas but also the impacts of a Park expansion on Dene people's settlements, homes, and lives in the areas where the plains bison had wandered.[46]

When word of the expansion circulated in early 1926, Indigenous residents feared it would restrict their movements, land-use, and lives. Indian Agents and missionaries tended to oppose the expansion for similar reasons.[47] A March 1926 telegram pointed to fears that the park extension would lead to bison destroying muskrat habitat, interfere with trapping, and lead to additional restrictions.[48] Dene oral histories also recount that, just like with the original Park establishment in 1922, the expansion occurred with little to no consultation with Indigenous residents and harvesters. When consultation did occur, Dene people may only have agreed if the expansion was presented by the Parks officials as a temporary loan. One Fort Chipewyan Elder told TARR researchers in 1974:

> Apparently, it was just loaned to them. After five years, the population of the buffalo grew in size. It was at this time the [federal] government had, as the provincial government for the land south of the Peace River and north of the Peace River is the old buffalo park, the provincial government also loaned the federal government the land south of the Peace River for the WBNP. Now that land is also filled with buffalo as far as the twenty-seventh baseline.[49]

Despite the clearly stated concerns of Dene people, Indian Affairs agents, and missionaries, the park's administration proceeded with the annex. In response to the 1926 petition, O.S. Finnie wrote a letter that justified the expansion, citing the clause of Treaty 8 that stated lands could be "taken up" from time to time for various purposes and suggesting the Park expansion would further benefit local Treaty Peoples by restricting white and Métis access to the area.[50] In the end, Elder Ray Ladouceur explained, Indigenous residents "had no choice. No choice after they [officials] brought in the other animals, the prairie buffalo." The Park was extended south of Peace River by Order-in-Council P.C. 634 on 26 April 1926, then further to include Buffalo Lake by Order-in-Council P.C. 1444, on 26 September of the same year.[51] This expanded the Park to a total of 44,800 square kilometers.

The New Permitting System: Inscribing Divisions

The Parks Branch did acknowledge the potential for "considerable opposition" should the new Park displace the many residents and harvesters, both Indigenous and non-Indigenous, with the annexation.[52] Rather than impose an outright ban on harvesting in the annex, a formal amendment to the Dominion Forest Reserves and Parks Act specified that some people could remain in both the original park and the annexed area on a permit-only basis. The amendment stated that

> No person shall enter the Wood Buffalo Park unless he holds a permit from the Superintendent of the Park authorizing his entry to the said Wood Buffalo Park; and any person found within the Park boundaries without the necessary permission from the Superintendent, may be summarily removed from the Park by order of the Superintendent.[53]

In June and September 1926, new access regulations were enshrined in Dominion law through Orders-in-Council P.C. 1444 and 2589: "all Treaty Indians who formerly hunted and trapped in the Park will be allowed to continue to do so, but must first secure a permit from the Park Superintendent. In the new area south of the river, whites and half-breeds, who formerly hunted and trapped there will also be allowed to continue."[54] The park was thus split into three zones with varying levels of access, and each with a different set of game laws: Zone A in the Northwest Territories, Zone B in the Alberta

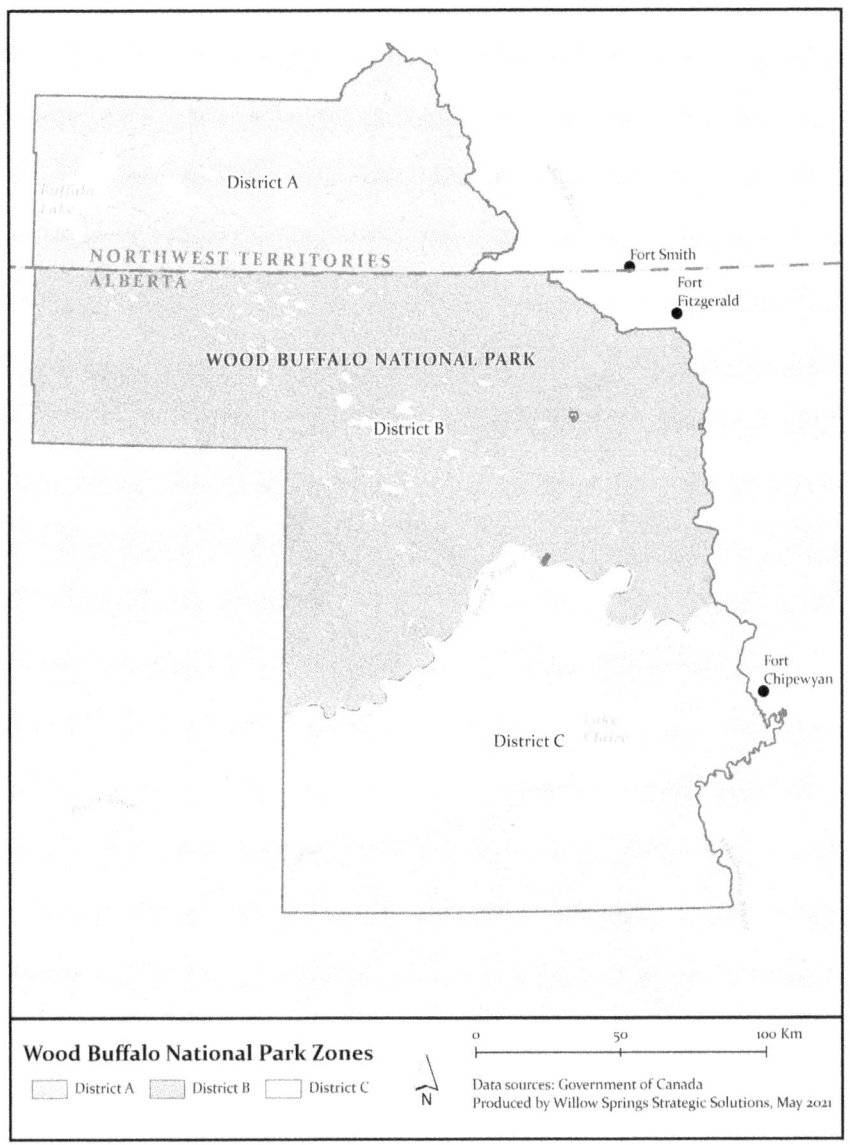

Fig. 3.7 Map of permitting zones A, B, and C established to differentiate among access rights for harvesting after the 1926 expansion. Map produced by Emily Boak, Willow Springs Strategic Solutions, 2021.

section of the original Park north of Peace River, and Zone C in the annexed section south of Peace River. Treaty harvesters could continue to access Zones A and B if they procured permits. Those who resided in Zone C at the time of the 1926 annex could apply for permits to stay.[55] White and Métis harvesters could only apply for permits in Zone C.[56] Parks administrators believed that this permitting system granted special privileges to permittees who would be protected from competition from other trappers and hunters who could not obtain permits. O.S. Finnie wrote that "this Order-in-Council will practically make a monopoly for them. They may continue to hunt and trap, but no new-comers will be allowed to do so."[57]

But far from creating a generous monopoly free of competition, the regulations were damaging to Dene families. The new Orders-in-Council gave park administrators a great deal of latitude to distribute or withhold harvesting and visiting permits; this continued throughout much of the twentieth century. A 1954 consolidation of game laws summarized the unilateral power of superintendents and parks officials to grant, deny, or revoke Indigenous rights to the Park: "The Minister may . . . cancel, suspend, or refuse to issue or renew any license or certificate of registration for any cause that to him seems sufficient."[58] Most of the members of the Cree Band, now Mikisew Cree First Nation, who resided in the Park annex in 1926, were able to obtain permits and remain at their homes on the Peace River. However, not all Dene families with a strong connection to the area in the expanded Park boundaries happened to be residing or harvesting in the Park at the time of the annexation—whether because they were staying near relatives outside the Park or harvesting in the wider Delta region outside of what became expanded Park boundaries. Several Dene families therefore did not apply for permits in the early years. As a result, the permitting system essentially split those who were members of the Chipewyan Band in half, separating families and the community between those with and those without access. Over time, permitting laws and the warden system that upheld them, combined with the shifting array of other colonial processes at work in northern Alberta, obstructed Dene lives in their homelands taken up by the Park and surrounding region.

Permit applicants had to make a strong case to obtain a permit under strict criteria: they must be "bona fide residents of the Park area" and be "dependent upon the game supply of the Wood Buffalo Park for their livelihood."[59] But many applications were refused. The reasons for declining permit applications were fairly inconsistent and could include a wide range of justifications such as a perceived shortage of game or the perception that an applicant was in some way "undesirable." For example, in 1935 Adam Boucher was denied a permit "owing to his gambling tendencies," and he and his wife Victoire Boucher and mother-in-law Sophie Ratfat were evicted from the Birch River settlement even though the family had cabins in the Park and had harvested there for generations.[60] Chief Jonas Laviolette was denied a trapping permit in 1928 and 1933 because his name was not added to the list of permittees when the permitting system was first established. The warden superintendent, M.J. Dempsey, felt that by granting Chief Laviolette a permit, he would be setting an unwanted precedent of granting permits to "a large number of treaty Indians who are in the same position as Mr. Laviolette as to having at some time trapped or hunted in the area which is now the Park, whose applications would follow closely upon the granting of a permit to Jonas Laviolette."[61] The permitting system regulating access to the Park was as much about exercising state control over Indigenous movement and lives as it was about conservation.

Visiting rights to WBNP were also restricted. Park laws required that those residing outside the Park boundaries must apply for a permit to visit family and friends in the Park. This restriction was similar to the pass system that had been introduced in Treaty 7 territory and elsewhere in the Dominion in 1885. According to Courtney Mason, colonial surveillance and control of Indigenous lives and off-reserve movements created through the pass system closely aligned with the Rocky Mountains Park Act, which "specified that the forceful exclusion and removal of 'trespassers' who did not adhere to the new park regulations was critical to the early development of the park."[62] While the pass system was not enforced in the homelands of ACFN at the time of the Park's expansion, Wood Buffalo National Park's permitting system played a remarkably similar role in limiting Dene movements and ways of life and subjecting them to colonial surveillance. Chief Jonas Laviolette had to apply for a permit to enter the Park to see his Nation's members who lived within its boundaries.[63] Wardens also limited visiting rights among the three park zones. Indian Agent John Melling relayed complaints from Cree and Dene peoples in the Park who had been warned against visiting family or friends in different zones and therefore "unanimously felt quite incensed over this restriction to their personal freedom . . . even relatives were denied the right of visiting each other."[64] Despite such complaints, Parks Canada administration declined to revise its policy around visiting, maintaining that "it does not seem unreasonable for the Wood Buffalo Park Officials to keep a check on the movements . . . by requiring any visitors to obtain permission from the resident Warden so that he may keep track of their movements."[65] As ACFN's oral histories relate, the permitting restrictions had profound implications for families whose movements in and out of the Park were closely watched and strictly limited, resulting in long-term impacts on community connectedness, kinship and family ties, and on connections to Dene homelands.

People who did not have permits to reside or harvest in the Park had to request permission even to use trails or roads that traversed the Park—even if their travels through the Park were transitory. Those travelling through the Park with harvesting gear, such as guns or traps, and evidence of furs were also required to declare these to Park wardens and Alberta Game Guardians before entering the Park. In 1948, for example, Park warden F.A. McCall reported Dene harvesters Theodore Bouchier and Pierre Piché, who both were considered "Alberta Indians," or people who did not have permits to reside and harvest in the Park, after he stopped them travelling from Poplar Point to Fort Chipewyan via the Park. Piche and Bouchier had furs, traps, and guns in their sleds, so McCall wrote them up and informed them of the need for permission to travel through the Park. He also informed the Indian Agent and Alberta Game Guardian of what had happened and asked them to ensure travellers without Park permits seek permission to use Park roads and declare any furs or gear before entering.[66] In many ways then, permitting regulations that were intended to restrict harvesting within the Park also restricted Dënesųłıné people's freedom of movement throughout their territories as well as their use of the network of pathways, portages, winter roads, and trails that Dene people had always used. These regulations had the effect of separating communities and families, alienating people from their territories, and increasing surveillance and disciplinary power of the colonial government.

Like the other policies governing Indigenous homelands in the twentieth century, the permitting system was characterized by inconsistencies and uncertainties and often was updated on an ad hoc basis and reactively. Confusion over the three zones and sometimes contradictory rules led to frustrations. Even some Park wardens recognized the problems policy inconsistencies could create: "[t]here are some doubts as to what the regulations really are, which may be a cause of friction," wrote Park Warden Dempsey to District Agent A.L. Cummings in 1935.[67] For example, there were often questions around permits for family members of existing permit holders. Marriage sometimes complicated things. At first, a person without a permit could not become eligible through marriage to a permit-holder who resided within the Park. Widows occasionally were granted permits, but women who grew up in the Park annex and later married non-permit holders faced specific challenges. Rules around marriage and Park access could cause a Dene woman to lose her access to her home and family in the Park, while the *Indian Act*, which stripped women of their Status if they married non-Status men, enhanced the power and longevity of these restrictions and cut women off from their families, lands, and communities. Some ACFN members' family histories shared in this chapter suggest several women eventually lost their permits and homes and had to leave the Park.

Additionally, the issue of granting permits to the sons of existing permit-holders was only settled after 1935, a decade after the annex occurred. Prior to that, the children of permittees could accompany their parents into the Park on harvesting trips, but administrators sometimes denied them their own permits after they turned 18. A 1935 law clarified and tightened the rules. It determined that if "the applicant is over eighteen years of age and . . . he is the son of a holder of a Wood Buffalo Park hunting and trapping permit," then his request should be granted.[68] But these young applicants were often denied if they did not apply for a permit immediately upon coming of age or if they were found to be making a living elsewhere and then, as Parks officials put it, they "suddenly decide they want to hunt and trap in the Park as their fathers do."[69] There was some uncertainty around adoption as well. One series of letters between wardens and officials in 1949 suggests that permits for adopted children would only be approved if the adoption had taken place "legally"—that is, documented and recognized by the systems and structures of the colonial state. This likely meant that adoptions according to local Indigenous kinship structures and customs were not taken into account.[70] In these ways, the new permitting system became a key instrument not only for controlling access to game and wildlife, but also for alienating people from their families, kinship ties, and lands and waters.

People could also have their permits revoked. Those who had received permits in 1926 but later harvested outside of Park boundaries, sometimes had their permits taken away.[71] Breaking game laws could also result in temporary revocations and sometimes permanent expulsions.[72] Numerous RCMP reports from the 1920s–1950s detail cases of Indigenous harvesters arrested and tried for breaking harvesting regulations; it was not uncommon for the defendants to lose their permits temporarily or permanently, have their game confiscated, and face fines.[73] Wardens reported Julian Ratfat, for example, for having two beavers in his possession during closed season in 1928; they revoked his license to trap temporarily and he and his family were expelled from the Park.[74] Sandlos counts at least forty people whose access "privileges" were revoked from 1934–1939.[75] The practice continued throughout the 1940s. Melling complained to Indian Affairs that people who lost their permits suffered: "the only source of livelihood for these Indians is derived from their work pursuant to hunting and trapping. There is practically no casual labor to be had in our settlement."[76] When harvesters lost their Park permits temporarily or permanently, he wrote, they were cut off from their main source of income and food. With few other options, many could not feed their families and were forced to rely on often insufficient government relief.

The oral history shared in this chapter discusses the history of the creation and expansion of Wood Buffalo National Park as they have heard it from their Elders. Their oral histories stress a lack of direct consultation and communication with local Indigenous Peoples when the Park was created and later expanded. ACFN Elder Edouard Trippe de Roche suggested that this was common practice at the time: "there was no consultation then." Elder Ernie "Joe" Ratfat agreed: "they didn't tell people back then. They just did whatever they wanted to do. Well, we had no say, when it came to government things, we had no say. They just did it." Elder Jimmy Deranger discussed his experiences as an interviewer for the Treaty and Aboriginal Rights Research team in the 1970s, an Indigenous-led initiative established by the Native Indian Brotherhood to conduct research about Indigenous perspectives and experiences of treaties, including Treaty 8. During interviews with Dënesųłıné Elders, many of whom were adults at the time the Park was created, Deranger learned that there was no systematic mode of local communication. Parks officials visited individual settlements and some families, but "there was no large assembly of them together . . . the official didn't say that 'I have gathered you here today, because we want to use the land for buffalos.' They didn't say that, they just went to camps I think . . . and told them." A Fort Chipewyan Elder confirmed in 1974, "Yes, our land was made to be part of the Park. It is like something sitting in the middle of a plate. They do whatever they want with the Park. They never consult us."[77] In much the same way as decisions were made about Indigenous lands and lives in what became national parks to the south such as Banff and Jasper, Treaty obligations and communication with Indigenous residents were ignored.[78]

Occasionally, indirect communication took place, typically involving Indian Affairs agents and missionaries claiming to speak on behalf of Indigenous residents. In a 1916 memorandum, Indian Agent Henry Bury wrote to the Deputy Minister of Indian Affairs that he had had a conversation with local Indigenous leaders about the original proposal for a bison sanctuary. According to his report, after conferring for a while about the matter, the "leading Indians . . . expressed their conviction that provided they were allowed some reasonable time during which to locate other hunting grounds they would not presume to register any claims for compensation, as they contended that the country was large and the game plentiful in other localities."[79] As Sandlos cautions in his analysis, Bury was an advocate of the Park, and therefore his conclusions were likely filtered through this lens rather than representing the actual views and words of Indigenous leaders with whom he spoke, and it is unclear from the memorandum who Bury spoke with beyond those he described as "chiefs and headmen," likely referring to those Indian Affairs understood to be political leaders.[80] His suggestion that Indigenous leaders were willing to consider being excluded from the area taken up by the proposed sanctuary without compensation does not align with the oral histories shared in this chapter.

According to the Elders speaking about the history of the Park in the 1970s and early 2000s, if Dënesųłıné leaders were consulted about the Park in the early days, they may have only agreed to it because they were led to believe that the lands would only be loaned temporarily for the bison sanctuary—they understood that their ability to continue moving and harvesting across the region would not be impeded. Indeed, oral testimony suggests that Parks officials promised residents and land-users that the land transferred to the Park would be returned. Some Elders were told that the loan would be no more than one or two decades, while others recalled oral stories of a 99-year lease. As one Fort Chipewyan Elder told interviewers in 1974, "apparently it was just loaned to [them]." Elder Alec Bruno stated decades later that "the Government had promised the trappers that they intended to use this WBNP area just for ten to fifteen years only. After that they will return the land back to Indigenous trappers to use it as they had done for many years before. Eighty plus years later, the WBNP is still in existence. Another broken promise to our people."[81]

As ACFN Elder Dora Flett explained, "They said that they'd have the park for 100 years. It's over 100 years now, so. Yeah. So I guess they [should] give it back now." A written record of this loan has not yet been identified in the archives. Whether the promise, like other Treaty 8 promises, was made orally in good faith by government officials and then broken, or the document was destroyed, is unclear. One way or the other, the oral record contains extensive evidence of this promise. The lack of communication and broken or forgotten Treaty promises were key components of the history of relations between the Park and the Dënesųłıné, shaping relations to the present-day and creating a general distrust of Parks administration and experiences of exclusion, misrepresentation, and dismissal.

Oral histories also suggests that some families were evicted from their homes in the Park after its expansion. While the archival documents contain ample evidence of permitting policies and permit revocations that restricted Dene people's access to their family homes and harvesting areas in what became the expanded Park, these texts do not mention forcible evictions. However, the oral archive has several stories of forcible removals of Dene residents who had lost their permits or otherwise were unable to prove to the administration's satisfaction their claim to be in the Park, even if they had family members with permits. Once evicted, some people's homes were burned down; they lost cabins and belongings. As Elder Edouard Trippe de Roche explained: "Once you leave, you can't come back. And the people that left their homes were burnt down. They went back [to] get some furniture or whatever they had, and they came back to a burnt home." In these ways, Park policy and practice became an important part of the encroachment of colonial power into Dene people's lives and homelands, resulting sometimes in dispossessions and violence to increase colonial power over lands, waters, and resources in northern Alberta in the twentieth century.

ORAL HISTORY

Chief Allan Adam (2 February 2021)

They brought in the buffalo and they gave all the rights to the buffalo. The buffalo were protected more than anything else, and [it was] pretty much 'save the buffalo, shoot the Dene.'

Only ACFN was the one that was kicked out. And ACFN members, they spread out and they joined other First Nations. You know when I went up, I became a Chief in 2008, but when I went up to Yellowknife in 2008 or 2009, I forget when it was, but I went up there for a water conference. And when I was talking to Dene people up there one guy told me that his parents were from Fort Chip. I didn't dig into the story because I knew right away, his parents were probably one of the ones that were kicked out of the Park as well. But they moved up north, and they became part of Wood Buffalo up in that area too. So, you know, and people from Salt River, people from Smith Landing, we're all members of ACFN pretty much, half of the population from Mikisew is ACFN you know. The history runs deep. It's like a vein. Right?

Horace Adam (19 March 2021)

Now, at that time, after the Treaty was signed, the federal government took over the National Park, so the Indigenous People didn't get access. So the Park was stolen. They took it, you know. . . . And it's so sad for the Indigenous people at that time.

Louis Boucher (1974)

Richard Lightning (RL):[82] There are many buffalo in the Park. Were your people ever allowed to hunt them before?

LB: No, it is difficult in the Park. A person could starve there. It is difficult for someone to get buffalo meat because there are park officials who guard the Park.

RL: Do you remember when the Park was first made or when the fence was built around it?[83] Maybe you could tell me about it.

LB: Yes, I remember. When I first arrived here, they hadn't brought the buffalo yet.[84] When the buffalo were brought, I was already married and had two children. They were brought from the south in 1922. But the wood buffalo were already there. That is across the lake from here, they were in the wood buffalo area before when we were trapping there. That place at Peace Point we are now looking at, is the area where I spent thirty-four years. It is upstream on the Peace River, and I trapped in the Buffalo Park. But it was difficult. We used to bring with us some goldeye [fish] which we caught during the fall. We travelled with pack horses when trapping. So there is no reason why I shouldn't be familiar with the country.

RL: Why was the Wood Buffalo Park established there?

LB: We feel it was a dishonest deal which was made with the Chiefs. When the Parks officials were going to bring the buffalo on to our lands, they [the Chiefs] had said, 'Yes.' That is the reason the Park was made. If they had refused, there would be no Buffalo Park.

RL: Do you remember the name of the Chief who they made the deal with?

LB: His name was Woy a Kash. His father was Chief first. His name was Nik Soo. Then it was Pierre Whitehead, but the buffalo had already been moved from the south.

RL: The Park was extended southward, what was the reason for this?

LB: The reason is that people who lived in the new park area were not allowed to go into the old park, not even to camp. Then the Chief, the one after Pierre Whitehead, made arrangements so the Indians could move back and forth from the old park across to the extended one.

Alec Bruno (n.d.)

The Government had promised the trappers that they intended to use this WBNP area, just for ten to fifteen years only. After that they will return the land back to the trappers to use it as they had done for many years before. Eighty plus years later the WBNP is still in existence. Another broken promise to our people.

The Elders often talked about how the WBNP was formed. Many Elders said they weren't aware of a WBNP being created. The Government officials came and surveyed the boundaries for the perimeter of WBNP and when that was done next came the bison which were barged in from the south. No one consulted or had any input to the formation of WBNP, because of this WBNP many of our members were lost to MCFN [Mikisew Cree First Nation] and others just moved elsewhere.

Many Elders recalled that no government officials ever came to them for consultation or input from the trappers and hunters of the region. So this proves that they, the government, didn't intend to share this with our people. Trappers and hunters weren't given any say in the formation of WBNP. We the ACFN are the biggest losers, not only in land but also many members to MCFN.

Our people, [ACFN] members, probably felt like they didn't exist in reality. Not only did they lose their rights to their traditions, way of life, they were told to leave the area of Birch River. Trappers were the ones that had the bigger loss. They refused to change bands, so they had no choice but to move elsewhere. This was their home base; families were raised from one generation to another.

In 1899, Treaty 8 was signed between the federal government and the First Nation People. Our people were promised that as long as the sun raised, river flows, and the grass grows, the people will never be interfered with as to where they lived and maintained their way of life, traditionally their land will never be taken away from them. Yet twenty some years later our people were told to leave their respected area and relocated elsewhere. As I see it the government had eradicated our people from their homeland just to be replaced by bison. This is unacceptable at any given time—the government had more concern for the animals than they did for our people.

Fredoline Deranger/Djeskelni (19 March 2021)

Wood Buffalo [Park] is not what we expected from the newcomers, because before Wood Buffalo, the Dënesųłıné, from day one, looked after all the Europeans when they came into Canada. They had . . . poor clothing, no roads, no machines at that time. So the Dënesųłıné went ahead and clothed them and fed them and looked after them for over 200 years. Yeah. So that's a common knowledge amongst the Dënesųłıné people of our country. . . .

They [the government officials wanting to create a park] came out of the blue. There was never direct dialogue between the [Park] people coming in and Dënesųłıné from Lake Athabasca. For 200 years we supplied them. We did everything for them. And they never consulted us.

Jimmy Deranger (24 March 2021)

In this passage, Jimmy refers to oral histories he had heard from Elders he interviewed as part of the Treaty and Aboriginal Rights Research in the 1970s.

Now some of our Elders are saying that that land [in the Park annex] is ours—you [Parks board] should just give it to us. There's no need for us to negotiate it. We let them use it for X number of years, and the use has expired. Now give it back to us. And they haven't even compensated them [the Dene people who were displaced].

They [the government] said they were going to give it back. That's what those Elders said. They were going to give it back after they used it for a certain period of time. So they should just give it back, we don't need, we shouldn't have to negotiate that land, that's ours in the first place, to negotiate it back. If we're going to negotiate, we should negotiate for compensation. But the premise of negotiating something that's already yours is pointless. They knew it was our land to begin with, the Treaty said it was our lands. The Elders said it was our lands. The Creator said it was our lands. And now they want us to negotiate back because of something legally. What makes sense to all of us, I think that they should compensate us for using the land for those number of years.

When I was with the TARR, Indian Association of Alberta Research Project, I was hired as a researcher, to interview Elders. I talked to Elders of both bands [ACFN and MCFN] because some of the Elders of Mikisew were Dene Elders. But they were Mikisew after the Park. Before that, they were Dene Elders. And they remembered what the officials who were representing the National Park, how they wanted to bring the buffalo in, and when they were bringing the buffalos in, and how long they were going to be on the land. And all that was done by like, sort of individual or families that were trapping in there or were using the land in Wood Buffalo Park. But there was no large assembly of them together. Got to our place and said—the official didn't say that, 'I have gathered you here today, because we want to use that land for buffalos.' They didn't say that; they just went to camps, I think. They went to the camps and then they told them. And like, the Shortmans, who are Mikisew, they were supposed to be Dene people, and the Ratfats, Peter Ratfat, and Pierre Ratfat and Claire Ratfat, were supposed to be Dene people but they were in Wood Buffalo Park [at the time of the membership transfer in 1944]—now Mikisew. [The] Vermillion [family] was also in Wood Buffalo but they were Dene. Then there was the Simpsons, some of the Simpsons were supposed to be Dene but there was Wood Buffalo Park. And some of the Denes were supposed to be Dene, but they were at Wood Buffalo Park too.[85] So that's what happened, like you know at that time when the Elders were talking to me and Salman Sepp, he was Wood Buffalo too, he is Dene.

So when the people [government officials] that came to talk to the Dene [the Indigenous residents], they were saying that buffalo was declining down south and they wanted land for the buffalo. And they could use that land for a number of years. And First Nations people in that region, in the area, on the land, can just go on doing what they want to do.

But after they [the government] got the land, things changed, yeah? They developed policies saying that 'you can't do this, you can't do that.' And, they [Dene leaders] were trying to tell the officials that it's not what the first official said.

And now, we're saying this. Then that's when the treaty question came up, when they were first saying that because the Elders at the time [of the TARR interviews], probably remembered some of the things that the government said on behalf of the government, between them, the Northwest Territories was then the Government of Canada [at the time of Treaty]. And then [Dene Elders] told them [the government officials], the Treaty says this: that if the land that's going to be opened up for forestry, agricultural mining, settlement, and other use, that the said Indians of that region, the said Indians of that land, were going to be consulted, and they [the government] needed the consent of them [the Dene people]. Before that, you can just go take it.

And they were supposed to be compensated because it's their land to begin with. But that always never happened. Because how they did it was, they didn't do it properly, I don't think they did it properly from what the testimony was of the Elders then, when I was doing the treaty research.

Dora Flett (19 March 2021)

They said they'd have the park for 100 years. It's over 100 years now, so it's time to give it back.

Leonard Flett (30 April 2021)

Yeah, they were removed from the National Park, I guess because the Park was established. And the Indian Agent, or the Parks Canada, went to my parents. That was my mum I guess—my dad wasn't even there, my dad was from a different reserve kind of deal. Kind of up the lake, I mean, up the river at Poplar Point . . . I think it wasn't right to her.[86] She didn't have a voice—she was just a kid, right? And my grandpa was there and my grandma.

Scott Flett (17 March 2021)

Yeah, I heard that too, I heard it's [WBNP] supposed to be built because the buffalo. When they made the Park, [it] was north of Peace and the buffalo start migrating south of the Peace into Lake Claire and that area. And they [Parks officials] said they're just going to borrow that area for a while for the Park. And the big dispute even with the Park boundary . . . so a lot of people are in dispute over the Park boundary. It was the Chip and stuff. But that's what I heard back—that's what they said—[the Park] is supposed to borrow [the lands] just for a while and that's how they told the people.

Felix Gibot (1974)

FG: It is like the Buffalo Park, when it was first established. I will tell you about it too. It was during the time a herd of buffalo was moved up here. They were taken far in the north country. Two seasons after that they made their way into our land. Those were the plains buffalo. When they came upon our land that is when the Park was established [expanded]. The Chief was asked, 'The buffalo entered your land. What do you think?' He replied, 'I don't know.' The Park official who was in charge, as there had been buffalo up north before, said, 'What do you think about the idea where they are going to include your land in the Buffalo Park, are you willing?' The Chief replied, 'No.' Park official: 'Will you lend it out or give it up?' The Chief told him he would lend it out, 'but I can't give it to you people. I'll just lend it to you.' The Park official told him that of all the buffalo that wandered into his land, the Indians could use them for a livelihood. They would multiply and they could live from the buffalo. If the Indians were experiencing difficulty, they could approach the Park officials and he would take charge. He told the Indians that they could kill them at their discretion whenever it was necessary, not anytime. I myself worked in the Park for a long time. We used to slaughter buffalo for the Indians and the missionaries.[87] That was the agreement on the Buffalo Park. But after a while it seems they [parks officials] didn't think that way anymore. If someone is caught killing a buffalo, he will get a 6-month sentence. That is not what they had agreed upon.

RL: They've already broken their promise.

FG: Yes, they broke their promise, after they made an agreement. My uncle was once lacking for food. They were very hungry out in the bush. They killed a buffalo. They were arrested and had to go to jail in Saskatchewan [Fort Saskatchewan].

RL: Did that legislation come from Ottawa?

FG.: Yes, the Park officials are hired through the government.

RL: Is anybody allowed to hunt buffalo today?

FG: Recently, 200 buffalo were slaughtered for the Indians.

RL: Does this happen every year?

FG: No, not every year. Some time ago, they slaughtered some. That was about three winters ago. It was only recently they slaughtered 200 for the Indians and Métis and Chipewyan.

RL: That land which you say is yours, does it enter the Park boundary?

FG: Yes, our land was made to be part of the Park. It is like something sitting in the middle of a plate. They do whatever they want with the Park. They never consult us, they own it.

RL: Thank you for talking to me.

FG: This discussion I just finished is all truth because I have seen it. I would be happy if my conversation could be heard somewhere. I thank you very much for talking to me. I wish to thank anybody, Indian or white man, who may listen to this conversation.

Ray Ladouceur (18 March 2021)

Well, those days a lot of those people that was in the Park here, the Dene, they didn't want a park, eh? Because it was their land. But when the white man came there and made laws, of course as the buffalo is down, trying to save the woodland buffalo. . . .

Yeah, prairie buffalos, they brought them in from the south. But the woodland buffalo always was there. Yeah, they pretty near cleaned out those woodland buffalos that's when they brought the prairie buffalos in. Oh, it helped people you know, but a lot of people had to poach to get a buffalo to feed their family. What else are you going to do, you know? You know you try to get something to feed your family, their family can't starve to death because there's thousands of those prairie buffalos, you know. That's what happened to woodland buffalo, I know. There was quite a few thousand, but what else did they have those days? They had to get those buffalos to feed their family.

They [the Dene people] had no choice. No choice after they brought in the other animals, now the prairie buffalo are totally different. They brought in quite a few thousand of those buffalos. I don't know, two, three thousand into the Park. And then that's why they increased them [the Park boundaries].

Some [of the buffalo] headed more further south, near Birch Mountain area here, the herd that they brought. But they migrated, some of them migrated to try to go back south.

Leslie Laviolette (22 March 2021)

I mean how many buffalo, two barges full of buffalo that they dropped off at Hay Camp, and mixed in with the real bison that were here for a long time. And that, this Ronald Lake [wood bison] herd here, I think there's about 300 original buffalo that have been here for a long time, got away from that herd. These ones migrate by themselves. And I think they became a—there's a little park there now they can't hunt or do anything to them.[88] So that's where we fought for. Cause those were original buffalo, the real bison.

Big John Marcel (18 March 2021)

Well, as far as I know, when Parks took over, and then when everybody had to get out of there if you don't belong to the Park, you know, they were burning houses and everything as far as I know. Parks did that.

Frank Marcel (n.d.)

From what I understand, the Government just went ahead and grabbed as much land as they needed for their own use—no input from the locals. People were not notified of the changes they will face because of this WBNP creation. They just came and took our traplines without telling us anything. Most of the trappers in the area of Birch River, Birch Mountains, and Peace River area were all ACFN members.

Keltie Paul and Edouard Trippe de Roche (25 November 2020)

KP: The park superintendents [each] had different ideas. Every time you get a new superintendent in, he's got a different idea based on probably another myth of what the Park is. At first, you know, people in Canada were saying, 'well, we have to save the Native populations.' And then, 'we have to save the buffalo. And this is how we're gonna do it.' And it's all based on nonsense. I would call it bureaucratic nonsense. That was based on a myth, total mythology, it has nothing to do with anything.

So they moved the people around, they moved the bison around, and very much you can kind of see parallels between moving the bison around and moving the people around to try to control everything. And they also have different ideas. One superintendent might think 'well, it'd be [a] really good idea to have the Park for trophy shooting the buffalo. We get a whole bunch of money from rich Americans, and we let them shoot our buffalo and then they take a head home.' Honest to goodness, this is what some people thought. And then the next superintendent will come in and he'd go, 'well, you know, this isn't what we're here for. We're here to preserve and protect the bison. And then that means that we have to come down on the Native people,' because they were kind of treated like the wolves. I don't know if you know this, but this has been causing controversy over on the other side, about the wolves and the caribou? So they treated the Native people like wolves. They said, 'okay, you can't, you're not supposed to hunt bison here, you don't hunt bison there.' The only thing was that if they got outside the Park, which is another story entirely, then they could shoot them and eat them if they were free of disease.

So, I guess that's what I'm trying to say, is there was, there's been a lot of different superintendents coming in with very many different ideas. There's been a lot of epochs: the conservation epochs, the preservation epoch, and the management epoch. And in each of those three time periods, there's all these people coming in with very different ideas, and remember, superintendents get replaced, then somebody goes to another national park, etc. And when you have a regime change like that, you get a whole different somebody coming in with a whole different idea about what they should be doing. But I think the basic thing was that they were basing it on bad data . . .

ST: Do you know if there was any point where government officials were looking for input from the community when they created the Park?

ER: There is no consultation then.

KP: Nothing. They plopped everything down. Just—they had no consultation; they didn't say anything to anybody. They really considered that—when you look back on it—and all of the things that they were doing *with*, I would say, *for* the Native People, not *with* the Native People, the expansion of the residential school, based on that data, everything that they were doing back there, they're justifying by saying, well, it says here . . . so they went with, I guess, prevailing mythology of the time, which was not well formed, not well executed, certainly not researched. And based on [that], I would call it hearsay. . . .

In a lot of ways, they sort of put the bison very much ahead of the people. Their livelihoods, their belief system, and ways of knowing, the ways of knowing that was passed on to their children, their culture, everything.

Ernie "Joe" Ratfat (19 March 2021)

ER: They brought up other ones [the plains bison]. They're smaller buffalo. Yeah.

ST: And that's when they made the Park bigger, too?

ER: Yes.

ST: Did they ever tell anybody that's what they were going to do?

ER: No, they just—they don't tell people back then. They just do whatever they wanted to do. Well, we had no say, when it came to government things, we had no say. They just did it.

Alice Rigney (16 March 2021)

I did hear something about a commitment for 100 years [that the lands were being leased for the Park], which is coming up next year. And it sure would be nice to find the document if it does exist and present it to the Parks. And never mind the apology, just give us back our land....

And they did that, you know. They were there and bringing those diseased prairie buffaloes here, I mean they were diseased because of their travel from Wainwright or wherever it is, and then on a train and then on a barge to here, you know, to put them in the Park. I remember going to Hay Camp in the Park, my sister actually lived with a park warden there and how they used to corral them, and they used to slaughter so many and that was for, they would ship them south. The hides would be sent south for tanning [as part of the commercial slaughter in the 1960s and 1970s]. But the buffalo there were not slaughtered for the people, for the community here.

Mary "Cookie" Simpson (11 March 2021)

CS: There was no consultation at all. That word didn't even exist a long time ago [for talking to Indigenous Peoples]. They never came to my grandpa or my uncles or my father, and they never ever did say, 'hey, we're going to be expanding, we're going to be bringing buffalos in, and we're going to take this land.' That was their [the Indigenous Peoples] traditional land and they just lost everything...

ST: And one other thing that we've heard about when the park was made, we've heard from a couple of Elders, that they were told that the Park would be just temporary?

CS: Yes, yes. That's what my dad always said. He said, 'when are they gonna leave anyways?' he would say, 'because it's only temporary.' And that's what they said when they first brought the buffalo in, when they first made the Park. They said it was just temporary and the land would go back to them, to the people. And that was it. He always said that, and my uncles always said that too . . . they're all gone now. But they [the Elders] would talk about it, and I would sit there and listen to them. That was one of the main things they said when we talked about the Park, was that it was just on loan.

ST: And do you know how long it was supposed to be before they gave it back?

CS: No, I never heard them say a date.

ST: So that means that all that land right now, that's up there that Parks Canada has, it's all loaned, it's not theirs?

CS: That's right. It's not theirs. They just took it. They just took it, and they never even gave anything to the Aboriginal People that were living there. They never give them nothing. They told them they couldn't shoot the animals. They couldn't shoot the buffaloes that they brought in. They didn't even get reimbursed for nothing. They just took their land and that was it. You know, they're just so evil.

Beverly Tourangeau (21 March 2021)

The Park had, from my understanding, from what the Elders have told me that have passed on, they had a 100-year agreement. The Park signed an agreement, a 100-year agreement. Well, that should be coming up soon. I think it was 1929 when they signed that 100-year agreement. But, from my understanding, the Park was established in 1922. You know, that agreement [that the Park lands would be returned to the people after the 100 years had passed] should become an absolute.

And, because the Park did this, they established the Park without consulting with the Native people. You know, they should have consulted with the Native people. Now they have eleven different First Nations [who are members of the Park's Cooperative Management Committee]. They're called Indigenous Partners, and ACFN is one of them. And they're from Alberta and NWT. But, in the beginning, they never consulted with First Nations or with anybody in Treaty 8. They just established the Park. And they had released the buffalo in 1929, by Buffalo Landing by Hay Camp, Stony Island. That's how little I know. But from what I heard, people were kicked out of the Park and out of Birch Mountain, but I was told by an Elder there's lots of ACFN graveyards in by Birch Mountain.

Leslie Wiltzen (21 January 2021)

Leslie discusses the oral histories shared by his uncle Elder Pat Marcel about the impacts of losing access to harvesting areas in the Park after the 1926 expansion. A portion of this interview is available as a digital audio recording online.[89]

SCAN TO LISTEN

When [the Park] was expanded, [that] was when the Dene people, the Chipewyan people of Fort Chip, were really affected—through the expansion, because the original boundaries of Wood Buffalo National Park were the Peace River. The Peace River north was the original boundaries when it was formed in 1922. And it was not until the bison crossed the Peace River into the Peace-Athabasca Delta that the Park boundaries were expanded to its present-day borders.

And that's when we were really affected because although we were on, as our Treaty says, 'the Chipewyan Indians of the Athabasca, of the Birch, the Slave, the Peace, and the Gull,' were already on the Peace and were all already on the Slave . . . and that expansion of the Park, from the Peace River boundaries to its current-day boundary, that's when it really affected [the Dene]. That's when everybody was forced [to leave]. And, you know, talking with my Uncle Pat and oral history that I have, that he had written, it explains that. It explains really a lack of desire of the Dene peoples to go [to leave their territories in the Park] originally because . . . you know, hunting in the Park and the Delta, that was a good area for providing food and a living for families of Dene people. And then with the expansion, now they had to go out and leave that area of the Park where it was good hunting. They had to go into areas where there was more non-Aboriginal hunters and trappers coming down the Athabasca River from more southern populated areas, expanding into their traditional territory. So when they were given the option [to transfer], when they were asked to leave, Uncle Pat said that was the harder part for them. They knew it was going to be rougher on the outside [of the Park boundaries] because the furs had been depleted by non-Aboriginal trappers coming down. So, resources and, you know, if you're hunting along the river system . . . you're hunting for fur-bearing animals, but you're also hunting moose, you're hunting all the animals that you need to survive. And you get a large group, like a First Nation group, where there's many families to feed, I mean, one moose doesn't go far. So they knew that there was going to be hardship, and it's in those oral histories. That's what he told me, that they were really reluctant to leave, but they were forced to leave, they weren't given the choice.

And that's what I recall from the stories, is that they knew there was going to be hard times in the years that followed. After they were forced to leave the Park were very, very, trying times for the people, the Chipewyan people of that area, because food was scarce, furs were scarce and just being able to provide food for your family was difficult. . . .

You know, the question that's always, always on my mind is, we go back to that expansion of Wood Buffalo National Park, and for some reason, the Chipewyan people took the brunt. It's our traditional territory, like I said previously, we've got documentation that verifies that Dene people have been in that area for tens of thousands of years. It is truly traditional territory.

Anonymous Fort Chipewyan Elder (7 February 1974)

One Elder had told me of this. His name was Pierre Whitehead. He was a Chief. The land was loaned to the government for the buffaloes. This was mentioned to me by Philip Gibot. It seemed to me that the land was given to them, but apparently it was just loaned to them. After five years, the population of the buffalo [in Buffalo National Park in Wainwright] grew in size. It was at this time the [federal] government had, as the provincial government for the land south of the Peace River, for the Wood Buffalo National Park. Now that land is also filled with buffalo as far as the twenty-seventh Baseline.

Anonymous ACFN Elder (11 March 2021)

A long time ago, there were two parks, a long time ago. That first park they made is across Peace River [north of the river]. And, when they brought in buffalos, 1925, 1930 maybe, then they took the other park in the Delta [south of the Peace River]. That's the old-timers—they call it the old park and new park. They [the government] wanted to bring buffalos here, to the Delta. And then the story is, what they said, my Elders, they said they would borrow it, they were going to give it back. They never gave it back yet . . . and they borrowed, took over the Park. They took a big one.

They borrowed it, so they have to give it back. You borrow, you have to give it back. That's the stories anyway.

Anonymous ACFN Elder (16 March 2021)

Yeah, it's not fair at all. You know what I mean? Our people never went to the Parks after that [after the expansion]. [In the] '60s and '70s, my mom, I mean my dad and my brothers never went hunting there. You don't even dare go across the river. You know what I mean? [My family would] jump on their dogs and they went to north shore. We weren't allowed. We weren't even thinking that way. That's how much they brainwashed the Indians there. We could go to north shore, but I mean on the rivers, on the Park side, we never did go there.

So like, I don't know nobody, even today, I will not go to the Park. I wouldn't even think of going to the Park. You know what I mean? Yes, I mean all our family, nobody goes to the Parks. Nobody. Even today, I wouldn't even go to the Parks. I'd rather go up to our [ACFN's reserves] country. Like my dad won't talk about it but, they will not do it, they will not go. We had our own area to go, us guys, but we never shot a buffalo. Our family never saw the buffalo, put it that way. Because no one knows in those days, eh? And most of controllers were white. They didn't care how us Indians [were] those days. Right?

4

1944 k'e nánį denesųłiné ʔená bets'į nųłtsa k'eyághe ts'én nílya

One of the most profound changes following the 1926 annex and the establishment of the Park permitting system was a membership transfer that took place in 1944, through which about half of the ancestors of ACFN were transferred to what is now MCFN. This chapter's Denesųłiné title literally translates to "in 1944, some Denesųłiné were placed in the Cree reserve." This event is in some ways unique in the history of national parks in Canada. Through this transfer, thirty-six Dënesųłıné families who had been living in the Park—a total of 123 individuals—were transferred from the Chipewyan Band's treaty payroll list to the Cree Band's treaty payroll list "through the stroke of a pen," as ACFN Elder Leslie Wiltzen put it. Most of the families who were transferred had resided and harvested at the Birch River and Peace Point settlements, which had been home to the Dene for hundreds of years— as Elder Frank Marcel called it, "their traditional land where they've homesteaded for many years."[1] Oral histories suggest that a number of the evictions of Dene people from their homes in the Park occurred immediately after the membership transfer.

There is little evidence to be gleaned from the government records to reconstruct why or how the transfer occurred. The few extant archival records suggest the transfer took place quickly and quietly, without the knowledge or consent of most Dene residents. Indian Agent Jack Stewart's diary entries from June 1944 refer to a meeting in which an unspecified number of Dene leaders requested the transfer and Stewart approved their request: "Had a meeting of the Cree Band in office today. Talked over the election system and also the reserve they have asked for. Part of the Chipewyan band was also here, and they put in an application for a transfer to the Cree Band."[2] Stewart updated the band lists, and the transfer was made official between June and December 1944. The 1946 treaty annuity paylists for the region listed the number of members who had transferred, and the 1949 Indian Census report showed a total population reduction for the Chipewyan Band from 259 to 161 between 1944 and 1949.[3] At the time of the transfer, the full population of the Fort Chipewyan Cree Band (now MCFN) and about half of the Chipewyan Band's population resided at Peace Point and Birch River/House Lake within the Park. In oral histories, Elders note several Dene family names that are now typically included on MCFN's list of family names, and the 1946 annuity paylist indicates the family names and total number of family members of those who were transferred: Adams, Baptiste, Beaulieu, Bouchier, Cheezie, Dene, Evans, Fontain, Freizie, Gladue, Nadary, Piche, Poitras, Ratfat, Sepp, Shortman, Simpson, Trippe de Roche, Tourangeau, Vermillion, Waquan, Watsharay, and William.[4]

McCormack argues that the establishment of the Registered Fur Management Area (RFMA) system, often referred to as traplines, outside Park boundaries in 1942, may have driven Dënesųłıné leaders within the Park to request the transfer.[5] The punitive nature of the prevailing wildlife management system—especially its power to expel people from harvesting areas within the Park if they were perceived to be breaking rules—put people living within the Park at risk of hardship and hunger. Tensions between harvesters within and outside the Park rose after 1926, as permitting rules limited access to the Park and resources outside the Park grew scarce due to an influx of fur trappers from the south of the province during the Great Depression. With the RFMA system established, places where people could trap outside the Park were effectively unavailable to Park residents, including those who lost their permits and were expelled for any reason after 1942. Furthermore, those Dene and Cree families living in the Park in the 1940s had little hope of establishing a reserve within the Park to protect their rights (MCFN did not obtain reserve land at Peace Point until 1986), partly because officials claimed that those living in the Park already had special privileges that others did not and that they were adequately provided for: "the Park is a wonderful game reserve for them and they have good hunting and trapping privileges," wrote one official in 1945.[6] Because of these unique challenges, McCormack and Sandlos argue that Dene people living in the Park were forced to "throw in their lot" with the Cree Band and that leaders requested the transfer as an act of desperation to protect members within Park boundaries. McCormack suggests that, given that Cree and Dene people within the Park shared common interests and had longstanding peace treaties and kinship connections already in place, an alliance through a band transfer made sense.[7]

The oral histories shared below suggest more complicated dynamics were at play. Some Elders believe that the transfer was forced by the Parks administration and Indian Affairs and may have been a deliberate effort to further limit who could access the Park. Several also contend that only a small number Indigenous leaders knew about the transfer, but there was little to no consultation with those residents who were most affected by the transfer. Some Elders and members believe that the transfer was intended to remove Dene people altogether from their rights and territories in the Park by cutting off kinship connections between those Dene families who had access to the Park and those who did not . Many Dënesųłıné people within or outside the Park did not know the change had occurred, and to this day do not know how it happened. "There's no documentation that shows that our Chiefs negotiated and allowed for that to happen, because they would never have done that," Leslie Wiltzen stated. Chief Adam also notes: "people weren't consulted about it whatsoever, because my granny said it just happened just like that . . . she wasn't told of it, nobody was told of this. All they were told [was] that if you want to stay in a park, you become Cree band. If not, leave. That was her consultation." Thus, as Elder Horace Adam explained, people were left with no choice but to transfer bands in order to maintain access to their harvesting areas within the Park: "They told them they could move or they become the Cree band. So most of them did become Cree band just to keep their land, their traplines. That's what happened."

Some members, like Leslie Wiltzen, believe the decision was in part intended to reduce Indian Affairs' administrative labour by consolidating multiple communities with claims to the lands in the region. Ray Ladouceur's oral history suggests the transfer was the result of administrative oversight and ignorance about the differences between the communities, because families within the Park were fluent in both languages and were often also closely connected by marriage: "They [the administrators] didn't know that and because they [the Dene people in the Park] spoke Cree, I guess, 'oh, they're all Cree in Birch River," [so] that part of the country, that area they took for Crees. And Dene was out of there." According to these oral histories, those who did not change their membership in 1944 were told they had to leave the Park and relocate to Big Point, Old Fort, Jackfish Lake, Point Brulé, or Poplar Point. Some families who were evicted had to move several times to maintain an adequate livelihood. Thus, Park policies of division and exclusion displacing Dene peoples from their lands and severing their family connections became further entrenched. What may have seemed to be a minor decision, made with just "the stroke of a pen," had profound and long-lasting effects on the community.

ACFN members' family histories suggest that women often bore the brunt of the impacts of this transfer. Several oral histories shared for this book explain that Dene women who married outside of the Nation or married non-Status men—thereby losing their Status under the *Indian Act*—before the transfer took place were not permitted to return to their family homes and family members within the Park later in life. This was the case for Helene Piche, Chief Allan Adam's grandmother, and Elizabeth Flett, Garry Flett's mother, whose stories are related below. The combination of the 1944 membership transfer and the gender-based discrimination of the *Indian Act's* Indian Status rules meant that several Dene women and their families lost access to their homelands within the Park and were severed from their kin. Their descendants still experience and feel the impacts of these exclusions. For those who had to transfer because they refused to move out of the Park, the forcible identity change had long-lasting, harmful effects. Alice Rigney explained that some MCFN members maintain their connections to their Dënesųłıné heritage: "the families here in Fort Chip are aware, you know, the Simpsons know they're Denes, the Tourangeaus, the Grandjambs, the Piches, the Ratfats, you know, they know, but it was the government that made them that." Chief Adam stated that this knowledge is painful: "how much of Mikisew members suffered the burden that I suffer when our people got ripped apart? . . . You know, the struggle of being Mikisew Cree First Nation when their heart belongs to Dene."

The oral testimonies shared in this chapter contains members' general reflections on and histories of the membership transfer and relates specific family histories. These stories suggest that the membership transfer, regardless of the intentions behind it, divided families and the community, disconnected many members from their heritage and language, entrenched existing government-imposed separations between the people and their territories, and led to long-term emotional trauma and harmful impacts on health and well-being. Furthermore, some Elders suggest that the population loss had long-term political impacts for the First Nation. With a reduced population, they suggest ACFN's bargaining power at government tables has decreased and that the Nation receives reduced per-capita government transfer payments. Nevertheless, ACFN members and some of their Dënesųłıné kin living in the Park boundaries are adamant that, despite this traumatic event, their identities as Dene will never disappear. As Donalyn Mercredi summarized, "If you're born a Dene, you'll always be a Dene."

ORAL HISTORY

Helene Piche's story

ACFN Elder Alec Bruno's mother, Helene Piche, left the Park after marrying a man who did not have a permit for the Park. Alec Bruno was Chief Allan Adam's father. Chief Adam shared in detail his granny's oral history of the transfer and eviction and Alec Bruno's telling of the history follows.

Chief Allan Adam (2 February 2021)

The only things that I had known about Wood Buffalo National Park when I was a kid growing up, was that we were not allowed to go and hunt in Wood Buffalo. My dad was known back then [as] being [an] ACFN member—which was Chip Band 201 was the legal name—and the people that belonged on Chip Band 201 were the people that were outside of Wood Buffalo National Park. And that carried on for a while until I got older. And then I asked my dad, I said, "how come we're not allowed to be in the park?" And this was back in the '80s, and my dad told me a story about what had happened.

And my granny was still alive. My granny passed away in 1989 at the age of 89 years old. And the funny thing, the tragic thing about everything, was that my granny survived the pandemic [the influenza and smallpox epidemics in the 1920s], and I think her husband perished just at the later stages of the pandemic, and that would be around year 1922. She brought her husband into town [when he became sick] according to what my dad said. That would be my granny's first husband. She took him to town. [Before that], she was staying out at House [Lake], I think it is. She had a two-storey house. She had everything, they had a garden there. Everything.

When members of the Piche family grew up, they were wealthy people. They provided for their kids and everything. There was families there, certain groups of families, and my granny was one of them. Her last name was Piche at the time, Helene Piche. I forget who her husband was, but he did give me it [his name], it could have been Pierre Piche, I don't know. But in a way, when he got sick, [she] brought him to Fort Chip from House River or Birch River area that side over there, his ailment, his illness got worse, and he perished here in the community. And my dad said that after he perished, my granny did what she had to do, bury him and everything and stuff like that, then she wanted to go back home. She wanted to literally go back home to Birch, to

House River, and when she notified [Parks] people that we're going back to the park, the warden came there and told her that she's not allowed to go back to the park unless she changes her identity. Meaning that if she goes back, she'll have to become a Cree band member, to give up her identity. My granny said no. But she was insisted to go home because it's the only home she had, was a two-storey beautiful house and everything that was there. They refused her to go back. And you know she was still determined to get home. And so, they just burned her place down and told her that there's nothing there, we burned your house down and everything.

That's when she realized—this was probably about the year [19]20, [19]23 around there, maybe [19]22—and she realized she had her husband, her husband's deceased now, she had a house before her husband was deceased, she had her family there and cared for and living there and everything. They had a roof over their head. They had a garden. They had all the wildlife and everything, and it was abundance.

It's one of the richest countries in the world in this area right there. And she lost all that. Not only her, but other family members as well that were told to leave the Park and never come back, and she never went back. We were told after from finding out from history and everything that if my granny had went back, they were going to kill her because they were ordered to kill anybody if they resisted to leave, and that mainly meant ACFN members, Athabasca Chipewyan First Nation, known as Chip Band 201 back then. . . .

Then I hear stories about other family members. After we were relocated from the Park, my granny moved to Big Point. And then she was relocated again to Fiddler's Point. And then she was relocated to Jackfish Lake. And then she relocated to Old Fort, only to be put back in Fort Chip, in 1954, '56. My dad said they moved into town in 1958, '59. So from 1922 to 1959 my granny, with her family, relocated five times before she went back to Fort Chip.[8] That's the legacy and the story that I have to bear. That's the story I'll have to tell because that's the story that was told to me from my grandma and my dad and oral history at its best. That's why I guess I have a keen memory about things that were told to me, and I hardly ever forget stuff. So that's where we're at right now, and that's as much as you know. I [have] given you all the information that I know about it and everything, but my granny said that she was forcefully moved, and [her] house was burned to the ground.

. . . People weren't consulted about it whatsoever because my granny said it just happened, just like that. She wasn't told of it. Nobody was told this

[was] to happen. All they were told, that if you want to stay in a park, you become Cree band. If not, leave. That was her consultation. And that's when she fought to go home. And that's when they said no and they deemed her as radical. They were probably going to shoot my granny if she went back home. That's when they decided to burn her house down. That's the exact words of what my dad told me.

Alec Bruno (Dene Laws Interviews, 2015)

Remember, I told you a story about my mom, when she got kicked out of her house. To me, that is unrealistic for Parks Canada to do: who gave them the rights to tell people? My mom was born and raised across from Lake Claire close to Birch River at a little place called House Lake. We went there about 4 years [ago] with Parks Canada to the site where we had lived. It was Dene people that lived there. My mom was born there, raised there, got married there, and two of her oldest boys are buried there at the graveyard. After WBNP was created in 1922, shortly after that, things started to change, and then by 1928, her husband got sick. Back then when people got married, the men [were] way older than the girls and same with my mom. Like my mom was born in 1900, by 1922 when WBNP [was established], she was already 22 years old, and she got married, she had kids, she said she got married very young. Maybe 15 or 16. You know, what [are] they called, pre-arranged or something like that? The guy comes and tells your mother and father, "I like your daughter and I want to marry her." She didn't like that but that's the way it was, but she said he was a good provider. A good hunter, a good trapper. But he got sick, and he died in 1929, I think, here in town.

Now she wanted to go back home, back to her place, and that's when Parks Canada intervened and said you can't go back there, that's Wood Buffalo Park now. The only way you could go back now is if you promise—you have to join the Cree Band if you want to go back there.

But who gives Parks Canada the rights to tell people? Who gave them the rights to say, "well, you join the Cree Band?" I asked that question many times. Nobody ever gave me an answer yet, especially when it comes from Canada or the government. Pat [Marcel] and I always talk about that. Pat's granny [Ester Piche, whose story follows] was my aunty, she was my mom's sister. She was from there too. I mean, mom used to cry sometimes, wanting to go back there. Nothing but the things she lost. She wanted to go back and see the gravesites too, her two boys, and she wasn't allowed to do that. . . .

Well, at the signing of the Treaty, it says, we will never take your land away from you, right? Okay, that's what Canada said, we will never take your land away, but we will share I; but with my mother it was different. She was told not to go back to her house. She had a house there, all her things, and she couldn't even go back to collect them.

Ester Piche's story

Alice Rigney (née Marcel) and several other Marcel family members shared a similar story about Ester Piche (Alice's grandmother, and Helene's sister), who also had grown up at the Dene settlement at Birch River. After refusing to transfer Bands in 1944, Ester Piche was required to leave the Park.

Alice Rigney (16 & 17 March 2021)

I'll think about my granny living at House [Lake], probably the most beautiful forests, and then being told to move and her moving to Old Fort and making a home there. I have a beautiful picture of my granny, you know, and . . . I get my strength from her and my mother. Their life was anything but easy.

At present, we [Alice's family] don't have anything to do with the Park because our traditional land is in the Delta on the Athabasca River, at a place called Jackfish Lake, by the Jackfish Lake, too. But in the past? Yeah, my grandmother lived at House Lake. My grandmother Ester Piche. I couldn't say for sure exactly the years, but it had to be probably in the 1920s, when the Park invaded us with their rules. You know, it's just a maddening situation when you think of all the wrongs that were done to our people.

Yes, my grandmother was living there. I don't think my mother was there because my mother was also in the residential school, in the mission. I know [she was in residential school] from 1926 to [19]32 and was like six consecutive years without going home. So I believe it was during that time that my grandmother had remarried. And when she left House [Lake], she moved to the south shore of Lake Athabasca at Old Fort Bay at a point which we call Poplar Point, which is across from Moose Point. So that's where she raised her daughters, and my mum took us there, showed us that little cabin that they lived in. . . . And that's where she lived and then when my mother married, and my auntie, they moved to Jackfish Lake, and my granny moved there too with them, because she lived with my Auntie Liza. . . .

Well, once you're evicted from your home, I mean, for what reasons? I mean, these guys, with the papers in their hand to say that the government is creating a park and you have a choice—you either can stay and join the Mikisew Cree First Nation, or you have to leave. She left. I mean, she's Dene. And there's many, many [Dene] families that stayed in the Cree band, you know, the Simpsons, the Tourangeaus, and the Ratfats. You know, there's many families that, they're Dene, but chose to stay [in the Park]. So, I mean, it was the Parks demanding people, "you either become this or you become that." And our people . . . they believed in these people [government officials]. And I mean, if in this day and age you tried that, there'd be riots and whatnot, you know. But in those days, you were told, and okay, well.

My late brother, Pat, went out to House Lake with a few family members, and Parks Canada—it was a Parks project, I believe—and they went there, and they saw what was left of the remains in the cemetery there, and they had a little community there when they had to leave. And so there was antiques, artifacts there, that they were not allowed to touch or bring home.

You know, my brother Pat [Marcel] had said they saw sewing machines there [at House Lake] and copper pots, and it's all gone. They could not take it with them, and they more or less had to leave just with what they could. I mean, how would anybody feel, being told, "okay, you have to move because we are the government, because we are the Parks"? You know, and they're obedient, but they lost the trust of the white people again. And I mean, this has been going on, now we're standing up you know, we're standing up through the colonization. I mean, you're hearing more and more of our people speaking up and it's issues like this. You know, if I was to put myself in my granny's shoes, and probably she only owned just a few items for herself 'cause she made all her own dresses, you know, meaning she had to get material from the store. She had to make clothes for her children. She used rabbit skin to make jackets and caribou hides to make clothing, moose hides for moccasins, because you couldn't go buy these things. So she utilized the land wherever she was. And if I pictured myself in my granny's shoes, I don't know how I would feel . . . I mean she had to pack her child and cross Lake Claire and Lake Mamawi, and then find a place to start over again.

The Ratfat family

The Ratfat family resided at Birch River and Peace Point and were transferred to the Cree Band in 1944. Elder Ernie "Joe" Ratfat shared his history about the impacts of the transfer here. To this day, he maintains that he is Dene at heart, even if he is MCFN on paper.

Ernie "Joe" Ratfat (19 March 2021)

Well, I'm with the Mikisew Cree. But I am Dene. Yeah, that's one of the things that happened to us. Kind of messed me up all my life. Those people changed my life without even asking. My dad always told me I was Dene . . . but on paper it says Mikisew Cree. Yeah, there's a lot of families that, at Fort Chip, belong to Mikisew Cree that are Dene. My dad is Peter Ratfat. And, like he always told me I was a Dene, and we always spoke Dene in our home. . . .

I've been trying to get back to the Dene Nation. And, my chief, they wouldn't let me go. They have the last word if we're going to be transferred. So I just kind of gave up. I just gave up and accepted the fact that on paper I am Cree. But my soul is Dene, and it will always be that way.

The Simpson & Flett Families' Stories

Some Flett and Simpson family members, whose relatives are historically connected by marriage, shared their families' experiences with the transfer as well. Most Simpson family members, with the known exception of Elizabeth Flett (née Simpson), whose story is shared by ACFN member Garry Flett below), transferred to Mikisew Cree Nation in 1944.

Mary "Cookie" Simpson (11 March 2021)

When they made the Wood Buffalo National Park, the Indian Affairs decided it was so good for their books to move everybody, all the trappers living in the Park area, to the Cree band, [so] they just moved them without their consent. So we got moved again to the Cree band . . . like we were moved first to the Chip Band then we're moved to the Cree band. They just did that on their own without consent, consenting of the people. And I know that the Trippe de Roche, too, were moved and . . . there was a lot of families that were just moved from different bands into the Cree Band because of the Park. Everybody trapping in the Park would be moved to the Cree Band according to the Indian Affairs—which is not even right, I don't think. They shouldn't be screwing around with people's livelihood.

If they refused to transfer, then their park license and hunting and trappers license would be taken away. And so they had no choice. People had no choice. They were just moved, which is not right. I don't agree with that . . . But after I learned about the history, I thought, holy, that's really wicked. So it's either of the Park or Indian Affairs in cahoots with each [other] that just moved people....

They took the people away [from ACFN], like us [the Simpson family]! We were, when they created the Park there, we were in the Chip Band. And then they just moved us without our knowledge or without letting us know. That's what my dad said anyways. He said, they just moved us, they just moved us to a different band just like that, he said.

Elizabeth Flett's Story

ACFN member Garry Flett's mother, Elizabeth Flett (née Simpson), shared her oral history of the membership transfer with her son. She was born the same year that the Park was established, 1922. Her grandfather, Edouard Shortman and his son Isidore Simpson (Elizabeth Flett's father) were Dene. They had been granted permission to live in the Park in 1925 and built a cabin at Peace Point the following year. Elizabeth grew up at Peace Point, and all her brothers hunted and trapped in that area. She married a non-Status man, lost her Status, and left the Park to live elsewhere. Following the transfer, Elizabeth Flett's situation was particularly challenging. After Bill C-31 was passed in 1985, changing the Indian Act provision that had stripped Indigenous women of their Status for marrying non-Status men, Elizabeth applied to regain her Status. The Department of Indian Affairs reinstated her to ACFN, where she had been a member at the time of her marriage, rather than to MCFN, to which all of her family had transferred after she lost her Status. Because of this, Elizabeth was refused access to her family home in the Park, and Garry and his siblings been barred from entering the Park to harvest as an ACFN member. Thus, he and his siblings, children, nieces and nephews are excluded from the Park, even though his grandfather's cabin, still standing, is a physical symbol of his family's claim to the live there.

Garry Flett (6 December 2020)

So we'll go back in history a bit too when my mother married my father. All of my mother's family were with the Athabasca Chipewyan First Nation, or known as the Chip Band at that time. So when my mother married my father, she had to leave the reserve, and she had to relinquish her Status rights because she married a non-Status person, which would be my father. At that time, when she was basically booted out of the reserve, it was ACFN. So, as time went by, and then back in 1986, when there was a challenge to the federal government by a lady [Sandra Lovelace] in Manitoba, who went after the government to get her rights back . . . her challenge was successful. And she got her rights back and she was reinstated into her band.⁹ So I challenged the government on behalf of my mother to do the same thing.

But when my mother was out of the Band, she was with ACFN. During that time, and after that, Parks Canada came in and said [to ACFN members in the Park], "in order for you to continue hunting and trapping in the Park, you had to become MCFN, Mikisew, or the Cree band." So it was of no significance to my mother because she was then non-Status. She already had been pulled out of the band sort of thing. In 1986, when we challenged, she was allowed back in, but she was put right back to where she started from [to ACFN, from which the rest of her family had been transferred]. She was kicked out of the Chip band, so she was reinstated back into the Chip band and meanwhile, all of her family were transferred over to the Cree band during that time. So that is why my mother is the only one out of all of her siblings that remained Chip band. All my uncles and aunts are all Mikisew Cree. . . .

It sounds like something you'd read in a novel, but you never experienced it until you had experienced it. And what was the thinking back then? It certainly wasn't on the side of women. Women were, their rights were told to them . . . not just the women, but pretty well everybody. Your rights were told to you and delivered to you by the federal government.

Garry Flett (16 December 2020)

So I spent my years, if you were going to hunt in the Park, I couldn't go with you. Even if they were my first cousins. They can all go but I couldn't. And members of my family could. So yeah, that's the piece that when I said that it affected me personally, that's what it is. So I had to stay away from there, from the Park side. To have that as your sole lifestyle, to hunt and trap and fish in the Park, it wasn't for us. I couldn't even dream about it. I wasn't allowed to because of what transpired there. But . . . my first cousins were—it was easy for them. They just got a park license and described who they were and who they belong to as members of the Cree Band or the Mikisew Cree Band. And they were granted those licenses. I would go back and say "well, that's my mom's brother's children" and "that's my first cousins" and they just [replied]: "no, not you. You're ACFN. Your mom was ACFN . . . you are not entitled."

GENERAL ORAL TESTIMONY ABOUT THE TRANSFER

Horace Adam (19 March 2021)

The people that occupy that area was the Cree. The Cree, yeah the Cree. And they, and there's a few Dene like the Ratfats, are the ones that were there. Because they had no choice . . . the treaties was signed and then the Dene people had their traplines there in the Park, at that time. They [Parks] told them they could move or they [could] become the Cree band. So most of them did became Cree Band just to keep their land, their traplines. That's what happened.

There was a lot [of Dene residents in the Park] at that time. There was Dene. There was a lot people from Fort Chipewyan. The Dënesųłıné that was out there on the land. And, I can't recall all their names because I didn't really know lots of people at that time. They stayed [in the Park], they stayed and so they become Cree Band.

Leonard Flett (30 April 2021)

We were treated like—I don't know what. Who are they to tell us to relocate from where my mom was born [at Birch River], move us to the reserve [at Jackfish]? I don't know, it just pisses me off when I think about it. And, when I go to the National Park today in Fort Chip, I don't go ask for their permission, I just go. And that's our right. We're entitled to it. I don't think the government should tell us to move away or else become—this is the part that really pisses me off—they had the rights to make [ACFN] members become Mikisew members. That really pisses me off. I mean, who are they to decide that, right? I mean, we signed a Treaty agreement back in 1899. And they can just go in there and do whatever they wanted. It is not right.

Scott Flett (17 March 2021)

That's really where they were, like House [Lake] on the Birch River area and stuff. That's where there was kind of little settlements and stuff. That's where lots of—I remember the Ratfat family, they were Dene before and then when the Dene people were forced out of the Park then they had to become a Cree Band member. There was about—I forget how many families there must have been. I know there is Vermillion, Simpson, Ratfats. I know there's a couple more that didn't switch over. And that whole area was like, they'd signed a treaty you know, like I said, Birch River, Gull River, south of Lake Claire also. The whole side of the south of Lake Athabasca and Lake Claire and stuff, that was all Dene territory. It's all Dene. . . . They didn't want to move, to get out of the Park. And I think the Simpsons and the Vermillions were in that area north of Peace side.

Fred (Jumbo) Fraser (12 March 2021)

What happened in the Park, I guess when they formed the Park [the expansion], south of the Peace, that's when they [Chipewyan Band members] had a choice of switching from ACFN to Mikisew if they wanted to trap in the Park. And I know some ACFN members did switch over, they went to Mikisew so that they could continue to stay in the Park and trapping. So the Métis were also kicked out of the Park because, you know, it's a brand Park, just freshly formed and the chief at the time for Mikisew said, no, the Métis do not leave, they stay in the Park.

As far as I know it's the Parks [who were responsible for the membership transfer]. Like I said, because they gave them [Dene residents in the Park] a choice, you know, like saying, "you could change from ACFN to Mikisew if you want to stay in the Park." You know, some did change and, like I said—Simpsons they had their trapline on the Peace River by west of Fort Chip. And they had a big house on the river, a two-storey building you know, and they had a very big family. Vermillions, they trapped up on the Peace River. They still own that trapline, one of the Simpsons still owns the traplines today. Not that anybody goes trapping. Vermillions, they have their traplines still up there.

Ray Ladouceur (18 March 2021)

Oh, it was mostly Dene [living in the Park], it was supposed to be all Dene, and the government when it came down here, most of them were people that was in Birch River, they [the government] called them Cree. Yeah, they called them Cree, but most of them belong to same Dene . . . But they call them Crees and they [the Dene residents in the Park] spoke Cree, so. They went under the name of Cree then. There's Vermillions and all those people there, they were Dene people at one time. Yeah, they [the Park] went and just went ahead without, well, of course they won't say anything, they wanted to do whatever they wanted to do.

At Birch River, people were mostly Dene, but then when the white man come in this part of the country, I guess there was a few Crees so they took that whole area, Birch River and the Peace River, all for the Cree. They [the white men] called them Cree 'cause they spoke Cree too, and their family, now they're all Cree. They don't call them Dene.

My understanding is, when the white man came over and took over the Park, it was Dene at Birch River. You know that same Dene that, to our area where we settled down, eh, same [thing—it was] Dene. But they [government officials] called them [the Dene living in the Park] Crees. Of course, there was—they were mixed with Cree. They called them Cree so that's where they got their name from, Cree. Most of them are Dene, you know. Yeah, that's what happened . . . the white man. They [white people] didn't know that [the Cree and Dene people were different] and because they [the Dene residents in the Park] spoke Cree, I guess, and [officials assumed] "oh, in the south they're all Cree in Birch River," that part of the country. That area they took for Crees. And so Dene was, you know, out of there.

Big John Marcel (18 March 2021)

Well, you know what it was—it was so many things that happened when Parks took over. And then, you know, I was told by the Elder people and my dad, when Park took over, most of our [ACFN] band members were all trapping in that area. Toward Birch River. And then, when things changed . . . all the band members that work there had to go back to our reserve. And they also—Fort McKay [Band] used to trap around that area, too.[10] And then Parks told most of the people that I know were trapping there, they were trapping, and then parks says to them, "if you want to go back to the Wood Buffalo, okay, you have to change and go back to the Cree band." So, most of these people that I know, just like the Simpsons and Vermillions, and there's quite a few families, joined the Parks because they wanted to trap in that area.

Charlie Mercredi (n.d.)

Elder William Laviolette used to tell me lots of stories; like one day we were in Old Fort just the two of us, everybody else went to Fort Chip for supplies, and the old man said nobody here but us. I asked him what he meant, and he said one time there used to be lots of people, now not anymore; after WBNP we lost many of our people to MCFN.

Donalyn Mercredi (11 March 2021)

And that was their home, so they didn't want to leave their home. So they have no other choice, I'm guessing that they had no other choice. Like I wouldn't want to leave my home. So they probably just transferred to the Mikisew Band. Which I don't think it's fair. They were stripped of their Dene [identity]. They're born Dené; however, they were stripped of it just over their homestead. And they had to transfer bands to another band. Which they really didn't belong to in the first place.

Leslie Wiltzen (21 January 2021)

Leslie began his discussion of the membership transfer reading the 1946 treaty payroll list document, which lists the names of families and number of members [123] who were transferred from the Chipewyan Band to the Cree Band.

There's a lot of names so I can tell you, roughly I'll just give you . . . I'll just read a few of the names off here.

We got Lucien Vermilion, it says two transferred to the Cree Band 170. Then we got Salman Sepp, two transferred. We have Cheezie, Marcel Cheezie, one transferred to Cree band. We have Jonas Nadary, one transferred to Cree band. We have Paul Shortman, two transferred to Cree band. We have Germain Ratfat. Isidore Shortman, four transferred. Joseph Fontain, four transferred. Napoleon Freezy, two transferred. John Volio, one transferred. Louisan Poitras, three transferred. Maragine Poitras, Valentine Piche, Lucien Cheezy, Salma Shortman, Alex Ratfat, Isidore Shortman, Peter Ratfat, Mary Ann, Pauline and Archie: fourteen. Joseph Poitras, William Simpson, Alexander Vermillion, Marjorie Magloire Vermillion, Philip Evans, Isidore Shortman, Moses Nadary, Eugene Poitras, Peter Ratfat, Joseph Bouchier, Ambrose Bouchier, Archie Simpson, Pierre Simpson, Willie Waquan, Francis Waquan, Leonard Leon Bouchier, Joseph Dene, Martin Tourangeau, Willie Waquan, Mary Rose Deraso, Fred Vague. You look at these guys, [they] were all ACFN members that were transferred over to Cree band.

And you know a lot of people unfortunately, it's really sad because, when you look at it today, there's a lot of youth both on the Athabasca Chipewyan First Nation and on the Mikisew Cree First Nation that really don't know their history. There's a lot of kids today that don't realize—don't know that history of what occurred in the Wood Buffalo National Park.

There's no documentation that shows that our chiefs negotiated and allowed for that to happen, because they would never have done that. They would never, ever give their people up. So that was done without any consultation, without any negotiation. If there was negotiations or if there was consultations that took place it was obviously just amongst the federal government and the agents. It never occurred with the Athabasca Chipewyan First Nation. It was never okayed and allowed to happen based on any written documentation, or any oral history that I've heard of or ever seen.

... From my understanding, the only details I have on that come from my Uncle Pat [Marcel] and from oral history. And from what I was told, was basically the federal government didn't want to have to deal with three people, three groups [two Nations in the Park and one outside the Park]. Right? So you have Mikisew there and then you have the ACFN that was asked to leave, and the majority took the option and left. And them that stayed, the federal government didn't want to have to deal with it, with the Chipewyan Indians anymore. They felt, they managed to convince the chief, the main part when he left, the federal government felt that they didn't want to have to deal with the other members. So they couldn't get them to leave. So it would be dealing with three groups. So they did that [Indian Affairs made the membership transfer]. That's why, that's where someone made the decision that we just turn them into Cree band members. My Uncle Pat used to say it really, really more thorough and complete, but that's kind of the oral history that I got out of it. It's not, again, it's not written anywhere. But that's all that's from my understanding, it was one of the main reasons there. And there might be more reasons that we don't know or never will know... It's funny when you read about all this. I mean, the federal government has a document—I've got a list. We know that these people were ACFN members. When we look at when the Treaty was signed, it showed the numbers of Mikisew members, and the members have drastically changed after that membership has changed. So we know there is a big transfer. It's in the federal government's archives. It's recorded in history. But [there's] nothing indicating what led up to that transfer and reasons that were made to transfer. It's like a book where you're reading a good story and then somebody rips out three pages and you never know what happens in those three pages. And that's what happened with the federal government. Why wasn't that more thoroughly documented, where we see that?

5

edeghą k'óíldé íle ajá ú nuhenéné thų́ bek'e náidé

In addition to the permitting system that accompanied the 1926 annex, the extensive suite of game conservation and land management policies governing Indigenous lives across the Park and province grew significantly after 1926. These were upheld through increased surveillance, enforcement and punishment measures overseen through a warden system that also began to expand after 1926. As the oral testimony shared in this chapter suggests, many Dene people perceived the new, and frequently changing, restrictions as infringements of Treaty 8. Furthermore, the hardship people outside the Park experienced after the annex and membership transfer was only amplified by conservation and wildlife management regulations. By the 1930s, parks officials perceived that the bison population in the Park had been sufficiently restored for the Park's central policy focus to shift from preservation of bison to developing a state-controlled wildlife management structure intent on conserving other game populations, especially fur-bearing animals, and on controlling and restricting Indigenous People's lives and movements, and ultimately, eroding Indigenous sovereignty and attempting to erase their presence from the land.[1] This shift proved to be especially challenging for those Dënesųłıné people who were excluded from the Park after the annex, who watched as fur-bearing populations dwindled and competition for furs increased significantly, and as their ways of life fell increasingly under the surveillance of administrators and wardens within and outside the boundaries of the Park. Dene people found themselves less free to live, move, and stay on the land, as the Dënesųłıné chapter title indicates: "We ceased being free or in charge of ourselves, and we couldn't manage to stay on our land (to use it)."

As ACFN Elder Alice Rigney's oral testimony shared in this chapter relates, the creation of the Park precipitated the development of a colonial regime of wildlife management intent on removing Dene people from the land and waters, separating them from kin and culture, eroding their ways of life and stewardship practices, and restricting their freedom and movements. Alice Rigney explained: "When Parks was created, it became a whole new level of government with their rules and whatnot. No one was allowed—you could not hunt at certain times." As Alice's oral history suggests, policies that increased provincial and federal control over the environment went together with attempted erasures of Dene people, ways of life, stewardship laws, and sovereignty.

This is something with which Indigenous Peoples barred from or restricted in parks and nature sanctuaries across Canada were familiar. As Tina Loo writes of Canadian conservation in the twentieth century, these kinds of policies ultimately had the effect of "marginalizing local customary uses of wildlife" as well as Indigenous stewardship laws and ways of relating to the land.[2] David Neufeld writes of similar experiences for the Southern Tutchone peoples in what became Kluane National Game Sanctuary in the southwest Yukon: colonial governments both denied and dismissed "not only the validity, but even the existence of the long tradition of deep local contextual knowledge" that shaped Indigenous ways of knowing the environment.[3] In WBNP, colonial officials increased restrictions and surveillance of Dene lives and relations to the land, based on the assumption that they had the claim to superior knowledge about land, water, and wildlife.[4] In these ways, Park exclusions and the other conservation laws that provincial and federal governments imposed contributed to processes of colonial elimination through the erosion of Dene connections to homeland and kin and refusals of Dene knowledge and connections to place.[5]

New or evolving regulations included bag limits—restrictions on the total number of animals people could harvest in a season— and closed and limited seasons for fur-bearing animals, birds, and large game.[6] Bison hunting remained prohibited throughout the twentieth century. Across Canada, the *Migratory Birds Convention Act* in 1916 had banned egg collecting, imposed game seasons on some migratory birds, and closed hunting of some birds altogether.[7] Within the Park, big game and non-migratory bird hunting was restricted by seasons (and prohibited altogether for some species).[8] Laws were particularly stringent when it came to fur-bearing animals, especially muskrat and beaver, whose populations had declined steeply in the 1930s and 1940s. Beaver season was closed for several years during the 1930s and

1940s, and occasionally marten and muskrat season were closed as well. At one point, muskrat season was shortened so much that Dene leader Benjamin Marcel (Elder Pat Marcel's father) complained to authorities in 1942 that the people could barely survive on what little trapping was permitted.⁹ As Elder Magloire Vermillion told interviewers in 1974, restrictions had serious implications for Dene people: "we were slowly being restricted with game regulations, preventing us from trapping, hunting, and fishing. [Before the Treaty] there were no such people as park wardens. . . . [After] we were not as free to hunt and trap as we were used to because of these regulations that were made."

It was not only subsistence harvesting that was limited. Dënesųłıné burning practices, which had been essential to the creation and maintenance of bison habitats, were outlawed in 1925 (and discouraged by the pre-Park buffalo rangers before that). Park law dictated that anyone responsible for starting a fire in a National Park would face fines, imprisonment, or hard labour.¹⁰ Harvesting timber within the Park for fuel was also restricted. Such laws criminalized the Dene stewardship practices described in Chapter 1 that had been a critical part of the Dene people's ways of living and caring for the environment. As Cardinal Christianson et. al. write, this kind of interruption of Indigenous stewardship practices "can be thought of as *cultural severance* . . . an act, intentional or not, that functionally disrupts relationships between people and the land."¹¹

Decades-old assumptions that Indigenous land users were dangerous and irresponsible underpinned many of the twentieth century's conservation and land management policies within and around the Park. Further, as McCormack observes, "Aboriginal People were never allowed to be managers of the programs that were supposed to protect the resources on which they relied."¹² Conservation proponents often claimed that new harvesting regulations were being imposed "for their own good."¹³ As one official wrote in 1947, "We can not [sic] . . . allow the Indians to hunt and trap indiscriminately if we expect to provide animals for him to hunt and trap now and in the future."¹⁴ Furthermore, Park officials often took the position that Indigenous harvesters—especially those who had permits to trap and hunt in the Park—had been granted special "privileges" that white trappers and hunters did not enjoy. For this reason, R.A. Gibson wrote to Secretary of the Indian Affairs Branch, T.R.L. MacInnes, in October 1939 dismissing Indigenous leaders' concerns about the restrictive laws: "We are at a loss to understand," he wrote, "why the Indian chiefs consider the regulations unfair."[15] Changes to policy also usually proceeded with little communication or consultation with the resident Indigenous communities, and was "enforced . . . with inconsistency and whimsy."[16] Policy was often imposed from a distance, communicated through written notices in English, distributed on paper through Indian Agents or missionaries, and rarely translated to Cree or Dënesųłıné.[17] Considering that breaking regulations could result in the loss of a Park permit and, potentially, one's source of subsistence, the failure of the administraton to clearly communicate consistent rules to Indigenous residents could have dire consequences.

Regulations were often generated or updated reactively, with little standardized order or unity between the Park and provincial regulations. This caused confusion for harvesters and administrators alike, who sometimes struggled to reconcile disparate game laws between the Park and the province.[18] Indian Agent P.W. Head and Park Warden Dempsey both recognized the potential consequences of such inconsistencies and confusion. Dempsey noted in 1935 that "there are doubts as to what the regulations really are, which may be the cause of so much friction."[19] Head wrote to Secretary MacInnes in 1938 that harvesting laws were causing harm to people within and outside the Park:

> After hearing all the complaints that come from one source and another I would strongly suggest an investigation of the whole trapping situation and a drawing up of a uniform set of laws for both the Park and all of Alberta north of the 27th Base Line. The situation is becoming very acute and I fear that unless something is done in the near future the outlook for the Indians will be very black [sic] and we will have to carry a large number on relief.[20]

As Head's remarks suggested, inconsistencies and arbitrary policy changes were often deeply frustrating to harvesters. For example, where beaver season might be limited outside the Park, it was at times closed altogether within. In these instances, Park permit-holders could leave the Park to continue trapping beaver and take advantage of the longer provincial season.[21] This loophole created a double standard, as the option was not available for those who lived outside the Park without a Park permit because they could not enter the Park to harvest if they were unsatisfied with provincial game laws.[22] At one point, trappers complained that the open beaver season only applied to "heads of families," leaving out trappers who were single or did not have dependents.[23]

Oral histories point to Dene residents' frustrations about the double standards and inconsistencies embedded in harvesting policies, which tended to disproportionately affect Dene residents and harvesters. For example, Elder Edouard Trippe de Roche explained that people relied on burning wood for energy, and only a small percentage of families used other sources of fuel when he was young. But after the Park was created, Dene people were denied the ability to harvest firewood in the Park. Meanwhile, those who remained in the Park were granted permits to harvest firewood, and some commercial sawmills operated in the Park throughout much of the twentieth century to provide fuel for the residential school, Indian Affairs, and other nearby institutions. Commercial fisheries were permitted to operate in some lakes within the Park, depleting fish stocks, but Dene people saw their own harvesting rights denied and eroded. Warden reports in 1947 and 1948 point to the friction this caused. For example, Dene people living in the Park petitioned against the establishment of a commercial fishery at Lake Claire, one of the important places in Dene homelands in the Birch River area, where some Dene families were allowed to continue to fish and hunt even after most Dene people had been displaced from their settlement there. Wardens and Indian Agents kept records of local opposition and of the sometimes sour relations between Indigenous fishers and the company, but commercial fishing activity continued.[24]

In addition, although bison hunting was prohibited, Parks administration allowed for a limited number of bison to be hunted each year (usually by wardens) to provide meat for the Fort Chipewyan hospital and residential school, and eventually, as described below, to sell meat in the south of the Province—to the Province's profit. While Parks officials continued to express the view that "as long as we allow the Indians to hunt in [the Park], it can never fulfill its full purpose," they did approve of the scheme for a limited number of non-Indigenous hunters to slaughter some bison to distribute meat to the hungry.[25] According to oral histories, the bison meat ration program also had inconsistencies that put Dene people at a disadvantage. Edouard Trippe de Roche noted in his oral history that the bison rations distributed through the Indian Agents or residential schools often did not reach Dene children but were given only to Cree children. He recalled that his sister, who was married to Indian Agent Jack Stewart's son, was able to get bison meat for her family only because of that connection. Such double standards embedded in the management regime within and around the Park demonstrate that colonial policy frameworks were as much about controlling Indigenous People's lives, movements, and ways of life as they were about maintaining control over resources.

A related example of inconsistencies in the policy governing Dënesųłıné territories took the form of a commercial bison slaughter program after World War Two, that lasted roughly from 1945 to 1967. Sandlos, who describes the program in detail, notes that after the war, Park officials shifted their discourses "from an appeal to save an endangered species to a contention that the buffalo must be exposed only to certain kinds of regulated butchery."[26] They set out to commodify bison meat through agriculturalized herd management, partial bison enclosures and a regulated slaughter program. Officials saw this program as a lucrative economic opportunity with a potentially large consumer base to the south. Wardens, and occasionally hunters from the south who were permitted to enter the Park to hunt bison for this program, slaughtered hundreds of Park bison from 1946 to 1967. Meat was either shipped south for sale or distributed as rations at the hospital and residential school in Fort Chipewyan. Indigenous harvesters were usually excluded from the hunts and from receiving meat, and subsistence bison hunting remained illegal. The controlled slaughter program demonstrates the contradictory and fundamentally racialized logic that drove conservation policy in and around the Park. While Indigenous ways of life were disparaged and prohibited, some harvesting activity, undertaken typically by white settlers, was considered an acceptable form of "efficient and controlled exploitation."[27] Meanwhile, subsistence harvesters were prohibited from hunting bison in the Park to feed their families and communities. As McCormack concludes, "except for the Department of Indian Affairs, all government agencies gave priority to economic activities that involved the exploitation of northern resources by outsiders."[28] These priorities took precedence over the rights and livelihoods of Indigenous residents and placed additional pressure on the Dene families and land users who were excluded from the Park after 1926.

In the oral histories shared in this chapter, Dënesųłıné Elders explained that reactive, poorly informed, and inconsistent regulations contributed to the attempted erosions of the sovereignty and a disconnection from knowledge for Dene land users, who intimately understood the patterns and ecology of the area. As such, regulations played a critical part in the colonial elimination that guided policy in Alberta's north in the mid-twentieth century. Elder Pat Marcel said that through most of the twentieth century, Dene knowledge was never considered when designing conservation policies. The ban on controlled burning and regular Park-sponsored wolf culls, which some Dene people strongly opposed,[29] are examples of this disconnect. Wardens and parks officials frequently wrote about how they struggled to convince local Indigenous hunters to kill wolves—some of the oral testimony in this chapter explains why. Some harvesters were also concerned with the use of poison to cull the wolves. As Ed Trippe de Roche explained, the way that wolves were culled often had devastating impacts for many other species; introducing poison into the environment put smaller, fur-bearing animals at risk of poisoning as well. Furthermore, according to McCormack, wolf culling in the 1930s and 1940s may have increased the rates of tuberculosis and brucellosis infections in the bison as the diseased portions of the bison population grew without wolf predation.

In the 1940s, officials dismissively argued that "every Indian who is not entitled to trap in this area is always ready to give advise [sic] and criticize Wood Buffalo Park management."[30] Indigenous experiences, concerns, and knowledge about the environment were treated as suspect rather than taken seriously.[31] Not all conservation policies regulating Dene land use were directly imposed by the Park, but the full suite of federal and provincial conservation and land-management policies from Park's Canada and provincial regulations exacerbated the existing impacts of the 1926 Park annex and permitting system. Chief Jonas Laviolette's 1927 statement clearly articulated the impacts: "If this country had been left to us here there would still be fur today and we would not be so poor and miserable today. Thirty years ago, it was a fine country because just the Indians lived in it."[32]

Registered traplines

Alongside the imposition of harvesting laws governing land use in the Park and province, the province's Registered Fur Management Areas (RFMA) program, colloquially known as the trapline system, emerged in the 1940s. The program fundamentally altered how and where many Dënesųłıné harvesters could interact with the land and water. In an effort to more systematically control the trapping economy throughout the province, Alberta established a system (not applicable in the Park) in 1942 under which fur trappers paid for annual permits to trap in designated areas. Proponents of the trapline system felt it could protect Indigenous trappers from the growing encroachment of southern white trappers in their territories. "Having regard to the welfare of these people we are anxious for a solution of the difficulties with which they must contend," wrote one official in 1938.[33]

Yet Dënesųłıné trappers outside the Park struggled to obtain a trapline under this system and had to compete with white harvesters who often applied for and received the best trapping areas.[34] After travelling through northern Alberta to assess the new trapline system, provincial Fur Supervisor J.L. Grew wrote that white trappers probably had the advantage over Indigenous trappers in identifying their trapping areas:

> A great deal of work remains to be done in Alberta before the Indians become firmly established on registered lines that are extensive enough to provide them with a sufficient amount of fur with which to support themselves and their families. . . . As previously stated many of the lines now registered should be reviewed in order to ascertain whether the Indian trapper has been provided with his traditional hunting ground or whether this ground has been pre-empted by white trappers.[35]

Some trappers and Indian Agents also complained that officials favoured the applications of white trappers, who were more interested in profits, over Dene applicants, who were trapping to feed their families. As Fortna finds in historical studies of traplines in Alberta, "the provincial government refused to provide any special consideration to Indigenous trappers, who continued to treat trapping as a vocation."[36] The province also had the power to revoke trapping certificates and redistribute them.[37] Sometimes, lapsed, cancelled, or revoked certificates held by Dene trappers were redistributed to non-Indigenous trappers.[38]

Although suggested as early as 1939, it took until 1942 for officials to recommended the establishment of larger group trapping areas that protected more land from encroaching non-Indigenous trappers and could stay within families long-term.[39] This approach eventually became the primary trapping management system within the Park, and Parks officials opted to establish group trapping areas within the Park as well.[40] During talks leading up to the establishment of traplines in the Park, Indian Agents and park wardens reported that harvesters residing within the Park generally wanted their traplines within the Delta area, where harvesting was better. As one warden wrote in 1947, "very few would consider other regions in the Park."[41] Group trapping areas were officially established in 1949; under this new system, Indigenous harvesters within the Park found themselves with even less freedom to move and harvest across the area.[42]

Dënesųłıné people were gravely disappointed with the trapline arrangement. As Indian Agent Head wrote in 1940, "the commencement of a Registered Trapline System in Alberta has led to a lot of controversy and complaints from the Indians in the Delta."[43] The provincial trapline system created unique problems for harvesters who had originally harvested in the Park but were later evicted or otherwise lost their permits to harvest there. As Indian Agent Melling wrote to Indian Affairs in June 1942, "before the registered trap-line area and trap-line system was in force in Alberta, these expelled Indians had little difficulty in finding new trapping grounds. . . . But since the institution of the registered traplines it has become impossible for these newly expelled Indians to find lands or lines upon which they might make anything that approaches a living," and the area where they might move has "all the hunters and trappers that it can now support." As a result, "these families are destitute or near destitute and it is essential to provide them with relief."[44] Melling's remarks suggest that the RFMA system led to hardship and hunger for some and exacerbated growing tensions between residents and harvesters within and outside the Park, creating significant difficulties for people on both sides of the Park boundaries.[45] Restrictions on access, previously produced through the permitting system and now enhanced with the new trapping areas, placed further restrictions on the capacity of some Dene people within and outside the Park to access the places that had always been part of their homelands. This resulted in greater competition between harvesters within and outside the Park, and between Indigenous and non-Indigenous harvesters over the environment and resources.

Traplines remain important spaces where people stay connected to Dene ways of life, land and waters, and language and identity, despite a wider environment of colonial policies that have dispossessed and sought to erase Dënesųłıné lives and cultural traditions. Much of the oral testimony and history shared in Chapter 1 discusses the ways of life and connections to land that Dene families have maintained on their families' traplines. Yet the RFMA system has also continued to present serious challenges, adding to the harvesting restrictions and limitations on movement and access that were already eroding Dene Treaty Rights. Over time, as Treaty and Aboriginal Rights researcher Bill Russell writes, "the Indian trapper and hunter was forced . . . to comply with the provincial registered trapline system, which in its early years did not even fend off the itinerant trappers [trappers who travelled temporarily into the region to trap for profit] . . . the majority were left to scramble for placement in a Provincial registration system imposed without their understanding or consent, and indeed without even the full co-operation of the DIA [Department of Indian Affairs]."[46] Combined with other wildlife management policies, Park restrictions, and the growth of the warden system, the fur management system became a means of shoring up state control over wildlife resources while eroding Dene sovereignty and connections to the land.

Wardens: "It was like living very, very stressfully under a nasty regime"

The Park's warden program, first established in 1911, expanded over time alongside the growth of the wider wildlife management system, with wardens in Wood Buffalo Park granted significantly more power over surveillance and enforcement by the early 1930s. At the time of the Park annex, supporters of expanding the warden system felt it was necessary for keeping a close watch on Indigenous Peoples. As Supervising Park Warden J.A. McDougal wrote in 1926, "the present warden system [should] be increased to such an extent that every Indian in the Park could be closely watched, no matter what place in the Park he might be."[47] In a similar way, another supervising warden's letter to the Superintendent of Forests and Wildlife twenty years later suggested that a key impetus for the operations of the warden system in Wood Buffalo National Park was the surveillance and control of Indigenous lives. "Unless we have many more wardens to keep a constant check on every Indian," Warden I.F. Kirkby wrote, "it is impossible to know whether game birds and animals are taken out of season, so long as the Indian can roam the entire park at will."[48] McCormack explains that, shortly after the annex, wardens became "the immediate agents of supervision" over Indigenous land use and harvesting within and around the Park.[49]

The extensive trail of documents left by wardens and their superiors in patrol reports, warden diaries and the summaries of these forwarded monthly from the chief warden to park administrators, sheds light on the daily activities, attitudes, and motivations of Indigenous Peoples living in the Park. Park wardens often worked alongside the RCMP and provincial game guardians and had a range of responsibilities such as managing permitting for trappers and hunters, monitoring wildlife, managing fires, patrolling assigned areas, monitoring the movements and activities of permittees and Indigenous residents, facilitating the supply of rations and medical assistance for local families, and killing for the bison slaughter relief program.[50] Wardens enforced the permit system and game laws with varying levels of severity, issuing warnings and fines, confiscating harvesting equipment, arresting people they deemed trespassers, and suspending or permanently revoking permits and expelling people from the Park. Reports across the decades recorded warden patrols with detail. In one day in 1948, for example, warden F.A. McCall reported travelling 225 miles and checking five areas where people had cabins, including the Birch River settlement. McCall made thorough searches of any cabins where people were home or that were unlocked. On another day, he reported flying in a patrol plane over trappers working at Ruis Lake, Birch River, Baril Lake, and Quatre Fourches, "to let them know that we were interested in what they were doing." [51] McCall's reports insinuated that patrols often occurred simply so that Indigenous harvesters knew they were being watched.

Oral histories express Dene people's frustration with wardens' behaviours that reflected the administration's working assumption that Indigenous harvesters were hiding something. Alice Rigney's oral testimony in this chapter explains that trust was rarely a defining characteristic of this relationship: "Yeah, there was no trust,' she said. "Parks Canada was able to go into anybody's home and check and see if you had buffalo meat." She explained that her mother-in-law used to say she and her family felt taunted by the people in uniforms. Oral histories and archival documents alike suggest that relations between local Dene people and the WBNP wardens have often been strained, with trust lacking on both sides. ACFN member Scott Flett's oral history shared below summarizes Dene experiences with wardens who, along with police, exercised significant power in the restriction and surveillance of Dene lives: "they had lots of power, like they can do whatever they want, eh? People were kind of scared of them back in the day." These are experiences that Indigenous oral histories elsewhere in Canada point to as well. For example, Roberta Nakoochee writes that Southern Tutchone Elders she interviewed described aggressive intimidation tactics that wardens in Kluane Game Sanctuary used in their interactions with Tutchone locals, including examples of low-flying helicopters or wardens approaching families with their firearms visible.[52] In these ways, wardens became part of a system that criminalized treaty-enshrined rights to harvest unimpeded throughout their territories.

As Dene oral histories indicate, restrictions on local ways of life and on Indigenous relations to the land were violations of Treaty 8 and had significant and harmful impacts. Elder Magloire Vermillion, who was born at Birch River and whose oral testimony is shared below, explained in 1974: "Even since the treaty was signed, we were slowly being restricted with game regulations, preventing us from trapping, hunting, and fishing. There was no such thing as Park wardens [before Treaty]. . . . along with these buffaloes [from Wainwright] came the Park wardens."[53] As this Elder's oral history suggests, restrictive game regulations and the increasingly powerful warden system became a key instrument in the expansion of state control over Indigenous People's lands and lives—and in attempted colonial erasures, after the Treaty.

Oral histories refer frequently to instances of wardens abusing their power, but official archives are sparse in details about abuse. As ACFN member Garry Flett said, "they're undocumented for sure. I mean, it would be self-incriminating if they put some of this stuff in there." There are occasional exceptions with indirect references that align with the memories and histories of Dene people communicated through the oral testimony. A 1947 letter points to Indian Agent Jack Stewart's view of the discriminatory attitudes of some wardens:

> Mr Stewart indicates that he has spoken to Park Wardens and Game Guardians . . . and he divides the opinions into three categores *[sic]*, those who believe the Indians are too lazy to fish for a living; those who believe the Indian as a ward of the Government and not a human being; those who take a broad view of the matter.[54]

Stewart's description of varying warden attitudes points to some of the motivations for their interactions with Indigenous Peoples. Another 1953 government letter stated that some wardens "acted and conducted themselves in a ruthless and arrogant manner."[55] Although the RCMP and Parks officials usually refuted such claims, it is conceivable that warden behaviour and abuses of power, especially toward Indigenous harvesters, were under-reported or

Fig. 5.1 *Camp for police dogs and Wood Buffalo park wardens' dogs, 1952.* Provincial Archives of Alberta, A17163.

even omitted from official records. Yet there is no shortage of examples in the oral histories of these types of actions and behaviours, as demonstrated in the testimonies shared here. Elders stressed that people live in fear under this system. This is a clear opportunity to honour oral histories by challenging erasures in the written archive that privilege mythologies that marginalize and do violence to Indigenous experiences and knowledges.[56] As historian Winona Wheeler tells us, the best way to understand community histories and experiences often are "found within the community itself."[57]

Some ACFN members noted that not all Park wardens were "bad guys," and some were only "doing their job." They suggested that some wardens were more understanding and lenient than others, and sometimes Dene residents were on friendly terms with wardens and assisted them with their labour. Some ACFN members also have noted that a newer generation of wardens with different views on Indigenous rights and ways of life has been slowly replacing the "old guard" in recent decades.[58] Archive documents suggest that some wardens acted as intermediaries between Indigenous residents and the Park's administration, communicating Indigenous People's frustrations

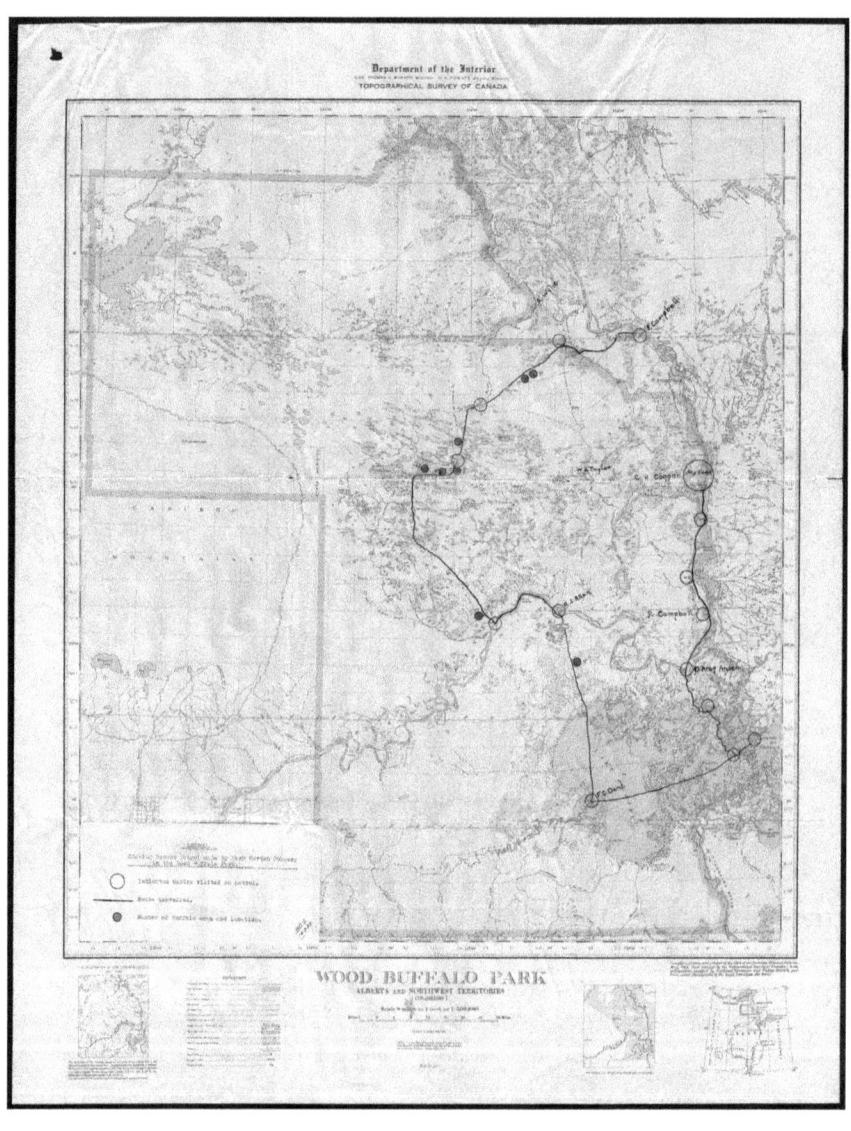

Fig. 5.2 Map of Warden Dempsey's patrol, including sites checked. Attachment to a memorandum from Hume to Rowatt, 28 March 1933. LAC RG85-D-1-A, Vol. 152, File 420-2.

with harvesting laws and decrying the hardships they faced. For example, Dempsey wrote to McDougal in February 1931 that he was deeply discouraged by the hunger and hardship he had witnessed during a recent patrol, arguing that the conditions were a direct result of the Treaty obligations not being adequately fulfilled. He wrote, "the Treaty with the Indians is simply another SCRAP OF PAPER."[59] Sometimes wardens facilitated Dene practices of helping people in need. In 1935, for example, Warden Robert Allen reported that Isidore Simpson (a Chipewyan Band Member and Councillor whose family lived at Peace Point and was transferred to the Cree band in 1944), had reported a bison had fallen off a cliff. When Allen went to investigate, he found the bull still alive but unable to move, so he killed it. He determined that the meat could be salvaged. Apart from one hind quarter that he felt would not be fit for human consumption because of shattered bones, Allen gave all the meat to Isidore Simpson, who in turn divided it among the needy in his community, especially the Elders and widows. Such reports suggest that relationships between Dene people and wardens were varied and complex. Although some wardens frequently complained about the conditions Indigenous Peoples faced, their reports did not usually suggest that they saw themselves—or the system that they enforced—as part of the problem.

Ultimately, through the permitting and warden programs, Parks administration had established a system in which abuses of power against Indigenous Peoples and erasures of Indigenous lifeways were tolerated, normalized, and even encouraged. O.S. Finnie wrote in 1925 that a warden's lack of popularity or trust among the local people should be considered a strength, suggesting that not having a positive relationship with local residents and harvesters would ensure a warden could do their job without prejudice.[60] Specific instances of warden abuse, even when not fully documented, were written into imposed colonial laws that empowered officials to intimidate residents and harvesters and criminalized Dene people's rights to move, live, and harvest freely throughout their homelands.

In the oral history section that follows, community members describe the power that wardens wielded in and around the Park throughout the twentieth century. They recount personal stories of interactions with wardens in more recent decades. Much of the oral testimony shared in this chapter relates personal examples of members' experiences with the restrictive and punitive system within and around WBNP. Speakers emphasized that the system was critical to advancing colonial control over Dene lands and waters and aimed to erase Dene people and ways of life from their homelands. These oral histories situate the Park and the surrounding wildlife management regime as instrumental in the histories of colonial elimination in northern Alberta.

ORAL HISTORY

Louis Boucher (1974)

Yes, it [the system controlling land use] has changed a lot. At first there were none, but now they have enforced many regulations. Whenever some white man comes here, a new regulation is in effect. It is a big change since I came here at first up to now.

Alec Bruno (2015)

ON WOLF CULLING

I never hunt, I never trap wolf. I killed two, all the years that I trapped. I caught one in a lynx snare, and I caught up to him [after he ran]. He hung; he wrapped the wire around the tree. I wanted to cut that wire but they wouldn't let me come close, so I had to shoot him. Twice I had to shoot a wolf like that to kill, cause, you know, I couldn't . . . because my dad always told me that wolves are very, very smart animals, very wise, they are just like humans. They have the strength to kill a moose or anything to eat, just like humans, he says. We go hunting and we don't give up until we kill caribou to take meat home. Men and wolves are almost equal. They don't live together but what they do out on the land is pretty well the same thing.

Well the old timers used to tell us the animals, wolves, caribous, moose, same thing. They're all just like humans because they all share. Wolves have to kill caribou to eat and many times you heard these stories. Any time a wolf kills an animal, a moose or caribou or bison, they usually get after the old and the sick. They know. The reason for that is, for them, killing the sick and the old is to maintain a good stock. Leave the young ones alone. It's their way of maintaining a good health, stock, herd together, you know, by killing the old and the sick. I watched, I seen a documentary on wolves that Parks Canada did a couple years ago, and they were with this pack of wolves for about a week. They watched everything they do. They kill, they were trying to, they killed one bison. He was an old one. They waited, they got him out of the herd to kill him and then they went hunting again and these guys [film crew] were in a chopper, and they said all of a sudden they were following this herd of buffalos and all of a sudden they stopped. There was only about four wolves, four or five wolves. They stopped, they turned around and took off, they started running. Now these guys didn't understand why they done that.

Bison were just ahead hey? So, they followed these buffalo, these wolves. They never stopped, they just ran and ran and ran and ran. They ran about 30 km, 37 km is the way they put it. They went into the bush and they came about a dead buffalo. He just died. Just fresh. That bison just died, maybe sick or something, I don't know. How did the wolves know this 37 km away? You'll see that sometimes when you watch shows about animals, wolves, how they hunt. I think it's done here in this area, I think around Lake Claire somewhere. How did they know this bison was dying 37 km away? They ran 37 km to just find this bison just freshly died. So, with all these things that happen, you have to think about it, it makes you think, why do animals do these things? Their ways pretty much tell you that wolves think like a man. That's what my dad you used to say. My dad was the one who used to say, don't ever trap wolves if you can, because wolves and man pretty well think alike. They strike—you strike as a hunter or a trapper to get what you want, and wolves are the same thing.

ON TRAPLINES AND HARVESTING RESTRICTIONS

There was no traplines before the Alberta government got involved. People went wherever they wanted to go. There was an open land out there. You'd take your family and go wherever you want and that's how you'd trap. And then after government got involved, then they start issuing traplines. Back in Richardson country, your trapline, the only rights you'd have to that thing is to trap and hunt, nothing else. There's a fine for trapping [outside the trapline or trapping season]. It started in November, and it ends February, so you only got about four months to do that, and then you come back to the Delta and trap muskrats for another two months, so you're trapping six months out of a year. That's what Western science, law, did to the people when they started giving them traplines. These traplines, you'd give it to Rene [Bruno] or whoever, you got to go out there every year. Harvest that land and if you miss one or two years, they'll take it away from you and give it to someone else... Like I said, the way I believe, is when the trapline [system] was issued, government knew that one day down the road this trapping thing would be [lucrative]. There is still a lot of fur out there, but there was no price so people quit going; but they still claim their trapline, but they don't go out. What Alberta government is doing now is bringing in sports fishing, bear baiting, stuff like that on the same trapline [where trappers no longer go] that we'd get into trouble [for doing], and they're getting away with it, making money from it and these guys [the trappers] are make nothing out of it.

Jimmy Deranger (25 March 2021)

Some Dene people were killing the buffalos like when they left the Park, right? And then some of them were charged for that. They spent time in jail I think for that. Because they killed the buffalos that were not even in the Park. "The buffalos," they were saying, "it was ours anyways to begin with." But still they charged them, right? With the regulations that they used in Wood Buffalo Park.

Yeah. And they said that the rules had to be followed. There were these rules; [if] they were going to change those rules, why didn't they come and tell us that they were going to do it? Why didn't they sit down with us and say, "we're going to do this: what do you think? What do you think?" That didn't happen. They just made the rules.

I remember once this thing that happened to me. Magloire Vermilion and Basil Vermilion [Dene Elders who are members of MCFN because of the membership transfer] were in the Parks. You know, even though they were Dene, they were recognized [by the government] as Cree. And I was coming back from Edmonton in January, and they were going back to Fort Chip. And they had cut wood for their homes in Fort Chip. And I was passing by when they were cutting wood. And they said, "why don't you come and get this wood for us and bring it into Fort Chip." I said, "okay, as soon as I drive and take my stuff off the truck, I'll come back." It's only about a forty-minute drive, maybe less than that. So I did, took my stuff back and then I came back and got it, their wood, and then I loaded all their wood into my truck and I drove out. And then drove in the bush across the river and there was a snye [a side channel]—this snye usually freezes right to the ground. Because it's not very much water, there's only about three feet of water.

And when I was there, I guess somehow they [wardens] heard that the Natives were cutting wood over there, bringing it to Fort Chip. They said they assumed it was for sale. I saw them and I went barreling past them, I wasn't going very fast, but it seems like you're going fast when the snow is flying, right? And when you have a load and then it sort of blows up more snow and I went past them, and they passed me. And then I drove it all the way to Basil's house, unloaded, and as I was going back to my house, I stopped there and they stopped behind my truck, and they're looking inside my truck and they saw woodchips. They asked me, "where'd you get that from?" I said this, "Basil told me to bring his wood in, so I brought it in."

"Oh, we have to charge you, we have to take your truck," they said. And then they went over to Basil's house and took the wood. And then, that pissed me off. And I went back and then they charged me. Said they were going to hold my truck. But I went to Calgary and then I went to see a lawyer that was working for the Indian Association, TARR—Bob Young—and I told him. He says, "I'll make a phone call for you," he said. So, he made a phone call and he said, "you can go get your truck now," he said, "they are in Fort Chip." And then they [wardens] turn around, they said they was trying to say it was my wood, [even though] it wasn't even my wood. They were looking for evidence. But they charged me ten dollars, they fined me ten dollars. So now, that was just in the '70s, so that means that whatever happened with the First Nations People, in their activities on the land at Wood Buffalo, they were probably charged for something that was ridiculous, like the one that they tried to charge me with.

Garry Flett (6 December 2020)

GF: I mean, it was common back then for a lot of the—I shouldn't say just Aboriginal People—people in general that harvested a bird in the Park or that were caught doing that sort of thing, or even picking a flower, got you into some crap with the Park. I don't know all the personal details into it, but I know growing up, it was common to hear about the court dockets of people that were fined for doing those things. So, it was not uncommon.

The only other interaction that I had with a warden that was negative was the one time when my oldest child was born, and my wife was in the vehicle with me. We were coming back from Fort Chip to Fort Smith, and we got stopped by a park warden, and it was cold—it was really cold. And my son was, I would say three weeks to a month old then. He was born in December, so it was in January sometime. But I'll never forget the cop's name, the warden's name either.

He stopped me and he said, "everybody out of the car."

And I said, "No. Sorry. I'll get out for you. What are you looking for?"

And he said, "I heard that you have buffalo meat in the vehicle?" I said, "I have none." He said, "Everybody out of the car." And I said, "No I'll get out, but I have a baby in there and a wife and they're not getting up."

And things escalated from there. He said, he accused me of being deaf. That I didn't hear him properly. And I accused him of being deaf because he didn't hear me. And he went to put his hand on me to move me out of the road. And I pushed him back. And there was another warden there. He came and got in between and de-escalated the situation.

But my expectation after that was that I would be stopped by the RCMP as I got into the community and questioned over this incident, because I did push him out of the road. When he meant to move me, I shoved him. Just the wrong thing to do, but it was just the heat of the moment. But you know, nothing ever transpired out of that. Nothing. The cops didn't come and see me. Never heard any more from it.

And I thought it just was nothing, it just went to bed, other than a fella came to me a week later and said, "I heard this happened," and he described a situation. And I said, "Yeah, it did." And all he said was "congratulations, the little bastard needed that," he said. "Oh okay." And that was it, and I never heard a thing again about it. I expected that I would be trying to explain myself in the court of law too.

ST: You never had to? And they never searched your vehicle in the end?

GF: No, no. I had nothing to hide anyway. But no, they didn't search it. Because I told him, they had the truck that was plugging off the highway. It was only a narrow little winter road sort of thing to the Park, and they had the highway closed off with their truck. By then my temper was flared, and I said, "get your truck off the road or I'll push it off the road." Anyway, they moved the truck and I was gone. . . . Yeah. Well, the good old days. They were, I don't know if they were empowered or just thought that they were empowered with the same powers that the RCMP had. But they did—they were bullies out there. I can't think of another word, another term for them other than they threw their weight around quite well.

[These types of incidents] are undocumented for sure. I mean, it would be self-incriminating if they put some of this stuff in there, right? At the end of the day, they're just as human as you and I are, and there's some of them that took advantage of the positions that they were put into and used that to bully their way through the system. And for me, we were ACFN. I didn't belong there.

Scott Flett (17 March 2021)

Back in the day, the priests and the game warden, and RCMP, boy, they had lots of power. Like they can do whatever they want, eh? People were kind of scared of them back in the day . . . I remember my Grandpa said he used to hide and stuff. He had to hide. If the park warden was coming along and they [the people] want to eat. If you want to—even the beavers, [there] were only so many beavers you could get per harvest, and ducks are out of season, you're not supposed to hunt ducks out of season. Oh my God, there's just, it's really bad.

I think there's some people who went to jail or something. I mean, they got a fine and stuff for breaking the rules or breaking the regulations. I heard a story. I think there's some people that were hiding ducks and stuff and then you know, there was a story about these guys, had some ducks or something, and the Park warden came with his dog, and they hid the ducks, but the dog went, sniffed out the ducks or something. I don't know if they got a warning or a fine.

ON BISON SLAUGHTERS

They had a great big laboratory [in the Park], I think they called it. One at Sweetgrass and one at Hay Camp where they had these big corrals and stuff, they used to bring in the buffalo, and they used to check them out for brucellosis and TB and stuff. And then even one time back, what year was that? That was September because school was—it was maybe '73 or something... they'd go pick up a truck, and they drove to Sweetgrass, and they brought a whole bunch of buffalo meat into town and they gave people buffalo meat.

Yeah, and they give not just rations like I said. I think it's only a one-time deal, but they're trying to sell buffalo meat down, down south, eh? They're trying to sell the beef to stores and stuff. And they had this big operation on Sweetgrass and, like I said, corrals all over, and then I think even one time they used to use these old Bell helicopters and just herd them by helicopter, and then they had to stop that because there were some buffalo breaking their legs or something. It was kind of cruelty, so they had to quit that process.

Fred (Jumbo) Fraser (12 March 2021)

FF: I think I heard them [local Elders] say anytime they'd kill moose they used to keep the moose bone. Because you never know when them rangers would come around, eh. So, they kept that. And then the rangers I heard were really bad. They'd go and check where the dogs are tied up and everything and look for bones. That's what I heard, anyway.

ST: So they would keep the moose bones so that the ranger didn't know about the buffalo. Is that what you mean?

FF: Yeah. If there was moose bones, but there was no buffalo bones, I guess there's a difference. They were bad rangers.... In my mind, too, I think they were pretty—how do you say it? Like, they always wanted to catch somebody. Yeah, I don't think they were good.

ST: What kinds of things did they do to the people who lived there?

FF: Oh, they're coming, nosing around, I guess. You know, look for something wrong. Always looking for dirt, I guess.

ST: What happens if they catch you?

FF: I don't know, you go to court, go to jail probably.

Leslie Laviolette (22 March 2021)

So [the relationship with Park wardens] was just like watching the movies, like cowboys and Indians. We used to hide. We'd see the cowboy ride by in a big jet boat, and us, we'd come out in the canoe, and we'd paddle away from them. You know, it was playing, well sort of playing with the law, I guess. Because they always seemed to get some guy and so we'd just go that extra mile not to get caught. But yet I don't know why we had to run like that and be scared of that. We never had to before.

And this is what my parents and my grandpa [Jonas Laviolette] and all these guys argued about that we're here now, second generation, third generation. I see all these changes that—what my grandfather and the other chiefs like Uncle Fred [Marcel] and all them seen before that, but [the Park officials] never listened. And then when the Park came, well the Park was the sheriff, he had the badge, and he did what he wanted. Cause when you [the wardens] have a badge, well you got to listen to them. They're not gonna listen to me. I don't have no badge, I'm just a trapper and that's it, cause I'm just a number.

Pat Marcel (2013)

ON WOLF CULLING

What we're talking about now, when the federal government came down, and said the only way we can conserve the caribou and the bison is to corral them and put them in a fenced area. But the people were very upset about that. Their [the government's] next move was to cull all the wolves that were preying on the caribou, because then there would be less predation by the wolf pack. But the Elders said that by culling the wolves, the caribou are now susceptible for diseases, because there is no keeping the herd strong by culling the wolves.

A caribou can outrun a wolf, unless they are old and sick or young. The herd is kept to a certain state so that the caribou will never eat themselves out of a home. The herd stays in the set numbers.

This is what we understood, and the white men could not understand. They culled wolves, in the past, mostly in Saskatchewan, in N22.[61] And the trappers would be reporting that they would be cutting open caribou, and they would be affected by it [by the poison used to cull wolves]. The wolves and even the ravens [who] would eat of that poisoned caribou carcass, would be dead [from Strychnine poison].

An old trapper told me that he killed a moose and put the poison into a caribou carcass, and he got twenty-seven wolves. This was happening in the Parks. A lot of terrible things were done, without thought of what will happen if we [the government] did this. No consultation with First Nations Elders. The government would just announce that, "this year we are going to cull wolves," and poison would be used. The government didn't think how this would be bad for the trappers and the wolves. Poison doesn't discriminate. And it kills whatever it touches.

Keltie Paul (25 November 2020)

I'm going to tell you a story. I had to change my shirt because I got strawberry jam all over it. So, I went into my bedroom, and I could hear this low-grade humming sound. And I took off my shirt and I put on another shirt. And then I turned around and, my cabin was right on the river, the curtains were open, and these damn men were in a helicopter right outside my window watching me change. And pointing at me and laughing. They were that close. So, they lowered their helicopter and then I went outside because I was really mad, and I started shaking my fist at them, so they moved off to the next cabin. And here they are with their little binoculars, and everything and they're looking into people's houses. Peeping Tom. And that was just an intimidation tactic. And they would, you know, they just insisted on doing things that would harass people. Would make people feel less than. Would make people feel that they were not being listened to. Because they would say, "well you don't belong here," and yet they knew they belonged there. They knew their Ancestors were from there. But these guys had different ideas to what things were [i.e. who belonged and who did not], and they'd use it to intimidate, to harass, to bully.

Ernie "Joe" Ratfat (19 March 2021)

Well, I remember [wardens] always enforced . . . if you're caught shooting a buffalo, that they had a fine to pay for or else I think there's a jail term too. Yeah, and they would come into your home, and they would check your meat, you know? If that fat, you know, the buffalo fat? Like it's kind of like a yellowish color. So, if they see that, you're charged.

Alice Rigney (16 March 2021)

ON WARDENS AND REGULATIONS

There was no trust. Parks Canada was able to go into anybody's home and check and see if you had buffalo meat. And if you had buffalo meat,` they could sentence you to jail. I mean that kind of rudeness and impolite[ness] and power over the people. And I mean, my family did not, we don't live in the Park. We never did.

And I hear a lot of stories about how they used to have to hide buffalo meat, because Parks Canada could just go to your tent and search through your coolers and your sheds to see if you have any caribou meat. I heard of an Elder who shot a duck out of season and he went to jail for a week or so—you know, stories like that. Where the intimidation was so strong that I mean, people live there in their homelands you know, even though House River [Birch River/House Lake settlement] is just a memory now, I mean, they lived listening for a motor. My brother had a friend living at Quatre Fourches—the Mikisew Cree have a little micro-village there now—and it's not very far from town, it's in the Park. And my brother Joe went out to visit one of his friends. And when he pulled up to his cabin, [his friend] wasn't there, so Joe thought, well, there's a fire going. And then his friend comes out from behind the house carrying a pot, and in that pot was buffalo meat. And he had heard a boat and he took that pot of meat and went to hide it. That kind of intimidation . . . And, I mean, this is the guy who hunted and trapped all his life and here he is hiding a pot of buffalo meat. That is the lowest way of hurting people, you know?

When Parks was created, it became a whole new level of government with their rules and whatnot. No one was allowed—you could not hunt at certain times. You could not do this, you could not hunt. Can't shoot ducks in the summer, you know, crazy things like that.

ON WOLF CULLING

I mean, there's no glamour in Wood Buffalo National Park. And the introduction of the buffalo in 192[6] just caused disease, and then [Parks Canada] they started exterminating the wolves without listening to people. I mean, what was wrong with the way it was? Why couldn't they just leave it alone? Let Mother Nature look after Mother Nature.

And just, there's that concept that white people think different than the land users, you know? We protect the land, as all of us, we were taught to protect the land and save it so that our children and grandchildren can use it as they have. It's destroyed now. You know, we can't do it [can't protect it like we used to]. So, we're trying to fight back. And as long as the government allows all this pollution and Parks, I mean, they have lifted a lot of the limitations and allowed Dene people to hunt in the Park, but most of us don't go there. We go to our traditional hunting spots.

It's the interference and the way of thinking that the Parks warden thinks that they could—they're trying to change Mother Nature by introducing a new breed [of bison] to this breed here. Mother Nature has a way of looking after what she has. The local people here know that when they go hunting, they only take what they need. They do not leave any behind. And there's always that sharing. So that's how it always was, and then [Parks] bring in all this [Wainwright] herd. And they got diseases and whatnot. And then they introduced [Wainwright plains bison], and then to get rid of the wolves, they start poisoning them. Well, you poison the wolves, it's just a vicious cycle. In the middle of that vicious cycle, is a big question mark. Like, why? Why did they even bother? I mean, because they're scientists? And because maybe they have these fancy letters behind their names that they think they know more than the local people. I mean, this is something that's being done all over the world.

ON THE BISON SLAUGHTER PROGRAM

I remember going to Hay Camp in the Park, my sister actually lived with a park warden there, and how they used to corral [bison] and they used to slaughter so many and that was for, you know, they would ship them south. The hides would be sent south for tann[ing]. But the buffalo there were not slaughtered for the people, for the community here. It was sent out and later on they did have one or two years where they did slaughter buffalo and distributed the meat in town.

Mary "Cookie" Simpson (11 March 2021)

ON HARVESTING REGULATIONS

MS: And then they had their stupid rules. They had all kinds of different regulations. They brought the buffalo in, and you couldn't shoot them, even if you were hungry, or even if it was there, which is not right. Because I know my family did not just go and kill just for the sake of killing lots of animals. They only took what they can eat, and they used every part of the animal.

ST: What would happen if you broke the rules?

MS: Well, they would throw you in jail. They would take you . . . and you had to feed your family. Somebody had to stay and feed their family. They couldn't afford to go to jail. So of course, they just forced our people into following their stupid regulations.

ON WARDEN INTIMIDATION

It's always a threat. Every time you see somebody with—what do you call their outfit—on? You think, "oh shit, they're gonna come and give us shit or they're going to come and arrest us." You know, there was not even a good relationship with them. Like today you can have a good relationship with a cop or somebody, but long time ago you couldn't. It was always the threat of something bad is going to happen. Sudden doom is going to come to you if you see somebody with one of those green outfits on.

And then, yeah, they didn't care for the people. There was nothing like caring and whatever. Like the Aboriginal People still cared and shared and whatever, but not with them. There was nothing with them, they just came to rule. They came and they had the regulations that they had to follow and that's what they did. There was no give or take anything. You've never ever heard of anybody just saying, "you know I guess I'll let you go this time or whatever," you never heard nothing like that.

ON BANNING INDIGENOUS CEREMONIES UNDER THE 1951 INDIAN ACT

ST: So, you have to be pretty careful, I guess, hey?

MS: Yes. That's right. And then you couldn't even practice your culture or your drumming or whatever. Because the park wardens would come and they'd hear your drum or whatever, then they'd go back and tell the RCMP. And they would come over and say, "oh, you were heard. Your drums were being heard." And then so, you had to hide all that.

Cause my dad and my grandpa's house there, where my dad and them all lived, they have a cellar in there. And in that cellar, there's a secret compartment where they had to keep their drums. If somebody would check that house out, they'll know there's a secret compartment, because it's still there. Because we checked it out a couple of years ago, well when my brother Charlie [Simpson] was still alive. We went in and checked it out. And sure enough, there was a drum frame in there. The hide was eaten away on the sides. But even that, like—they [the authorities] were bad. You couldn't practice anything.

ST: So you couldn't even drum?

MS: No, that was banned for about 75 years, at least three generations. You couldn't practice your culture. You couldn't have your Sweats or anything.

ST: Right. Yeah. Because the *Indian Act*, eh?

MS: Yeah. And of course, those park wardens, they were out there more than the RCMP, right? So, they would hear that [drumming] and they would see that, so of course, they'd go back and tell on us. And that's why nobody likes them.

Edouard Trippe de Roche

A portion of this interview is available as a digital audio recording online.[62]

Yeah, I know for a fact there was, back in the '50s, '60s, everybody in Fort Chip was burning wood. Maybe two or three percent of people burned fuel—you know like Indian Affairs, the Park, the RCMP, police, the Hudson's Bay Company. So, people were saying, the residential school ought to burn wood for heat and cooking. They were allowed to get wood in the Wood Buffalo Park, and they'd buy, I don't know how many cords of wood, I don't know how many cords there is, thousands—the state harvest in the year. But we weren't allowed to harvest any firewood from the Park to bring into Fort Chip.

But yet again, in the '60s probably late '50s, early '60s, they had sawmills in the Park and they were permitted to log on the Cree side of the Park, and to my understanding, their permit is still valid today and yet we Natives cannot put a sawmill in the Park. And I know of four sites that there were sawmills, four or five sites in the Park.

As for harvesting fur, I think my dad had a permit but I'm not sure if I can still use it today if I had to. I don't know if it's passed on from one generation to the next. But he used to trap in the Park. I don't know if it was with other people or by himself, but by his own area and I know that there were some people were allowed to harvest a buffalo here and there. And I know of two people that were charged for harvesting buffalo. But I guess it's all right if you ate it in the Park. But they brought it to Fort Chip, so they got charged for that. Back in the '60s, my cousin Gilbert got fined $100 which would be something like, what, $10,000 today, probably. And one of them, the other guys, got his meat taken away. So, they [wardens] took all his meat. He had moose meat in there. A friend of mine and I helped them get some meat back. We told him to meet us—it was at the RCMP station. And we hauled all this buffalo meat out, so when he went to court there was just this moose meat, so they had to throw it out of court. But, you know, there was things like that, and at the residential school, we ate buffalo meat.

Magloire Vermillion

On one occasion I was with my family, and we were low on supplies. It was then I decided to hunt for ducks, so I had killed six ducks and, at the same time, by coincidence, the Park wardens came. Not really knowing what their action would be, thinking that they would not react to my killing of the ducks, I proceeded to go home with my ducks in my boat. They were following me, but I thought they were just going to go by, but apparently, they followed me home. When I got home, they took my ducks and gun. Along with these, a fine was imposed for me to pay in the amount of $14.00. They had also taken my boat. My gun was barely given back to me.

Another incident was when I killed a beaver in early spring. I put my beaver in my sled and proceeded home with my beaver. It was getting very late, so I came upon this camp where some Crees were staying. They had no meat of any kind. I was going to camp there anyway. I had this beaver in my sled, so I went out to get it. We skinned the beaver and boiled the meat. After that I camped there. The Cree had told the game warden that I had killed the beaver out of season.

Shortly after that I came to Fort Chip. It was then the Park warden had told me to turn in my permit. I was not to trap, hunt, and fish in the Park for one whole year.

I was very frustrated and disappointed. My permit was taken from me, my only source of livelihood. All my trapping, hunting, and fishing supplies were in my cabin at Peace Point [inside the Park, where he could not go without a valid permit]. There was nothing that I could do about the incident.

It was in early summer. I had thought the whole situation over.

I then made up my mind that I would personally see the district superintendent myself. So I moved to go to Fort Smith, since the district office was there. I went by boat to Fitzgerald. From there, I left my boat. I proceeded to Fort Smith which is about 22 miles by foot. I went directly to the district office. I went into the office. There was this district superintendent who used to be a Hudson's Bay clerk. I knew the man personally when he used to be the clerk. Now he is the district superintendent. I told him about the incident. I could not understand how I could have killed a beaver out of season when it was early spring. I told him that Philip Burkque [the warden] and his assistants had told me to turn in my permit. So I turned my permit over to him. I also told him that this permit that I handed in was the only source for me to provide for my family since we lived off the land. Philip Burkque was in the same office that time, but in a different room. He [the district superintendent] then called him [Burkque] into his office. Philip then sat down in a chair with no impression of any sort of incident. It appears that he had no knowledge of why I was there.

I told him [the district superintendent] that it was the warden that is sitting in the chair along with his assistants who told me that I [un]lawfully had killed a beaver out of season and told me to turn in my permit. The district superintendent then questioned him to cross-examine the situation—but apparently what happened was the intention of showing their authority [Park's authority], rather than for the principle [of conservation]. They both started to blame each other for the so-called illegal principle, not knowing who should take the blame. But this confusion was a coverup. I was then given back my permit.

The district superintendent couldn't see the point during this confusion. So he told his wardens that he could not see how this Treaty Indian had killed a beaver out of season when it was early spring when the beaver season expires late spring. So he told him to turn the permit which was in his hands, back to me.

I then proceeded back to Fort Chipewyan. I stayed for a short period, and during this short period, Philip Burkque came up to me and told me while he was laughing, that I could have my permit back. I went to his office with him to get my permit. He then told me that he was told from the district office that was to turn over my permit to me.

[Burkque explained], "In the future if you're trapping, hunting, and fishing, we are not to interfere with your Treaty."

If I had not decided to act on the so-called violation, I probably would not have gotten my permit back.

Leslie Wiltzen (21 January 2021)

ON HARVESTING REGULATIONS

In the first portion of this excerpt, Leslie discusses how some of the state-imposed harvesting regulations (in this case seasons for migratory bird hunting) were incongruous with Dene subsistence practices and Traditional Knowledge, and often did not make sense in the context of the north.

You know, when you start talking about stuff like that [harvesting regulations], you talk about, in springtime, the people of Fort Chipewyan—it's the people of the North. In springtime you have a mass migration of waterfowl that come from southern areas to northern areas to nest. But you have both male and female species that come in abundance, great abundance. Like I said, when I spoke to you earlier, it was like a cloud. A cloud of geese lifted up. You could hear the thunder from the wings flapping together. Huge, huge amounts of birds. [Yet] you know, the regulations indicate that you couldn't have a bird in the springtime when they're at their most; you have to wait for fall. And, you know, birds in the spring—that's when they're the most, that's when they're [in] the best shape as they've been down in certain areas, feeding on corn, feeding on farmers' fields where food was plentiful. So when they go up north, they lay their eggs, the females lay their eggs, the young are born, they're all skinny. When they go back south in the fall time, they're in their worst shape, right? Because they've depleted all that resources that they built up down south for that long migration flight, and then to have their young and then migrate back.

So when you're hunting for food in the springtime, and the wardens come along and start taking your birds away and say you can't kill birds, or you have to start hiding your birds for fear of being charged. And in 1899 when you [Indigenous leaders] negotiated your treaty [Treaty 8], it indicated that you would be able to carry on your traditional way of living, to make a livelihood to feed your family, as you did regardless [as though you had never taken treaty]. And then all of a sudden again, here's another roadblock: we've just formed the Park but also you can't kill these birds now. So again, you know those are hardships.

Now we kill a duck, people long ago, those bones after you're all done [with the duck], those bones you don't want to have around your house. So you take them and you go somewhere in the bush and you throw them away. You throw them away because you have fear that if the wardens come around, they're gonna ask you "where did you get that bird?" They're gonna try to prove that you're guilty [of] taking that bird when you're not supposed to, even though your stomach says you need that bird. See, that's how it was. And when you look at those regulations, long ago, they were imposed. They were developed, again without consultation, without any input of how they would affect the day-to-day living of the Chipewyan people.

So again, there's a good [amount] of regulations that were put in place, they don't work. They work in southern jurisdictions, but they don't work in the northern parks. Because in the south populations, like say now you go around Elk Island [near Edmonton, Alberta], you're [in] an urban park surrounded by urban people. You're not a park that is surrounded by Aboriginal People that have traditionally harvested food for as long as time immemorial, right? So, Elk Island National Park . . . you know, it's been modernized and commercialized to a point where that's what it is. People don't make a living there [from the land] anymore. People can't make a living anymore. So that's why I say it works. Those laws work good, those laws. When you look at the laws of Wood Buffalo National Park, the regulations of Wood Buffalo National Park, and you look at the regulations of Elk Island, they're similar in design and their approach when they were written. They're written for white people, right? Written for Canadians. But never took the treaties the Aboriginal People signed into consideration. That when we signed treaty, it said that "as long as the rivers flow, and the sun shines" we'll be able to fish, hunt, and trap. But when those regulations came into effect, our rights were stomped on. Again, no consultation, no input by the Aboriginal People.

ON RELATIONS WITH WARDENS

I started working with Parks Canada on the fire crew back in the late '80s or early '90s, and I myself have gone through the federal park warden training program. I've gone through the RCMP Depot Division [training program] and I became a full-fledged park warden in Wood Buffalo National Park. So I know the regulations and I know all the red tape, right? So, you know, it's frustrating. It's frustrating to see how little progress from even in 1990 to today. If we hadn't had certain court cases that dictated how the federal government would react to Aboriginal People, I feel, I still think we'd be in a situation where the federal government would still be trying to dictate to us what we were to do, and how to do it, and how we were to react.

Because, you know what, there's a lot of people in this Park I find that have been here long, long enough. I call them old school park wardens. They're starting to fade out, which is nice to see. It'll be a good day when they're all gone. Because you need new people to come and take on a new perspective. When you come to Wood Buffalo National Park, as an employee from another part of the country . . . we haven't always had people that have been cooperatively willing to give the Aboriginal People the benefit of the doubt in this park. And it's always been a struggle. And when you come to Wood Buffalo National Park starting your career, and you have that mindset, then all of a sudden you have a few court cases that dictate otherwise of how you are to think and how you are to react with Aboriginal People. It's hard to change on a split of a dime and change your thinking. In your mind you've always got that old school thinking, "this is what we used to do." And I still find today a lot of the people that are old school will push the envelope to the point where "what can we get away with?" With knowing the boundaries that have been set by precedent, courts that have set precedents. But they'll still push, still push, still push.

Anonymous ACFN Elder (11 March 2021)

Elder: The park rangers, this is a little way back, you know, they were pretty strict. But now, no, because they only got about one ranger here, or two.

[They were pretty] strict, yeah. They were, they were. Long time ago, we couldn't even go to the Park. We got to get a permit. You know, and that's how they were doing that. You can't go. You can't go to the Park. . . .

PF: So what did people think of them?

Elder: Well, the warden, you were scared of him. Well not me, I wasn't scared. . . . But they don't let you hunt or trap or do anything. They won't let you camp out there or nothing.

Anonymous ACFN Elder (16 March 2021)

Elder: Okay, I was gonna ask you a question. How come the Roman Catholics could shoot a buffalo? They took pictures in there, and us Indians from Fort Chip can't shoot a buffalo. It makes sense to you?

ST: I think they had that relief program so they could shoot a buffalo and then they distribute the meat in the mission or in the hospital?

Elder: Ok. Yeah, I'm just asking. To me, it didn't seem right as a Dene... You know, how come a white man can shoot a buffalo and the Dene can never really shoot one?

ST: And sometimes they even sold the meat down south too.

Elder: Yes? Oh I didn't know, like I read that, looked at that book, and I was thinking about that. And how come they have the right to shoot a buffalo and we can't? And they have big pictures of them shooting buffalo.

Anonymous ACFN Member (21 March 2021)

I did hear stories that they [harvesters] will lose [have confiscated if they broke the rules] all their trapping stuff, you know? And, what do you call even—like, if they were stopped in their vehicle out in the Park with that, they'd lose their vehicle, their guns, everything. And they'd go to court, and they could go to jail. But I never heard of anyone. Because I was young that time, so I was, I didn't really know.

I did hear stories that they will lose all their trapping stuff, you know. They had to get a license to hunt beaver from the Park in 1912. And that's where some people didn't have license, so they ended up starving. Because they weren't able to hunt in the Park.

6

t'ąt'ú náídé nuhghą hílchú ląt'e kúlí ąłu̱´ dene k'ezí náídé

Combined with the increasingly strict system of harvesting laws enforced by the warden system, exclusions from Dënesųłıné territories taken up by the Park created serious problems for people living outside the Park. Many people faced periods of severe hardship, some even to the point of starvation. Meanwhile, those who could remain in the Park fared somewhat better because competition was limited. Dene people in the Delta, however, did not benefit from the protections afforded to Park residents and faced serious challenges. Hunger and hardship became realities for Dënesųłıné people in the Delta, especially those who had been evicted from the Park. After the expansion of the Park, many were forced to take government relief, whereas only a few decades earlier they had provided for themselves from the land. Chief Jonas Laviolette's 1927 letters to Indian Affairs officials emphasized the challenges people were facing: "There are lots of men here looking after the buffalo, no one looking after us. . . . No one seems to care if we starve or not." His letter continued, "sometimes the Police give us a little rations . . . but we cannot live on that all the time. Since the fur has left the country, you don't know how poor we are, not only in food but clothing and blankets too."[1] As Indian Affairs officials had feared from the start, Dene families were often forced to rely on government assistance because they were unable to freely harvest as they had always done.

Faced with these challenges, Dene people frequently and clearly resisted government officials, asserting their concerns through protest, petition, and requests for government support. They indicated that new state-imposed regulations and evictions from the Park not only interfered with their livelihood, leading to widespread hardship and hunger, but also were violations of their Treaty and hereditary rights. As Sandlos describes, through letter writing campaigns, political delegations, protests, and subversions of harvesting regulations, Dene residents and land users have always articulated "a set of cultural and political values rooted in the notion of customary use rights, hereditary land title, and ... a treaty guarantee of the right to hunt and trap."[2] Dene oral histories allude to the strength and resistance of Dene people who used many different means and forums to express their concerns about restrictions on harvesting and the resulting suffering they experienced, and to resist and challenge attempts at eliminating their sovereignty and ways of life. As this chapter's Dënesųłıné title states, "the way we lived was taken from us; however we still live/stay there as Dene people."

Extensive letter-writing campaigns were a key form of Dene activism from the time the Park was created. Letters written by harvesters and leaders indicated that Indigenous residents opposed laws imposed from afar and without their consent or regard to their needs and rights. Letter writers repeatedly stated the concern that their Treaty Rights were being violated and that this was causing extreme difficulty. In 1926, several Indigenous and non-Indigenous residents contested the Park annex in a memorandum to Charles Cross: "So unnecessary is any such establishment in the area in question, and so harmful would it ultimately prove to be to those now resident in that area and vicinity that we pray that the above-described terrain shall under no circumstances be set apart as a Buffalo Park, or as an annex."[3] They continued, "As you are doubtless aware, when the Treaty was first made ... the members ... were given the solemn assurance that they would be as free to hunt and fish after the signing of the Treaty, as if they had never entered upon it."[4]

After the annex, a 1927 letter from Chief Jonas Laviolette called on officials to respond to Dene demands for the establishment of the reserves promised in Treaty 8 to his Nation, which would protect the people from increasing trapping competition and the hunger that resulted from game laws.[5] Numerous other letters throughout the period expressed people's frustrations with the regulations, encroaching white trappers, their fears of starvation, and concerns for their families' health and well-being.

Delegations made up of leaders and residents asserted Dene rights and concerns to government officials. Chief Jonas Laviolette travelled to Edmonton more than once to state his concerns directly to officials, sometimes taking a delegation of other leaders with him. A 1935 delegation of Cree and Dene chiefs stated their view to Austin L. Cumming, District Agent and Park Superintendent, that the revised permitting regulations were infringing on Treaty Rights.[6] At Treaty Days, leaders repeated their concerns to Indian

Fig. 6.1 Chief Jonas Laviolette, pictured here, spent much of his leadership defending the community's rights and interests in the face of stringent and exclusive colonial environmental policy in the twentieth century. He also frequently spoke out about the harmful impacts of WBNP's boundaries. *Jonas Laviolette, Ft. Chipewyan (1948–1954)*. Provincial Archives of Alberta, A17118.

Agents on a yearly basis.[7] Some refused treaty payments to protest the Park and game laws.[8]

Another common form of resistance was to ignore or break state-imposed game laws. Some Dene harvesters continued trapping and hunting in the Park as a political act, "an attempt to return to the time before an arbitrary and largely impersonal state bureaucracy" dispossessed them and restricted their movement and lifeways, as Sandlos explains.[9] By harvesting as they had always done in areas currently restricted through colonial law and refusing to share information with Park wardens, he argues, Dene harvesters expressed "collective dissent against the arbitrary application of state power over traditional hunting rights in the region."[10] Historians connecting Parks with colonialism in Canada often draw this conclusion from their reading of archival sources; Wood Buffalo Park warden diaries and patrol reports from the 1920s to the 1940s contain evidence to support the assertion. In 1930, several Indigenous harvesters were tried and found guilty of hunting bison in the Park and were sentenced to three months of hard labour at the RCMP Barracks in Fort Chipewyan. The trial generated widespread interest among local Indigenous communities; according to warden Dempsey's notes, roughly sixty Indigenous residents were in attendance. According to Finnie's summary of the proceedings, the convicted men argued that they would not have hunted bison if the government wasn't starving them, and further that "the Indians were not advised when treaty was made that buffalo from Wainwright Park would be imported."[11] Finnie dismissed this defence as irrelevant, missing the point. The harvesters' argument implied that they perceived the importation of plains bison and subsequent Park extension and accompanying regulations to be a violation of Treaty 8. By hunting bison, they were exposing this violation while also asserting what they knew to be their treaty rights.

Numerous other instances of harvesting in the Park and breaking regulations are evident from Park records; wardens tracked these instances meticulously. A 1935 report by Warden Dent to Supervising Warden M.J. Dempsey suggested that Dene residents in the Birch River area were hosting their kin from Fort McKay. Dent reported that Peter Ratfat and Vzckial Ratfat had visited Adam Boucher and his two sons at the Birch River settlement and that they were reported to be trapping without permits there. When Dent questioned Adam Boucher and his sons, they denied the reports. Dent wrote, "It is evident that someone is not telling truth. As you are aware, the Birch River Indians are related to some of the McKay Indians, so really it is difficult to get them to convict one another."[12] Two years later, in 1937, warden Dempsey reported people trespassing in the Birch River area.[13] These may have been assertions of Dënesųłıné harvesting rights in the area from which they had been removed or perhaps an attempt to return to the homes from which they had been evicted. One warden reflected in 1947 that in his interactions with local trappers, he learned that many were "extremely suspicious of new or proposed regulations" and that if those regulations were generally considered harmful, "individuals gain personal merit by breaking them and not being caught."[14]

The oral histories shared in this chapter also explicitly document these sorts of acts of resistance. Elders and community members shared examples of Dene people entering the Park to harvest despite the regulations banning them from doing so. Some Dene harvesters might enter the Park with a Métis or MCFN trapper who held a permit. Others recalled that some harvesters would wait until dark to enter the Park and harvest a bison and then store the meat throughout the Park, such as in rat houses or in residents' freezers,

Fig. 6.2 Photo of ACFN's Flag at ACFN Elders' Meeting, June 2022, Fort Chipewyan. Photo by Peter Fortna.

under a pile of moose meat, to avoid being caught. "They made sure it was all hidden," said one Elder. Other times, harvesters found that wardens did not know the difference between moose meat and bison meat and would capitalize on that ignorance. Two Elders shared accounts from the 1980s to the early 2000s in which they entered the Park to hunt or fish with the aim of initiating legal action. They notified Parks officials of their plans to harvest in the Park, including details of when and where, with the intention of getting arrested to initiate a lawsuit. While wardens met them and ordered the men to return home, they did not arrest the harvesters. Nonetheless, this is an important example of Dënesųłıné assertions of their uninterrupted and treaty-protected rights throughout their territories.

Assertions of Dënesųłıné rights and concerns like these were ignored, dismissed, or punished by provincial and federal authorities. The 1935 Edmonton delegation of Chiefs was dismissed by officials who told them that "there were no drastic changes in the Wood Buffalo Park regulations."[15] Officials sometimes responded to Dene activism by increasing warden surveillance. In 1937, after Dempsey had reported trespassers in the Birch River area, one official wrote, "I am asking Park Warden Dempsey to have wardens patrol this area as much as possible this winter to try and prevent any trespassing by unwarranted persons."[16] When residents suggested revisions to the permitting and harvesting laws, they were often denied. For example, in 1937 leaders in the Northwest Territories requested permission for heads of families to kill a bison if their families were starving. They were refused on the basis that "the privilege would be abused" and that "the Government was preserving the buffalo for the Indians' own good."[17] Chief Jonas Laviolette's letters went unanswered. He described a generally dismissive attitude characterizing the federal administration's responses: "I have been waiting long to hear from you that I think you have forgotten all about me and my people from Fort Chipewyan. Four years ago, I went to Edmonton on purpose to see you about my people and my country. Times were hard then but now they are worse. My people are very miserable because they cannot make a living anymore from the fur."[18] Thus, a central component of the history of the Park's relation to ACFN, especially after 1926, was the dismissal of Dënesųłiné rights and concerns. Dene protests and petitions, as well as the intimate knowledge they had of the land and water, were mostly ignored, and the struggles resulting from physical displacements went unnoticed and uncompensated by the government.

Establishing Reserves: Delays and Denials

In addition to refusals and dismissals, government officials took decades to secure the reserves promised in Treaty 8. Families who were evicted from the Park needed protected space where could safely reside, harvest, and practice their rights. Although the park administration itself was not directly responsible for the long delays, park restrictions and evictions were a central reason Dënesųłiné leaders fought to secure reserves in the first place. They saw reserves as a key space where the people could survive physical displacements, restrictive game laws, and erosions of their Treaty Rights. As McCormack notes, without the potential protection of a reserve, and facing the influx of outsiders and newly imposed restrictions on land use and mobility, people found themselves living "in a condition of total insecurity, at the mercy of the park administration, which they distrusted."[19] Chiefs Alexandre Laviolette and Jonas Laviolette had lobbied the government for reserves since the signing of Treaty 8 to mitigate these issues. But as the Treaty and Aboriginal Rights Research report concluded, "repeated Indian demands for protection from

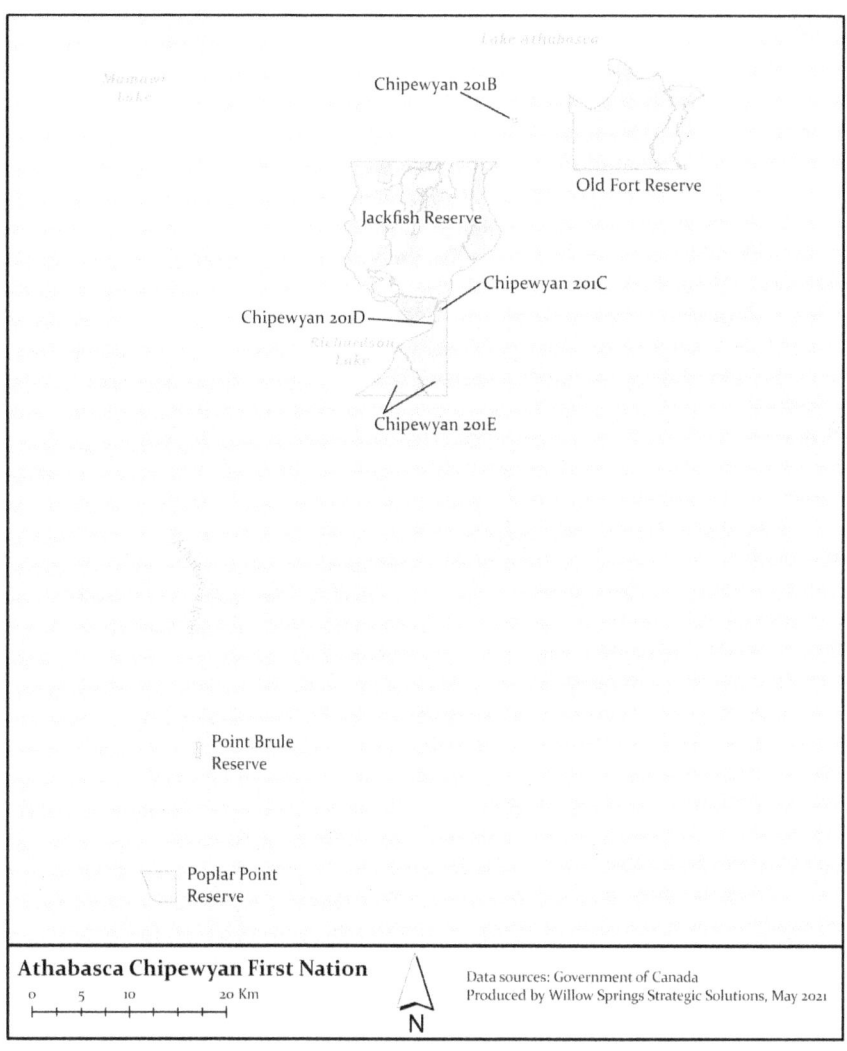

Fig. 6.3 Map of ACFN IR201 reserves. Map produced by Emily Boak, Willow Springs Strategic Solutions, 2021.

unregulated, irresponsible and sometimes illegal outside competitions—by the establishment of preserves—had been fruitless" for many decades.[20]

Indian Affairs eventually acted on Dene leaders' urgent and repeated requests for a reserve in 1931—thirty-two years after the Nation signed onto Treaty 8 and nearly a decade after the Park's creation. However, the province of Alberta challenged the proposed allotment size, which was almost 34-square kilometres larger than the Nation's Treaty entitlement required. The province was particularly reluctant to transfer control over prime muskrat trapping terrain in one section of the proposed reserve. It was not until 1937 that federal Order-in-Council 1399/27 granted certificates of title for the surface rights to 200 square kilometres of land for the Chipewyan Band (now ACFN) reserves in the Athabasca Delta. The province retained control over waterways, mines and minerals, and fishing in the Band's IR 201A-G reserves. Surface rights were not officially transferred from the province to the federal government until 1954.[21]

The negotiation of the reserve allotments occurred largely without the input or consultation of Dënesųłıné leaders and land users. The original, larger allotments that leaders had previously negotiated were ultimately reduced and re-negotiated by the provincial and federal governments without consultation. As one Elder explained, "when the Dene were kicked out of the park, the government gave the Dene a piece of land over here. . . . We didn't have a choice on where we wanted to be, you know. They put us over here by Jackfish Lake, Old Fort, and up the river a couple of other places. . . . So I was telling the chief we should pick some reserves or a piece of land or lands somewhere where we want to live, not where they want us to live. We want to decide rather than the[m] telling us where to live." As the various levels of government argued over reserve boundaries, Dene people who had been removed from the Park continued to face hunger and economic hardship with little recourse or help.

The 1935 Order-in-Council to protect Dene Harvesting Rights: Another Broken Promise

In 2013, Elder Pat Marcel related the oral history of another effort by Dënesųłıné leaders to mitigate the harmful impacts of the Park and the conservation restrictions after 1926. He explained that, as the IR 201 reserves were being negotiated, Chiefs lobbied the government for the establishment of protected harvesting reserves outside the Park, in addition to the IR201 reserves. Indian Agent Card wrote to Indian Affairs in 1927:

> On behalf of the Chipewyan Indians, under Chief Jonas Laviolette, Jackfish Lake, Ft. Chipewyan, I would call the attention of the Department to the wishes of the band . . . to have, *independently of these special reserves*, the survey, in the coming spring of the reserve, for the band, guaranteed by Treaty, June 21st, 1899. I might add that they are very urgent on this matter, as there is a prospect of rats [muskrats] coming back and they wish to protect the marsh grounds surrounding their homes.[22]

By 1931, officials were still discussing the request: "For many years the Indians of the Chippewyan [sic] band at Fort McMurray have been pressing to have a game reserve set aside for them," wrote one official.[23] As Elder Pat Marcel explained, Dene leaders and land users were determined because they knew that "most of the better lands [outside the Park] would be taken up" by non-Indigenous trappers competing for harvesting space, and by a growing industrial presence in the region.[24]

Due to Dene activism, the 1935 Order-in-Council 298-35 set aside a large, protected conservation area in addition to the IR201 reserves. The Order-in-Council closed trapping to anyone but local residents in the following area:

> Beginning at a point where the Inter-Provincial boundary between Alberta and Saskatchewan joins the south boundary of the North West Territories, thence southward along the Inter-Provincial boundary to the 27th Baseline, thence west along the said 27th Baseline to the Athabasca River; thence north along the eastern boundary of the Wood Buffalo Park to a point where it joins the southern boundary of the North West Territories, thence east along the southern boundary of the North West Territories to the point of intersection of the Inter-Provincial boundary.[25]

The oral histories indicate that this area was exclusively intended for Indigenous residents, and Dene leaders saw it as an important space to protect Dënesųłıné people who had been expelled from the Park. As Elder Pat Marcel stated, "I am sure that Chief Jonas Laviolette convinced the government that if we didn't have that agreement, then the white population would run rampant and kill everything off, and we would not have anything to survive. So this is what happened with the 27th Baseline and our land."[26] However, the province abandoned this Order-in-Council, likely shortly after the Registered Fur Management Area (RFMA) system came into effect in 1942.

A series of letters among government officials from 1935 to 1942 suggests that the administration struggled to manage the complex and sometimes contradictory trapping arrangements within and outside the Park, including for this new preserve. The 1935 Order-in-Council added controversy to confusion by excluding non-resident harvesters from trapping or hunting in the large preserve. Both Indigenous and non-Indigenous harvesters who resided south of the Delta region were not permitted to harvest within the preserve boundaries, which frustrated Dene harvesters who resided south of the area but had relatives in the Delta.[27] After 1942, the province no longer acknowledged the Order-in-Council that set aside preserve land; trapping throughout the area was subsequently managed through the RFMA as with the rest of the province.[28] In this way, another attempt by Dënesųłıné people to protect themselves and their rights after being expelled from the Park was thwarted by government authorities. Pat Marcel's oral history of these events is quoted at length later in this chapter.

ACFN members continue to challenge colonial systems of land and resource management in Dene homelands. In Spring 2022, a WBNP warden ordered ACFN member Melissa Daniels to stop travelling to the Park's salt flats to harvest salt for wellness products she creates through her small business Naidie Nezu. The roughly 200 square-kilometre salt plains are a distinguishing feature of the region and are among the elements of Outstanding Universal Value for which Wood Buffalo National Park was designated a UNESCO World Heritage Site in 1983.[29] Indigenous Peoples in the region have harvested in the salt deposits for various purposes such as for food preservation since time immemorial. Parks Canada took issue with Daniels' purpose for harvesting. Harvesting salt for personal use was not an issue, according to the communication, but "commercial harvesting" was not permitted. Indicating that she never had plans to mass-produce or widely distribute the Naidie Nezu products and that harvesting salt for any reason was a Dene right, Daniels took the exchange to the public. As she told a CBC reporter in April 2022: "The implication that my land-based, hand-harvested practice is a threat to the natural environment is insulting to me, our Nation, our

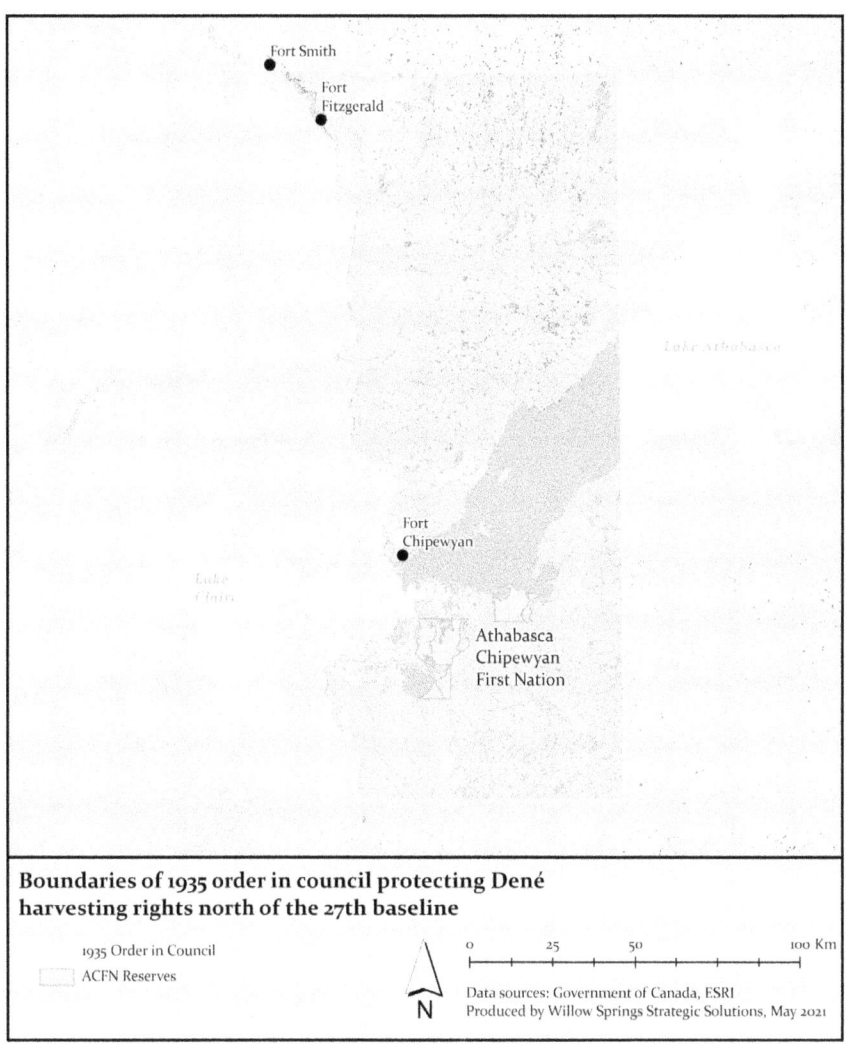

Fig. 6.4 Map of the boundaries of the preserve set by 1935 Order-in-Council 298-35 Map Produced by Emily Boak, Willow Springs Strategic Solutions, 2021.

Fig. 6.5 A Round Dance at ACFN's Treaty Days, 2018, Fort Chipewyan. Photo by Peter Fortna.

ancestors and the land itself."[30] Daniels argued that this was a blatant refusal of Dene people's Indigenous and Treaty Rights and their land-based ways of life, stating that she would not stop harvesting. As she noted publicly, "colonialism is colonialism is colonialism" and that this situation demonstrated the need for "a radical reconfiguration of environmental dynamics."[31] By excluding Indigenous Peoples from their homes and homelands and restricting their movements and ways of life, while supporting extreme extraction outside of Park boundaries, Canadian authorities continue a legacy of environmental racism. Daniels explained that she had no plans to stop harvesting and that supporting the business and soaking in "forbidden bath salts" itself could be seen as an act of resistance, of "soaking in a century worth of reparations."[32]

In the oral testimony shared in this chapter, Elders discuss efforts to challenge encroachments on Dënesųłıné rights and homelands, and to respond to the harmful impacts of the Park's and province's policies.[33] Dene people have engaged in activism and resistance in organized forums and in their everyday lives. Whether by harvesting salt, passing down oral histories, exposing tailings leaks that industry and regulators have kept hidden from Indigenous Peoples and the public,[34] teaching Dene language classes, or writing this book—the Dënesųłıné have always resisted and challenged colonial attempts at elimination. They continue to express and maintain Dene knowledge, rights, ways of life, and relations to the land and water.

ORAL HISTORY

ACFN Elder Leonard Flett (30 April 2021)

In this discussion, ACFN Elder Leonard Flett described an interaction with Parks Canada in the 1990s. Leonard deliberately entered the Park and practiced his right to fish there in hopes of being arrested and charged, to initiate legal proceedings and thereby demonstrate and establish his rights to harvest in the Park in court. While he was ticketed and took the case to court, it was ultimately dropped.

LF: I was robbed. Yeah, highway robbery, I guess. Everything. Our culture and the land. We were there and stuff, right? And took years and years till I put my foot back in [the] national park. I kind of disagreed with it. I fought it back in the '90s for ice fishing so I can practice my right. I was charged by the National Park and went as far as the court door, didn't go anywhere else.

PF: They dropped the charges?

LF: Yeah.

PF: Or, they still charged you?

LF: Yup, they took my chisel away, they took my fishing rods, whatever else I had there. I went walking out there [to where I fished]. I didn't take my skidoo or anything. Cause I [knew] that was a challenge I took. My mother was very, very upset for me to go out there and that's the kind of guy I am, I guess. I want challenges.

PF: Can you take me back to that time when you were deciding—what made you decide that you wanted to go back to the Park?

LF: I just wanted to practice my rights, my hunting rights, my fishing rights, a lot I had before, right? I even called [the] national park, I told them I was going at a certain time and they met me out there while I was fishing, yeah.

PF: And so, was part of it you wanted to reconnect kind of with your past too?

LF: Yeah. I'm entitled to.

PF: And so, what did the parks guys have to say when they picked you up?

LF: They didn't say much. They just gave me a ticket and they offered a ride back to town. And I said, no, I'll walk. I came walking out here, I walk back to town.

PF: What did you think about on that walk?

LF: It's good, it was a challenge. It was. I defeated the national park.

PF: And then, I guess you got your tickets? So you're getting ready for court and stuff. What were other people, like your mom was upset, but what were other people thinking?

LF: My mom was very upset. Cause, anybody [who] violated the Park way back in the day they're probably jailed, right?

PF: So she thought that was gonna happen to you?

LF: Yeah. But I stood my ground. And I have people from Northwest Territories that were challenging [the] national park [WBNP] for their hunting rights. Like the Métis Association of Alberta. And I called them up and told them, and they backed me up and said, "go ahead, do it." And then when are you going to resolve it?

PF: And so, what about people in your community, were they backing you up too?

LF: There aren't much people involved, and I just involved my mother, that's pretty well it. And I got a hold of Indian Association out of Treaty 8, they got me a lawyer and stuff like that. So, I went to court. It didn't go anywhere.

PF: So you were getting ready to go to court. And then what happened? They just told you it was dropped?

LF: Yeah, it was dropped right at the court door that day. Yeah.

PF: Did they say why?

LF: No.

PF: What do you think?

LF: I think they were defeated. I don't think they had a chance. I don't think they had a chance, you know? And that's the reason why I took it [this cause] up. I took journalism before, so.

PF: Okay. Did you ever write anything about it?

LF: Uh, no, I haven't. One of these days, I will.

PF: Okay. Yeah, it sounds like it'd be a good story. So have you gone back since?

LF: Yeah, I built a cabin in the national park. I gave it to my son. There's other memberships that have built cabins in the park. My sister and her husband used to live in Peace Point, used to teach in Peace Point which is the national park back in the '80s. So we maintain our rights, I guess.

PF: How do you feel about having the cabin now and having been able to pass it on to your kids and, or your son and stuff?

LF: Feeling proud.

John H. Marcel (30 April 2021)

John was explaining to the interviewer that he often used to visit the Park and called it home, sometimes hunting there to assert his rights to the territory taken up by the Park. He suggested that sometimes when he does so, he gets resistance from some MCFN members who are permitted by Park policy to call the Park home.

I like going there [to the Park], but I don't. It seems like I'm not welcome in that place. And then I just bug them sometimes. I get this little thing that where—the hell with the way you feel—my granny was born up that way [at] Birch River. My granny is the one—she was born up that way. My granny and my other grandfather, her side was from that way so that they'd all come to the Park after, eh? But in a way, that's why, when I go there, I always say, hey, I'm coming back home, I always bug a Cree member. But them, they don't get what I'm saying. I never told them why I'm saying that, like, "hey, I feel like I'm happy I'm getting home, the way home, you know?" I'm just fooling around with them.

But, when you get there, you get, "what is this guy doing here?" Just like about that time when I'm saying I'm going back home, we stopped in a cabin, right about this time of the year [in the Spring], with a lot of birds going north, that's what we're going for. It was in the Park right by Lake Mamawi, and when I stopped there, I know everybody, they're all from here, Fort Chip, but they all look at me, "what the hell is this guy doing here?" Right? You know, I know right away, just by the look of it. But I didn't care . . . it doesn't bother me, if they think that way, to hell with them, it's no longer my land. I just laugh at them. That's all I do. I'm only there to hunt, right? I'm not there to go put a cabin right next door to you, so I'm there for two hours or a few days, then I go home. And I'm probably going to do that not too long from now, the next couple of weeks you know, exercise our right. I might go for a cruise [a boat ride] up that way and bring my little tent and stove and what I need. Talk about [how] I'm going to go for when the birds come in, eh? Yeah, go for a little hunt there.

Pat Marcel (2013)

The following is an extensive excerpt from Pat Marcel's oral history about negotiations for ACFN's reserves and the 1935 provincial Order-in-Council 298-35 setting aside an additional preserve north of the 27th Baseline to further protect the rights of those Dene individuals without access to the Park. In 2013, he shared this history with Arlene Seegerts, a researcher who, at the time, was working with Pat to record his family oral histories about Treaty 8 and the 1935 Order-in-Council. Pat's grandfather was Chief Jonas Laviolette, who, along with his brother Alexandre Laviolette and son-in-law Benjamin Marcel, Pat's father, was instrumental in negotiating the establishment of this preserve.

The story that I am about to recall [is] about Chief Jonas Laviolette, in negotiations for reserve land. Reserves like 201A to 201G.[35] When the government proposed these reserves, Chief Alexandre Laviolette saw immediately that the land was too small for ACFN to survive on. Negotiations continued, not only for N22, but also for a bigger area in Alberta, where we could practice Treaty Rights and use the land for conservation, because the land around the Delta was being invaded by people who had no regard for fur bearing animals, and the moose and other big game animals that the Chipewyan survived on.

When Chief Alexandre Laviolette first started negotiation for protected land, this was the outcome, in 1935. When most of the negotiation for land started, he knew that most of the better lands [outside the Park] would be taken up. . . . He wanted to make sure that there would always be game and fur-bearing animals because he was already preaching conservation, back then. The Chiefs, starting with Alexandre, always had an interest in the future, in order to survive off the land in fifty or one hundred years. He did not see ACFN surviving on agriculture. He did not see ACFN surviving on commercial fishing, as seen by McGinnis [fishery] bringing in their own people to fish, not ACFN.[36] So that is why he wanted to protect land for the sole use of ACFN into the future.

These negotiations went on and were picked up by Chief Jonas Laviolette, after his brother [Alexandre] died, and he and my dad, Benjamin Marcel [a Chipewyan Band leader , were able to negotiate with the province with the help of the federal government. It was through legislation with the Alberta government that this land was set aside for ACFN to practise our Treaty Rights and conservation. And [it] was set up as [a] huge tract of land, right up to the Northwest Territories. . . . This land, they talked about for many years. They [Dene Elders] called, time and time again, the importance of keeping this land, and to be sure that we would never lose this land for as long as ACFN needs the land to practise our Treaty Rights and conservation.

The Chief knew in those days—he was a very wise man—[that] what he puts in place with the Alberta government has to go right into the future, so we will always have a place where we can hunt. For the conservation, so we will always have game. This is what the Chief talked about all the time with my Dad. They had already signed the agreement, that legislative agreement. That was three years before I was born. And as I grew up, right until I was sixteen or seventeen, I trapped with my Dad, in the very same area, and he described this very same land. And he was very adamant: "You can never lose this land." That we must hang onto this—"forever."

I have not forgotten what my dad put into my head, and what Chief Jonas Laviolette used to come over and talk to my dad about; that that [1935] Agreement was an achievement for ACFN to practise Treaty Rights and also for conservation. I am sure that Chief Jonas Laviolette convinced the government that if we didn't have that agreement, then the white population would run rampant and kill everything off, and we would not have anything to survive. So this is what happened with the 27th Baseline and our land. And I tell the people, "Do you think it is coincidence that all of our traplines [RFMAs—the means whereby the province has managed trapping activities outside reserves since 1942] end on the 27th Baseline, but not outside of this land?" The traplines all ended on the 27th Baseline.

I heard Chief Laviolette speak about how we must not let Alberta Game take our land. He was looking at Reserve #201 to #201G, that those lands, called "the reserves," are so small that we could not survive off it. So this land [under the 1935 Order-in-Council] has been set aside by the Alberta government, by an Order-in-Council, by the *Games Act*, which was [the] first time at the agricultural side, but was put into the Games Act for enforcement.

In 1935, an Order-in-Council was passed by the Province setting aside the area in the Fort Chipewyan district, north of a line beginning at the south-east corner of Buffalo Park running directly east to the Saskatchewan border. This area is for the exclusive use of the Indians and settlers living north of the above-mentioned line and no trapping licenses have been issued to outsiders for that area since that time.

The Alberta government was not doing this—giving us land—from the goodness of their hearts. They were doing that because they knew that they had disrupted all family life at House Lake, by removing us from the park. So when we were given this piece of land to practise our Treaty Rights on, it was for us to pass the test of time—for our use—that Chief Jonas Laviolette made sure that this land would be able to be there for us. To pass the test of time. It would still be there for one hundred or two hundred years into the future. That there would be somebody to speak for it, and that the government would support ACFN, to have this land that was set aside.

The fact that Chief Jonas Laviolette and my dad would always go back and talk about this land was to make sure that the future generation knew about it. And that we could still pressure the Alberta government, to make sure that this land was always there for us, for our use. Chief Jonas Laviolette was my grandfather, and he would come to my house and talk to my father and tell him, "That knowledge cannot be lost."

Edouard Trippe de Roche (25 November 2021)

Edouard Trippe de Roche described the establishment of reserves promised in Treaty 8. He suggested that, although the 201 reserves were important for protecting Dene rights as other areas in the territory were being taken up, the reserve allotments came together without the knowledge or consent of many of the Dene residents and land users. He concluded that ACFN's experience with unsatisfactory reserve allotments was not an isolated event—referring to the similar experiences of Blackfoot Nations in southern Alberta.

When the Dene were kicked out [of] the Park, the government gave us, or gave the Dene, a piece of land over here. We didn't have a choice on where we wanted to be, you know. They put us over here by Jackfish Lake, Old Fort, and up the river a couple of other places. And there's high water—we're losing so many acres. Even these last floods here, just this summer. Now, if you want to call land, land, you can't call our reserve there across the lake, 201, "land," because it's all under water, so we didn't actually have a reserve. So, I was telling the Chief we should pick some reserves or a piece of land or lands somewhere where we want to live, not where *they* want us to live. I know down south they've given the Blackfoots, they put them all in rocky hills, you know, rolling hills. They have places, sure they have small places to farm but not like where they were kicked out of the prairie. That's what happened out west here. So that's just one of my points.

Anonymous ACFN members (2021)

1. I think as you go along, you might find some—not just cautionary tales, but things that I would call passive aggressive. People going hunting bison

outside the Park and then inviting everybody outside the Park for two days while you eat the bison and have a really great time. And I've done it, I didn't shoot bison, but I've gone to the feast, and I had a great time. Everybody just crowds around—oh maybe I shouldn't say this, sorry—they crowd around the fire, and you know, tell tales and stuff like that and everybody just eats. But this is something, feasting is something that has always been there and it's a thing that people love to do. But they don't shoot inside the Park because of course the Park wardens, if they found out, would kick everybody out. And I think you'll find among the [Dene] there's been some very, very strong passive aggressive actions taken. Because you just can't live without resistance.

2. Yeah, I did hunt buffalo and buffalos used to come out from the Park, eh? But you can't go and hunt in the Park. But sometimes people they go in and get themselves a buffalo or two in the park too, well, in a bad storm. Well, you got to survive somehow, you know. You'll starve yourself. [They] tell you, "you can't go and shoot this buffalo in that Park" and what else is there to eat? And they had to poach buffalo out in the bush and then try to hide it. Everything they can hide, to survive. That was wrong, you know? That they'd [Parks officials] do that to other people.

Yeah, you keep it from the rangers, fish and wildlife. They [Indigenous harvesters] don't squeal on one another either. Somebody gets a caribou, everybody gets a piece of it. They help one another feed themselves. That was really good. Those were the good happy old days in one way. Oh, yeah, they help one another as much as they can for survival, to try to survive. Can't see a person starve to death, you know?

But Native People survive on the land. They had to do what they had to do to survive and sometimes they don't follow the white man's law. They can't, otherwise they'll starve their family. They go and poach too, we did. But still, we used to go and hunt. You had to survive. We had no choice.

3. I will tell you what I used to do, I mean, whether you bring it out [in the government report] or not doesn't make any darn difference—it's all gone now. But I—there was about three or four of us on a boat. We'd wait till Parks get to Chip and they're back [until the wardens have left the park], and they bring all their boats off. Well, I noticed about six o'clock, seven o'clock they're all in. And then we go out and hunt the buffaloes. Yeah. Oh, my God, I think I better darn keep quiet here. Shit, all of a sudden, the Parks, you come here one night, and they lay charges on me for all the information I've given you guys.

4. I shouldn't say that they never ever, ever come into the Park. There's a few of the guys went in just to go poaching—waterfowl.

5. Well, I think of one story my grandpa told me where they waited right till about dark. They knew where the buffalos are there, and then they took all the meat and they worked all night.... They cut all the meat up and stored it all over the place and even the buffalo they say, they took a [musk]rat house away and then put the buffalo into the rat house and covered it back up. Covered all their tracks and stuff to make sure there's nothing. They had the meat. I think they hid it from the dogs or they'd hide some meat for themselves and stuff. But they made sure it was all hidden. Or they made dried meat right away, you know, dried meat can be stored easily in a cabin and stuff. Yeah, they were kind of scared back in the day. But they did it, they poached them.

6. I'll tell you a little story. I used to live with my partner at the time. And they, well me too, I like eating buffalo meat, eh? We're not supposed to kill them, but my partner had killed one and then it just happened that the Chief at that time there, he came there with the Park wardens. They come to visit and so when they came there, in here, I was boiling a big pot of buffalo ribs and some moose meat. They asked me what it was, and I told the Chief, I said, "you should know it's moose meat," I told him, "have some." "Okay," he said. He just smiled and looked at me, big smile on his face 'cause he knew what it was. The Park warden, I invited him. I said, "have some moose with us." He said, "oh it tastes so good" and all that. He was eating buffalo meat, he didn't even know the difference.

Yeah, they went to an Elder's [house] here in Chip one time, because somebody reported he had shot a buffalo [in the Park]. And then, well, he did but already he had packaged the meat and put it in the bottom [of the freezer] and he had some moose meat and he put it on top. So by the time the Park came over there, Park wardens came there, they wanted to check his deep freeze. So the Elder opened the deep freeze, said, "okay, go ahead," he said. There's moose meat there and you could see outside there, like part of the moose, like the bones and stuff like that, he hadn't gotten rid of yet. So Parks said, "oh, okay, we just had to check." And he said, "I know not to kill buffalo," he said. Closes his deep freeze and he left, but at the bottom was all the buffalo meat. So yeah, they don't know—these people.

ST: And what would happen if they did get caught?

Elder: They'd get charged, you're not supposed to, I guess. I don't know what they did now, but you're not supposed to kill buffalo. Yeah, because you're not supposed to kill it in the park because it's considered endangered or whatever they say. But you know, if they come this way towards Alberta, we're gonna go, not me, but you know, the guys are gonna head out there. Yeah, it tastes good that buffalo meat.

7. I mentioned earlier my father was sixty-one when he perished, and he left thirteen in our family and for sustenance purposes—my mother didn't have any advanced education, and it was difficult. So, I had uncles who would harvest a buffalo or a moose, but most of the time it was buffalo. We weren't allowed to, but they did anyway, and they would provide for my mother who was their sister, and they would bring food, which would be buffalo and fish and that sort of thing.

And in the summers, I know that on one occasion, and I'll never forget it, we went into the Park. I had an older brother that was going to get a buffalo in the Park because we needed meat. So away we went, and he dropped me at a place called Salt Plains which was west of Fort Smith. It was in the Park, and in order to get in there, there was a couple cabins near a place called Salt River and we had to sneak around those cabins with the vehicle so they wouldn't hear us or see the lights or turn us in.

So we went and we got into the salt flats and he gave me a pot and something else, and he dropped me off, and he said, "when you see me flash the lights you start coming towards the lights and make lots of noise, okay?" So I did that. What I was doing was pushing buffalo to him and then he'd turn the lights on, and "bang, bang," and we had a buffalo. So, then we would carve it up and load it up and get out of there. But that was in the Park.

So, I would daresay, we weren't the only ones doing that. I mean he must've learned it from somebody else too. But most of it was for subsistence reasons. That was our meat. That's how I grew up.

8. I mean, you know there's been cases over the years where people hunt bison or they hunt geese. Even when I was younger to go hunting in the Park, we knew it was illegal, we knew it was illegal, but it was where all the birds were. It was where the migratory route was—was in the Park. So you know you risk being criminally charged from the federal government through the warden services for doing activities like that.

7

t'a nuhél nódher sí nuhenéné bazį́ chu t'ąt'ú nuheba horená duhų́, eyi beghą dene hé́ł hoílni

The Dënesųłiné title of this chapter translates to "what happened to us regarding our land and how we are in difficulty today, about that we tell our story to people." The title highlights the central intention of this chapter and of *Remembering Our Relations*: to tell the story of the intergenerational impacts of the Park on the Dënesųłiné people.

During much of the twentieth century, Wood Buffalo National Park was one of the only national parks in Canada that allowed some Indigenous Peoples to harvest within its boundaries. Yet, despite Parks officials' contention that the Park and its policies existed for the good of Indigenous Peoples, exclusions from WBNP were especially damaging to Dënesųłiné residents and land users. Dënesųłiné oral histories emphasize that the impacts of Wood Buffalo National Park's creation, expansion, and management throughout the twentieth century have been severe and long-lasting, complex, and multi-layered. Virtually all ACFN members who shared testimony for this project described in detail direct and cumulative impacts, both past and present. The impacts of the Park touch on many areas of Dene lives and well-being, with demonstrable long-term effects on the community's connections to Dene homelands, sovereignty, community dynamics, family connections, identity, and overall health—physical, spiritual and mental. The oral testimony shared in this chapter describes these complex, multidimensional, and multigenerational impacts cut "of Park policy."

A Holistic Understanding of the Impacts of Wood Buffalo National Park

Dene oral histories place the impacts of the Park within the wider context of colonization in Northern Alberta. The physical displacements and separations of Dënesųłiné families due to Park policy occurred within a wider historical context of drastic changes that Dene people in Northern Alberta were already facing, including the Residential School System, devastating epidemics, the influx of settlers and extreme extractive activity, the destruction of the Peace-Athabasca Delta and the many habitats it sustains (especially of fur-bearing animals) after the construction of the W.A.C. Bennett Dam in 1967, and the increasing power of the Canadian state over northern Alberta. Because ACFN members do not separate the impacts of the Park from this wider context, describing instead how other colonial processes, institutions, and policies compounded issues created by the Park, the oral histories in this chapter include excerpts that may not appear to directly pertain to WBNP's relationship with Dene people. These are indicated by subtitles like "On Residential Schools" or "On the Bennett Dam." It is important to honour this testimony because, as Chief Allan Adam puts it, "It was all part of it. Everything played into it. Residential [school] was created there to take the people off the land and everything because the government knew that land was full of resources, rich in resources—that people were living good." Chief Adam's statement suggests that the wider context of colonial eliminationism in Dene territories was directly tied up with the specific impacts of the Park. According to the oral histories, the Park was a major player in a history in which "an originally healthy and relatively affluent society ... has been colonized and disenfranchised and has been losing traditional lands" over the past 250 years.[1]

A series of influenza and smallpox epidemics from 1916–1928 devastated Dënesųłiné communities in the region. Tuberculosis also devastated the community at various times throughout the twentieth century. In some cases, entire families were lost. As one ACFN Elder explained when recalling the oral history he had learned, Elders and children were the most vulnerable to these diseases. The loss of Elders was profoundly harmful to the well-being and continuity of the community because it is the Elders who hold and pass on the language, knowledge, ways of life, and oral histories and traditions. Further, he explained, if diseases hit the residential school, many children died as well, but priests and nuns usually survived the epidemics. A strain of the Spanish flu in 1920 hit the Holy Angels residential school and also killed Chief Alexandre Laviolette at age 41 in 1921.[2] Another flu epidemic arrived in 1922, taking the lives of children, Elders, and sometimes entire families. Roughly ten percent of the population was killed by this epidemic. It is probable that Dene leaders Julien Ratfat and Sept Hezell, both of whom were active at the negotiation of Treaty 8, died from influenza.³ Another tragic flu epidemic hit Dënesųłıné families outside the Park again in 1928, leading to such population declines that Indian Affairs agents feared it would be impossible for many families to provide for themselves in advance of winter.⁴ Several Elders spoke of epidemics and mass graves when discussing the oral histories of the Park. Numerous gravesites including one in Fort Chipewyan and others near the Birch River settlements and elsewhere in the Park are physical markers of these devastating losses. As ACFN's oral histories suggest, throughout the history of the Park, the Dënesųłıné population shrank, and leadership, families, and communities were devastated by disease. The severe impacts of Park policies throughout the twentieth century only amplified the tragic situation.

Elders also spoke of the genocide caused by the Residential Schools System. Many Dene families in Northern Alberta and Saskatchewan have their own traumatic histories with residential schools, with many children forcibly taken from their homes and sent to Holy Angels Residential School in Fort Chipewyan. In 2021 and 2022, ACFN undertook ground-penetrating radar research to confirm the presence of numerous unmarked graves to which Elders and survivors have been pointing for decades. A number of Elders interviewed for this research are residential school survivors. Several shared their personal stories, while others described the experience in more general terms. Elder Ernie "Joe" Ratfat explained:

> They never asked anybody about the residential school [Holy Angels] too. They just decided to put it there. Yeah. That messed up so many families . . . And also they lost languages and our cultural ways. You know, they had a really big impact on us. I was in the residential school. We had no choice. And if we didn't go there, then our parents would be thrown in jail.

The testimony about residential schools encapsulates the devastation they wrought on families and the community at large. The loss of children and the Dënesųłıné language, the restrictions on cultural practices, the violence and abuse teachers and administrators committed against children, the deaths that often went unreported, and separations from family and land created harmful, intergenerational impacts.⁵ These were only enhanced by the Park restrictions after 1922. Displacements and treaty violations related to the Park went hand-in-hand with the trauma of residential school and epidemics.

In addition, significant economic and environmental transformations occurred in Northern Alberta from the 1920s to the 1960s; these had serious impacts on Dënesųłıné lives and livelihoods and were acutely challenging for those who were evicted from the Park. Victor Mercredi's diary described some of the impacts of these dramatic shifts in the 1960s:

> Many years have pulled by. Time passed. Old Fort Chipewyan was affected by the tide that swept past it. The fur trade has diminished. The wavies [snow geese] are leaving the place, the fishing is not as good as years ago. The old place of the H.B.Co. [Hudson's Bay Company] near the rock is abandoned. All the buildings are now worn and a store more modern was built in a situation more convenient to the people. Fort Chipewyan was the northern Indian life play[ed] out. Nowadays Crees and Chipewyans keep more around the Fort and they give up the ways of their fathers.[6]

Dene participation in the fur trade declined significantly after the Park expansion, in part due to declining fur populations, and in part due to increasingly restrictive conservation policies imposed from the 1930s onward and the establishment of the registered fur management area (RFMA or trapline) program across the Province in 1942 (discussed in Chapter 5). Dënesųłıné trappers also found themselves competing for trapping areas with an increasing number of trappers from the south, which peaked in the 1930s. Archival and oral sources alike suggest that, whereas Dënesųłıné trappers struggled to secure enough furs to feed themselves and their families, white trappers were often reported to be over-trapping to maximize profits. They used poison, destroyed Dene harvesters' traps, ignored conservation practices, and depleted fur stocks; their aggressive approach put Dënesųłıné land users at a significant disadvantage. As provincial fur supervisor J.L Grew summarized in 1945 Indigenous harvesters outside of the Park were being "crowded out." "It must be remembered," he wrote, "that these people for the past thirty or forty years and particularly in the past fifteen or twenty years, have been losing their hold over extensive trapping areas by white settlement and the intrusion of white trappers and have felt that at any time they might be crowded off their traditional hunting grounds."[7]

The influx of trapping competition also brought a wave of tensions and violence that particularly affected people who had become excluded from the Park after 1926. Newcomers aggressively protected the trapping areas they claimed within Dënesųłıné territories. For example, an extensive series of official memoranda and letters described the activities and behaviour of Grant Savage, a white harvester who moved into the Park to trap in 1926, as well as his interactions with local Indigenous harvesters. He frequently complained to the Park administration, claiming that Indigenous locals were encroaching on the trapping area he had claimed. Due to his aggressive behaviour, the administration eventually wearied of him, and Savage was banned from the Park in 1941. This forced him to move his enterprise outside the Park, where he continued harassing the Indigenous residents and harvesters who had been pushed out. Wardens and Park officials documented his behaviour. Although Savage may be an extreme example, the frustrations expressed by Dene letter-writers and leaders, and recalled in the oral histories, suggest that he was probably not the only white trapper violently oppressing Indigenous harvesters in the region during those decades.[8]

The "nail in the coffin" for the northern fur trade—indeed an environmental catastrophe with sustained impacts on life at the Peace-Athabasca Delta—was the construction of BC Hydro's WAC Bennett Dam in 1967 on the Peace River. This dam destroyed the habitats of fur-bearing animals and many other species, resulting in irreparable damage to Dene trapping economies, relations to land, and the community's health and well-being for generations afterward. Several Elders lamented the total loss of the ways of life they had grown up with. Alice Rigney's poignant discussion of the profound, intergenerational impacts of the dam is quoted at length in this chapter. Some members also mentioned their current concerns about the new Site C dam, a $16 billion project under construction about eighty kilometres downstream of the Bennett Dam on the Peace River and slated for completion in 2025. Members fear the impacts of this dam will be as bad or worse than those of the Bennett Dam and perceive it as an infringement on their Treaty Rights and a threat to the well-being of future generations.

Amidst the decline of the fur trade in the mid-twentieth century, other intense extractive activities took centre-stage in the landscape of colonialism in Dënesųłıné homelands. What Westman, Gross and Joly call "extreme extraction" has had significant impacts on the many ways that the Dene people have always related to the land and water and all life they support. State-supported extractive activity—including the extraction of bitumen, oil, sand, gravel, and minerals such as uranium as well as through commercial fishing and harvesting timber and pulp—across Indigenous territories has placed increasing pressure on Indigenous lands, waterways, and communities. Some ACFN members and Elders see extreme extraction as colonialism in its most recent guise—further restricting where and when they can safely travel and harvest and resulting in harm to the health and quality of the animals and plants that people harvest. Leslie Laviolette concluded, "the land was healthy. Now the land is polluted today." With waters warming and increased air pollution, the migratory patterns and movements of both migratory birds and river fish have shifted; fish have also become too toxic to eat.

One ACFN Elder indicated that few benefits from the extraction economy flow to Dene people: "You know, people they don't use the land very much anymore . . . we're poor, everything's polluted, and there's no water, nothing, they killed it, the government." He continues, "But there's still more, more, and more, you know, more industry, more companies, like that's what happened, we get nothing—we should get something out of it. Government's getting all the money." As the Dënesųłıné have watched their livelihoods and lands harmed by intensive industrial activities, they have also had to manage the impacts of being evicted from their homes and harvesting places within the Park since 1922. Park evictions and permitting regulations, as well as a strict system of harvesting laws, have combined with the ecologically harmful activities described above to erode Dënesųłıné connections to and sovereignty over the land and water.

Impacts of the Park

Displacement

Displaced from their homes at the Birch River/House Lake and Peace Point settlements and from other areas throughout what became the Park, such as at Moose Island, Lake Dene and Lake Mamawi, along the Birch Mountains and all the rivers identified in Treaty 8 as Dene territory, Dënesųłıné people lost the freedom to practice their deeply rooted land-based ways of living. Not only were many forced to leave their homes in the Park as a direct result of its creation and expansion (and many were refused the ability to return).

The permitting and harvesting laws also restricted access to their hereditary harvesting areas in the wider territory, including places where people harvested fish, mammals, birds, medicines, and other plants. Displacing Dene people from their homes and harvesting areas within the Park—fragmenting their wider homelands and territories—Park exclusions and the colonial land-management regime as a whole caused harm on many levels. ACFN Elders and Members' testimony shed light, for example, on erosions of Dene sovereignty and self-determination; losses of physical homes and belongings; alienations from Dene ways of life; interruptions of the intergenerational transmission of language and knowledge; losses of some members' senses of identity, pride of culture, and self-esteem; and separations of families and the fragmentation of widespread kinship networks. In turn, as the oral histories in this chapter show, Dene people have suffered at physical, emotional, mental, and spiritual levels.

One significant outcome of the displacement has been an erosion of Dene sovereignty and self-determination. The oral histories shared in Chapter 1 suggest that Dënesųłıné stewardship laws and legal orders have guided Dene ways of life and relations to the territory, as well as governed the active management of lands, waters, and wildlife for generations. After 1922, evictions from the Park, permitting and harvesting regulations, trapline arrangements, and the warden system worked together to limit and erode the community's sovereignty over a substantive portion of their homelands. As Sandlos writes, "decisions that had previously been made locally about what species to hunt and the best time of year to take particular game animals were now at least partly circumscribed by a formal legislative and regulatory framework that emanated from Ottawa."[9] Park policies and boundaries that excluded and alienated Dene people, as Joly and other scholars of WBNP describe, were part of a system intended to eliminate their legal orders from the landscape.[10] In these ways, Park policy was key to attempted erasures of Dene authority over land-based decision-making, sustainability practices, subsistence harvesting, seasonal mobility, and wildlife management.

Displacement also led to hardship. Archival and oral records demonstrate that some families removed from the Park experienced scarcity and hunger, sometimes to the point of starvation, especially from 1930s to the 1970s. In *Footprints on the Land*, Elders confirm that for those who were denied access, "the park eventually became a major contributor to hardship."[11] Hunger and economic strain became a reality that Dënesųłıné people in the

Delta, especially those who had been evicted or otherwise refused access, faced throughout the twentieth century. Steep competition for dwindling furs, restrictive game laws, and a lack of alternative economic opportunities made for challenging times for Dene people outside the Park after 1926.

Park officials largely remained obstinate, and policies remained the same. When missionaries and Indian Agents petitioned on behalf of those facing starvation, officials often dismissed their concerns. As one official flippantly claimed, "with regard to an Indian starving, the word 'starving' with the Indians here, does not necessarily mean total hunger."[12] When, in 1937, some hunters requested permission to kill one bison in the case of very serious need, they were refused because the officials believed people would start to fake "a starving condition very quickly" if given the opportunity.[13] Elders and members quoted in the oral histories in this chapter draw direct connections between the creation of the Park, and the evictions that followed it, and the severe hardship people faced. Their testimony clearly connects Park policies and exclusions with colonial elimination in the form of starvation; something that scholars of genocide and elimination in Canada argue was central to colonial politics of genocide.[14]

Furthermore, much of the oral history indicates that families and individuals who were forced to leave their homes within the Park, or who were refused access through the permitting system after 1926, lost their houses, cabins, and belongings. Some members said that their families' cabins were burned down by Parks Canada after they were forced to leave the Park. Through threats and intimidation, Parks Canada officials kept Dënesųłıné residents from returning to their physical homes in the Park after evictions. This was a reality that many other Indigenous Peoples in Canada faced throughout the history of national parks in Canada. For example, Dene oral histories about being forcibly removed from the Birch River area and leaving behind belongings—and coming back to find their cabins burned down— are strikingly similar to what happened to members of the Keeseekoowin Ojibway Nation in Manitoba during the creation of the Riding Mountain National Park in their territories.[15]

In some cases, the oral histories make direct connections between being denied freedom to move and live in the lands taken up by the Park and the physical, mental, and spiritual health and challenges that ACFN sees in the community now. Loss of access to Dene homelands not only cut harvesters off from trapping, hunting, gathering, and fishing areas within the Park that were key to Dënesųłıné lives and subsistence but also led to alienation from sacred places, areas of cultural and spiritual importance, and access to medicines.[16] Being able to gather medicines, carry out cultural practices, and access spiritual sites, as ACFN Elders explained, is fundamental to Dene relations to the land and water and is critical to health and well-being.[17] As Keltie Paul noted, "you can't put a price on that. So where do these people . . . who get thrown out [go]? Well, where would you go for that? It's like . . . it's not just a pharmacy, it's a hospital. It's a spa." Some oral testimony in this chapter demonstrates the deep significance of being cut off from the cultural and spiritual resources of the land and water within the Park.

This is only compounded by the mental, spiritual, and emotional trauma resulting from strict Park policies of exclusion and accompanying warden surveillance and policing practices. Community testimony indicates that, even today, fear and stress about entering the Park or harvesting persist, as well as feelings of landlessness, disconnection, a loss of home, sadness, and deflation. Some Elders explained that even though Dene people have been allowed to go into the Park after the laws changed in 2005, a sense of caution and trepidation persists. One ACFN Elder stated that people are still afraid to enter the Park, and they are keenly aware of ongoing surveillance as Cree residents and Parks officials watch who enters and exits the Park.

Another significant impact that is described in the oral histories has to do with the intergenerational transmission of knowledge, language, and ways of life. Elders and members explained how Park-imposed displacements and boundaries have limited the abilities of Dene people to share knowledge and to learn and grow through travelling and using the land.[18] As McCormack notes, "on-going land use is critical to the transmission of the historic stories, to understanding the relationship of these stories to specific places, and to maintaining the spiritual relationships between people and land. . . . The very government regulatory systems that alienated Chipewyans from much of their traditional territory have over time contributed to a diminished ability . . . to learn about new lands by personal experience, the most important source of this knowledge."[19] The intergenerational transmission of Dene knowledge includes the transmission of the Dënesųłıné language, which some Elders and members note was interrupted in the twentieth century as a direct result of displacements from the land. This only compounded the deliberate work of residential schools to eliminate Indigenous languages and ways of life. Park displacements and restrictions have led to alienation not just from the physical land and water, but from language, way of life and senses of identity since the continuity of these are intimately tied to relationship to homelands.

When combined with the membership transfer in 1944, the effect of the Park's displacements and restrictions on people's senses of identity is also a critical theme expressed in the oral histories. As ACFN writes, "The identity of a people is ultimately defined by their relationship to the land. . . . The core of their [the Dene people of Athabasca Chipewyan First Nation] identity and culture is still tied to their traditional use . . . and spiritual understanding of the land."[20] Relations to and knowledge of the land and water is both a key determinant of Dene health and well-being and a central part of Dene identities. Many members express the view that, being cut off from their kinship relations, homes, and territories within the Park, the community's connection with the "core of their identity and culture" has been affected. This loss has led directly to profound, intergenerational harm. ACFN social worker Lori Stevens explained that she sees this impacts in her work every day. She noted that disconnection from the teachings due to Park policy and boundaries has "huge implications" for the mental health of ACFN members to this day: "you're no longer who you are. You're no longer allowed to be what you know. So it definitely shows the mental, spiritual, emotional impacts [of] uprooting somebody." Elder Joe Ratfat's story of the impacts of landlessness on his identity poignantly summarizes how alienation from homelands, Dene ways of life, and ways of knowing the world led directly to intergenerational trauma with serious implications on individuals' and families' health and well being. In his oral history, Joe described the profound impacts of displacement on his mental health, his sense of self-esteem, and his pride in his identity and culture. He discussed his battles with alcoholism and his time being houseless as a youth and explained this was all because of the harms caused by the creation and expansion of Wood Buffalo National Park. "They really wrecked a lot of families," he concluded.

Separations of families and severance of kinship connections

Park regulations restricted and impeded Dënesųłıné connections to land and water, but also affected the family and kinship connections on which the health and resilience of the community depend. The permit system divided families between those who were allowed to stay in the Park and those without access. Even immediate relations between parents and children, siblings and spouses, were severed if one family member was denied a permit. The 1944 membership transfer extended and reinforced these separations. As such, Park policy led to "dramatic changes to community, kinship, and cultural relationships."[21] "Our families are all connected," ACFN member Lori Stevens stated, "but kind of like split up now because of the Park, right?"

Members identify several layers of harm cascading from family separations, especially emphasizing disconnections from Dënesųłıné identity that some people have experienced. Park exclusions and the 1944 membership transfer explicitly contributed to colonial attempts at what Matthew Wildcat calls "social death": the eliminationist processes that "undercut or destroy the collectivity of Indigenous Peoples" and the destruction of the "social vitality of a community that gives meaning to life."[22] He describes disruptions of social and kinship relations that have sustained Indigenous communities, like those of the Dene people of the Peace-Athabasca Delta for generations, as an enactment of eliminationism on the part of the colonial state.

Oral testimony shared in this chapter suggests that the forced identity changes and family separations resulted in deep emotional trauma. After the implementation of the 1926 permitting system and the membership transfer in 1944, some families whose lands were taken up by the Park were split in half, and many extended families experienced fragmentation. These separations happened in both a legal and physical way: on paper, Indian Agents and Parks officials kept track of family members with and without access to the Park, while wardens maintained the system whereby people were physically barred from entering the Park, even to visit family. Many ACFN members and Elders are working to reclaim their Dënesųłıné identity and address this profound impact of the membership transfer. Relatedly, some Dene families for generations after the membership transfer learned to speak Cree rather than Dënesųłıné as their first language; this created generational communication divides among community members who could speak both languages and those who could only speak one. This affected families' capacity to transmit knowledge, language, and cultural practices, especially after the prohibition on Indigenous language use in residential schools. Few fluent Dënesųłıné speakers remain in 2021 and language revitalization efforts are being keenly pursued by some Elders.

Population losses

Finally, some members and Elders note that the permitting system essentially cut the community in half in the 1930s, separating those with and without access to the Park, and then the 1944 membership transfer enshrined this separation in the treaty payroll lists. As a result, ACFN lost roughly half its recorded population. As Elder Pat Marcel related in 2013, "so, what you see here is the government being guilty for forcible removal from the Park, but also reducing our membership, by forcing our members to join the Cree band. The numbers of the Cree band, right now to the present day, I would assume that almost half are of Dene descent and are Dene members."[23]

Drastic population changes like this have social and political impacts. Some Elders concluded that the loss reduced ACFN's political weight and bargaining power in negotiations with government and industry. In part, this is because the loss of membership meant a loss of potential leaders. Elder Charlie Mercredi wrote that if it were not for the membership transfer, "ACFN membership would be bigger and we would have stronger voices in all negotiations.... Due to the loss of our members to ACFN we are a much smaller band and for that we tend to have a weaker voice and get fewer benefits from the feds."[24] He continued: "Elder William Laviolette use to say if we didn't lose that many people to MCFN he was sure that most of Birch River area would have been included in our reserve land."[25] Other members stressed that a loss of membership translates directly to reduced per-capita-based transfer payments from government for the Nation. Finally, some oral testimonies suggest that the divisions resulting from the Park boundaries and permitting systems exacerbated tensions between members of AFCN and MCFN. Some community members feel Mikisew Cree's claims to the Park were privileged over ACFN's. While members generally maintain respectful relationships, resentment remains.

In 2018, Stoney Nakoda Elders told historian Courtney Mason that exclusions from Banff National Park have had traumatic and long-term impacts, similar to those that Dene people experienced throughout the history of Wood Buffalo National Park. As one Elder said, "It cut off all the circulation that was providing us of life . . . when we lost access to the area this meant straying away from all of our roots and our physical and spiritual energy."[26] Like in the context of other Parks, the impacts of Wood Buffalo National Park's creation, expansion and management throughout the twentieth century on the Dënesųłıné are complex and multidimensional. The oral history and testimony shared below indicates that these impacts are direct and cumulative—compounded in a wider history of changes in Dënesųłıné territories after Treaty 8—and intergenerational, experienced by individuals, families and the community as a whole to this day. They touch on relations to land; Dene language, culture, and knowledge; Indigenous self-determination and sovereignty; community and family dynamics; and health and well-being. Given the diverse range of impacts discussed in the passages that follow, we have occasionally indicated specific topics using sub-headings, noting for example, when members are discussing the impacts of specific aspects of the Park's history, residential schools, or the W.A.C. Bennett Dam. The permitting system restricting movement and harvesting in the Park after 1926, the suite of strict harvesting regulations and the powerful warden system, and the 1944 band membership transfer had direct, profound impacts on Dënesųłıné people on both sides of the Park boundary. As Alice Rigney said, the community's strength, resistance, and resilience have ensured their survival throughout this history—but the impacts are still keenly felt across generations.

ORAL HISTORY

Allan Adam (2 February 2021)

But there are quite a lot of people that were affected by it—in ways where we did lose our belongings and lose our stuff. We lost a community basically, two communities: House Lake and Birch River. And those were Dene-populated, the water people. History was removed. But the legacy still lies within myself and my brother, my family. Lies with the stories that are still there. And you probably can see for yourself that just thinking of the hardship of what my granny went through still touches me, even though I wasn't there, one hundred years later. And when I tell this to my kids, my kids get very feisty and they want to fight. Because they see. And I tell them, "just leave it alone. I'll take care of it." Maybe that's my job. Maybe that's why I was given so much information. And that's why I'm still the Chief today. I'm a human being like everybody else. I'll keep on promoting that I'm a human being. I feel, I hurt, I cry, I laugh. You know, it's all part of human growth. Some had it tougher than others. Some had it better than others. You know, and I'm just grateful that the good Lord always looks after us and keeps on guiding us where we're supposed to go, and there will be closure on this one day. It might not be [in] my time but it's very close. Could be even sooner. I don't know. That's what we're working on. . . .

The impact that happened was that our people were displaced. Like I said, my granny had everything and then she struggled for a while, moved five times, five locations back until 1958. She struggled to maintain and everything, but the impacts were hard on everybody. The ones that were affected deeply. They had to move, to go places. In 1920-something, I forget what year, 1930-something, ACFN chief Jonas Laviolette wrote to Ottawa and said "I want to create reserve 201 out of Delta because our people are all over the place. We don't have no fish and everything." And it's all highlighted. It's all written in the archives. And he pleaded with the government. He said that "my people are starving because we're being encroached [on]." We got kicked out of over here and people are still coming over here. And we have no land base.

I remember now because I read that story. I read the letter that Chief Jonas sent to Ottawa and that's when they created the reserve. And it was officially mapped out I think in 1935. I've seen all the legal documents and everything and stuff like that. So it was hardship, and it was—people were just being pushed around. Ever since Wood Buffalo National Park kicked us out of the Park, out of our homeland, it just seemed like anybody else that just came along and seen our people just pushed us around.

And now you're making me mad, now I get really pumped up here because I don't like being pushed around, and I see this that's happened and what they've done in the past and how they've done it. And I'm glad that Chief Jonas Laviolette, he did what he did. And he secured our homeland. He put us back right there. And you got to remember Alexandre Laviolette, his brother, who was the former chief who died in the pandemic in 1918. Our Chief, original Chief, was buried in Edmonton with four other bodies on top of him. You know, and how do we bring them home? This happened, like it just happened. We lost our Chief in 1918, we didn't get another Chief. I forget when he [Jonas] became chief, in 1922 I think. . . . So we were without a chief for a while in that span of time when they'd taken the Park over from us. We had no representation, nothing whatsoever. A pandemic was going on. A lot of stuff were happening back in the day. No communication, nothing like we have here today.

So there was a lot of people that were impacted by it, because I still talk to all the Mikisew First Nation members who were supposed to be ACFN. They tell me that today, "you're my Chief, you're supposed to be my chief." How much of Mikisew members suffered the burden that I suffer when our people got ripped apart? My heart just got torn. I still feel it today. You know, I look at them and I feel for them and I see the hardship that they go through. You know, the struggle of being Mikisew Cree First Nation when their heart belongs to Dene. How do they feel when they walk around every day? Knowing they belong to the Mikisew Cree First Nation, but their identity tells them who they are. Their DNA tells different story.

And look at all the wealth and all the benefits that are generated over the years. It was one of the richest prime lands of hunting, trapping, and fishing. You know, everybody that lived in the Park benefited from it. But ACFN we plummeted. We lived in poverty, our people struggled.

ON RESIDENTIAL SCHOOLS

It was all part of it. Everything played into it. Residential was created there to take the people off the land and everything because the government knew that land was full of resources, rich in resources, that people were living good. The thriving people, the Dene people, were very healthy at the time.

Horace Adam (19 March 2021)

ACFN Elder Horace Adam described the implications of Park boundaries on the seasonal movements of Dene people whose traditional harvesting practices depended on access to extensive and well-known routes along the rivers that were taken up by the Park. For many who could no longer access the Park, well-known travel routes had to change, and harvesters had to go elsewhere.

Oh yes, it was hard for them. Because, the Fort Chip people, it used to be [that] there was no Park [but then] the Park's at their back door. And they can't go out the way they usually go on the west side of the river. Both sides, the west side of the Athabasca River, Peace River, and the Slave River, all those were in the park. Our people used to go all the way up, a far way to our territories, they'd go to Fort Resolution . . . then they had to go to Saskatchewan, on the west side, to go hunting moose and that. It was pretty hard for us First Nations to go.

Alec Bruno

Our people, [ACFN] members, probably felt like they didn't exist in reality. Not only did they lose their rights to their traditions and way of life, they were told to leave the area of Birch River. Trappers were the ones that had the bigger loss [if] they refuse[d] to change bands, so they had no choice but to move elsewhere. This was their home base; families were raised from one generation to another.

    I mean, mom used to cry sometimes wanting to go back there. Nothing but the things she lost. She wanted to go back and see the gravesites too, her two boys [who were buried at Birch River] and she wasn't allowed to do that. Till today I always think about it.

Jimmy Deranger (24 March 2021)

Jimmy Deranger described what he sees to be the biggest change resulting from the creation of the Park.

JD: The land use. Over the park boundary, which we had used for hundreds of years, we were no longer allowed to use that area of land. And because of that, there was some degree of scarcity on our side, regarding animals for food and the use of the resources for ourselves. When I say resource, I mean that the living resources—not the mineral resources—the living resources like the different animals and also the berries and the vegetables, the natural vegetables, and also more importantly, the medicines of the land.

PF: So, sounds like it caused pain that was felt at the time but still felt today.

JD: Yeah, there was pain at that time. And then the young generation never got to understand it. Because they were in a residential school, Holy Angels residential school, throughout the land, all the land knowledge was never given to them. Traditional land use knowledge of the resources, the living resources, were never given to them. Only in pieces. But not the full.

Dora Flett (19 March 2021)

ON RESIDENTIAL SCHOOLS AND BEING CUT OFF FROM THE LAND

I was raised up in residential school and taken from my home, my bush life, from 1946 to 1950 [from the ages of six to ten]. After that I lived in town, so I forgot my traditional ways of living off the land. I didn't know nothing about bush life—I forgot. By my 20s is when I learned how. I had lots of fun because I made lots of mistakes. I learned how to make moose hide, and dry fish and dry meat. I was learning how to make moccasins and mitts. I had lots of fun doing them. Oh, the mistakes I made making moccasins!

My husband came back from hunting on the trapline, and I said, "here's the moccasins I made for you." I gave them to him, and he put them on. The moccasins were big on him, they were just round. He just laughed at that. Then, I made him mitts with the other hide, I told him to put them on the table. The thumb of those mitts didn't go down, they just stayed sticking up.

I didn't know nothing. Then I made him a fur hat. It was supposed to cover the ears. He put it on, and it only covered his head, the ears were just sticking out. I'll freeze my ears, he said, you go to fix it, he old me. Because I didn't know nothing, I had to learn. I had lots of fun doing things though, making mistakes and then I learned after.

Garry Flett

Garry talks about a Group Trapping Area within the Park that belonged to his grandfather, Isidore Simpson, who was once a Chipewyan Band Member but was transferred to the Cree Band along with many other Simpsons in 1944 (as described in Chapter 4). Because of the rules that later excluded his mother from re-entering the Park, Garry and his siblings have never shared access to his maternal family's harvesting areas, while his cousins maintain their rights there.

The main piece that really affected me on how all this came to light was . . . all of my relatives that were in the Cree Band and the Mikisew Band were able to hunt and trap on that line, but culturally and historically that line had belonged to my grandfather. But when I went to Parks Canada to get a hunting license for [the Park], what they call the Parks hunting license, I was denied because I had no affiliation with Parks Canada. And they said, "no, maybe try becoming a member of the Métis and you could try again. But ACFN, no, you're not [allowed]." So I was bewildered by it. I knew little of the history and approached my mother, and she was livid about it. But there wasn't much we could do.

So, I spent my years—if you were going to hunt in the park, I couldn't go with you. Even if they were my first cousins. They can all go but I couldn't. And members of my family could. So yeah, that's the piece that when I said that it affected me personally, that's what it is. So, I had to stay away from there, from the Park side.

But, you know, it affects everybody uniquely I suppose. . . . I would love an apology from them to say, "I'm sorry that we denied you access to exercise your rights in the Park." My mother went to her grave being denied access to the Park and without an apology. Without doing anything wrong. She, I'm not saying that was front and center of her thinking, but I know it was. She hated the park because of it. I think it was just the alienation of the parks to members of the ACFN and where she grew up—she was unentitled to be, to have any further affiliation with that area. For that, I think that the Park missed the boat in apologizing to my mother.

I just know that she was wronged, and she went to her grave being wronged. So, not just her, if you look at others that were raised in similar situations. It's just wrong.

John Flett (18 March 2021)

Back in the day, this was twenty years ago, us ACFN, we couldn't even go to the park and hunt and anything like that. We were restricted back in the days . . . there's one place where like, you were born [but now] you can't go [to] the river and exercise your rights there. They're just taking [it] away from you—it's our land. I've been rerouted. And yet, that land up there belonged to ACFN. Yeah, and that's good, good land up there, it's high ground. That's why we should be up there.

The Park formation wasn't good. Way back in those days, the members, they wanted to go back there, and they wanted to live in the Park back then. It was our Elders and that's how they talk about it when they would sit around having coffee. They'd talk about the bush, and a lot of them, that's where they wanted to be, in the Park, back then.

Leonard Flett

I lost knowing the country that my mom was born in, Birch River and that area. I would like to go back there and look at it. Maybe camp out there. . . .

That's why you call it Indian discrimination. It's just unacceptable. They had no rights to do that, you know? Absolutely none. It's just, what they did to my mom, it's unacceptable.

Scott Flett (17 March 2021)

I heard some stories about—they had to come back into town here and go to Indian Affairs and try to get some food and stuff [after being denied access to the Park]. Some flour, I guess, and maybe, I don't know if they had meat or something to give away or some rations I guess, from the stores and stuff. That's the only thing I heard about.

[It's] like the same feeling when they get kicked out of your home or something. And you've been there for so long and then, that's your home, and then you have to go live someplace else. I guess, back in the day, it's lucky that our reserve, 201, had plentiful of rats back in the day, eh? So that, when they made that reserve there, people were forced over there, they had, especially at Jackfish, they had fishing right there. And then they had their muskrats and you're right in the Delta. . . . But they weren't allowed after, back in the Park. Even I remember back in the day, people from ACFN couldn't even go in the Park to hunt. I mean to hunt birds or anything in the spring. Or even moose hunt. And like I said, the next thing is some person comes in here and marries, or even stays with a Native girl here that belongs in the Park, they could go into [the] Park and then these other people that were born and raised in Fort Chip couldn't go. How do you—how does that make you feel? Makes you feel not so good.

How you could word that is, you know, it was always yours and then somebody else comes out and takes it away from you, but still it's yours and you're a part of it. Like it [the Park] was part of the culture and part of the traditional harvesting areas that you could use.

ON EPIDEMICS

My grandfather was born in 1899 and he ... got enlisted to join the army ... him and that other guy, John Gladue, I think his name is, enlisted in the army, the barracks or something in Edmonton. And they were like going for training and stuff then the next thing the war was over, eh? In 1918. So they came back through Fort McMurray by train or something and sit around McMurray. I think they got the flu there. I think they were kind of sick or something and they were wrapped up with something, with this Hudson Bay blankets and stuff and they finally made it back to Chip. But that's when the flu, well like it came after, that's why they call it the Spanish Flu ... because it came mostly from the war veterans, eh? Brought it in from, well they came back from fighting in Europe.

But he came here and then, he used to bury like at least, the cemetery just behind the northern ridge over there. They have, you know, sometimes there's six or eight people buried in one grave because he couldn't dig fast, dig it right fast enough when the ground is frozen, eh. No backhoe back then, eh. They had to dig a hole ... burn the wood and thaw it out and dig it down and burn again. Like it takes, a long process to make a grave, eh? Yeah. There's so many dead there and then like six people in one grave so when the spring came along, summer came along, you smell the stench of the decaying people, eh? But they said that in Birch River, like somebody went over the Birch River and they, I guess this cleaned out the whole community that was there.

Fred "Jumbo" Fraser (12 March 2021)

When the Park kicked them out, they [the Dene people who were kicked out] just said "to hell with you" and they went. You know, never even bothered trying to come back in because I just don't know of anybody that tried.

Leslie Laviolette (22 March 2021)

It's all bush and different country that you see and you know, you can start on the east side of the lake [Athabasca] and end up at the west side in the Park. Like we used to travel. And all that was taken away. Once the Park came up, that was shut down for us. And then we moved to Richardson area, Jackfish Lake area, Old Fort area. And then we had Point Brulé and Poplar Point. We had those areas that we could go and harvest whenever we wanted. As long as you were on the reserve back then. If you are off the reserve, you had to watch because if it wasn't Fish and Wildlife, it was Parks down on your back. . . .

And even to get into the Park back in the day, you couldn't. You had to go through the paperwork and everything. And it was a certain group that didn't want us in there. They kept avoiding our application. There was a lot of rules and regulations that we had to learn and how to get around all this stuff to get our food. We shouldn't have had to hide or sneak around corners to get our food.

Now we're just in the corner now. And the government made more profit off our land than we did. We're still struggling today, and the Park doesn't want to acknowledge that, that they did wrong to us because compensation-wise they would have to pay lots . . . whenever they admit it, that they did wrong to us.

ON RESIDENTIAL SCHOOLS

They said that if we didn't come out of Jackfish or out of the bush, the cops are gonna come there and get all of us kids and put us in jail. So the parents right away, "well okay, go on to the mission." And when you got in the mission, man, you got a bunch of abuse there. From the father that's supposed to be working for God and the nuns giving you a lickins and abusing you. That's all we had to learn, cause we didn't talk then.

I went home and told my parents what was happening in school. [They responded] "oh those are God's people, don't talk like that, it's not nice." And I said, "why, why are they allowed to do this then?" That's why I keep saying like . . . I've seen some nuns there and the priest and I thought man you know, if I had a big stick right now, boy I'll give you guys a good lickin, just to give you that licking that you gave me. You know, show them how it feels. But then right away, a little light went off and "no, don't do that. Forgive and forget." But I still have to hold the pain.

I went, and my grandpa is the one that got me out. I just went through the door. I just made it through the door and two of my buddies were ahead of me and they had long hair too like me and all of a sudden they come out around the curtain and they're bald. Then it was my turn and all of a sudden, somebody tapped me and I turned back and my grandpa right there, he said they could take me home, they could look after me he said, so let's go. "You don't belong here," he said. But I ended up in day school for ten years. And went through all the abuse. Or had the priests and the brother abusing you and the two school teachers. Two male school teachers, and that still haunts me today. That's why I say today, now when I'm around kids, it's like, kids are gonna get whatever they want because I didn't have it. And I went through the abuse part. And it took me just about forty years just to talk about it. I could talk about it now. Before I couldn't—it was something that made me cry.

Big John Marcel

Well, as far as I know, when Parks took over [is] when everybody had to get out of there. If you don't belong to the Park, they were burning houses and everything as far as I know. Parks did that.

ON EPIDEMICS

Big John and many other Elders shared stories passed down to them by their relatives who worked as gravediggers during the epidemics in the first two decades of the twentieth century. Many of these stories emphasize how emotionally and physically traumatic it was for gravediggers to face the number of casualties they did on a daily basis. In many cases, they resorted to digging mass graves. ACFN has recently commissioned archaeologists to identify these graves in their territories.

My grandfather was telling me when I was young when that flu came around, he said, people were just passing out. One time he said, there were seven boats [carrying] people they brought to Chip that had passed away and that they were buried there. And, in one spot he said, "my boy," he said, you know what he said? "There were seven people [who had died in one day], they couldn't keep up with it, so they have this one big spot. They put several people in there."

Charlie Mercredi (n.d.)

I do feel the loss of membership to MCFN had a big impact on our membership. Elder William Laviolette used to say if we didn't lose that many people to MCFN he was sure that most of Birch River area would have been included in our reserve land.

If WBNP was not created, many of these people would still have access to their traditional land. Because of WBNP, these people were denied access to their homeland. This to me is not right, people should come first before the bison.

Marie Josephine Mercredi (1998)

It would be better to live like old times, live off the lake—the land. The children used to listen to you. We used to all pray before bed. If things were the same, my children might have been still alive—better off.

Keltie Paul (25 November 2020)

I think identity is our core. I think that they [the government] sold their [ACFN's] identity [through the membership transfer and the displacement], and they made them assume another identity. It messes up with everybody's identity. "Who am I really? Who am I?" People spend their whole life trying to answer these questions that become a psychological problem, because people who lose their identities lose their footing, their space, their reasoning sometimes. Identity is our core. And when you just pick up and steal somebody's identity and then force them to live like somebody else, it's going to cause all kinds of psychological problems, networking problems, problems within families. . . . You become something you're not and then somebody says, "Well, if you're not this, I'm going to disown you." I mean, that's a horrible thing to happen.

ON RESIDENTIAL SCHOOLS

Well, they moved a lot of people out of different areas in the Park when the public schools came into existence. And one of the tactics that DIAND [Department of Indian and Northern Affairs] and other people used, was to threaten to withhold the family allowance. And the family allowance, I think came in '48? Am I right on that? It was around that time, I know it was post-war, and the family allowance came in, and it was a godsend for people. You gotta realize they have big families, and then they got family allowance. So, they really had a stake, that they could use that money for food, for the nutrition for the family. And to be threatened with having [that taken away], I mean, nowhere else in Alberta were people threatened to have their family allowance taken. My parents were living out on a farm, we never got threatened with something stupid like that.

And yet, they threatened to take this monthly allotment away from them if they didn't move into Fort Chip or Garden River, because they wanted kids to be educated [assimilated into the colonial system]. So, a lot of people came in off the trapline. That doesn't mean they didn't go out; they did go out in winter, and sometimes, that they had to have like a residence in town in order to be counted for the public school, enumerated for the public school. So that was going on at that time. . . . So, it's just one thing after another that they're trying to use to get people to sedentarism. Because they believed that sedentism is, quote, "civilizing the savage"—those are in air quotes. And that's what they were trying to do even up into the '60s and '70s.

Ernie "Joe" Ratfat (19 March 2021)

Joe Ratfat's family's experience with the 1944 band membership transfer is described in Chapter 4. The harmful impacts of the transfer also combined with the intergenerational trauma of residential school that took Joe away from his family and homelands for his adolescent and adult life. His story is a clear example of the ways that park displacements and the forced membership transfer worked together with other colonial institutions and residential schools to alienate people from their lands and families, disconnecting them from their lives, histories, and homelands. A portion of this interview is available online as a digital audio recording.[27]

SCAN TO LISTEN

I've lost a lot of things. As far as my pride and things like that. I didn't know who I was, I couldn't speak Cree and I was supposed to be a Cree member. And I was too brown to be white. So, I didn't fit in anywheres, you know. I ended up on the street, you know, like —alcoholism. Through alcoholism, like I said, a lot of my family members passed away from alcoholism. I'm the only one left now in my family. Everybody else has gone and they all had a really rough death of alcohol.

So I looked at different areas to look after myself, to forget alcohol and drugs and other things. And, through Sweat Lodges and other ceremonies that I ran across when I was out—I've never heard of before in our hometown [St. Paul, Alberta, where Joe was sent for school as a youth]—that's how I got a sense of pride So, that's where I'm at right now, and even my marriage broke up because of alcoholism. And that's all coming from being displaced. Yeah, going back and being displaced, and having—don't know who you are. It's all from that. And those people should pay for it. Those people should do something about it because they really wrecked a lot of families. . . .

And myself, I had no land base. It really hurt. It hurts me. It does hurt.

ON RESIDENTIAL SCHOOLS

Yeah, they never asked anybody about the residential school too. They just decided to put it there. That messed up so many families. . . . And also they lost languages and our cultural ways. You know, like they had a really big impact on us. I was in the residential school. We had no choice. And if we didn't go there, then our parents would be thrown in jail.

Alice Rigney (16 and 17 March 2021)

A portion of Alice Rigney's interview is available as a digital audio recording online.[28]

Well, one thing that happened because of the dislocation and being evicted is loss of trust, once again. And maybe it wasn't, you know, our Elders were not so verbal in those days. Because my granny did not speak any English at all. She never had any formal education. Her education was on the land. She was very good. She was a very excellent land user . . . but they lost trust [in] the white people again.

ON THE W.A.C. BENNETT DAM

A portion of Alice Rigney's interview is available as a digital audio recording online.[29]

The Bennett Dam was a curse to our land, to our people. I mean by them taking our water at this end and flooding it by the man-made lake and other side of the Bennett Dam, where they totally destroyed Aboriginal homes—you know graveyards. I mean, that was all, I think they were given like forty-eight hours to move out. I mean, I talk about power of the Europeans. I don't know what else to [call] it, but you know, for them to write a letter to us saying that our Delta would not be affected, makes us feel—my Uncle Fred [Marcel, a member of leadership at the time the dam was built] believed them. And we saw the results almost right away. The lake here has dropped at least three meters. And this is the lake, and so the Delta, which depends on the floods, not every year, but every other year. So, we would get a flood that would replenish the

Delta, the snyes, and inland lake. You know, so the muskrats and beavers were plentiful. And that was all taken away. The water dried out, the lakes dried out, and my dad saw that. Not only my dad, most of the people here who are land users noticed that.

Because, in the early '70s we were swamped with scientists that came to check, they called it the Delta project. And we had scientists doing fish count and duck count and all kinds of samples of what was happening to our land as the water dropped. The reports are someplace out there. We've been interviewed to death about the death of our Delta, there've been documentaries made about it, stories told about it. And this was before the influx of the tar sands. So our water from the Peace River was held back by the Bennett Dam, which did damage to the farmers there. With no consideration because they saw the water as a way—[as a] resource....

And you know, issues like the Bennett Dam was just another tactic that they used—that our say was not worth anything. So, the Bennett Dam did a lot of damage. That was just like the resources. But when you think about the people that were affected, the families that were affected by a loss of a way of life, where trapping was taken away from them, they had to move off the land. Well, they were more or less forced to move off the land and into the community. And idle hands turn to the wrong things—alcohol and that.

And many of those trappers were the best. We used to call them the riflemen and because they were such sharpshooters. Their families were well off, living off the land. And then to have that taken away and forced to move into matchbox houses, and our way of life that was on the land diminished over time. People start eating less and less traditional foods and going with fast foods. Of course diabetes is on the rise. We have a community of 1200, [and] I think we have about 200 diabetic people. And so, I mean a lot of children do not want to eat the food from the land, they prefer chicken nuggets and fries and stuff like that.

So, the impact of the Bennett Dam is not just the loss of the water, it's all that and more that happened after the fact, when you think about it, and it's still ongoing. It's getting to the point—last summer we had lots of water, we all got flooded out you know, which is an unusual year. There was a lot of snow runoff in the mountains. I have a home in the Delta and my clearing where my husband and I had our tourist campus totally destroyed. And I mean, I'm a widow now and so I'm not going back to move there. I'm just going to move out, but everyone that had a cabin out in the land in Wood

Buffalo National Park, we were all flooded out. I was not flooded out as bad as those in the Park because they built on flat ground and so they were—their homes—they had water in the houses. So you have all those things from the Bennett Dam. . . . And so, the Bennett Dam changed our way of life here. Took away our resources, created a lot of social problems for many families, a lot of alcohol related deaths, alcoholism on the rise, and drug use now. . . .

It's just, everything has changed because we have our water taken away from us. But last summer, we had high water, I mean we talk about global warming. This is the winter that the lake never fully froze. It's open. Right now, I can see open water and usually we don't have open water until probably the end of April. I remember when they were first building it [the dam], my husband and friend and I always talked about how we knew—we were quite young—but we knew what was going to happen, because we could see it happening.

I was a social worker, I dealt with a lot of the issues that came out of all the damages done by the Bennett Dam, by the family breakdowns. You know, the trappers having to sell their snowmobiles, their boats, their guns, their traps, you know, for alcohol. And now a lot of them, now the new trapline is the oilsands [where people now go to make an income].

ON OILSANDS EXTRACTION

I'm an environmentalist. I strictly oppose the dirty oilsands. It hurts to see what they're doing. It's a destruction. It's not a blessing. I live at Jackfish. I'm still a land-user. I'm seventy years old. My son is buried there. It holds dear to me. But the changes I've seen of the land really hurts. But every day is a blessing—that is how I see it.

Mary "Cookie" Simpson (11 March 2021)

They were robbed of their land, they were robbed. Robbed of their traditional land. And for many years, they couldn't even come to the Park because only Cree Band hunters and trappers were allowed to hunt in the Park, right? Allowed to have their trapline in the Park. And so, the Chipewyan lost out on that, they lost out in going into the Park.

ON RESIDENTIAL SCHOOLS

They said that everybody had to put their children in. They had to move to Fort Chipewyan so their children can go to school. They had a residential school there. And then if you didn't put your child in residential school, because education was the law, then you'd end up in jail as long as your kids were not in school. And then they would come and throw you in. And take your kid anyway. There was so many wrongs.

And then my dad said he had a brother named Marvin. And they all had to go to residential school. There was about four or five of them that had to go to residential school. All of a sudden, my dad said, they took Marvin, and then they never seen him ever again. And then when my mushum, my grandpa, went to pick his kids up, Marvin was missing. They said that he died of influenza.

There was a lot of impact on everybody. Because all of a sudden now you had to move to Fort Chip because your children had to go to school, right? So you weren't in the bush too often. And then, you kind of lost your children, I suppose. Because they were all now in residential school, otherwise, you'd go to jail. So that was a big impact on the people. And then when your children were in residential school, then they couldn't speak their language. So they'd go home and you'd try speaking Dene to them and then of course, they wouldn't understand you because they had to block it in order for them to survive it in residential school. They'd have to block their own language. And so, it had a big impact on the families.

Lori Stevens (25 May 2021)

Portions of Lori Steven's interview are available as a digital audio recording online.[30]

SCAN TO LISTEN

ON THE MEMBERSHIP TRANSFER

LS: Just how, you know, mixed up people are because like Cree and Dene are two completely different people with different values, different family systems. . . . And then you're switching these families into different family structures. So those roles are different. So where does that leave those people? What does it look like for traditions and medicines, prayer, spirituality? We are not the same and a lot of the Elders they'll tell me, you know—ribbon skirts, like everybody's buying ribbon skirts and everybody wants it. And the first thing they tell us is, "you can get that, you can show it for your ceremony, but that's not our way." I'm constantly hearing, "that's not our way. That's not our way." And then it's like, well, jeepers, what is our way? Because it feels like this *is* our way, but in my opinion, it's because of that transition of some of those Dene people going to Cree. Because now they're muddled, and they're passing on those traditions. And saying, "this is our way," but in reality, you know, 100 to 150 years ago, it wasn't our way. So, that's what I hear the most about is, "that's not our way. That's not our way. That's not our way."

ST: So it's impacting on people's identities, really, and how they're understanding... culture and their heritage?

LS: Yeah, and our drumming. Our prayers, when we're giving thanks to the land, we do it differently. Medicines. So a big one that an Elder told me is... skunk pee? I don't know if you've ever heard of skunk pee. She was like, "we don't use that. Everybody's using it. But that's not our medicine." And I'm like, oh, thank gosh, because I'd never want to drink it. But little things that are popping up and then it's like, well, jeepers, what is our identity? Okay, we don't Pow Wow but we Tea Dance, and what are the dances for the Tea Dance? Who knows these tea dances because all we're seeing is Pow Wow right? So, the jingle and the fancy [dances], and that's not us. So, it's kind of like well, what is us? What is the Dene people of Fort Chip? Because it feels like we're just so muddled, for lack of a better word.

ST: Have you heard about any connection between the loss of language speakers as well because of the transfer? The loss of Dene-language speakers?

LS: Yes, for sure. Because now you have all these individuals who have to identify as Crees, so they're all speaking Cree. So they're not passing down Dene. They were passing down Cree. And like a lot of those Indian Agents, they all spoke Cree because Dene is a hard language to learn, right? So more people were going with Cree than actually our Dene language. Yeah, there's not a lot at all, especially with what it would have been like in our dialect. Because, if you go to Janvier [a small rural community 123 kilometres south of Fort McMurray], they speak real fast and nasally and they can understand each other, but somebody else speaking Dene, trying to understand what they are saying, they have to slow it down. And then when you talk to the Dene in the Dene-Zaa area[31], they're slow [speakers]. I did some training with them and when they were speaking, I was like, "oh, my, I could probably learn from you because you're speaking so slow that I can probably pick it up now, right?" And so, it's kind of, what was it [the dialect of Dene spoken] here? We don't have that many people. We also have Elders who spoke it but didn't pass it down because they married somebody who was Cree. So, if you were a female, you went to Cree Band [i.e. because they married a Cree man]. So, they passed on that Cree language versus that Dene language. So, there's not many—I can only think of a handful of people who actually speak it. My adopted dad does speak it, and he's from Fort Fitzgerald. So, he can speak it, but he doesn't pass it on. And there's shame in that too from him, right? Like, when we're like, "oh, teach us," he's not about to, but when it relates to this, I don't have anybody in my family close to me—I have cousins who are relearning it, but I don't have any Elder who speaks it.

ON DISPLACEMENT

Well, from then, [some members of the community] probably didn't even realize [the displacement was happening] because of the different types of—we didn't have that type of ownership, right? They probably didn't understand at all that you would not allow us to come back to where this really good hunting ground is. "You're trying to starve me" is basically probably what was going through their heads, and then also trying to relocate their families. So, these are a lot of families who had multiple children. What did that look like for them to move? And did they even know where to move? Like we hear stories of the Métis and Big Point and Alexandre Laviolette giving space on ACFN land to the Métis because they were like "where do we go?" And so, it was probably the exact same thing. So that's why you would see a lot . . . of the families just outside of the Park and trying to stay close to those better hunting grounds that were in the Park without stepping on that boundary.

And now, there's just this unsung rule of, you don't pass that [Park] boundary. Don't really know why, or there's not given much of a definition as to why you can't, it's just, "you're Chip Band and so you don't get to go there." Basically, you don't get to hunt there. You don't get to have your traveling there. Just that boundary has just hindered that cultural aspect of the trapping and the fishing and of that migration of following the animals. And then culturally, like I did [already] say, you're going from one identified person of Dene to now Cree, which is completely different. Different way of talking, different way of knowing. Just because everybody is Indigenous does not mean that they are the same. . . . And like, did that contribute to so many Dene people getting sick with the flu and that, because they did not have access to the wildlife or the hunting grounds that they knew? So, they had to go and try and figure out where to hunt now. So, there's most likely a correlation as to why so many Dene people were sick and when they were forced out. . . .

With respect to their identity, we see a lot of addictions, mental health, trauma from just identity—where do I belong? So a lot of people will speak of it, like with CFS [Children & Family Services], like these people don't know where they belong. Well, that could be incorporated for being pushed out of your homes and your traditional hunting areas, just the same. Like you're no longer who you are. You're no longer allowed to be what you know. So it definitely shows the mental, spiritual, emotional impacts that uprooting somebody [has]. And not only for some people who chose not to become Cree, uprooting them and changing everything about them.

But also, for those who now have to identify as a completely different person. That's like me going and saying "I now identify as Australian" or something, right? It's completely different. So, they'd have probably a lot of stress, of one minute I'm this, next minute I'm not. So, I've definitely seen it. And you can see it in the compounding issues of what we see today with mental health issues or addiction issues, people just don't know where they belong. And this definitely plays into it.

ON EPIDEMICS

Growing up, I remember the mass graves in Jackfish for the children who passed away from the Spanish flu, and my uncle, Charlie Voyageur, who's passed, he was telling us about how the kids were just all dying, and that it was mostly the Dene who had passed. It wiped out a big population in Fort Chip. And they talked about there was like, big strong men that at the beginning of the day would seem like they were okay and by the end of the day, they were dying. Ones who were like helping to dig these graves and stuff like that, didn't show any signs and by the end of the day, they had the flu, and . . . the next day they were gone, is what they were saying. It just hit them fast. And these were, according to Uncle, strong, young, healthy people, right? . . . I just remember we went to go clean the graveyards and there was lots of like the last name Laviolette . . . and then there was like these big, long fenced off mass graves. And then there's multiple little kids in there. And then, they died so quickly that they had to put the fence up.

Beverly Tourangeau (21 March 2021)

Well, a lot more people moved into town. You can't really just go out there just hunting, whatever, because everything was just kind of drying up . . . their traditional way of life. They had to come into town and there was no more like trapping and all that. Because the Delta and that was all drying up. So, all—like where do you go for all the fur-bearing animals? Can't trap, so people just went different places to go look for work. . . .

Well, it's kind of like, my sense, the way I felt was we didn't belong there. You know? So it's kind of like, there's separation even though some people are getting married Cree. They're slowly—that separation between ACFN and MCFN, there's still that separation.

Edouard Trippe de Roche (25 November 2021)

I just know one incident where this woman was married to this guy and they were trapping in the Park. Her husband died, so she remarried another guy who trapped at the Athabasca Lake, and she went back to retrieve her belongings. They both went over there, and her cabin was burnt. I guess her marrying somebody that's trapping out in the Park didn't sit too well with the Park wardens or the Park guards or whatever you want to call them.

Leslie Wiltzen (21 January 2021)

Well, I think, you know, always the big part [is] the people being disconnected from the land. That's a big thing, right? Because I mean, like I said when I go back to the words of Treaty [8], where it says "the Athabasca, the Chipewyan people, the Athabasca, the Birch River, the Peace River, Slave River, Gull River," those are all territories that were once ACFN members,' right? That's where they always— that was their homeland. Now imagine being taken away from your homeland and forced to go outside. Long ago in—when you go back to the 1920s—getting around wasn't an easy thing. Most people traveled by canoes. You know, fast machines weren't around. Fast boats weren't around like today. I mean today, you can go from Fort Smith, Fort Chip, in one day—four hours. Just going from Fort McMurray to Fort Chipewyan. But you know, if you go on a map, and you start looking at the size of Lake Claire and you start looking at [the] size of Lake Mamawi and that traditional territory now, when you're familiar with an area where to go hunting, you know how long it takes to get there. You know how many days you need to get there, how many days you need to get back. You know how many days you need to hunt. So by removing ACFN members, you force them to learn a whole new area of the Park that traditionally [they knew] . . . But to force everybody to relearn things like that, that's a hardship.

And you know, that's one of the hardships but for me, enduring being disconnected from the land. That's a big thing. It's hard to describe. And it's hard to say how you've been affected because you're affected—you're affected. I mean, all your life, you grew up knowing that you're not allowed in a certain area where traditionally, for thousands of years, the generations before you lived there, then all of a sudden now you're not allowed. And people tell you you're not allowed there and then you become a criminal by even thinking about it. So now I mean, so how do you put—how do you describe that in words? How do you justify something like that? I don't know. It's a good question.

Anonymous ACFN Elder (16 March 2021)

ON THE W.A.C. BENNETT DAM

Elder: Oh, that's a big one, that one there. Put it this way: at that time, us Indians, when I was young, we set up a garden at Jackfish Lake, okay, we had potatoes growing. We had the whole field full of potatoes and it was waiting for growing. Then we come back to Chip on Friday, Saturday, we went back Monday, and it was covered with water. The Bennett Dam said nothing of reopening the water. So we come back Sunday night, and it was covered with water. All that work for nothing.

ST: You lost everything?

Elder: Yes, we lost everything. They never said a word to nobody. I mean, we didn't know, eh? So we put our guts into that garden because we were going to start a five-acre farm in those days. So we lost everything.

Conclusion: t'ąt'ú erihtł'ís hóhlį eyi bet'á dene néné chu tu ghą k'óílde ha dúé

Much of the history of Wood Buffalo National Park has been driven by outsiders vying for control over Dene homelands—people who held the firm belief that their management plans were in the best interests of the land, water, animals, the Dominion, and, at times, the planet. The sentiments at the heart of Maxwell Graham's 1912 proclamation that creating a human-free bison sanctuary was in the interest of the "entire civilized world" have carried weight even today.[1] As the oral testimonies shared in this book demonstrate, such perspectives have almost always resulted in systemic exclusions and harm to Dene people who since time immemorial have stewarded the territories the Park takes up.

Federal management practices of this and other national parks shifted in the second half of the twentieth century, and provincial and international authorities advanced their own concerns about the Park. However, ACFN members have experienced what appear to be changing (and sometimes competing) layers of management of their homelands as a continuities in the longer history of exclusion and displacement of which WBNP has always played a central role. One ACFN Elder summarized the community's frustration with this: "Like now, I'm baffled: who's the Park? And how come they got to own Dene Nation land? And this control? And they're in control, I'll tell you that much." Likewise, the Dënesųłiné title for this chapter translates to "the way that laws (papers) were made, because of that we cannot manage Dene lands and water." From many directions over time, external entities have imposed their intentions and desires for the Park, resulting in erosions of Dene self-determination and of disconnections from Dene homelands and ways of life. This has also coincided with ongoing refusals of Dene knowledge and experiences—something this book, and the research that preceded it, has actively aimed to address.

Shifts in Park management and co-management arrangements

In the early 1960s, the Park's administrative structure was transformed. Until then, it had been largely administered by the Northern Affairs arm of the Department of Indian Affairs and Northern Development. From 1964 to 1969, however, full administrative responsibility for the Park was gradually transferred to the National and Historic Parks Branch. McCormack explains that after decades of intense government interference, the Park management policy shifted once again to embrace an ethos of "non-interference, allowing natural processes to proceed unhindered."[2] That non-interference approach was not new—it was simply another iteration in the ongoing program of state control over Dënesųłiné territories.

In a 1963 memorandum to cabinet, Minister of Northern Affairs and National Resources Walter Dinsdale wrote that "the management of this last great buffalo herd—which must be regarded as a national responsibility—requires [Federal] control of the land over which they range."[3] Dinsdale was responding with hesitation to formal requests from Alberta ministers to "return" the land within the Park to the Province, transferring to the Province control over resource management, including development and extraction, in the significant land mass taken up by WBNP. Alberta Minister of Lands and Forests, Norman Willmore, had proposed in 1962 that the status of the Park be changed to a provincially managed buffalo conservation area "which would recognize the multiple use principle in resource development and exploitation."[4] Willmore's recommendation and Dinsdale's response reflect one of the many ways that outsider perspectives on and interests in lands and resources in Dene territories—whether to exploit or conserve them—have almost always taken priority over Dënesųłiné people's knowledge, concerns, and interests by excluding, dismissing, or silencing them.

Only two decades after the province's request was denied, Park administrators introduced the concept of co-management. This concept had first appeared in the 1984 Wood Buffalo National Park Management Plan, the Park's first long-range management plan, a result of efforts to conform WBNP policy and management with management structures common across other national parks. A Northern Buffalo Management Board was established in 1991, conceived as a multi-stakeholder committee for community-based planning, and it included nine local Indigenous representatives. This management plan, however, was never approved. The Park's management plans have since been revised several times since 1984. The 2010 WBNP Management Plan incorporates commitments to reconciliation and co-management with Indigenous communities and other stakeholders in the area. Parks officials meet annually through a cooperative management board that includes representatives from ACFN and all other local Indigenous communities and governments with ties to the Park.[5] In 2014, the Committee for Cooperative Management of Wood Buffalo National Park (CMC) was formed to align with the 2010 Management Plan and provide space for dialogue and information sharing between Parks Canada and Indigenous communities with claims to the Park. The 2010 Plan indicates a commitment of the Park to collaboratively revise game regulations and work toward resolution of various park-related issues through more Indigenous engagement. It states, "efforts are underway to expand working relationships given the impact of the park on the region and there is great potential to coordinate park activities with neighbouring provincial, territorial and Aboriginal governments."[6] As Parks has moved toward co-management arrangements and commitments to reconciliation, they have invited ACFN representatives to the co-management table.

ACFN members contend that recent co-management arrangements do not adequately acknowledge or address their unique experiences or the history of displacements, exclusions, and elimination over the past one hundred years. Since 2005, the Park has conceded that all members of Treaty 8 Nations have the right to enter and hunt in the Park, but feelings of disconnection and experiences of exclusion remain for many ACFN members. Despite stated intentions of collaboration and reconciliation, community members' oral testimony suggests the new co-management regime continues to push Dene concerns to the sidelines. Government officials continue to make decisions that affect Dene harvesters, and this style of management has, as East puts it, "fostered a climate of distrust and cynicism which continues to this day."[7]

Leslie Wiltzen, who has been involved in co-management and advisory roles for many years, described his experience:

> The federal government did what they wanted to do. Right from the get-go. And you know what, even today I'm heavily involved with the events of Wood Buffalo National Park. I represent ACFN on anything that has to do with the UNESCO recommendations. I mean, whether it be with, where we're dealing

with hydrology . . . and science and monitoring, or cooperative management committees.

I still get discouraged. I am discouraged with the federal government's inability to adjust, to accommodate what First Nations wish for. All we want is an opportunity to sit equally at a table and to have input that will benefit our people in a proper way. But time and time again, the federal government has an ability to overlook that and do exactly what they want, even though we can be sitting at the table.

He continued:

> I'll tell you a good example . . . I sit on the Cooperative Management Committee of Wood Buffalo National Park. That committee is made up of eleven First Nations that utilize Wood Buffalo National Park, right? So it's the Mikisew Cree, [ACFN], Métis from Fort Chip, you have the Little Red First Nation from Garden River, you have Smith Landing, Salt River, the Métis from Fort Smith, you have the K'atl'odeeche and so on, so forth from Fort Res[olution] to Hay river.
>
> So, at this table now, for years we've been talking about trying to implement something in Wood Buffalo National Park from an employment perspective [that] would benefit and hire local [Indigenous people] . . . We aimed for years on entry level jobs with Wood Buffalo National Park, to a place where local Indigenous people, whether it be from Fort Chip, Fort Smith, Garden River, Hay River, Fort Res, it doesn't matter, as long as their traditional territory's in the Park, they'd have a first chance at these entry-level jobs.
>
> Do you know what? Time and time again we told that to Parks. And they say 'yes and yes, yes.' It's so hard. It's like pulling teeth. It's just a process that they say yes, turn around and say one thing and the next day turn around and do another and you say, 'why did you just do that? Why did we just all discuss this whole thing and agree to do this, and you turn around and do this?' So . . . when they negotiated Treaty in 1899. Again, same thing, you sign one agreement, and then fifteen years later, you'll

[the government will] say, 'nope, sorry. Even though we faithfully negotiated this treaty and we agreed on these terms, but now they're no good. Get out of the Park' ... I mean, we say we want local employment, but you know, they'll bring in people from southern Canada and eastern Canada to fill these entry level jobs. Why? Because they do what they want to do, when they want to do it, and to whom they want to do it.

As Leslie's testimony demonstrates, co-management and reconciliation talk can conceal broken promises, a general lack of interest to address Indigenous communities' desires and concerns especially when they do not align with state priorities, and the ultimate reality that the state continues to control land management in Dene territories.

Leslie's uncle, Elder Pat Marcel, shared this perspective 2013:

I've been trying to push co-management, from way back. From about 2000 and on, I've been working with the Alberta government, and I've been denied and told that, "We will never agree to co-management with any band."

So I said, "How can we survive?"

And they said that we have reserves. But that reserve is so small, there is no way we can survive with that many membership. The government had us in a really bad place. They know that there is nothing that we can do. They are the law ...

But what my dad taught me, many years ago, I have never forgot, because he was pushing on that. And because of my demands, they have come to know that what I am saying is true ... My grandfather and my father must have known why they kept harping on this story ... That is what it was: "Co-management." That's the memory of what made me remember this [1935] Agreement. All of my lifetime, I have a story in my head that I have never forgotten. I can talk about a meeting that happened twenty years ago and I have never forgotten. That is what oral history is about. I never take notes because this is how I have learnt. This all comes from Chief Alexandre Laviolette and was passed onto his brother, Jonas, who was my grandfather.

Pat Marcel worked extensively as an Elder and Indigenous Knowledge Holder with governments, industry, and Western scientists to co-monitor wildlife health and assess impacts of extractive industry on animals and their habitats. He described two monitoring programs for woodland caribou and the bison herds in the 2013 passage that follows. He noted that non-Indigenous authorities rarely took his knowledge seriously, as has been the case in many other parks. He explained:

> If you want our cooperation, work with us. We will help you collar the animals and track them. But when professors come from Calgary and don't understand the animals in our traditional territories, they don't understand what they see. Moose is not like caribou. I have seen moose in the spring of the year when they have all these ticks; some of them have no hair on their bodies, and it is actually bleeding where the collar is. They never ask the Elders what is happening. They suffer enough without having collars on them. I would also not agree to collaring the bison. My belief is that the bison is there, across from Poplar Point, are the true wood buffalo that have to be protected, because they are endangered.
>
> And these oil companies, their whole plan: they have to come through us. Teck [Resources, Ltd.][8] was hoping the whole herd [of Wood Buffalo outside of the Park] was diseased and they commissioned the study but they [the buffalo] came back healthy, just like I saw. We got to a discussion of numbers of possibly diseased. And I told the story of way back, we tested 198 and only 3 were diseased, way back in the 1960s. The [Ronald Lake] bison herd never had contact with Wood Buffalo [National Park Bison], and they are disease free. I told him I'll make him a bet. He said no bets. So I told him to take me with them, and they moved their kill zone closer to Wood Buffalo, but they ended up not getting anything. I explained to them that "when you see this herd here, when you see the bulls, you will see that they don't look nothing like the bulls around Fort Chip."[9]

Pat Marcel concluded that in interactions with Western scientists, government officials, impact assessors, and industry managers, Dene knowledge is often overlooked and silenced. During his leadership, Elder Marcel urged governments to consider a more empowering relationship "because the Dënesųłıné have always had the responsibility of living in balance with the natural environment, and there is much that both provincial and federal environmental resource managers can learn from them if they take the time to listen."[10] He was consistently ignored by Parks Canada administration, and co-management activities have rarely taken Dene leadership seriously.

Members of ACFN suggest that the new co-management and reconciliation agendas must do more to acknowledge and amend the past and work toward genuine, transformative efforts that centre Indigenous governance and self-determination. There are meaningful collaborative and Indigenous-led initiatives that could provide guidance for shifting the engagement model that has been in use until now. For example, the Conservation through Reconciliation Partnership (CRP) is an Indigenous-led organization that, with support from Indigenous and non-Indigenous institutions, aims to advance Indigenous-led conservation initiatives. A key element of the CRP's work is the Indigenous Protected and Conserved Areas (IPCA) program. IPCAs are Indigenous-managed stewardship initiatives, through which lands and waters are designated and set apart for protection, and Indigenous governments have the primary role in protecting and conserving them through Indigenous laws, knowledge systems, and governance. Several IPCAs have been established in Dene homelands in what are now called the Northwest Territories.[11] Another is being established in unceded Mi'kmaw territories near what is now called Cape Breton.[12] The CRP works with the IISAAK OLAM Foundation, which shares knowledge and builds capacity for IPCAs. In 2021, the Foundation secured $340 million dollars to establish and manage IPCAs. CRP also partners with the Indigenous Leadership Initiative (ILI), an organization focused on Indigenous land, water, and resource stewardship. The initiative runs a guardian program that trains and supports Indigenous Peoples to manage protected areas and to lead restoration and management projects.[13] IPCAs and the various initiatives supporting them elevate and advance Indigenous rights, responsibilities, ways of life, and knowledge. They present critical alternatives to the colonial conservation systems that provincial and federal governments have maintained.

To date, Indigenous communities' participation in the management of WBNP remains advisory in nature, and, as Sandlos notes, "the absolute power of the state to regulate the Native harvest remains intact."[14] In spite of the urging of Indigenous Peoples and even of the United Nations, Parks Canada and provincial governments maintain that existing co-management systems are working well, implicitly sidelining calls to the more rigorous and meaningful Nation-to-Nation arrangement that Dënesųłıné leaders desire. Historical distrust and a structure that tends to relegate Indigenous leaders to consulting or advisory positions, rather than to meaningful decision-making positions, has limited the potential of these approaches and left Dënesųłıné participants feeling dismissed, as has been the case in the administration of WBNP since its creation.[15]

International Oversight

WBNP gained international notoriety in 1983 when the United Nations Educational, Scientific and Cultural Organization (UNESCO) granted it status as a World Heritage Site. As the home of North America's largest population of wild bison, the world's only breeding habitat for the endangered whooping crane, the location of the world's largest inland delta, and "the most ecologically complete and largest example of the entire Great Plains-Boreal grassland ecosystem of North America," UNESCO points to many factors that make the Park worthy of the designation of "outstanding universal value" (OUV). The 1983 World Heritage nomination also indicated that the Park's size and remoteness provide "ample room for most ecological processes to continue undisturbed."

With the designation comes ongoing monitoring and regular recommendations to Canadian authorities to improve Park management, increase formal protections and address issues of concern that may threaten the integrity of the site's OUV. Since 1983, UNESCO has released twelve State of Conservation reports addressing the recommendations. These reports note for example UNESCO's concerns about proposed development projects adjacent to the Park, the cumulative impacts of upstream industrial activity, and the ongoing issue of tuberculosis and brucellosis infections in the bison herd. Most recently, in response to the formal petition Mikisew Cree First Nation submitted in 2014 to the World Heritage Committee (WHC) requesting that WBNP be moved to the List of World Heritage Sites in Danger, the WHC and International Union for Conservation of Nature and Natural Resources (IUCN) undertook a mission to assess threats to the Park's OUV. The final report stated that "considerably more effort will be needed to reverse the negative trends at a time when climate change combined with upstream industrial developments and resource extractions are intensifying" if WBNP was to avoid inclusion on the Sites in Danger list.[16] UNESCO listed the potential impacts of the Site C dam and downstream impacts of oilsands growth as key concerns that were not being adequately assessed by Canadian authorities.[17] In June 2021—the same month ACFN publicly released the initial report resulting from the WBNP research project—UNESCO reiterated its 2016 warning call. Despite federal promises to finance further protections for the Park, significant upstream impact of oilsands development and "governance challenges" have prolonged the risks UNESCO identified in previous years.[18]

UNESCO's discussion of Indigenous Peoples in relation to WBNP has changed over time. The technical evaluation preceding the 1983 World Heritage designation included Indigenous harvesters among the reasons the Park's ecosystems needed protection and international management: "the ecosystems also support populations of Native Americans who still continue some of their traditional ways of life, thus adding the human element to the completeness of the ecosystem."[19] Indigenous Peoples' presence in the Park and surrounding area, and their relations to the land, were positioned as evidence for the need for WBNP's inclusion on the World Heritage list—perhaps driven by what Sandlos describes as the common paternalistic position for Canadian Parks management through much of the twentieth century that assumed Indigenous Peoples were "as much in need of management [or, at times, protection] as the animals they hunted."[20] Restrictions on Indigenous harvesting were listed among conservation management practices important to maintaining the Park's integrity. In 2014 though, language in UNESCO publications shifted and began to position local Indigenous communities among those who should have authority to manage the Park, rather than being managed by it. Among the overarching concerns listed in the 2016 mission's final report, the authors point to "longstanding and unresolved conflicts and tensions between Aboriginal Peoples and governmental and private sector actors which call for a coherent management response in line with the legal framework and unambiguous commitments to reconciliation."[21] Every *State of Conservation* report following the 2016 mission has listed "lack of effective engagement with First Nations and Métis in monitoring activities and insufficient consideration of local and Indigenous knowledge" as factors affecting the OUV.[22]

UNESCO urged the Canadian government to reassess and reconfigure its relations with Indigenous residents in the management of the Park. In 2021,

UNESCO's Decision Statement re-urged Canada to "Adopt a clear and coherent policy and guidance to enable the transition to a genuine partnership with First Nations and Métis communities in the governance and management of the property [the Park]." It also noted "with regret" that the government's responses to date had been insufficient despite the "severe threats" to the property and its conditions of OUV.[23] Canada has consistently responded to UNESCO's concerns by pointing to work undertaken under the 2014 CMC, which, as Pat Marcel and Leslie Wiltzen discussed, has thus far demonstrated insufficient engagement with ACFN and has not addressed the unique and harmful impacts the Park has had on ACFN and their Dene ancestors.

Sandlos writes that the 1983 World Heritage Site designation has contributed to Canadian public discourse that celebrates the Park's "unique natural history" while also effectively masking its "more ambiguous human heritage: the litany of injustice inflicted" on Indigenous residents throughout the twentieth century.[24] And indeed, while UNESCO's more recent position on the Park's relations with Indigenous Peoples appears to have progressed since 1983 (and since Sandlos published his book), some ACFN members feel it is not enough. They perceive UNESCO discourse about the Park, like co-management arrangements advanced by Parks Canada or the Government of Canada's professed commitment to meaningful action on reconciliation, to be continuities in the century-long colonial patterns of land and wildlife management that have largely excluded Dene people's knowledge and perspectives and privileged those of outsiders.

Chief Adam spoke to ACFN leadership's hesitancy to partake in the new, reconciliatory management structures proposed by Parks Canada and recommended by UNESCO: "Now after one hundred years they're going just you know . . . they want ACFN to participate . . . And yet, all the years prior they did not want ACFN to participate in anything." The "unresolved conflicts" the 2016 mission report referred to must first be addressed, but members suggest that the experiences of each Indigenous community affected by Parks policy must be acknowledged and addressed individually rather than being lumped together. For them, the history of displacements and exclusions, with its particular impacts on Dënesųłıné land users and families, must be formally acknowledged—truth, many members suggest, is necessary before reconciliation. Beyond such formal acknowledgment, they also argue for specific and substantive reparative measures for the unique harms Dënesųłıné peoples suffered. For many members, this involves not only compensation and a restructuring of Park management and policy, but also a return of the land to those who lost access to it and sovereignty over it after 1926. As ACFN Elder Alice Rigney put it, "never mind the apology. Just give us back our land."

In closing: "For our relatives to be remembered"

In addition to their goals of obtaining reparations, ACFN members have emphasized that a central intention of this work has been to recover and re-centre their community's stories and experiences. Indeed, since the establishment of WBNP, non-Indigenous authorities—whether federal or provincial officials, international bodies, private sector representatives, missionaries or Indian Agents—have exerted control over narratives about the Park and surrounding environment, and thus over its management, for a hundred years. This had had specific implications for Dënesųłıné peoples who have witnessed their knowledge and experiences being misrepresented or ignored, their homelands "taken up" and connections to place interrupted, their families separated, and their rights and sovereignty eroded. Getting ACFN's story out there is key to challenging colonial omissions and the material harms they underpin. Chief Adam said, "You know that now ACFN is coming back in there, and you've got people pushing back against us now because they don't want us there, because they've lived too comfortable not knowing the history about what happened." Not knowing (or refusing to know) Dene histories and experiences with WBNP, colonial governments have avoided acknowledging the harms committed by the Park in Dene territories, thus avoiding addressing ACFN's claims. Control over the narrative leads to control over the land.

The oral histories and testimonies in this book demonstrate that Dënesųłıné people have never lost sight of their connections to and knowledge of their homelands taken up by the Park, even after one hundred years of exclusions and displacements. This book is testament to the community's collective memory of Wood Buffalo National Park's history and its relations to the Dënesųłıné peoples whose lands and waterways it takes up. The history and testimony shared here are part of a century-long work led by Dene leaders, members, Elders, and land users to keep that memory alive in the pursuit of justice, land back, healing, and reparations. Dënesųłıné oral histories challenge exclusions of local knowledge and attempted erasures of Dene voices from the historical record and Dene people from environment. They are a means to reclaim a narrative that has consistently been told without

Dënesųłıné knowledge, experiences, and rights at the centre—and to do so without "allowing the government to turn it all around," as ACFN member Donalyn Mercredi remarked. They are a call, Elder Ernie "Joe" Ratfat eloquently told us, for "our relatives to be remembered."

APPENDIX 1

Building a Community-Directed Work of Oral History

By Sabina Trimble, Peter Fortna, Willow Springs Strategic Solutions

Remembering Our Relations is a community-directed, collaborative work of oral history. The book has been one important result of a long-term, justice-oriented research initiative that the Athabasca Chipewyan First Nation (ACFN) community has been working on for several decades. We wanted to take some space here to discuss the work that led up to *A History of Wood Buffalo National Park's Relations with the Dënesųłıné*, the 2021 research report that resulted in this book, in order to highlight the relationships on which the work depended. In this appendix, we share the history of how the report and book came together and discuss the roles of members and staff of ACFN as the leaders and overseers of the project, as well as collaborators in diverse ways, and of us at Willow Springs Strategic Solutions (WSSS) as settler partners, researchers, and consultants. We also highlight some of the complexities and challenges, and the interesting possibilities, of working together in the context of a global pandemic that has necessitated separation and isolation.

Background to *Remembering Our Relations*

Much of the work that led up to *Remembering Our Relations* began before the idea for the book emerged. Members, ancestors, and relations of ACFN laid the foundation for the work by calling out and resisting colonial encroachments and passing down their oral histories. Indeed, Dënesųłıné people have been engaged in research and activism in direct response to the history of Wood Buffalo National Park for generations. Decades of research by the late

ACFN Elders Pat Marcel and Alec Bruno formed an important catalyst and starting place for this project. They spoke out often about their own families' traumatic experiences and what they saw to be Treaty 8 violations and widespread harms that accompanied the establishment and expansion of the Park. They pressed for many years for the community's oral histories to be gathered, along with government records and other documents, to tell the story of the Park from a Dene perspective.

In 2019, ACFN leadership, including the Elders' Council and Chief and Council, initiated a research project with the intention to tell the story of WBNP. The goal was to gather evidence to inform ACFN's plans to negotiate with Environment and Climate Change Canada (ECCC) and Crown-Indigenous Relations and Northern Affairs Canada (CIRNAC) for a formal, public apology and reparations for harms the predecessors of these branches committed against members of the community through the creation, expansion, and management of Wood Buffalo National Park. Much of the archival and oral history research at the heart of this book was initially completed for this larger initiative. Before the work began, ACFN established a steering committee to direct the work and keep it in line with the community's goals. The committee was comprised of ACFN Elders, staff, and youth, including the late Elder Pat Marcel, Rose Ross, Lisa Tssessaze, Olivia Villebrun, Leslie Wiltzen, Brian Fung, and Jay Telegdi. Later, Willow Springs and the Nation's legal and public relations teams, including staff at Counsel Public Affairs, Inc. and Larry Innes at Olthuis Kleer Townshend Law, also became involved with the committee. The committee was a cornerstone throughout all stages of the work and oversaw all phases—developing the project, managing its progress, navigating the research and writing processes, engaging with community on a regular basis, and bringing the report to the negotiating table, and eventually, to the publication process. Lisa Tssessaze, Rose Ross, and Jay Telegdi especially played leading roles in the coordination and development of the project.

Athabasca Chipewyan First Nation hired Willow Springs Strategic Solutions in late 2019 to begin documenting the history and intergenerational impacts of WBNP. Leadership and the steering committee wanted to build a strong case through extensive archival and oral historical research and through a systematic review of existing scholarly literatures and research previously conducted by the Nation and adjacent communities. In *Research as Resistance*, Susan Strega and Leslie Brown argue that transparency is key for any researcher wishing to work with communities in good relation.[1] As white settler researchers living and working in Indigenous homelands, and usually working in relation with Indigenous Knowledge, we understand that it is important to reflect on our positionality and privilege and to discuss our role in the process. Willow Springs is a settler-owned research consultancy that focuses on historical research; we often work with Indigenous communities in northern Alberta. Peter had worked with ACFN on several other projects over the previous decade, so he had an existing relationship with members of the community and ACFN leadership. This meant that we came to the project familiar with Elder Pat Marcel's foundational research, and other work that ACFN or other researchers had previously conducted that could assist in our work. The role of WSSS in this project was to gather stories and sources, help manage the project, and develop the findings and analyses into a report. Sabina Trimble, Peter Fortna and, Tara Joly (from 2019 to 2020), led the archival and oral history research. Sabina and Peter wrote the initial report drafts and the introductory text for the chapters of this book and helped with project planning and coordination.

Research in Indigenous communities by non-Indigenous peoples has often been extractive and violent. Māori scholar Linda Tuhiwai Smith famously describes research as "the dirtiest word in the Indigenous world's vocabulary." She points to the "imperial legacies of Western knowledge and the ways in which those legacies continue to influence knowledge institutions to the exclusion of Indigenous peoples and their aspirations."[2] Social sciences research has advanced harmful and discriminatory ideas that inform and justify oppressive policy, colonial dispossessions and eliminationism, and extractive activity around the world. Power is also inequitably distributed in research relationships, resulting in violence within the relationship itself and in the research outcomes. This is almost inevitable when the person holding the pen (or the audio recorder) has control over research questions, the time and place where research takes place, data analysis, and the structure of the narrative. Moreover, Métis historian Adam Gaudry contends that, "just as corporations aspire to extract resources from Indigenous lands, much research within Indigenous communities is an extractive process."[3] This includes the extraction of Indigenous knowledge and stories from communities and publishing those in the name of "academic freedom" with blatant disregard for sacredness, protocol, and ceremony, or for Indigenous People's individual and collective intellectual property rights.[4] Researchers who work with communities extract knowledge and stories and often benefit much more from the relation than the communities themselves, whose knowledge and experience are at the centre of the research. So, while researchers enjoy income, career advancement, awards, and public respect, community goals are rarely advanced.

Critics have called "for an end to research 'on' the marginalized" rather than 'with' or 'by' them. They have advanced community-led and -empowering, anti-oppressive, and collaborative approaches.[5] To realize the ethic of "nothing about us without us," critics argue, researchers must relinquish their assumed role as "expert" and "owner" and privilege local leadership, knowledge, and ways of knowing. "Indigenous knowledge," argues Gaudry, "is valid on its own terms and is capable of standing on its own."[6] All forms of knowledge-making and every historical source should thus be "read differently and evaluated on their own merits in a way that is not predetermined by their form," as community-engaged historian Madeline Knickerbocker puts it.[7] Anthropologist Leslie Robertson explains in her collaborative research with members of the Kwagu'ł Gix̱sa̱m Clan, the production of historical knowledge thus becomes "a long conversation" that honours and uplifts the "analyses, descriptions and explanations of knowledgeable partners in the research."[8] Moreover, researchers must "place community concerns above all others in the research process and put forward an empowering and decolonized view of the people with whom they conduct the research."[9] Community members centrally involved throughout the work, Gaudry argues, and "the final judges of the validity and effectiveness of the research."[10]

We agree. As paid consultants whose names are on the front cover of the book, there is no question we have benefitted from the work. But the intentions of the ACFN community have always been at the heart of our involvement. We aimed to work in a way that opposes harmful practice and is on the community's terms, within their timeline, and under their guidance. We attempted to balance our role between making meaningful and worthwhile contributions of our resources, knowledge, and capacity as a research consultancy and providing leadership where it made sense to do so, and foregrounding ACFN's leadership, knowledge, and experiences and, most importantly, advancing their goals. Our involvement with the steering committee and engagement with the wider community were important to navigating this balance. The central goals of the *History of Wood Buffalo National Park's Relations with the Dënesųłiné* report and of *Remembering Our Relations* have always been to honour and amplify the knowledge, stories, memories, and histories of ACFN members and their ancestors—this is why ACFN is listed as the first author. It is their stories, their knowledge, their interpretations and analyses, their goals that make this book what it is. The project was designed to be collaborative and to ensure that ACFN holds the authority over how and when the research proceeded, what questions were asked, how the narrative would be told, and where the information that went into the report—including all archival texts, secondary sources, and oral history recordings and transcriptions—would be held. Digital and physical copies of all the sources we had gathered are housed in the Nation's own offices and archives, as well as in a shared cloud space that WSSS administrates.

Doing the work

The work depended on engagement with many members of the community and close listening to the oral histories passed down from generation to generation. We also worked with an expansive written record housed across provincial and national archives, containing tens of thousands of pages produced by various government departments and branches, churches, and local Indigenous leaders. Early on, WSSS and the community steering committee together identified research questions and developed a phased plan to guide the project. We proposed several phases to approach the work, involving community engagement and extensive analysis of diverse written texts.

The first phase of the project, and a large role that WSSS played, was to gather copies of relevant texts to construct the research report and provide the ACFN with digital and physical copies of all texts, so the community could grow their local archives for future use. We conducted a deep review of archival texts and of prior research by ACFN, as well as in-depth reviews of other relevant academic literature and texts produced by other Indigenous communities, local industry, governments, and other consultants. Peter and Tara did most of the labour of identifying and digitizing textual sources that would be critical to this story, initially working with ACFN members and staff from Parks Canada. All texts gathered have been digitized and saved in multiple formats now housed by the Nation. Parks Canada staff helped identify, access, and prioritize non-digitized texts from relevant collections at Library and Archives Canada (LAC). The team also gathered records from the Provincial Archives of Alberta and ACFN's community records.

Our access to archival documents was strained in several ways. Archival records are not always easily accessible to remote Indigenous communities researching their histories. For projects like this, the limitations can be serious even though the stakes are high: communities are often working with restrictive budgets and narrow timelines to pursue research that could have long-term, material impacts on members. While LAC has digitized many non-restricted Indian Affairs files (RG10) and Parks Branch files (RG84), the same could not be said of the full extent of the Department of the Interior – Northern Affairs Branch (RG85) collection, where the pre-1950s documents related to the Park are housed.[11] Travel to archives in Ottawa, Winnipeg, or Vancouver and costly copy requests were the only means to access many of the files documenting the most critical decades in ACFN's history with the Park. These challenges were compounded by the global pandemic—something many historical researchers in Canada experienced during these years. Library and Archives Canada was closed to visitors for much of 2020 and 2021 and the copy request system was backed up for months. When the archives re-opened in summer 2021, physical access was by appointment only and spots were limited. We worked around these challenges through requesting digital copies of records from LAC and the Provincial Archives of Alberta, by working with copies of documents that Parks Canada shared with the team digitally, and by accessing copies that ACFN already had in their community records for other projects. The volume of material we amassed was substantive, notwithstanding the limitations. In summer 2022, after the report and an initial book draft were complete, we received copies of thousands of additional pages of archival materials that LAC digitized for us. We updated both the report and the book manuscript after receiving the new documents.

The second phase of the research plan was to focus on the oral histories. Sabina and Peter began, as discussed in the Introduction to *Remembering Our Relations,* by gathering and reviewing the existing transcriptions and audio recordings of oral histories that had been recorded for other community-led projects from the 1970s to the 2010s. With the leadership and coordination of the steering committee, Willow Springs also conducted the oral history interviews that occurred from 2020 to 2021. The interview questions were drafted by Tara Joly and then underwent several revisions by the committee. The oral history work progressed relatively smoothly until spring 2020, when the onset of the COVID-19 pandemic halted all plans of in-person community engagement, leading to delays and compromises. To ensure the health and safety of the community and all participants, in-person committee meetings and plans for oral history interviews and focus groups were put on hold. In

December 2020, ACFN leadership determined that the work must proceed remotely. This was in part so the team could time the release of the report so it would align with the national celebrations likely to accompany the 100th anniversary of the Park in 2022, and in part to keep the momentum going on the larger negotiations with the Government of Canada.

Recruiting community members for remote interviews presented logistical challenges in the initial months. It was difficult to decide on the most appropriate medium to complete the interviews. Video conferencing would have been preferred to conducting interviews over the phone, but internet connectivity in remote places and comfort with emergent (and changing) technologies posed challenges. In February 2021, ACFN hired Angela Marcel, a Nation member with strong connections across the community, to directly contact Elders and schedule remote interviews. The community made the decision to complete the remaining interviews over the phone, which removed a number of key barriers. Angela helped the team to schedule discussions with twenty-nine individuals from ACFN and the wider community. Along with committee members Lisa and Jay, Angela played a pivotal role in the community engagement and in keeping the work moving forward.

Remote interviewing is not always ideal. A key characteristic of oral history is its relationality—it is alive in ways that written texts are not. The interactive nature and physical and social context and delivery of the spoken word are as important as the words themselves. In-person conversations breathe with inflection, connection, emotion, gestures, facial expressions, and other forms of body language. Remote interviews can strip words from context, resulting in what some oral historians have termed disembodiment.[12] To some extent, this disembodiment is inevitable—even when interviews are conducted in person, disembodiment occurs at the point of transcribing oral interviews to writing—but it can be managed more effectively when talking to someone in person. Another challenge came as the committee worked out how to honour protocol and ceremony from a distance. Elders and community leaders provided suggestions such as tobacco offerings. When these could not be made in person, Elders suggested a digital tobacco offering. Others requested that the tobacco be mailed to them along with their interview transcription. Most members asked that we make offerings at our homes on their behalf and say a prayer for them. Everyone received honoraria in advance of their sharing. Where we had permissions, we digitally recorded the interviews and transcribed them. In two instances, interviewees requested that their interviews not be recorded, preferring instead that the interviewer take notes and only make general references to the interview rather than directly quoting them. Audio recordings and physical and digital transcriptions were sent to all members who requested them, and copies of the recordings and transcriptions are held and managed by the Nation.

Throughout the research process, we kept the dialogue open and frequent. The committee met remotely every week after the pandemic began. Where possible, we joined in larger community meetings to share and discuss progress, including meetings with the Elders' Council, Chief and Council, and other members of ACFN staff and membership. The committee decided we should send the physical transcripts, drafts, gifts, and thank you cards by mail, either directly to those who participated or to the Nation office to be hand-delivered to members during Treaty Days in June 2021. The packages included our phone numbers and email addresses with invitations to review and comment on the material at any time. We followed up directly with most of the interviewees by phone or email, and the committee communicated regularly with the wider community through ACFN's quarterly newsletter, the website and social media, and at other community gatherings. Committee members, Elders, and Chief and Council reviewed iterations of the report before ACFN submitted a strong draft in July 2021 to Ministers of ECCC and CIRNAC and made it public through social media and news outlets. The steering committee also decided to treat the online report as a living document that will evolve as additional feedback comes in, further evidence is established, and ACFN continues to make progress on the government negotiations.

Willow Springs staff regularly updated the writing based on community reviews. For example, after reviewing an early draft of the report, committee member and ACFN member Olivia Villebrun recommended that we place more emphasis on the intergenerational nature of the Park's impacts—especially on youth. Olivia described the loss of language that resulted from the 1944 membership transfer (described in Chapter 4) and the removals from the wider territory, which compounded the violence of residential schools. She explained that youth have suffered from this outcome in specific ways. Her important feedback dramatically strengthened the section of the report focused on impacts and led to an additional critical interpretation that we had not previously considered—that Dene youth members' connections to language and knowledge in the present are critically influenced by Park policies that had interrupted knowledge transmission from Elders to youth for generations. Many other important points of feedback from the steering committee, Chief and Council, Elders, and the wider community contributed to the strength of the final report. We resubmitted a revised report to the government in early 2023. Likewise, *Remembering Our Relations* has been shaped and reshaped by ongoing conversations.

Athabasca Chipewyan First Nation began discussions with representatives from ECCC and CIRNAC in 2022 to obtain formal, public acknowledgement and reparations for the damage caused to the Dënesųłıné people after the Park was created.[13] Once the negotiations started, Lisa Tssessaze emphasized that the team should find a way to highlight and honour the oral histories and testimony of Elders who have gone before. ACFN determined shortly thereafter that the initial research report should be reworked into a book manuscript that would be owned by the community. We then began to shift our focus to gathering everything together for *Remembering Our Relations*. The book manuscript developed over roughly two years. Like the original report, this book has also been centrally guided by the work of the steering committee, as well as contributions from leadership, community participants, Elders, and other ACFN members who had been involved with the report.

There are a few important differences between this book and the original report. The central distinction has to do with intentions: the report was written with the goal of informing negotiations with governments, whereas this book was written primarily to highlight and honour the oral history and experiences of the community. The second difference has to do with the format. The report integrates evidence from both written and oral archives with our analysis and interpretations throughout. Dene oral histories are, of course, deeply important to the report, and the key interpretations and themes of the report are based on the oral histories. However, we felt the traditional report style and the language used to communicate with governments was limiting, not only in the extent to which we could directly incorporate oral history excerpts, but also in the levels to which the report could speak meaningfully to community members. For this reason, we adopted a format in this book that emphasizes the oral history. The goal was to gather stories by the community, for the community, in ways that made some of the stories more accessible than the report format could allow. Elder and member voices form the core of the book. Because the steering committee also felt it was important to make some of the written sources accessible to readers, we worked with UCalgary Press to include copies of several archival sources as an appendix to the e-book. The steering committee also decided that samples of some of the interviews should be included as audio recordings so that the voices of speakers could be heard—especially the few that have been recorded in Dene. These passages are linked throughout the book and are available online for listeners. ACFN plans to host more digital audio recordings from the oral history interviews on its website in the future.

Much of the existing writing in the report formed the basis for the chapter introductions for this book. The committee and WSSS also took time to identify the oral history passages to be included in each chapter, with the help of interviewees. Oral histories included in each chapter were selected with explicit permissions from the speakers, who revised, removed, or added to their testimony up until the final submission of the manuscript to the press. For interviews with Elders who have since passed away that were recorded for previous community research projects such as the Treaty and Aboriginal Rights Research interviews in the 1970s, we requested permissions from members of the family and next-of-kin for inclusion in the work. The book manuscript also underwent multiple layers of community review in addition to the academic peer review process. The steering committee, with recommendations from Elders' Council, Chief and Council, and the ACFN board membership, appointed a community review panel with three Elders: Edouard Trippe de Roche, Keltie Paul, and Alice Rigney. Elder reviews and peer reviews were central to the revisions and development of the manuscript. Elders and members Rene Bruno, Jimmy Deranger, Kristi Deranger, Dora Flett, Garry Flett, Lorraine Hoffman, Julie Mercredi, Hazel Mercredi, and Les Wiltzen reviewed oral history transcripts and several sections of the manuscript. Several other ACFN Elders shared oral feedback during project updates at Elders' meetings and Treaty Days in Fort Chipewyan in 2021 and 2022.

ACFN Elders and members have made important contributions to the many other moving parts that brought this book together. During summer 2022 ACFN hosted a title and cover contest, inviting members to propose a title and design a book cover. ACFN Elder Leonard Flett's watercolour painting of wood bison won the competition and is the central image of the *Remembering Our Relations* cover. Staff member Josh Holden worked with Elder Cecilia Adam to develop titles in Dënesųłıné in summer 2023. This was a critical development since, as discussed in the Introduction, there are few

Dënesųłıné oral history recordings in this book, and the committee wanted to find other ways that the language could feature prominently. Youth members have been involved in the public engagement, including through sharing histories on social media and through an essay contest about the history and impacts of the Park, which ACFN hosted in 2022.

Rose Ross and Lisa Tssessaze coordinated the work of obtaining permissions and revisions from members whose testimony is included in the book, and from next-of-kin for those who have since passed. They also drafted many of the biographies included in the front matter of this book. Several members and Elders wrote their own biographies, and other ACFN members assisted in that process. Chief Allan Adam's Foreword and Elder Alice Rigney's Preface provided a powerful opening to the rest of the book, setting the tone for the narrative and demonstrating the intergenerational importance of telling this story.

Conclusion

There is no doubt that this research process has been filled with compromise, especially in the surrounding context of the pandemic. We worked hard to do things in a good way and in good relation, within the constraints the circumstances posed. Out of necessity spurred by short timelines and the pandemic, we sacrificed some of the long-term engagement and organic, close-up conversation that is so crucial to this kind of work. We have aimed nonetheless to approach our involvement with sensitivity and respect, taking Dene knowledge, memory, history, and experience seriously and holding space to ensure the community has the first and final say over the research process, the story, and the outcomes. The power of this book comes from the community members who graciously agreed to share their time and space, histories, and often difficult and traumatic memories.

Remembering Our Relations is a call to return the land and a concerted effort to honour, amplify, and reflect on the powerful work that has gone before and on this community's resilient ways of being and knowing. That this work continued in the face of deeply challenging global circumstances, and amidst the many other crises it has faced in the past two years—including the Imperial Oil tailings ponds leaks in Spring 2023 and a wildfire evacuation order in summer 2023—is a testament to its value and importance to ACFN. It is also evidence of the strength and creativity of Dënesųłıné people who have always courageously stewarded their homelands and endured and resisted the violence of colonial transformations. It has been a deep honour, a joy, and a great privilege to share in this journey.

APPENDIX 2

List of Oral History Interviews From 2020–2021[1]

Adam, Allan. Zoom interview with Sabina Trimble and Jay Telegdi, 2 February 2021. Fort Chipewyan: ACFN, 2021.

Adam, Horace. Phone interview with Peter Fortna, 19 March 2021. Fort Chipewyan: ACFN, 2021.

Deranger, Jimmy. Phone interview with Peter Fortna, 24 March 2021. Fort Chipewyan: ACFN, 2021.

Deranger, Fredoline Djeskelni. Phone interview with Sabina Trimble and Lisa Tssessaze, 19 March, 2021. Fort Chipewyan: ACFN, 2021.

Flett, Dora. Phone interview with Sabina Trimble, 19 March 2021. Fort Chipewyan: ACFN, 2021.

Flett, Garry. Zoom interview with Sabina Trimble, 3 and 16 December 2020. Fort Chipewyan: ACFN, 2020.

Flett, Leonard. Phone interview with Peter Fortna, 30 April 2021. Fort Chipewyan: ACFN, 2021.

Flett, Scott. Phone interview with Sabina Trimble, 17 March 2021. Fort Chipewyan: ACFN, 2021.

Flett, John. Phone interview with Peter Fortna, 18 March 2021. Fort Chipewyan: ACFN, 2021.

Fraser, Jumbo. Phone interview with Sabina Trimble, 12 March, 2021. Fort Chipewyan: ACFN, 2021.

Ladouceur, Big Ray. Phone interview with Sabina Trimble, 18 March 2021. Fort Chipewyan: ACFN, 2021.

Laviolette, Leslie. Phone interview with Sabina Trimble, 21 and 22 March 2021. Fort Chipewyan: ACFN, 2021.

Marcel, Big John. Phone interview with Sabina Trimble, 18 March 2021. Fort Chipewyan: ACFN, 2021.

Marcel, John H. Phone interview with Peter Fortna, 30 April 2021. Fort Chipewyan: ACFN, 2021.

Mercredi, Donalyn. Phone interview with Sabina Trimble, 11 March 2021. Fort Chipewyan: ACFN, 2021.

Ratfat, Ernie (Joe). Phone interview with Sabina Trimble, 19 March, 2021. Fort Chipewyan: ACFN, 2021.

Trippe de Roche, Edouard and Keltie Paul. Phone interview with Sabina Trimble and Jay Telegdi, 25 November 2020. Fort Chipewyan: ACFN, 2020.

Rigney, Alice. Phone interview with Sabina Trimble, 16 and 17 March 2021. Fort Chipewyan: ACFN, 2021.

Simpson, Mary (Cookie). Phone interview with Sabina Trimble, 12 March 2021. Fort Chipewyan: ACFN, 2021.

Stevens, Lori. Zoom interview with Sabina Trimble, 25 May 2021. Fort Chipewyan: ACFN, 2021.

Tourangeau, Beverly. Phone interview with Sabina Trimble, 21 March 2021. Fort Chipewyan: ACFN, 2021.

Wiltzen, Leslie. Zoom interview with Sabina Trimble, 21 January 2021. Fort Chipewyan: ACFN, 2021.

ANONYMOUS INTERVIEWS WITH TRANSCRIPTIONS

ACFN Elder. Phone interview with Sabina Trimble and Peter Fortna, 11 March 2021. Fort Chipewyan: ACFN, 2021.

ACFN Elder. Phone interview with Sabina Trimble, 16 March 2021. Fort Chipewyan: ACFN, 2021.

ACFN Elder. Phone interview with Peter Fortna, 16 March 2021. Fort Chipewyan: ACFN, 2021.

ACFN Elder. Phone interview with Sabina Trimble, 18 March 2021. Fort Chipewyan: ACFN, 2021.

APPENDIX 3

Digital Copies of Archival Documents

Scan QR codes to view archival documents online

CHAPTER 2

2.1 Text and transcription of Treaty 8 including statement of adhesion of the Chipewyan people of Athabasca River, Birch River, Peace River, Slave River and Gull River, and the Cree Indians of Gull River and Deep Lake. Government of Canada, *Treaty No. 8. Made June 21, 1899 and Adhesions, Reports, Etc.* [1899]. Reprinted from file the 1899 edition by Roger Duhamel, F.R.S.C. (Ottawa: Queen's Printer and Controller of Stationary, 1966). https://digitalcollections.ucalgary.ca/AssetLink/25f43867fk83nb613334663t3irs2448.pdf

CHAPTER 3

3.1 Memo from Maxwell Graham to J.B. Harkin, 7 December 1912. LAC RG 85, vol. 665, file 3912, pt. 2. https://digitalcollections.ucalgary.ca/AssetLink/l8papc01bj52mxxva35125a3suk6pyj8.pdf

3.2 Report by Maxwell Graham about the creation of Wood Buffalo Park. Maxwell Graham, "Statement as to the Causes That Led up to the Creation Of the Wood Buffalo Park," For the information of O.S. Finnie, 4 June 1924. LAC RG85, vol. 1390, file 406-13. https://digitalcollections.ucalgary.ca/AssetLink/eqr8a45y08mo32tb31fgj506358231k7.pdf

3.3 Article about the importation of the Wainwright bison, 14 September 1925. Maxwell Graham, "Canada's Repatriation of the Buffalo," 14 September 1925, LAC RG85-D-1-A, vol. 1391, file 406-13. https://digitalcollections.ucalgary.ca/AssetLink/apn0sq8oy63386c27kimlw601uj237p3.pdf

3.4 Order-in-Council that expanded the original Park, 24 September 1926. LAC RG85, vol. 1391, file 406-13. https://digitalcollections.ucalgary.ca/AssetLink/ai80a255vfr4kg8ff6ujc20j88swj17x.pdf

261

CHAPTER 4

 4.1 Journal entry of Indian Agent Jack Stewart, recording the transfer of the members of the Chipewyan Band to the Cree Band, 12 June 1944. "Daily Journal," PAA, Acc 71.11/2d. https://digitalcollections.ucalgary.ca/AssetLink/q8fm43t1nav38s1r8vad23n2cqj8x480.jpg

CHAPTER 5

 5.1 Consolidated list of laws that governed harvesting in WBNP, September 1945. Department of Northern Affairs and National Resources, Northern Administration and Lands Branch, Conservation and Management Services, "Office Consolidation of Regulations governing hunting and trapping in Wood Buffalo Park, Established under authority of O.C. of 14th December, 1933, P.C. 2589" 15 September 1945, LAC RG85-4-C-A, vol. 345, file 5. https://digitalcollections.ucalgary.ca/AssetLink/43xiea488c2vfi6i44it33364fcu7y10.pdf

 5.2 Letter from Park Warden M.J. Dempsey to J. Milner discussing increased warden surveillance and Chief Jonas Laviolette's application for a permit to enter the Park, which was denied in 1925, 1 March 1933, LAC RG85, vol. 852, file 7870. https://digitalcollections.ucalgary.ca/AssetLink/c8ed16kp0mpp1575653d0eba7y61ldd6.png

 5.3 Letter from Provincial Fur Supervisor J.L. Grew to D.J. Allen about warden surveillance, 19 March 1943, LAC RG10, vol. 8409, file 191/20-14-1, pt. 1. https://digitalcollections.ucalgary.ca/AssetLink/544i888l08150j4801hj0kx58164r31x.pdf

 5.4 Letter from Indian Agent John Melling to Secretary of Indian Affairs detailing the hunger and hardship Indigenous Peoples who had been expelled from the Park were facing, 12 June 1942. LAC RG10, vol. 8409, file 191/20-14/1, pt. 1. https://digitalcollections.ucalgary.ca/AssetLink/k4fqr8u88jv71kxae0c0o7x50f3xeo2i.pdf

CHAPTER 6

6.1 Letter from Chief Jonas Laviolette urging Indian Affairs to attend to the struggles the Dene people were facing as a result of the Park's creation, 20 February 1927. LAC RG10, vol. 6732, file 420-2B. https://digitalcollections.ucalgary.ca/AssetLink/807dvtt8128tl2wf12j28sq2610nn26x.pdf

6.2 Memorandum signed by Indigenous leaders protesting the planned expansion of the Park, 16 April 1926. Memorandum from John Wylie, Colin Fraser, James Fraser, ? Marcel, P. Mercredi to Charles Cross, "Re the setting-apart of a New Buffalo Park or the establishing of an annex to the existing Wood Buffalo Park; which is to be situated in the terrain North of the Quatre Fourches River, and on the West shore of Lake Mamiwi, North of Hay River and Lake Claire," 16 April 1926. LAC RG85, vol. 1213, file 400-2-3, pt. 1A. https://digitalcollections.ucalgary.ca/AssetLink/e2h77r66s2f750615n473457vn318eo1.pdf

6.3 Letter from Gerald Card to J.D. McLean about a request from Dene community members for the establishment of protected reserves independent of the Treaty reserves, 6 December 1927. LAC RG10, vol. 6732, file 420-2B. https://digitalcollections.ucalgary.ca/AssetLink/6y6cu03g808177ced0m4023ss7yy6v11.pdf

6.4 Letter from S.H. Clark (Game Commissioner) to M. Christianson (Inspector of Indian Agencies) about the 1935 establishment of a large, protected area for local Indigenous harvesters, 12 March 1935. LAC RG10, vol. 6733, file 420-2C. https://digitalcollections.ucalgary.ca/AssetLink/ao3olk0vf2o6b83ut712bkcperk1wv13.pdf

CHAPTER 7

7.1 Letter from Park Warden M.J. Dempsey to District Indian Agent J.A. McDougal about the hunger and hardship Indigenous Peoples were facing, 17 February 1931. RG85-D-1-A, vol. 152, file 420-2. https://digitalcollections.ucalgary.ca/AssetLink/2oc8a6r275vs25e7qgg76fjbf7xg302g.pdf

7.2 Notes from Wardens' diaries indicating the frustrations of local harvesters about game laws, 20 April 1938. "Notes from Wardens' diaries, Wood Buffalo Park, received with letters of 9th and 25th March 1938, from the Fort Smith Office," 20 April 1938. RG85, vol. 153, file 420-2, Warden Patrol Reports 1936–44. https://digitalcollections.ucalgary.ca/AssetLink/257j554547wm2nrrmt008jr3166g000h.pdf

7.3 Report by Provincial Fur Supervisor J.L. Grew about the need for registered traplines, 11 March 1943. J.L. Grew to D.J. Allen, *Report on Registered Trap Lines in Alberta*, p. 6, LAC RG 10, vol. 6733, file 420-2-2 2. https://digitalcollections.ucalgary.ca/AssetLink/i44g2vjmnqxqi7ks531712eq1ws25s3r.pdf

7.4 Report on low trapping yields, March 1949. W.A. Fuller (Mammologist), "Monthly Report for March 1949," LAC RG10, vol. 8409, file 191/20-14-1, pt. 1. https://digitalcollections.ucalgary.ca/AssetLink/np761428nvd821au5w44eg1722pqm30v.pdf

Notes

NOTES TO PREFACE

1 Alice is referring to the Dene settlement near Lake Claire and Birch River that was taken up by (incorporated into) the expansion of Wood Buffalo National Park in 1926.

2 Another name for Holy Angels Residential School, located in Fort Chipewyan, Alberta.

3 Ester Piché had to relocate to Jackfish near Frezie Lake in the Peace-Athabasca Delta. This is now Chipewyan 201, an ACFN reserve.

NOTES TO ACFN ELDERS' DECLARATION

1 The Lower Athabasca Regional Plan (LARP) was developed by the Alberta government in 2012 as a regional plan meant to guide "future resource decisions while considering environmental, social and economic impacts." Many Indigenous communities expressed concerns with the plan when it was first adopted by the government, concerns which, by and large, have yet to be meaningfully addressed. Many (though not all) of ACFN's concerns with the plan are well documented in ACFN, *Athabasca Chipewyan First Nation Advice to the Government of Alberta Regarding the Lower Athabasca Regional Plan*, Provided to the Land Use Secretariat, 22 November 2010, https://landuse.alberta.ca/Forms%20and%20Applications/RFR_ACFN%20 Response%20to%20LARP%20Panel%20IR%206%20-%20Advice_2014-11-14_PUBLIC. pdf.

Additional recommendations can be found in Pat Marcel, Carolyn Whittaker, and Craig Candler, *Níh Boghodi: We Are the Stewards of Our Land: An ACFN Stewardship Strategy for Thunzea, et'thén and Dechen Yághe* Ejere (Woodland Caribou, Barren-Ground Caribou and Wood Bison), (Fort Chipewyan, AB: Athabasca Chipewyan First Nation, 2012), https://landuse.alberta.ca/Forms%20and%20Applications/RFR_ ACFN%20Reply%20to%20IR%204%20Nih%20Boghodi_2014-12-01_PUBLIC.pdf.

NOTES TO INTRODUCTION

1 Canadian Parks and Wilderness Society (CPAWS), "On the 100th Anniversary of Wood Buffalo National Park, Chief Allan Adam Sets the Record Straight on Park Founder who Starved Indigenous People," news release, 12 December 2022, https://cpaws.org/ on-the-100th-anniversary-of-wood-buffalo-national-park-chief-allan-adam-sets-the-record-straight-on-park-founder-who-starved-indigenous-people.

2   We use two names in this book when referring the people of ACFN and their ancestors: Dënesųłıné and Dene. ACFN oral histories tell us that there are several names that refer to the people and their profound connections to the land, water, and all living and non-living relations in ACFN homelands, including Ethhen eldeli Dene, which refers to the relationship between the people and the caribou, and K'ái Tailé Dene, which translates to the "real people of the blanket willows." For this project, Elders told us that the preferred name is Dënesųłıné, referring to both the language and the people, and translating roughly to "the real people." They noted as well that it is common to shorten this to Dene. We typically avoid use of the name Chipewyan, which is a misnomer that government officials, church representatives, and academics have applied for many decades. The exceptions are when we directly quote a document or interview that uses the name or refer to the historical political designation for ACFN—the Chipewyan Band.

3   Andrew Woolford and Jeff Benvenuto, "Canada and colonial genocide," *Journal of Genocide Research* 17, no. 4 (2015): 381.

4   See Patrick Wolfe, "Settler colonialism and the elimination of the native," *Journal of Genocide Research* 8, no. 4 (2006): 387–409; Woolford and Benvenuto, "Canada and colonial genocide"; Matthew Wildcat, "Fearing social and cultural death: genocide and elimination in settler colonial Canada—an Indigenous perspective," *Journal of Genocide Research* 17, no. 4 (2015): 391–409.

5   Sabina Trimble and Peter Fortna, *A History of Wood Buffalo National Park's Relations with the Dënesųłıné: Final Report*, 10 August 2021, https://drive.google.com/file/d/1T8ZgZAwW4cHieI0R_EkLf5dVfMFicUhB/view. A discussion of the work of both ACFN and WSSS, and of the relationships, approach, and processes that led to the original report and this book, is included as "Appendix 1: Building a community-directed work of oral history."

6   Ramsar Sites Information Services, *Canada 7: Peace-Athabasca Delta, Alberta. Information Sheet on Ramsar Wetlands,* Last updated 2001, https://rsis.ramsar.org/RISapp/files/RISrep/CA241RIS.pdf.

7   Wood Buffalo National Park lists the following First Nation and Métis communities as its Indigenous partners in Alberta: Mikisew Cree First Nation, Athabasca Chipewyan First Nation, Fort Chipewyan Métis, Little Red River Cree First Nation, and Smith Landing First Nation. Northwest Territories partners are: Salt River First Nation, Fort Smith Métis Council, K'atl'odeeche First Nation, Hay River Métis Council, Deninu Kue First Nation, and Fort Resolution Métis Council.

8   Archaeological evidence and oral traditions suggest that the presence of ancestors in the area dates back at least 7,000 years, and there is archaeological evidence of the ways of life and movements specifically of the Taltheilei, whom ACFN considers direct ancestors, that dates back roughly 3,000 years. See ACFN, *Footprints on the Land*, 20–24. ACFN Elders have shared volumes of oral tradition, history, and knowledge about the territories and Dene ways of life in community histories, TLU studies, and many other forums. See for example Athabasca Chipewyan First Nation, *Footprints on the Land: Tracing the Path of the Athabasca Chipewyan First Nation* (Fort Chipewyan: ACFN, 2003); Craig Candler, the Firelight Group Research Cooperative and ACFN, *Athabasca Chipewyan First Nation Integrated Knowledge and Land Use Report and*

Assessment for Shell Canada's Proposed Jackpine Mine Expansion and Pierre River Mine (2011), https://ceaa-acee.gc.ca/050/documents_staticpost/59540/82080/Appendix_D_-_Part_01.pdf; Patricia McCormack, *Research Report: An Ethnohistory of the Athabasca Chipewyan First Nation*, 2 September 2012, https://ceaa-acee.gc.ca/050/documents_staticpost/59540/82080/Appendix_D_-_Part_03.pdf.

9   McCormack, *Research Report*, 131; see also ACFN, *Footprints on the Land*, 32.

10 ACFN, *Footprints on the Land*, 9.

11 Maxwell Graham to J.B. Harkin, 7 December 1912, LAC RG 85, vol. 665, file 3911, pt. 1.

12 Leaders of the Chipewyan Band (the former name of ACFN) signed Treaty 8 in July 1899. The understanding and intent of the Treaty from Dene perspectives is discussed at greater length in Chapter 2. According to oral histories and archival documents, Dene leaders resolutely negotiated with Crown representatives for several days to ensure their rights, lives, and ways of life would not be impeded by the agreement. Like other Numbered Treaties, one term of Treaty 8 was the Crown's agreement to pay annuities to those registered as members of the First Nations who had signed. The annuity payment was set at $25 for the Chief, $15 for those the Commissioners called "Headmen" in the records (councillors and other leaders) and $5 for other members. The transfer from the Chipewyan Band annuity list to the Cree Band annuity list referred to here took place in 1944 and is discussed at greater length in Chapter 4.

13 As cited in Claudia Notzke, *Aboriginal Peoples and Natural Resources in Canada* (Concord, ON: Captus University Press, 1994), 246.

14 See, for example, Megan Youdelis, "'They could Take You out for Coffee and Call it Consultation!': The Colonial Antipolitics of Indigenous Consultation in Jasper National Park," *Environment and Planning: Economy and Space* 48, no. 7 (2016): 1374–92; Megan Youdelis et.al., "'Wilderness' revisited: Is Canadian park management moving beyond the 'wilderness' ethic?" *Canadian Geographer* (2019): 1–18; Jason W. Johnston and Courtney W. Mason, "The Paths to Realizing Reconciliation: Indigenous Consultation in Jasper National Park," *International Indigenous Policy Journal* 11, no. 4 (2020): 1–27.

15 Johnston and Mason, "The Paths to Realizing Reconciliation," 4.

16 See, for example, Ted Binnema and Melanie Niemi, "'Let the line be drawn now': Wilderness, Conservation, and the Exclusion of Aboriginal People from Banff National Park in Canada," *Environmental History* 11 (October 2006): 724–50; John Clapperton, "Desolate Viewscapes: Sliammon First Nation, Desolation Sound Marine Park and Environmental Narratives," *Environment and History* 18, no. 4 (November 2012): 529–559; Tina Loo, *States of Nature: Conserving Canada's Wildlife in the Twentieth Century* (Vancouver: UBC Press, 2007); I.S. MacLaren, *Culturing Wilderness in Jasper National Park: Studies in Two Centuries of Human History in the Upper Athabasca River Watershed* (Edmonton: University of Alberta Press, 2007); Courtney Mason, *Spirit of the Rockies: Reasserting an Indigenous Presence in Banff National Park* (Toronto: University of Toronto Press, 2014); Roberta Nakoochee, "Reconnection with Asi Kéyi: Healing Broken Connections' Implications for Ecological Integrity in Canadian National Parks," MA Thesis (Guelph: University of Guelph, 2018); John Sandlos, "Not Wanted at the Boundary: The Expulsion of the Keeseekoowenin Ojibway Band from Riding Mountain National Park," *Canadian Historical Review* 89, no. 2 (June 2008):

189–221; John Sandlos, *Hunters at the Margin: Native People and Wildlife Conservation in the Northwest Territories* (Vancouver: UBC Press, 2007); Youdelis, "Take You out for Coffee"; Youdelis et. al., "'Wilderness' revisited."

For global overviews of literature on evictions of Indigenous Peoples for conservation, see Daniel Brockington and James Igoe, "Eviction for Conservation: A Global Overview," *Conservation and Society* 4, no. 3 (2006): 424–470; John M. Mackenzie, *The Empire of Nature: Hunting, Conservation and British imperialism* (Manchester: Manchester University Press, 1988); Robert Poirier and David Ostergren, "Evicting People from Nature: Indigenous Land Rights and National Parks in Australia, Russia, and the United States," *Natural Resources Journal* 42, no. 2 (Spring 2002): 331–351.

For specific examples of these processes across the globe, see: Phillip Burnham, *Indian Country, God's Country: Native Americans and National Parks* (Washington, DC: Island Press, 2000); Robert Keller and Michael Turek, *American Indians and National Parks* (Tucson, AZ: University of Arizona Press, 1998); Mark Spence, *Dispossessing the Wilderness: Indigenous Removal and the Making of National Parks* (Oxford: Oxford University Press, 1999); Ramachandra Guha, "The Authoritarian Biologist and the Arrogance of Anti-Humanism: Wildlife Conservation in the Third World," *The Ecologist* 27, no. 1 (January/February 1997): 14–20; David Himmerflab, "Moving People, Moving Boundaries: The Socio-economic Effects of Protectionist Conservation, Involuntary Resettlement and Tenure Insecurity on the Edge of Mt. Elgon National Park, Uganda," *World Agroforestry* (2006), http://apps.worldagroforestry.org/programmes/african-highlands/pdfs/wps/ahiwp_24.pdf; Roderick P. Neumann, *Imposing Wilderness: Struggles over Livelihood and Nature Preservation in Africa* (Berkeley: UC Press, 1998); Klaus Seeland, "National Park Policy and Wildlife Problems in Nepal and Bhutan," *Population and Environment* 22, no. 1 (September 2000): 43–62.

17 Maano Ramutsindela, "National Parks and (Neo) Colonialisms," in *The Cambridge Handbook of Environmental Sociology*, vol. 1, ed. Katharine Legun, Julie C. Keller, Michael Carolan and Michael M. Bell (Cambridge: Cambridge University Press, 2020), 208.

18 Youdelis et. al., "'Wilderness' Revisited," 2.

19 Youdelis et. al., "'Wilderness' Revisited," 2.

20 Wolfe, "Settler colonialism"; Wildcat, "Fearing social and cultural death."

21 Woolford and Benvenuto, "Canada and colonial genocide," 381.

22 Wolfe, "Settler Colonialism," 388.

23 William Cronon, "The Trouble with Wilderness; or, Getting Back to the Wrong Nature" in *Uncommon Ground: Rethinking the Human Place in Nature*, ed. William Cronon (New York: W.W. Norton & Co., 1995); Mark Spence, *Dispossessing the Wilderness: Indigenous Removal and the Making of National Parks* (Oxford: Oxford University Press, 1999).

24 See for example, Loo, *States of Nature*; Binnema and Niemi, "Let the line be drawn now"; John M. Mackenzie, *The Empire of Nature: Hunting, Conservation and British imperialism* (Manchester: Manchester University Press, 1988).

25 See, for example, Desiree Valaderes, "Dispossessing the Wilderness: Contesting Canada's National Park Narrative" in *Cultural Contestation: Heritage, Identity and the Role of Government*, eds. J. Rodenberg and Pieter Wagenaar (London: Springer International Publications, 2018), 145; I.S. MacLaren, "Introduction" in *Culturing Wilderness in Jasper National Park: Studies in Two Centuries of Human History in the Upper Athabasca River Watershed*, ed. I.S. MacLaren (Edmonton: University of Alberta Press, 2007); Sandlos, "Not Wanted at the Boundary"; Clapperton, "Desolate Viewscapes."

26 Binnema and Niemi, "Let the line be drawn now," 738.

27 In some cases, Parks Canada officials expelled non-Indigenous people from their homes for the creation of national parks. See, for example, Bill Waiser, "'A Case of a Special Privilege and a Fancied Right': The Shack Tent Controversy in Prince Albert," in *A Century of Parks in Canada, 1911–2011*, ed. Claire Elizabeth Campbell (Calgary: University of Calgary Press, 2011), 103–132; Ronald Rudin, *Kouchibouguac: Removal, Resistance and Remembrance at a Canadian National Park* (Toronto: University of Toronto Press, 2016).

28 Ramutsindela, "National Parks and (Neo)Colonialisms," 212.

29 Some of the critical scholarship on colonial genocide and elimination in Canada is helpful here. See, for example, Wolfe, "Settler colonialism"; Woolford and Benvenuto, "Canada and colonial genocide"; Wildcat, "Fearing social and cultural death."

30 Cronon, "The Trouble with Wilderness."

31 O.S. Finnie to R.A. Gibson, 9 December 1925, LAC RG85, vol. 1213, file 400-2-3, v. 1.

32 Valaderes, "Dispossessing the Wilderness," 151.

33 Binnema and Niemi, "Let the line be drawn now," 725.

34 MacLaren, "Introduction" in *Culturing Wilderness*, xxvii.

35 Sandlos, "Not wanted at the Boundary," 211.

36 Sandlos, "Not wanted at the Boundary," 211.

37 David Neufeld, "Kluane National Park Reserve: 1923–1974: Modernity and Pluralism," in *A Century of Parks in Canada*, ed. Claire Elizabeth Campbell (Calgary: University of Calgary Press, 2011), 235–272.

38 Neufeld, "Kluane National Park Reserve," 254.

39 Binnema and Niemi, "Let the line be drawn now," 740.

40 Loo, *States of Nature*, 6.

41 Valaderes, "Dispossessing the Wilderness," 145.

42 Sandlos, "Not wanted at the boundary," 215.

43 Sandlos, "Not wanted at the boundary," 214.

44 MacLaren, Introduction to *Culturing Wilderness*, xxii.

45 MacLaren, Introduction to *Culturing Wilderness*, xxiii–xxiv.

46   Binnema and Niemi, "Let the line be drawn now," 738.

47   Johnston and Mason, "The Paths to Realizing Reconciliation," 2.

48   Ferguson, Theresa A. "The 'Jarvis Proof': Management of Bison, Management of Bison Hunters and the Development of a Literary Tradition," *Proceedings of the Fort Chipewyan / Fort Vermilion Bicentennial Conference* (Sept. 23–24, 1988), 299–300. For an important, related discussion about local oral histories and ecological knowledge, see Theresa A. Ferguson and Frank LaViolette, "A Note on Historical Mortality in a Northern Bison Population," *Arctic* 45 (March 1992): 47–50.

49   Sandlos, "Not wanted at the boundary," 207.

50   Nakoochee, "Reconnection with Asi Kéyi," 116.

51   Patricia McCormack, "The Political Economy of Bison Management in Wood Buffalo National Park," *Arctic* 45, no. 4 (December 1992): 379.

52   Patricia McCormack, *Fort Chipewyan and the Shaping of Canadian History, 1788-1920s: "We like to be free in this country"* (Vancouver: UBC Press, 2010), 271–72.

53   Sandlos, *Hunters at the Margin,* 26.

54   Tara Joly, "Urban Buffalo: Métis-Bison Relations and Oil Sands Extraction in Northeastern Alberta," in *Extracting Home in the Oil Sands: Settler Colonialism and Environmental Change in Subarctic Canada,* eds. Clinton Westman, Tara Joly and Lena Gross (London and New York, Routledge, 2020), 140.

55   Tara Joly, "Urban Buffalo," 148–9.

56   See McCormack, *Fort Chipewyan;* Liza Piper, *The Industrial Transformation of Subarctic Canada* (Vancouver: UBC Press, 2010); Ann Keeling and John Sandlos, eds. *Mining and Communities in Northern Canada: History, Politics, and Memory* (Calgary: University of Calgary Press, 2015); Clint Westman, Tara Joly, and Lena Gross, eds., *Extracting Home in the Oil Sands: Settler Colonialism and Environmental Change in Subarctic Canada* (London and New York: Routledge, 2020).

57   Although we are focused here on McCormack's 2010 book, we refer to her much larger corpus of work throughout this book.

58   McCormack, *Fort Chipewyan,* 202.

59   McCormack, *Fort Chipewyan,* 210.

60   McCormack, *Fort Chipewyan,* 224.

61   McCormack, *Fort Chipewyan,* 272.

62   Clint Westman, Tara Joly and Lena Gross, "Introduction" in *Extracting Home,* 1–22; Allan Greer, "Settler Colonialism and Beyond," *Journal of the Canadian Historical Association* 40, no. 1 (2019): 61–86.

63   Greer, "Settler Colonialism and Beyond."

64   Westman, Joly and Gross, "Introduction" in *Extracting Home,* 11.

65   Westman, Joly and Gross, "Introduction" in *Extracting Home,* 13.

66   Zoe Todd, "Foreword" in *Extracting Home,* ix.

67   Westman, Joly and Gross, "Introduction" in *Extracting Home*, 14.

68   Tara Joly, "Growing with Muskeg: Oil Sands Reclamation and Healing in Northern Alberta," *Anthropologica* 63, no. 1 (2021): 6-7.

69   Jennifer Huseman and Damien Short, "'A slow industrial genocide': tar sands and indigenous peoples of northern Alberta," *International Journal of Human Rights* 16, no. 1 (2012): 216-237.

70   Hereward Longley, "Uncertain Sovereignty: Treaty 8, Bitumen and Land Claims in the Athabasca Oil Sands Region," in *Extracting Home*, 35.

71   Longley, "Uncertain Sovereignty," in *Extracting Home*, 23-47.

72   Westman, Joly and Gross, "Introduction" in *Extracting Home*, 3.

73   See, for example, Candler et. al., *Athabasca Chipewyan First Nation Report*; Pat Marcel, Carolyn Whittaker and Craig Candler, *Níh Boghodi: We Are the Stewards of Our Land: An ACFN Stewardship Strategy for Thunzea, et'thén and Dechen Yághe Ejere (Woodland Caribou, Barren-Ground Caribou and Wood Bison*, (Fort Chipewyan, AB: Athabasca Chipewyan First Nation, 2012); Pat Marcel and Arlene Seegerts, *The Rights to Practice our Treaty Rights & The Importance of Co-Management with the Province of Alberta* (Fort Chipewyan: ACFN, n.d.); McCormack, *Research Report*; Adams & Associates, *Fort Chipewyan Way of Life Study* (Stuart Adams & Associates, 1998).

74   ACFN Elders, "ACFN Elders' Declaration on Rights to Land Use," in Marcel et.al., *Níh Boghodi* (Appendix 1), 12.

75   There are many important Indigenous-authored and community-driven works that honour and centre oral histories. For example, ɬaʔamin Elder Elsie Paul's life history, which she shared with Harmony Johnson and Paige Raibmon, centres oral history and tells the story of her community and homelands from a ɬaʔamin woman's perspective. See Elsie Paul, in collaboration with Paige Raibmon and Harmony Johnson, *Written as I remember it: Teachings (ʔems taʔaw) From the Life of a Sliammon Elder* (Vancouver: University of British Columbia Press, 2014). Similarly, Joan Scottie's history of uranium mining and Inuit resistance, co-written with Warren Bernauer and Jack Hicks, is a collaborative work based on the experiences of an Inuit woman. See Joan Scottie, Warren Bernauer and Jack Hicks, *I Will Live for Both of Us: A History of Colonialism, Uranium Mining, and Inuit Resistance* (Winnipeg: University of Manitoba Press, 2022). Treaty 7 Elders and Tribal Council aimed to "provide an opportunity for the Elders to speak" on their knowledge and history of Treaty 7, which had been extensively documented by lawyers and academics who rarely included the voices of Elders. See Treaty 7 Elders and Tribal Council, Walter Hildebrandt, Sarah Carter and Dorothy First Rider, *The True Spirit and Original Intent of Treaty 7* (Montreal/Toronto: McGill-Queen's University Press, 1996). Other important examples include Julie Cruikshank in collaboration with Angela Sidney, Kitty Smith and Anny Ned, *Life Lived Like a Story: Life Stories of Three Yukon Native Elders* (Vancouver: UBC Press, 1991); Harry Robinson and Wendy Wickwire, *Write it on your Heart* (Vancouver: Talonbooks, 1992); Camille Fouillard, Mushuau Innu Band Council, Naskapi Montagnais Innu Association, *Gathering Voices: Finding Strength to Help our Children* (Vancouver: Douglas and McIntyre, 1995); Andrea Laforet and Annie York, *Spuzzum: Fraser Canyon Histories, 1808-1939* (Vancouver: UBC Press, 1998); Kim Anderson, *Life Stages and Native*

Women: Memory, Teachings, and Story Medicine (Winnipeg: University of Manitoba Press, 2011); Robin Ridington and Jillian Ridington in collaboration with Elders of the Dane-Zaa First Nations, *Where Happiness Dwells: A History of the Dane-zaa First Nations* (Vanvouver: UBC Press, 2013).

76 Gregory Younging, *Elements of Indigenous Style: A Guide for Writing by and about Indigenous Peoples* (Edmonton: Brush Education, 2018).

77 Daniel Heath Justice, *Why Indigenous Literatures Matter* (Waterloo-Kitchener: Wilfrid Laurier University Press, 2018).

78 McCormack, *Fort Chipewyan,* 246.

79 Winona Wheeler, "Narrative Wisps of the Ochekiwi Sipi Past: A Journey in Recovering Collective Memories," in *The Canadian Oral History Reader,* eds. Kristina R. Llewellyn, Alexander Freund, Nolan Reilly (Montreal/Toronto: McGill-Queen's University Press, 2015), 285.

80 Interpretations of the TARR research can be found in *The Spirit of the Alberta Treaties,* ed. Richard Price (Edmonton: Pica, Pica Press, 1987). Copies of the original interviews can be found at the Lesser Slave Lake Indian Regional Council TARR Program Archive. For more information please visit https://lslirctarr.ca/archives/.

81 Readers can access the recordings via the QR codes and links provided throughout the book.

82 Ferguson, "The 'Jarvis' Proof," 299.

83 Victorine Mercredi, interview with Lorraine Hoffman, translated by Yvonne Hoffman (Mercredi), 20 January 1998, tape 2, 45 (Fort Chipewyan: ACFN Archives, 1998).

84 ACFN Elder Alec Bruno, written questionnaire, "ACFN Elders on Wood Buffalo National Park" (Fort Chipewyan: ACFN Community Archives, date unknown).

85 Patricia McCormack reaches this conclusion in Patricia McCormack, "Chipewyans Turn Cree: Governmental and Structural Factors in Ethnic Processes," in *For Purposes of Dominion: Essays in Honour of Morris Zaslow,* eds. Kenneth S. Coates and William R. Morrison (North York, On.: Captus University Publications, 1989). Sandlos agrees with McCormack's conclusion in *Hunters at the Margin.*

86 Alec Bruno, interview, written questionnaire.

87 Wolfe, "Settler colonialism," 388.

88 Wildcat, "Fear of cultural and social death," 394.

89 UNESCO World Heritage Convention, World Heritage Nomination: International Union for Conservation of Nature and Natural Resources Technical Review, 256 Wood Buffalo National Park (April 1983), https://whc.unesco.org/en/list/256/documents/.

90 UNESCO World Heritage Convention, Decision 39 COM 7B.18, Wood Buffalo National Park (Canada) (N256) (2015), https://whc.unesco.org/en/decisions/6275; UNESCO World Heritage Convention, Decision 44 COM 7B.190, Wood Buffalo National Park (Canada) (N256) (2021), https://whc.unesco.org/en/decisions/7906.

91 UNESCO World Heritage Centre, 41 COM, and International Union for Conservation of Nature, Mission Report Wood Buffalo National Park (Canada) (N 256) "Reactive Monitoring Mission to Wood Buffalo National Park, Canada" (24 September–4 October 2016), https://whc.unesco.org/en/list/256/documents/.

NOTES TO CHAPTER 1

1 The title of this section is drawn from the language used in Treaty 8 to designate the territories of the Dene people of the Peace-Athabasca Delta region (whom Treaty commissioners called "the Chipewyan Indians") who signed onto Treaty 8 in 1899. We have replaced the term "Chipewyan" with "Dene."

2 ACFN Elders, "ACFN Elders' Declaration on Rights to Land Use," in Marcel et.al., *Níh Boghodi* (Appendix 1): 12.

3 ACFN, *Footprints on the Land,* 31-32; McCormack, *Research Report.*

4 Fort Chipewyan Elder interview with Jimmy Deranger, Fort Chipewyan, 7 February 1974, Alberta. Treaty and Aboriginal Rights Research, Indian Association of Alberta, Fort Chipewyan, ACFN Archives, 1974. The Caribou Mountains, so named because they are a favoured habitat for the woodland caribou, are the highest mountain range in northern Alberta and are bounded on their north and east side by the Park. They have always been an important part of Dënesųłıné homelands; access was interrupted and cut off through the establishment of the Park.

5 McCormack, *Research Report,* 131; see also ACFN, *Footprints on the Land,* 32.

6 The title of this section is drawn from a comment by ACFN Elder Alice Rigney after she reviewed an early draft of the book. Personal communication with Sabina Trimble, Rose Ross, Lisa Tssessaze, Jay Telegdi, and Edouard Trippe de Roche, 4 April 2022.

7 Laura Peterson, "Exploring the Egg Lake/ ?Eghés tu Landscape and the Lake One Trail: A Collaboration with Knowledge Holders in Wood Buffalo National Park," (unpublished master's thesis, University of Alberta, 2018), https://doi.org/10.7939/R3NZ81611.

8 Peterson, "Exploring the Egg Lake," 73.

9 Marcel and Seegerts, *The Rights to Practice,* 18.

10 Amy Cardinal-Christianson, Colin Robert Sutherland, Faisal Moola, Noémie Gonzalez Bautista, David Young, and Heather MacDonald, "Centering Indigenous Voices: The Role of Fire in the Boreal Forest of North America," *Current Forestry Reports* 8 (2022): 257, 261.

11 Henry T. Lewis, *A Time for Burning: Traditional Indian Uses of Fire in the Western Canadian Boreal Forest* (Edmonton: Boreal Institute for Northern Studies Occasional Publication, No. 17, 1982), 47. See also Theresa A. Ferguson, "In Search of the Elusive: traditional native prescribed burning in the Northeastern Wood Buffalo Park Area," (discussion paper presented to the University of New Brunswick Fire Science Centre, 1989).

12 ACFN, Dene Laws, https://www.acfn.com/chief-and-council.

13 Donalee Deck, *Archaeological House Lake Project, 2011*, prepared for Wood Buffalo National Park (Winnipeg: Cultural Science Branch, Parks Canada, August 2012), 7.

14 Deck, *Archaeological House Lake Project*, 6.

15 Deck, *Archaeological House Lake Project*, 14–21.

16 Deck, *Archaeological House Lake Project*, 22–49.

17 M.J. Dempsey to John A. McDougal, 21 October 1930, LAC RG85-D-1-A, vol. 152, file 420-2.

18 ACFN Elder Fredoline Deranger/ Djeskelni (Fred's Dene name is Djeskelni), telephone interview with Sabina Trimble and Lisa Tssessaze, 19 March 2021.

19 Lees & Associates Landscape Architects with Regional Municipality of Wood Buffalo, *Regional Municipality of Wood Buffalo Urban and Rural Cemeteries Project: Phase II Consultant Report: Inventories and Interviews*, Fort Chipewyan: ACFN Community Files, 23 July 2010.

20 Marie Josephine Mercredi, interview with Lorraine Hoffman, translated by Yvonne Hoffman (Mercredi), 20 January 1998, tape 2, 45, Fort Chipewyan: AFCN Archives, 1998.

21 Rene Bruno, "Oral History of Treaty 8," recorded by Nicole Nicholls, translated by Arsene Bernaille, Fort Chipewyan: AFCN Archives, 8 February 2010.

22 Cardinal-Christianson et. al., "Centering Indigenous Voices," 271.

23 Alice Rigney, personal communication with Sabina Trimble, Rose Ross, Lisa Tssessaze, Jay Telegdi, and Edouard Trippe de Roche 4 April 2022.

24 ACFN, *Footprints on the Land*, 29.

25 ACFN Elder Marie Josephine Mercredi, interview with Lorraine Hoffman, translated by Yvonne Hoffman (Mercredi), 22 January 1998, Fort Chipewyan: ACFN Archives, 1998.

26 Rene Bruno, Alec Bruno, Beverly Tourangeau, and Charlie Mercredi, interview with Melissa Daniels, 5 May 2015, Fort Chipewyan, Alberta. Dene Laws interview collection (Fort Chipewyan: ACFN Archives, 2015). Audio recording: https://digitalcollections.ucalgary.ca/AssetLink/ht4qw765nh77x344t5yk5623501coj00.mp3.

27 Rene Bruno, Alec Bruno, Beverly Tourangeau, and Charlie Mercredi, 5 May 2015. Dene Laws interview collection. Audio recording: https://digitalcollections.ucalgary.ca/AssetLink/ht4qw765nh77x344t5yk5623501coj00.mp3.

28 Jim Deranger, phone interview with Peter Fortna, 24 March, 2021. Audio recording: https://digitalcollections.ucalgary.ca/AssetLink/131d7of5rn51bpq1ow06841s670gk648.mp3.

29 Keltie Paul is married to ACFN Elder Edouard Trippe de Roche. Keltie and Ed shared their testimony in a joint interview.

30 Uranium City is a settlement in Saskatchewan, located on the northeast side of Lake Athabasca. It sits in ACFN's core homelands. It was established in response to the uranium mining boom in the Beaverlodge area in the 1950s. Some Elders shared

memories of their families and other Indigenous workers and families from the Athabasca area who travelled to the town for work during the 1950s and 1960s.

NOTES TO CHAPTER 2

1. Government of Canada, *Treaty No. 8. Made June 21, 1899 and Adhesions, Reports, Etc.* [1899], reprinted from file the 1899 edition by Roger Duhamel, FRSC (Ottawa: Queen's Printer and Controller of Stationary, 1966), https://www.rcaanc-cirnac.gc.ca/eng/1100100028813/1581293624572#chp4.

2. Patricia McCormack compiled a helpful list titled "Promises made by the Treaty Commissioners in 1899 about Lands and Resources," which indicates numerous occasions at which treaty commissioners promised that rights to treaty lands would remain with Indigenous Peoples. See McCormack, "Studying the Social and Cultural Impacts of 'Extreme Extraction' in Northern Alberta," in *Extracting Home*, 188.

3. Fort Chipewyan Elder Louis Boucher, interview with Richard Lightning, 6 February 1974, Treaty and Aboriginal Rights Research, Indian Association of Alberta (Fort Chipewyan: ACFN Office).

4. ACFN Elders, *ACFN Elders' Declaration*.

5. Bruno, "Oral History of Treaty 8."

6. *Treaty No. 8.*

7. As cited in Fumoleau, *As Long as this Land Shall Last*, 79–80.

8. Chief Jonas Laviolette to James K. Cornwall, February 1928, RCMAFS, file. Cornwall, as cited in René Fumoleau, *As Long as this Land Shall Last: A History of Treaty 8 and Treaty 11, 1870–1939* (Calgary: University of Calgary Press, 2004), 339–340n104.

9. Victorine Mercredi, interview.

10. Rene is referring to the steamship transportation industry that centred on hauling freight by steamship or barge along the Athabasca River and connected river systems. This system was central to the northern fur trade, had a strong influence on migration and settlement patterns around Fort McMurray and Fort Chipewyan, and was an industry in which many First Nations and Métis men worked throughout the late nineteenth and twentieth centuries. Elders from ACFN like Rene are among those who worked on the barges, including loading and off-loading barges and captaining them.

NOTES TO CHAPTER 3

1. Alec Bruno, written questionnaire.

2. Graham to Harkin, 7 December 1912.

3. Harkin's memorandum is referenced in another 1915 memorandum that recounted some of the earlier conversations and controversy surrounding the proposal to create a sanctuary. See memorandum to J.G. Mitchell, 23 September 1915, LAC RG85 vol. 1390, file 406-13, WBNP General file (Clippings).

4. Memorandum to Mitchell, 23 September 1915.

5   See for example, Maxwell Graham, *Canada's Wild Buffalo: Observations in the Wood Buffalo Park, 1922* (Department of the Interior, Northwest Territories and Yukon Branch. Ottawa: F.A. Acland, 1923), 11. https://babel.hathitrust.org/cgi/pt?id=mdp.39015006571528&view=1up&seq=1. See also O.S. Finnie to J.W. Martin (Commissioner of Dominion Lands Administration), 14 April 192?, LAC RG85, vol. 792, file 6276.

6   Graham to Harkin, 7 December 1912.

7   Graham to Harkin, 7 December 1912.

8   Sandlos, *Hunters at the Margin*, 39. See also John Sandlos, "Landscaping Desire: Poetics, Politics in the Early Biological Surveys of the Canadian North," *Space and Culture* 6, no. 4 (Nov. 2003): 395–414.

9   Valaderes, "Dispossessing the Wilderness," 151.

10 See for example, Marcel and Seegerts, "The Rights to Practice," 21.

11 McCormack, "The Political Economy of Bison Management in Wood Buffalo National Park," *Arctic* 45, no. 4 (December 1992): 368.

12 For example, Sandlos cites several letters and reports, including Radford to Hooper, 20 June 1911, LAC RG85, vol. 665, file 3911, pt. 2; Henry Bury, "Report on Buffalo Protection," 25 October 1915, LAC RG85, vol. 665, file 3912, pt. 1; George Mulloy's patrol report to Robert Campbell, 9 July 1913, LAC RG85, vol. 665, file 3912, pt. 1; Charles Camsell, "The Wood Buffalo Range of Northern Alberta," 21 November 1916, LAC RG85, vol. 1390, file 406-13, pt. 1. See Sandlos, *Hunters at the Margin*, 38.

13 See, for example, comments by Indian Agent Gerald Card to Parks officials and others, including J.B. Harkin and F.H. Kitto, in 1921. "Stenographic report of a portion of the Meeting" (sgd.) H.L. 12 April 1921, LAC RG85 vol. 1390, file 406-13.

14 Wardens frequently reported these kinds of interactions with Indigenous Peoples in their diaries and patrol reports. See LAC RG85-D-1-A, vol. 152, file 420-2. Wardens' Patrol Reports, Wood Buffalo National Park (Maps), 1928–1936; LAC RG85, vol. 153, file 420-2, Warden Patrol Reports 1936–44; and LAC RG85-C-1-a, vol. 761, file 4878, Pt. 1 (Warden M.J. Dempsey's Journals, 1925–1948).

15 Sandlos, *Hunters at the Margin*, 53.

16 Ferguson, "The 'Jarvis Proof," 299.

17 See Proposed Order in Council for Creation of Wood Bison Habitat Into a National Park, Description of area approved by Surveyor General, 3 July 1916, LAC RG85 vol. 1390, file 406-13, WBNP General file (Clippings) 1914–25. See also Maxwell Graham, "Statement as to the Causes that led up to the Creation of the Wood Buffalo Park" for O.S. Finnie's information, 4 June 1924, LAC RG85 vol. 1390, file 406-13 WBNP General file (Clippings) 1914–25.

18 Graham, "Statement as to the Causes," 2.

19 Arthur Meighen, "Address of Welcome," in *National Conference on Conservation of Game, Fur-Bearing Animals and Other Wild Life, 18–19 February 1919*, ed. Commission

of Conservation of Canada (Ottawa: King's Printer, 1919), 5. https://www.canadiana.ca/view/oocihm.82935/16?r=0&s=1.

20 Graham, "Statement as to the Causes," 3.

21 Graham, "Statement as to the Causes," 6.

22 F.H. Kitto, *Report on the Natural Resources of the Mackenzie District and Their Economic Development*, Natural Resources Intelligence Branch, Department of the Interior, 1920, LAC RG10, vol. 4092, file 548-036, 5.

23 Kitto, "Report on the Natural Resources," 21.

24 Memorandum from F.H. Kitto to J.B. Harkin, with map attachments, 12 January 1921, LAC RG85 vol. 1390, file 406-13, WBNP General file (Clippings) 1914–25.

25 Copy of Resolution [Regarding the setting aside of the wood bison range as a sanctuary], 18 June 1920, Advisory Board on Wild Life Protection, LAC RG85 vol. 1390, file 406-13, WBNP General file (Clippings) 1914–25. The Resolution is also cited in a letter from J.B. Harkin to Duncan Campbell Scott, 23 November 1920, LAC RG10, vol. 4085, file 496, 658-1A Minutes, Advisory Board in Wildlife Protection, 18 June 1920, LAC RG10, vol. 4085, file 496,658-1A.

26 Memorandum from W.W. Cory to F.C.C. Lynch, 8 May 1922, LAC RG85 vol. 1390, file 406-13, WBNP General file (Clippings) 1914–25.

27 Graham, "Statement as to the Causes," 7.

28 This is evident from a lengthy series of memoranda and telegrams from September to October 1922, mostly between Graham and Finnie, LAC RG85 vol. 1390, file 406-13, WBNP General file (Clippings) 1914–25.

29 Memorandum to J.G. Mitchell, 23 September 1915.

30 Graham to Finnie, 16 January 1923, LAC RG85 vol. 1390, file 406-13, WBNP General file (Clippings) 1914–25.

31 See, for example, Binnema and Niemi, "'Let the line be drawn now'"; MacLaren, *Culturing Wilderness;* Sandlos, "Not Wanted at the Boundary"; Nakoochee, "Reconnection with Asi Kéyi" and others discussed in the Introduction to this book.

32 Finnie to Graham, 28 December 1925 with memorandum from Finnie, 21 December 1921 attached, LAC RG85-D-1-A, vol. 1391, file 406-13. Wood Buffalo National Park – General file, 1921–27, 1928–36.

33 Graham to Harkin, 7 December 1923, LAC RG85, vol. 665, file 3911, p. 3.

34 Graham to Finnie, 27 September 1923, Archival source unknown. Copies available at ACFN community archives, Fort Chipewyan, Alberta; Graham to Finnie, 17 July 1924, LAC RG85 vol. 1390, file 406-13, WBNP General file (Clippings) 1914–25.

35 R.I. Eklund to R.F. Battle, 4 January 1955 and R.I. Eklund to Regional Supervisor of Indian Agencies, 4 August 1954, LAC RG10 vol. 8409, file 191/20-14-1, pt. 2.

36 Finnie to R.A. Gibson, 9 December 1925, LAC RG85, vol. 1213, file 400-2-3, v. 1.

37   Finnie to Graham, 28 December 1925, LAC RG85-D-1-A, vol. 1391, file 406-1, Wood Buffalo National Park – General file, 1921–27.

38   Finnie to Graham, 28 December 1925.

39   Duncan Campbell Scott, 29 December 1925, cited in memorandum by O.S. Finnie, 8 November 1928, LAC RG85, vol. 792, file 6276, p. 3.

40   J.A. McDougal to O.S. Finnie, 2 March 1926, LAC RG85, vol. 1213, file 400-2-3, pt. 1.

41   W.W. Cory to James Harkin, 26 May 1923, LAC RG85, vol 1390, file 406-13, pt. 1. See also memorandum from Graham to Fyle, 5 January 1923, LAC RG85, vol. 1390, file 406-13.

42   Strong and widespread opposition to the importation scheme (and Graham and Finnie's continued dismissal of that opposition — even as the main concerns about the scheme eventually came to pass), are extensively documented in LAC RG85, vol. 1391, file 406-13. For example, see W.E. Saunders to Cory, 15 April 1925, RG85-D-1-A, vol. 1391, file 406-13, Wood Buffalo National Park – General file, 1921–27, 1928–36; Saunders to White, 11 April 1925, RG85-D-1-A, vol. 1391, file 406-13. See also Professor J.D. Detwiler to Prime Minister Mackenzie King, 10 June 1925, RG85-D-1-A, vol. 1391, file 406-13. See also Dr. James Ritchie, "The American Bison: A Questionable Experiment." Article copied from *Supplement to Nature,* 20 February 1926. Clipped in RG85-D-1-A, vol. 1391, file 406-13.

43   W.F. Lothian, *A History of Canada's National Parks,* vol. IV. (Ottawa: Parks Canada, 1981), 33–35. See also Jennifer Brower, *Lost Tracks: Buffalo National Park, 1909–1939* (Edmonton: Athabasca University Press, 2008).

44   See for example McDougal to Finnie, 24 July 1925 and memorandum from Finnie to Cory, 13 August 1925, both from LAC RG85-D-1-A, vol. 1391, file 406-13, Wood Buffalo National Park – General file, 1921–27, 1928–36.

45   Telegram from Finnie to McDougal, 1 February 1926 and then from McDougal to Finnie, 2 February 1926. LAC RG85-D-1-A, vol. 1391, file 406-13, Wood Buffalo National Park – General file, 1921–27, 1928–36.

46   Memorandum for file by O.S. Finnie, 16 February 1926, LAC RG-85-D-1-A, vol. 1391, file 406-13.

47   J.A. McDougal to O.S. Finnie, 25 March 1926, LAC RG85, vol. 1213, file 400-2-3, pt. 1.

48   Telegram from McDougal to Finnie, 22 March 1926, LAC RG-85-D-1-A, vol. 1391, file 406-13.

49   Fort Chipewyan Elder Jimmy Deranger, interview 7 February 1974, Treaty and Aboriginal Rights Research, Indian Association of Alberta (Fort Chipewyan: ACFN Office).

50   O.S. Finnie to ?, 30 June 1926, archival source unknown (likely LAC RG85). Copies of source available at ACFN community archives, Fort Chipewyan, Alberta.

51   Order in Council PC 1444, 18 September 1926, LAC RG85 vol. 1391, file 406-13.

52   See, for example, Finnie to Gibson, 29 March 1926. LAC RG85-D-1-A vol. 1391, file 406-13; Finnie to Cory, 31 March 1926, LAC RG85-D-1-A vol. 1391, file 406-13.

53 Order in Council PC 1444, 24 September 1926, LAC RG 85 vol. 1391, file 406-13.
54 R.A. Gibson to D.J. Allan (Superintendent, Reserves and Trusts, Indian Affairs Branch), 23 September 1938, LAC RG85 v. 1213 file 400-2-3, v.1. This permit system bears a striking resemblance to the Indian Pass System, which was instituted on the prairies between 1877 and 1935. Keith Douglas Smith, *Liberalism, Surveillance, and Resistance: Indigenous Communities in Western Canada, 1877–1927* (Edmonton: Athabasca University Press, 2009); F. Laurie Barron, "The Indian Pass System in the Canadian West, 1882–1935," *Prairie Forum*, vol. 13, no. 1 (1988).
55 O.S. Finnie to R.A. Gibson, 23 April 1926, LAC RG85, vol. 1213, file 400-2-3, pt. 1.
56 R.A. Gibson to D.J. Allan, 23 September 1938, LAC RG85 v. 1213 file 400-2-3, v. 1.
57 Memorandum from O.S. Finnie to R.A. Gibson, 18 June 1926, archival source unknown. Copy of memorandum available at ACFN community archives, Fort Chipewyan, Alberta.
58 Department of Northern Affairs and National Resources, Northern Administration and Lands Branch, Conservation and Management Services, Wood Buffalo Park Game Regulations, Office Consolidation, Ottawa, 1 June 1954, LAC RG10, vol. 8409, file 191/20-14-1, pt. 2.
59 Memorandum from [unknown] to R.A. Gibson, Department of Interior, 29 February 1936, LAC RG85, v. 1213 file 400-2-3, pt. 2A, p. 2.
60 Report from M.J. Dempsey to M. Meikle (Agent and Superintendent), 20 February 1937, LAC RG85, vol. 845, file 7744, pt. 1, as cited in Sandlos, *Hunters at the Margin*, 71n107.
61 M.J. Dempsey to J. Milner, 1 March 1933, LAC RG85, v. 852, file 7870.
62 Mason, *Spirit of the Rockies*, 52.
63 M.J. Dempsey to J. Milner, 1 March 1933.
64 J. Melling, *Report of Meeting with Chief and Councillors of Indians Living in 'B' and 'C' Areas of the Wood Buffalo Park*, LAC RG10, vol. 8409, file 191/20-14-1, pt. 1.
65 J.L. Grew to D.J. Allen, 19 March 1943, LAC RG10, vol. 8409, file 191/20-14-1, pt. 1.
66 F.A. McCall, January Wardens' Reports, 4 February 1948, Fort Chipewyan, Alberta. RG85-D-1-A, vol. 318, file 420-2/199-1, Wardens Reports – Fort Chipewyan (1946–53).
67 M.J. Dempsey to A.L. Cumming, 12 August 1935, LAC RG85, v. 1213, file 400-2-3, pt. 2A.
68 [Unknown] to R.A. Gibson, 29 February 1936.
69 M. Meikle to R.A. Gibson, 15 April 1937, LAC RG85, v. 1213, file 400-2-3, pt. 2A.
70 See, for example, R.A. Gibson to J.W. Burton, 22 December 1949, LAC RG85-C-1-a, vol. 846, file 7744, pt. 4, applications to hunt and trap (1950–54).
71 Meikle to Gibson, 15 April 1937.
72 See Government of Canada, Department of the Interior, "Regulations governing hunting and trapping in Wood Buffalo Park Established under authority of the Order-in-Council of the 14th December, 1933, P.C. 2589," LAC RG10, vol. 8409, file 191/20-

14-1, pt. 1. See also W.G. Brown to G.E.B. Sinclair, 20 July 1951 "Illegal Beaver – Wood Buffalo Park," LAC RG10 vol. 8409, file 191/20-14-1, pt. 2, p. 1.

73 See, for example, Royal Canadian Mounted Police, *Reports on Conclusions of Case*, Form 264B, 19 March 1942, LAC RG10 vol. 8409, file 191/20-14-1, pt. 1; W.G. Brown to G.E.B. Sinclair, 20 July 1942.

74 Telegram from J.A. McDougal to O.S. Finnie, 4 January 1928, LAC RG85, v. 1213, file 400-2-3, pt. 1A.

75 Sandlos, *Hunters at the Margin*, 71.

76 Indian Agent John Melling to Secretary of Indian Affairs, 15 October 1942, LAC RG10 vol. 8409, file 191/20-14-1, pt. 1.

77 Fort Chipewyan Elder Felix Gibot, interview with Richard Lightning at Fort Chipewyan, 5 February 1974, Treaty and Aboriginal Rights Research, Indian Association of Alberta (Fort Chipewyan: ACFN Office).

78 For example, Treaty 7 Elders explained in 1996, and Stoney Nakoda Elders told Courtney Mason two decades later that: "'At the time [1877] nothing was ever mentioned about the cutting up of the land here and there into recreational areas and parks. The government didn't tell them it would eventually be doing this. It is because of these special areas that we can't go hunting' (Hildebrandt et al., 1996, 90). The government never consulted with or informed Nakoda peoples about the formation of the reserve or the national park." See Mason, *Spirits of the Rockies*, 53.

79 Henry Bury to Deputy Minister of Indian Affairs, 13 April 1916, LAC RG85, vol. 664, file 3910, vol. 1.

80 Bury to Deputy Minister of Indian Affairs, 13 April 1916.

81 Alec Bruno, written questionnaire.

82 Richard Lightning was one of the field researchers/interviewers for the Treaty 8 research under the Treaty and Aboriginal Rights Research initiative in the 1970s.

83 Lightning might have been referring to the fenced enclosures where bison were rounded up for monitoring or slaughtering, or he may be referring to the harvesting laws and permitting restrictions that kept Dene people out of the Park.

84 Boucher is referring to the plains bison that were imported from 1925 to 1928.

85 Dené is a family name belonging to one of the Dënesųłıné families within the Park that was transferred to the Cree Band.

86 Leonard's mother, Liza Piche, was among the Piche family members who had to leave the Park after the 1926 expansion.

87 Felix Gibot and other local Indigenous workers were hired by the Park to assist with the distribution of bison meat at the time of the scheduled slaughters. Some Indigenous workers found employment in the Park in other capacities throughout the twentieth century, working as guides and interpreters and at the fisheries and mills.

88 Leslie is referring to Kitaskino Nuwëné Wildland Provincial Park, located on the southeast boundary of WBNP, in the heart of the Ronald Lake bison herd's range.

The 161,880-hectare protected area was established in 2019 following collaborative discussions amongst Indigenous governments (including MCFN and ACFN) and the Government of Alberta. The Park is planned to be cooperatively managed and was created to "support the exercise of Treaty and harvesting rights for First Nations and approved Métis harvesters" as well as to steward "many many natural values important to Indigenous People's culture and well-being, including the Ronald Lake bison herd — a critical species for many Indigenous Peoples in the region who share a cultural relationship with the herd." For more information see Alberta Parks, Kitaskino Nuwënë Wildland Provincial Park, "Decision to Establish Kitaskino Nuwënë Wildland Provincial Park," https://www.albertaparks.ca/albertaparksca/about-parks/public-engagement/archives/kitaskino-nuwenëné-wildland-provincial-park/.

89   Les Wiltzen interview on oral histories about the Park expansion January 21, 2021. Audio recording: https://digitalcollections.ucalgary.ca/AssetLink/21ivrjx1eoi18672587 w2d1ri52dvdn1.mp3.

NOTES TO CHAPTER 4

1   Frank Marcel, written questionnaire, "ACFN Elders on Wood Buffalo National Park," (Fort Chipewyan: ACFN Community Archives, date unknown).

2   Indian Agent Jack Stewart, "Daily Journal, 1944," PAA, Acc 71.11/2d.

3   See Jacques Whitford, *Treaty Entitlements Research — Update Report*, Tables 1–4 (Fort Chipewyan: ACFN, 2006).

4   Written questionnaires by ACFN members; see also Whitford, *Treaty Entitlements Research*.

5   McCormack, "Chipewyans Turn Cree," 132–133.

6   M. Meikle to R.A. Gibson, 27 June 1945, LAC RG85, Vol. 1214, file 400-2-3, pt. 3, as cited in Sandlos, *Hunters at the Margin*, p. 86.

7   McCormack, "Chipewyans Turn Cree."

8   Helene Piche and her family relocated many times out of necessity, moving to where they could continue to continue to find suitable wage labour and harvesting areas.

9   Garry is referring to *Sandra Lovelace v. Canada*. Lovelace is a Wolastoqiyik woman who was a member of the Tobique First Nation, until, like Elizabeth Flett, she was stripped of her Indian Status under the Indian Act after marrying a non-Status Indigenous man. She brought forward an application to the United Nations Human Rights Committee in 1977, arguing that the Act was discriminatory on the basis of sex because the law, which did not apply to men who married non-Indigenous women, stripped Indigenous women of their Status, First Nations' membership, and access to funds and programming. It also cut women off from traditional hunting and fishing rights and the cultural benefits of living in their community. The UN Committee found that Canada had interfered with Lovelace's right to enjoy her culture and that stripping her of her Status was a violation of the International Covenant on Civil and Political Rights. Canada's response was to amend the *Indian Act* via Bill C-31 in 1985. Garry attempted to make his family's case for access to the Park after this revision.

10   Big John may have been referring to the Simpson family and other Dene families from Fort McKay who relocated to the Delta to trap before the transfer.

NOTES TO CHAPTER 5

1. See for example, Mackay Meikle, "WOOD BUFFALO PARK: Notice to native hunters who have permits for the Wood Buffalo Park," 15 March 1939, LAC RG85, v. 1213, file 400-2-3, p. 1.
2. Loo, *States of Nature*, 6.
3. Neufeld, "Kluane National Park Reserve," 254.
4. Ferguson, "Jarvis Proof," 300.
5. Wolfe, "Settler colonialism," 388.
6. See "Regulations governing hunting and trapping in Wood Buffalo Park Established under authority of the Order-in-Council of the 14th December, 1933, P.C. 2589." LAC RG10, Vol. 8409, File 191/20-14-1, pt. 1; see also Department of Northern Affairs and National Resources, Northern Administration and Lands Branch, Conservation and Management Services, *Wood Buffalo Park Game Regulations, Office Consolidation*, Ottawa: 1 June 1954, LAC RG10 Vol. 8409, File 191/20-14-1, pt. 2; "Precis for Northwest Territories Council: Representations of single Indians for Wood Buffalo Park beaver permits." N.d. LAC RG85, v. 1213 file 400-2-3, pt. 2A; unknown author to Hugh Conn, Fur Development, Indian Affairs, 19 July 1950, LAC RG10 Vol. 8409, File 191/20-14-1, pt. 1.
7. Government of Canada and Government of United States of America, *Convention for the Protection of Migratory Birds in the United States and Canada*, Ratified 7 December 1916, amended in 1999. https://www.canada.ca/en/environment-climate-change/corporate/international-affairs/partnerships-countries-regions/north-america/canada-united-states-protecting-migratory-birds.html
8. Privy Council, Order in Council P.C. 1955-940, *Amendment to the Wood Buffalo Park Game Regulations*, Ottawa: 23 June 1955, LAC RG10 Vol. 8409, File 191/20-14-1, pt. 2.
9. John Melling, "Diary of Treaty Trip," Athabaska Agency, 4 July 1942, LAC RG10 Vol. 8409, File 191/20-14-1, pt. 1; see also R.A. Hoey to R.A. Gibson, 11 May 1946, LAC RG10 Vol. 8409, File 191/20-14-1, pt. 1.
10. O.S. Finnie to J.A. McDougal, 6 March 1925, LAC RG85, Vol. 1213, File 400-2-3, v. 1.
11. Cardinal Christianson et. al., "Centring Indigenous Voices": 270.
12. McCormack, *Fort Chipewyan*, 234.
13. Act. Sgt. G.T. Makinson's Report, "Re — Treaty Indians — Resolution, NWT. Refusal to Accept Treaty Payment," 3 July 1937, LAC RG85 Vol. 1213, File 400 2-3, Vol. 1; See also E.G. Oldham to R.A. Gibson, 15 September 1947, LAC RG85, Vol. 1214, File 400-2-3, vol 3A.
14. E.G. Oldham to R.A. Gibson, 15 September 1947, 3.
15. R.A. Gibson to T.R.L. MacInnes, 4 October 1939, LAC RG10 Vol. 8409, File 191/20-14-1, pt. 1.

16 As cited in Notzke, *Aboriginal Peoples and Natural Resources*, 246.

17 See for example F.C. Dent to J.A. Urquhart, 22 February 1940, LAC RG10, Vol. 8409, File 191/20-14-1, pt. 1; R.A. Gibson to H.W. McGill, 13 March 1940, LAC RG10, Vol. 8409, File 191/20-14-1, pt. 1.

18 For example: Game Commissioner to O.S. Finnie, 12 December 1925, LAC RG85, Vol. 1213, File 400-2-3, v. 1; D.J. Allan to R.A. Gibson, 16 September 1938, LAC RG85, v. 1213, file 400-2-3, v.1; R.I. Eklund to Regional Supervisor of Indian Agencies, 4 August1954, LAC RG10 Vol. 8409, File 191/20-14-1, pt. 2.

19 M.J. Dempsey to A.L. Cumming, 12 August 1935, LAC RG85, v. 1213, File 400-2-3, pt. 2A.

20 T.R.L. MacInnes to Deputy Commissioner, NWT, 6 June 1938, LAC RG85, v. 1213, file 400-2-3.

21 See T.R.L. MacInnes to R.A. Gibson, 1 September 1938, LAC RG10 Vol. 8409, File 191/20-14-1, pt. 1; R.A. Gibson to T.R.L. MacInnes, 27 September 1938, LAC RG10 Vol. 8409, File 191/20-14-1, pt. 1; Mackay Meikle to R.A. Gibson, 25 October 1938, LAC RG10 Vol. 8409, File 191/20-14-1, pt. 1; R.A. Gibson to H.W. McGill, Director of Indian Affairs Branch, 9 November 1938, LAC RG10 Vol. 8409, File 191/20-14-1, pt. 1; T.R.L. MacInnes to P.G. Head, 8 December 1938, LAC RG10 Vol. 8409, File 191/20-14-1, pt. 1; S.C. Knapp to J.P.B Ostrander, Attn: Hugh R. Conn, 9 July 1954, LAC RG10 Vol. 8409, File 191/20-14-1, pt. 2.

22 M.J. Dempsey to A.L. Cumming, 12 August 1935.

23 Park Warden J.A. Routh noted this complaint in 1938. See memorandum by Cumming. "Notes from Wardens' diaries, Wood Buffalo Park, received with letters of 9th and 25th March 1938, from the Fort Smith Office," 20 April 1938. RG85, Vol. 153, File 420-2, Warden Patrol Reports 1936–44.

24 See Warden F.A. McCall "June 1948 Report," 9 July 1948, Fort Chipewyan, LAC RG85-D-1-A, Vol. 318, File 420-2/199-1, Wardens Reports — Fort Chipewyan (1946–53); Report of Warden F.A. McCall "February 1947 Report," LAC RG85-D-1-A, Vol. 318, File 420-2/199-1, Wardens Reports — Fort Chipewyan (1946–53).

25 Unknown author to W.W. Cory, 25 October 1928, LAC RG85, v. 1213 file 400-2-3, pt. 1A.

26 Sandlos, *Hunters at the Margin*, 101.

27 Sandlos, *Hunters at the Margin*, 76–77.

28 McCormack, *Fort Chipewyan*, 224–225.

29 As is apparent from some of the oral histories in this chapter, Dënesųłıné people share kinship and a strong cultural and spiritual connection with wolves and were reluctant to kill them. Parks officials observed this reluctance throughout the twentieth century. When offered pay to cull wolves to reduce wolf predation, few Dene harvesters took up the opportunity. Maxwell Graham wrote of this in his report to O.S. Finnie, "Statement as to the Causes."

30   A.L. Cumming to R.A. Gibson, 29 November 1940, LAC RG85, v. 1214, file 400-2-3, pt. 3, as cited in McCormack, "How the (North)West was won," 232.

31   Ferguson, "Jarvis Proof," 304. Elder Pat Marcel spoke extensively about the standard government response to Indigenous Peoples' concerns in his oral history, excerpted at length in this chapter. See: Marcel and Seegerts, *The Rights to Practice*. See also R.I. Eklund to Regional Supervisor of Indian Agencies, 4 August 1954.

32   Chief Jonas Laviolette to Indian Affairs, 20 February 1927, LAC RG10, vol. 6732, file 420-2

33   N.E. Tanner to M. Christian, Gen. Superintendent of Agencies, Indian Affairs Branch, 15 March 1938, LAC RG10, Vol. 6733, File 420-2-1.

34   Bill Russell, *Report to the Chipewyan Band of Fort Chipewyan on Treaty Land Entitlement and other Land Matters* (Ottawa: Indian Association of Alberta), 27.

35   J.L. Grew to D.J. Allen, *Report on Registered Trap Lines in Alberta*, (11 March 1943), 6, LAC RG 10, Vol. 6733, File 420-2-2 2.

36   Peter Fortna, *Cadotte Lake Métis: A Genealogical Narrative, 1850–2000* (Cochrane, AB: Willow Springs Strategic Solutions, 2021), 31. See also, Dawn Balazs, *A Short Analysis of the Transfer of Natural Resources to Alberta in 1930 and a Preliminary Study of the Registered Trapline System* (Treaty and Aboriginal Rights Research of the Indian Association of Alberta, March 1976), Chapter 3.

37   W.B. Skead, "Report on the Revision of Indian Registered Traplines and Registered Trapping Areas in Alberta," 20 January 1949, p. 1. LAC RG10, Vol. 6734, File 420-2-2 1.

38   W.B. Skead, *Annual Report — Alberta Fur Supervisor*, 1 November 1947–1 October 1948, p. 7. LAC RG10 Vol. 6734, File 420-2 1.

39   Skead, *Annual Report*. See M. Meikle, J.L. Grew, J. Dewey Soper, and M.J. Dempsey, "Recommendations of Committee Appointed to Enquire into Certain Fur Conservation Problems in Wood Buffalo Park," 16 July 1945, LAC RG10, Vol. 8409, File 191/20-14-1, pt. 1.

40   Skead, *Annual Report*. See also Memorandum Re: Open season for muskrats and registered trap lines, 12 June 1939, LAC RG85, vol. 1213, file 400-2-3.

41   Report of Warden F.A. McCall, January 1947.

42   See Memorandum Re: Open season for muskrats and registered trap lines, 12 June 1939.

43   Indian Agent P.G. Head to unknown, 21 March 1940, LAC RG10, Vol. 6733, File 420-2 5.

44   John Melling to Secretary of Indian Affairs, 12 June 1942, LAC RG10 Vol. 8409, File 191/20-14/1, pt. 1.

45   See Indian Agent P.G. Head to unknown, 21 March 1940.

46   Russell, "Report to the Chipewyan Band," 27.

47   J.A. McDougal to O.S. Finnie, 2 March 1926.

48   I.F. Kirkby to E.G. Oldham, 24 June 1947, LAC RG85-4-C-A, Vol. 345, File 5. Admin of WBNP, 1944–1947.

49 McCormack, "How the (North)West was Won," 203.

50 See for example Department of Northern Affairs and National Resources, Northern Administration and Lands Branch, Conservation and Management Services, "Office Consolidation of Regulations governing hunting and trapping in Wood Buffalo Park," 1933; and a lengthy series of correspondence between E.G. Oldham and Supervising Warden I.F. Kirkby, 1944–1946. RG85-4-C-A, Vol. 345, File 5, Admin of WBNP 1944-47.

51 F.A. McCall, March report, 1 April 1948 and April Report, 5 May 1948. LAC RG85-D-1-A, Vol. 318, File 420-2/199-1, Wardens Reports — Fort Chipewyan (1946–53).

52 Nakoochee, "Reconnection with Asi Kéyi."

53 Elder Magloire Vermillion, interview with Jim Deranger, 13 February 1974, Treaty and Aboriginal Rights Research, Indian Association of Alberta (Fort Chipewyan: ACFN Community Archives).

54 E.G. Oldham to R.A. Gibson, 15 September 1947.

55 Neil Walker to C.B. Carignan, 11 May 1953, LAC RG10 Vol. 8409, File 191/20-14-1, pt. 2.

56 See, for example, Wendy Wickwire, "To See Ourselves as the Other's Other: Nlaka'pamux Contact Narratives," *Canadian Historical Review* 75, no. 1 (March 1994): 1–20.

57 Winona Wheeler, "Narrative Wisps of the Ochekiwi Sipi Past: A Journey in Recovering Collective Memories," in *The Canadian Oral History Reader*, eds. Kristina R. Llewellyn, Alexander Freund and Nolan Reilly (Montreal/Toronto: McGill-Queen's University Press, 2015), 285.

58 Warden reports also contain frequent references to the help they received from Dene and other Indigenous Peoples, sometimes explicitly writing about friendly relations with harvesters.

59 M.J. Dempsey to J.A. McDougal, 17 February 1931, RG85-D-1-A, Vol. 152, File 420-2. Wardens' Patrol Reports, Wood Buffalo National Park (with maps), 1928–1936.

60 O.S. Finnie to Christie, 8 June 1925, RG85-D-1-A, Vol. 1391, File 406-13. Wood Buffalo National Park — General File, 1921–1927, 1928–1936.

61 N22 refers to an ACFN-controlled trapping block in northwestern Saskatchewan.

62 Edouard Trippe de Roche and Keltie Paul interview, November 25, 2020. Audio recording: https://digitalcollections.ucalgary.ca/AssetLink/36lsl083a4h1e566y0sj5 m472624g307.mp3.

NOTES TO CHAPTER 6

1 Chief Laviolette to Indian Affairs, 20 February 1927.

2 Sandlos, *Hunters at the Margin*, 74.

3 Memorandum from John Wylie, Colin Fraser, James Fraser, ? Marcel, and P. Mercredi to Charles Cross, "Re the setting-apart of a New Buffalo Park or the establishing of an

annex to the existing Wood Buffalo Park; which is to be situated in the terrain North of the Quatre Fourches River, and on the West shore of Lake Mamiwi, North of Hay River and Lake Claire," 16 April 1926, LAC RG85, v. 1213, file 400-2-3, pt. 1A.

4   Memorandum from Wylie et al. 16 April 1926.

5   Chief Laviolette to Indian Affairs, 20 February 1927, 3. For other examples of letters from Indigenous Peoples to Park officials, see St. Cyr to Urquhart, 29 December 1939, LAC RG85, vol. 845, file 7744, pt. 2, as cited in Sandlos, *Hunters at the Margin,* 72n106; Boucher to Wood Buffalo Head, 8 January 1937, LAC RG85, vol. 845, file 7744, pt. 2, as cited in Sandlos, *Hunters at the Margin,* 72n109; Mrs. Adam Boucher [née Ratfat] to Fort Smith, 27 February 1936, as cited in Sandlos, *Hunters at the Margin,* 72n109.

6   A.L. Cumming to J. Lorne Turner, 13 August 1935, LAC RG85, v. 1213, file 400-2-3, pt. 2A.

7   See for example, Melling, "Diary of Treaty Trip."

8   Act. Sgt. G.T. Makinson's Report, "Re — Treaty Indians."

9   Sandlos, *Hunters at the Margin*, 75.

10 Sandlos, *Hunters at the Margin*, 67.

11 O.S. Finnie to W.W. Cory, 7 August 1930, RG85-D-1-A, vol. 152, file 420-2. Wardens' Patrol Reports, Wood Buffalo National Park (with maps), 1928–1936.

12 F.C. Dent to M.J. Dempsey, 16 December 1935. RG85-D-1-A, vol. 152, file 420-2.

13 As stated in a memo from Mackay Meikle to R.A. Gibson, 23 December 1937, LAC RG85, vol.1213 file 400-2-3 pt. 2A.

14 F.A. Bryant to E.G. Oldham, 24 March 1947. RG85-C-4-A, vol. 345, file 5.

15 A.L. Cumming to J. Lorne Turner, 13 August 1935.

16 Mackay Meikle to R.A. Gibson, 23 December 1937.

17 Act. Sgt. G.T. Makinson's Report, "Re — Treaty Indians."

18 Chief Jonas Laviolette to Indian Affairs, 20 February 1927.

19 McCormack, "Chipewyans Turn Cree," 133.

20 Russell, "Report to the Chipewyan Band," 27.

21 This shift occurred under Orders-in-Council P.C. 1954-817 and P.C. 1954-900.

22 Gerald Card to J.D. McLean, 6 December 1927, LAC RG10, vol. 6732, file 420-2B. (Emphasis added). In the hopes of an increase in the muskrat population, leaders wanted to protect the region from excessive trapping and other human activities that could prevent a resurgence in the muskrat population.

23 Robertson to MacInnes, 11 February 1931, LAC RG10, vol. 6732, file 420-2B.

24 Marcel and Seegerts, "The Rights to Practice our Treaty Rights," 12.

25 Order-in-Council 298-35, 6 March 1935 and accompanying Report from the Minister of Agriculture, as cited in Marcel and Seegerts, "The Rights to Practice our Treaty

Rights," 24. See also S.H. Clark to M. Christianson, 12 March 1935, LAC RG10, vol. 6733, file 420-2C.

26 Marcel and Seegerts, "The Rights to Practice our Treaty Rights," 14.

27 See for example, letters between Indian Agent Harry Lewis, M. Christianson, and A.F. MacKenzie during March and April 1936, LAC RG10, vol. 6733, file 420-2C.

28 Marcel and Seegerts, "The Rights to Practice our Treaty Rights," 14.

29 UNESCO World Heritage Centre, 41 COM, "Reactive Monitoring Mission."

30 Joanne Stassen, "Indigenous entrepreneur defends right to harvest salt after warning from Parks Canada," *CBC* (April 14, 2022), https://www.cbc.ca/news/canada/north/melissa-daniels-won-t-stop-harvesting-salt-from-wood-buffal-1.6420471.

31 Leyland Cecco, "Salt spat highlights Canadian national park's troubling history," *The Guardian* (17 April 2022), https://www.theguardian.com/world/2022/apr/17/salt-spat-highlights-canadian-national-parks-troubling-history.

32 Cecco, "Salt spat."

33 Where a speaker discusses harvesting in the Park against regulations, their names, and the people of whom they speak, are kept anonymous to prevent possible repercussions from sharing their stories.

34 In May 2022, Imperial Oil identified a leak from one of its tailings ponds on the northeastern corner of the Kearl Mine Site, about 75 kilometres south of WNBP and five kilometres from the Firebag River. Tailings ponds are massive, engineered reservoirs that oil sands mines use to store tailings — the toxic by-product of oilsands extraction. Tailings ponds hold waters containing petrochemical waste from the extraction process, concentrated organic matter, sand, and silt. The water can be highly toxic due to high levels of organic acids, ammonia, lead, mercury, and benzene. Imperial workers identified pooled surface water outside the boundaries of the tailings pond, which contained a mix of groundwater and tailings material. In August 2022, the company found more discoloured water near a fish-bearing waterbody. Imperial Oil reported the leak to the Alberta Energy Regulator (AER), but it was never made public, and Indigenous governments were not informed. In late January 2023, there was a massive spill of 5.3 million litres from the tailings area of the same project. It took four days before the company detected the spill. The spill resulted in seepage of toxic industrial wastewaters into the boreal wetlands and nearby tributaries. The 2022 leak was not made public until the 2023 spill occurred, after the AER issued an Environmental Protection Order on 6 February 2023.

Representatives from ACFN and many of the other First Nations and Métis communities in the area publicly denounced Imperial Oil's and the AER's actions and silence on this matter. Among several other Indigenous leaders, Chief Allan Adam testified before the House of Commons in Ottawa in April 2023, calling the AER "a complete joke." He described the community's deep frustration with the events and grave concerns about the impacts of the seepage and spill. Federal and provincial investigations proceeded shortly after the hearings. See: Imperial Oil Ltd., "Kearl EPO Update #3," news release, 1 March 2023, https://www.imperialoil.ca/-/media/imperial/files/operations/kearl/kearl-epo-update-3-mar-1-2023.pdf; Gillian Chow-Fraser and

Nicole Doll, "Everything you need to know about the Kearl Mine tailings silent leak and then sudden spill," Canadian Parks and Wilderness Society – Northern Alberta Chapter, 16 May 2023, https://cpawsnab.org/everything-you-need-to-know-about-the-kearl-spill/; APTN National News, "First Nation in northern Alberta reports Kearl mine leak 'worse' than expected," *APTN National News*, 21 March 2023, https://www.aptnnews.ca/national-news/first-nation-in-northern-alberta-reports-kearl-mine-leak-worse-than-expected/.

35   Referring to seven of ACFN's eight reserves, which include Chipewyan 201 and Chipewyan 201A-G.

36   A commercial fishery with operations in the Park in the first half of the twentieth century, which Marcel suggests rarely employed ACFN people.

NOTES TO CHAPTER 7

1   Athabasca Chipewyan First Nation, *Footprints on the Land,* 9.

2   McCormack, *Fort Chipewyan,* 269.

3   McCormack, *Fort Chipewyan,* 270.

4   McCormack, "How the (North)West was Won," 156.

5   The genocide committed through Canada's residential school system, and its profound intergenerational impacts, have been extensively discussed in oral histories and survivors' memoirs, historical research studies, and in the final report of the Truth and Reconciliation Commission of Canada. See for example: Theodore Fontaine, *Broken Circle: The Dark Legacy of Indian Residential Schools – A Memoir* (Victoria: Heritage House Publishing, 2010); Bev Sellars, *They Called Me Number One: Secrets and Survival at an Indian Residential School* (Vancouver: Talonbooks, 2013); Joseph Auguste Merasty, with David Carpenter, *The Education of Augie Merasty: A Residential School Memoir* (Regina: University of Regina Press, 2015); Phyllis Webstad, *Beyond the Orange Shirt Story: A collection of stories from family and friends of Phyllis Webstad before, during, and after their Residential School experiences* (Unceded Sc'ianew, Lekwungen, and T'Sou-ke territory: Medicine Wheel Publishing, 2020); J.R. Miller, *Shingwauk's Vision: A History of Native Residential Schools* (Toronto: University of Toronto Press, 1996); John S. Milloy, *A National Crime: The Canadian Government and the Residential School System, 1879-1986* (Winnipeg: University of Manitoba Press, 1990); and Truth and Reconciliation Commission of Canada, *Honouring Truth, Reconciling for the Future: Summary of the Final Report of the Truth and Reconciliation Commission of Canada* (Ottawa, 2015), https://publications.gc.ca/site/eng/9.800288/publication.html.

6   Victor Mercredi, "Diary of Victor Mercredi," (Fort Chipewyan, 1962), PAA, ACC 71.369 SE PAA, p. 26.

7   J.L. Grew to D.J. Allen, 14 August 1945, "Report on Registered Trap Lines in Alberta and General Trapping Conditions," p. 11, LAC RG10, vol. 6734, file 420-2-2-3

8   See Dempsey to Gibson, 5 August 1937, LAC RG85, vol. 852, file 7869, pt. 1; Gibson to Urquhart, 13 August 1941, LAC RG85, vol. 852, file 7869, pt. 2; see also memorandum from Gibson to Cumming, 8 March 1940, LAC RG85, vol. 852, file 7869, pt. 2; Gibson to Urquhart, 28 October 1940, LAC RG85, vol. 852, file 7869, pt. 2; Savage to ?, 25 June

1940, LAC RG85, vol. 852, file 7869, pt. 2; W.B. Skead, RCMP Report re: Grant Savage, 17 March 1941, LAC RG85, vol. 852, file 7869, pt. 2.

9   Sandlos, *Hunters at the Margin*, 25.
10 Joly, "Urban Buffalo," 140.
11 Athabasca Chipewyan First Nation, *Footprints on the Land*, 64.
12 T.R.L. MacInnes to Richards, 7 June 1938, LAC RG85, v. 1213 file 400-2-3, pt. 1.
13 Makinson, "Re-Treaty Indians."
14 See for example James Daschuk, *Clearing the Plains: Disease, Politics of Starvation, and the Loss of Indigenous Life* (Regina: University of Regina Press, 2014); see also Woolford and Benvenuto, "Canada and Colonial Genocide."
15 See Sandlos, "Not Wanted at the Boundary." See also, for example, Mason, *Spirit of the Rockies* for examples of similar processes in Banff National Park.
16 Peterson, "Exploring the Egg Lake," 140–141.
17 Athabasca Chipewyan First Nation, *Footprints on the Land*, 13.
18 Athabasca Chipewyan First Nation, *Footprints on the Land*, 89.
19 McCormack, *Research Report*, 170.
20 Athabasca Chipewyan First Nation, *Footprints on the Land*, 13.
21 Sandlos, *Hunters at the Margin*, 75.
22 Wildcat, "Fear of Social and Cultural Death," 394 & 398.
23 Marcel and Seegerts, "The Rights to Practice Our Treaty Rights," 18–19.
24 Mercredi, written questionnaire.
25 Mercredi, written questionnaire.
26 Mason, *Spirit of the Rockies*, 58.
27 Ernie "Joe" Ratfat, phone interview with Sabina Trimble, 19 March, 2021. Audio recording: https://digitalcollections.ucalgary.ca/AssetLink/e3yeqao80712p243t 082262543dnlt4x.mp3.
28 Alice Rigney, phone interview with Sabina Trimble, 16 & 17 March, 2021. Audio recording: https://digitalcollections.ucalgary.ca/AssetLink/rs18km5bigb0jyxuxjt 0far4g0u4em34.mp3.
29 Alice Rigney, phone interview with Sabina Trimble, 16 & 17 March, 2021. Audio recording: https://digitalcollections.ucalgary.ca/AssetLink/wd0rvkk748ei0ti4e82 gmnge16r05475.mp3.
30 Lori Stevens, Zoom interview with Sabina Trimble, 25 May, 2021. Audio recording: https://digitalcollections.ucalgary.ca/AssetLink/sj81b7fh44qjr15tutr5rpx85m786717. mp3.
31 Whose homelands are west of Dënesųłıné homelands, with the Peace River at their centre. The territory crosses the border of what are now Alberta and British Columbia, spanning from the Rocky Mountains to near Fort Vermillion and as far south as the Wapiti River.

NOTES TO CONCLUSION

1 Maxwell Graham to J.B. Harkin, 7 December 1912.
2 McCormack, "Political Economy," 373.
3 Memorandum to Cabinet, Walter Dinsdale, Minister of Northern Affairs and National Resources, 30 January 1963, LAC RG84-A-2-A, vol. 2227, file WB2, Pt. 2.
4 T. O'Dwyer, Secretary Treasurer, White Hills Mining Corporation to Hon. Walter Dinsdale, 4 December 1963, LAC RG84-A-2-A, vol. 2227, file WB2, Pt. 2.
5 Peterson, "Exploring the Egg Lake," 6.
6 Wood Buffalo National Park of Canada, "Management Plan" (Fort Smith: Parks Canada, June 2010), 8.
7 As cited in Notzke, *Aboriginal Peoples and Natural Resources*, 246.
8 Teck Resources, Ltd. is a mining company that proposed to construct a $20 billion oil sands extraction operation 110 kilometres north of Fort McMurray in 2008, called the Teck Frontier Oil Sands Mine. The project would have involved the construction, operation, and reclamation of an oil sands surface mine with production capacity of about 260,000 barrels of bitumen per day and was expected to operate for forty-one years. The project was suspended in 2020.
9 Marcel and Seegerts, "The Rights to Practice our Treaty Rights," 20–22. In this excerpt, Pat Marcel was referring to the Ronald Lake Bison herd which is located south of Wood Buffalo National Park. It became a major topic of discussion in relation to the proposed Teck Frontier project. ACFN, and Pat Marcel in particular, have made numerous filings with regards to the importance of the Ronald Lake Bison herd which can be found in the *Canadian Environmental Assessment Act* Teck Frontier Mine Oil Sands Mine Project https://iaac-aeic.gc.ca/050/evaluations/proj/65505 as well as ACFN Submissions to the Lower Athabasca Regional Plan Land Use Secretariate; for example see: Melissa Daniels to LARP Review Panel, 30 November 2014, https://landuse.alberta.ca/Forms%20and%20Applications/RFR_ACFN%20Reply%20to%20IR%204_2014-12-01_PUBLIC.pdf.
10 Marcel and Seegerts, *The Rights to Practice our Treaty Rights*, 20–22.
11 These include Ts'udé Niḷiné Tueyata, a sacred area co-managed by the Dene community of K'asho Got'ı̨nę and the Fort Good Hope Métis Land Corporation #54, near what is now called Fort Good Hope, NWT; the Edéhzhíe Dehcho Protected Area, in Dehcho Dene homelands between Fort Simpson and Fort Providence; and Thaidene Nëné, a protected area in southeastern NWT, co-managed by Łutsël K'é Dene First Nation, Northwest Territory Métis Nation, Deninu Kųę First Nation, and Yellowknives Dene First Nation.
12 Mi'kmaq stewardship and conservation organizations established the Sespite'tmnej Kmit Knu Conservancy in 2021 and are currently working toward the establishment of an IPCA in an area of interest in what is not called Cape Breton, in unceded Mi'kmaq territory.
13 See Conservation Through Reconciliation Partnership, Indigenous Protected and Conserved Areas, https://conservation-reconciliation.ca/about-ipcas.

14 Sandlos, *Hunters at the Margin,* 107.

15 Some scholars and Indigenous communities have discussed the challenges related to Parks Canada's co-management and Indigenous consultation in recent decades across the country. See for example, Youdelis, "Take You out for Coffee"; Youdelis, et al., "Wilderness' revisited"; Johnston and Mason, "The Paths to Realizing Reconciliation."

16 United Nations Educational, Scientific and Cultural Organization, "Report of the joint WHC/IUCN Reactive Monitoring mission to Wood Buffalo National Park, Canada 25 September–4 October 2016," Convention Concerning the Protection of the World Cultural and Natural Heritage, World Heritage Committee. Forty-first session. Krakow, Poland: 2–12 July 2017, https://whc.unesco.org/en/documents/156893.

17 Judith Lavoie, "UN says Canada isn't doing enough to save Wood Buffalo National Park," *The Narwhal,* 14 June 2019. Available at: https://thenarwhal.ca/un-says-canada-isnt-doing-enough-to-save-wood-buffalo-national-park/.

18 "UNESCO says industry and poor governance 'likely' endanger Wood Buffalo National Park," *Fort McMurray Today,* 22 June 2021, https://www.fortmcmurraytoday.com/news/unesco-says-industry-poor-governance-likely-endanger-wood-buffalo-national-park.

19 International Union for Conservation of Nature and Natural Resources, Advisory Body Evaluation World Heritage Nomination: 256 Wood Buffalo National Park (15 April 1993), 2, https://whc.unesco.org/en/list/256/documents/

20 Sandlos, *Hunters at the Margin,* 104.

21 UNESCO, "Report of the joint WHC/IUCN Reactive Monitoring Mission."

22 See 2017, 2019, and 2021 World Heritage State of Conservation Reports for 256 Wood Buffalo National Park, https://whc.unesco.org/en/list/256/documents/.

23 UNESCO World Heritage Convention, Decision 44 COM 7B.190.

24 Sandlos, *Hunters at the Margin,* 108.

NOTES TO APPENDIX 1

1 Leslie Brown and Susan Strega, "Introduction," in *Research as Resistance: Revisiting Critical, Indigenous, and Anti-Oppressive Approaches,* 2nd edition, eds. Leslie Brown and Susan Strega (Toronto: Women's Press – Canadian Scholars Press, 2015), 7.

2 Linda Tuhiwai Smith, *Decolonizing Methodologies: Research and Indigenous Peoples,* 2nd Edition (London: Zed Books, 2012), xi, xii.

3 Adam Gaudry, "Researching the Resurgence: Insurgent Research and Community-Engaged Methodologies," in *Research as Resistance,* 244.

4 Younging, *Elements of Indigenous Style.*

5 Brown and Strega, "Introduction," 5. Among many other examples, see Smith, *Decolonizing Methodologies*; Shawn Wilson, *Research is Ceremony: Indigenous Research Methods* (Halifax: Fernwood Publishing, 2008); Margaret Kovach, *Indigenous Methodologies: Characteristics, Conversations and Contexts* (Toronto: University of Toronto Press, 2009); Jason Arday, "Dismantling Power and privilege through

reflexivity: negotiating normative Whiteness, the Eurocentric curriculum and racial micro-aggressions within the Academy," *Whiteness and Education* 3, no. 2 (2018): 141–61; Keith Carlson, John Lutz, David Schaepe, Naxaxalhts'i (Sonny McHalsie), eds., *Towards a New Ethnohistory: Community Engaged Scholarship among the People of the River* (Winnipeg: University of Manitoba Press, 2018); Sarah Nickel and Amanda Fehr, eds., *In Good Relation: History, Gender, and Kinship in Indigenous Feminisms* (Winnipeg: University of Manitoba Press, 2020); Linda Tuhiwai Smith, Eve Tuck and K.W. Yang, eds., *Indigenous and Decolonizing Studies in Education: Mapping the Long View* (New York: Routledge, 2019).

6   Gaudry, "Researching the Resurgence," 249.

7   Madeline Rose Knickerbocker, "Making Matriarchs at Coqualeetza: Stó:lō Women's Politics and Histories across Generations," in *In Good Relation*, 29.

8   Kwagu'ł Gix̱sa̱m Clan and Leslie Robertson, *Standing Up with G̱a'ax̱sta'las: Jane Constance Cook and the Politics of Memory, Church and Custom* (Vancouver: UBC Press, 2012), 16.

9   Gaudry, "Researching the Resurgence," 244.

10 Gaudry, "Researching the Resurgence," 248.

11 The Northern Affairs Branch of the Department of the Interior administered the Park for the first four decades of its existence until administrative responsibility was transferred to the Parks Branch in 1964.

12 See, for example, Serena Hillman, Azadeh Forghani, Carolyn Pang and Carman Neustaedter, "Conducting Interviews with Remote Participants," in *Studying and Designing Technology for Domestic Life*, eds. Tejinder K. Judge and Carman Neustaedter (Waltham, MA: Morgan Kaufman, Elsevier, 2015), 11–32; Jasmine R. Linabery and Stephanie A. Hamel, "Feminist Online Interviewing: Engaging Issues of Power, Resistance and Reflexivity in Practice," *Feminist Review* 115, no. 1 (2017): 97–113.

13 Government negotiations are ongoing as of summer 2023.

NOTES TO APPENDIX 2

1   Interview transcripts held in the ACFN Wood Buffalo National Park Apology Project interview collection. Fort Chipewyan: ACFN, 2021.

Bibliography

Athabasca Chipewyan First Nation Community Records and Other Historic Collections, Fort Chipewyan, AB

ACFN. *Athabasca Chipewyan First Nation Advice to the Government of Alberta Regarding the Lower Athabasca Regional Plan.* Provided to the Land Use Secretariat, 22 November 2010. https://landuse.alberta.ca/Forms%20and%20Applications/RFR_ACFN%20 Response%20to%20LARP%20Panel%20IR%206%20-%20Advice_2014-11-14_ PUBLIC.pdf.

ACFN Elders. "ACFN Elders' Declaration on Rights to Land Use." In Marcel, Pat, Carolyn Whittaker, and Craig Candler. *Níh Boghodi: We Are the Stewards of Our Land: An ACFN Stewardship Strategy for Thunzea, et'thén and Dechen Yághe Ejere (Woodland Caribou, Barren-Ground Caribou and Wood Bison),* Appendix 1, 12. Fort Chipewyan, AB: Athabasca Chipewyan First Nation, 2012. https://landuse.alberta.ca/Forms%20 and%20Applications/RFR_ACFN%20Reply%20to%20IR%204%20Nih%20 Boghodi_2014-12-01_PUBLIC.pdf.

ACFN Elders' questionnaire. ACFN Elders on Wood Buffalo National Park. Fort Chipewyan: ACFN, n.d.

ACFN Land-Use Plan interview transcripts collection. Fort Chipewyan: ACFN, 2009.

Adams, Stuart, *Fort Chipewyan Way of Life Study.* Stuart Adams & Associates, 1998.

Bruno, Rene. "Oral History of Treaty 8." Recorded by Nicole Nicholls. Trans. Arsene Bernaille. Fort Chipewyan, AB: 8 February 2010.

Candler, Craig, the Firelight Group Research Cooperative, and ACFN. *Athabasca Chipewyan First Nation Integrated Knowledge and Land Use Report and Assessment for Shell Canada's Proposed Jackpine Mine Expansion and Pierre River Mine.* Fort Chipewyan: ACFN, 2011. https://ceaa-acee.gc.ca/050/documents_staticpost/59540/82080/ Appendix_D_-_Part_01.pdf.

Deck, Donalee. *Archaeological Inventory: House Lake Project, 2011.* Report prepared for Wood Buffalo National Park. Parks Canada. Winnipeg: Cultural Science Branch, 2012.

Dene Laws Project interview transcripts collection. Fort Chipewyan: ACFN, 2015.

Lorraine Hoffman interview transcripts collection. Fort Chipewyan: ACFN, 1998.

Jacques Whitford, Ltd. *Treaty Entitlements Research — Update Report*. Fort Chipewyan: ACFN, 2006.

Lees & Associates Landscape Architects with Regional Municipality of Wood Buffalo. *Regional Municipality of Wood Buffalo Urban and Rural Cemeteries Project: Phase II Consultant Report: Inventories and Interviews*. Fort Chipewyan: ACFN Community Files, 23 July 2010.

Marcel, Pat and Arlene Seegerts. *The Rights to Practice Our Treaty Rights & The Importance of Co-Management with the Province of Alberta*. Fort Chipewyan: ACFN, n.d.

Russell, Bill. Treaty and Aboriginal Rights Research (TARR). *Report to the Chipewyan Band of Fort Chipewyan on Treaty Land Entitlement and other Land Matters*. Ottawa: Indian Association of Alberta, 1981.

Stuart Adams & Associates. *Fort Chipewyan Way of Life Study*. Stuart Adams & Associates, 1998.

Treaty and Aboriginal Right Research Interview Transcripts. Indian Association of Alberta. Fort Chipewyan: ACFN, 1974. Lesser Slave Lake Indian Regional Council TARR Program Archive.

Trimble, Sabina and Peter Fortna. *A History of Wood Buffalo National Park's Relations with the Dënesųłıné: Final Report Including historical narrative, impacts and critical interpretations, with appendices*. 10 August 2021 (Revised February 2023). https://drive.google.com/file/d/1T8ZgZAwW4cHieI0R_EkLf5dVfMFicUhB/view.

Published Sources

Anderson, Kim. *Life Stages and Native Women: Memory, Teachings, and Story Medicine*. Winnipeg: University of Manitoba Press, 2011.

Athabasca Chipewyan First Nation. *Footprints on the Land: Tracing the Path of the Athabasca Chipewyan First Nation*. Fort Chipewyan: ACFN, 2003.

Arday, Jason. "Dismantling Power and privilege through reflexivity: negotiating normative Whiteness, the Eurocentric curriculum and racial micro-aggressions within the Academy." *Whiteness and Education* 3, no. 2 (2018): 141–161.

Balazs, Dawn. *A Short Analysis of the Transfer of Natural Resources to Alberta in 1930 and a Preliminary Study of the Registered Trapline System*. Treaty and Aboriginal Rights Research of the Indian Association of Alberta, March 1976.

Barron, Laurie F. "The Indian Pass System in the Canadian West, 1882–1935." *Prairie Forum* vol. 13, no. 1 (1988): 25–42.

Binnema, Ted and Melanie Niemi. "'Let the line be drawn now': Wilderness, Conservation, and the Exclusion of Aboriginal People from Banff National Park in Canada." *Environmental History* 11 (October 2006): 724–50.

Brockington, David and James Igoe. "Eviction for Conservation: A Global Overview." *Conservation and Society* 4, no. 3 (2006): 424–470.

Brower, Jennifer. *Lost Tracks: Buffalo National Park, 1909-1939*. Edmonton: Athabasca University Press, 2008.

Brown, Leslie and Susan Strega. "Introduction." In *Research as Resistance: Revisiting Critical, Indigenous, and Anti-Oppressive Approaches*, edited by Leslie Brown and Susan Strega, 1-16. 2nd edition. Toronto: Women's Press–Canadian Scholars Press, 2015.

Burnham, Philip. *Indian Country, God's Country: Native Americans and National Parks*. Washington, D.C.: Island Press, 2000.

Campbell, Claire Elizabeth, ed. *A Century of Parks in Canada, 1911-2011*. Calgary: University of Calgary Press, 2011.

Cardinal Christianson, Amy, Colin Robert Sutherland, Faisal Moola, Noémie Gonzalez Bautista, David Young and Heather MacDonald. "Centering Indigenous Voices: The Role of Fire in the Boreal Forest of North America." *Current Forestry Reports* 8 (2022): 257-276. https://doi.org/10.1007/s40725-022-00168-9.

Carlson, Keith Thor, John Sutton Lutz, David Schaepe and Naxaxalhts'i (Sonny McHalsie), eds. *Towards a New Ethnohistory: Community Engaged Scholarship among the People of the River*. Winnipeg: University of Manitoba Press, 2018.

Clapperton, Jonathan. "Desolate Viewscapes: Sliammon First Nation, Desolation Sound Marine Park and Environmental Narratives." *Environment and History* 18, no. 4 (November 2012): 529-559.

———. "Naturalizing Race Relations: Conservation, Colonialism, and Spectacle at the Banff Indian Days." *Canadian Historical Review* 94, no. 3 (September 2013): 349-379.

Commission of Conservation Canada. *National Conference on Conservation of Game, Fur-Bearing Animals and Other Wild Life*. Ottawa: J.L. Taché, Printer to the King's Most Excellent Majesty, 1919. https://www.canadiana.ca/view/oocihm.82935/16?r=0&s=1.

Cronon, William. "The Trouble with Wilderness; or, Getting Back to the Wrong Nature." In *Uncommon Ground: Rethinking the Human Place in Nature*, edited by W. Cronon, 69-90. New York: W.W. Norton & Co., 1995.

Cruikshank, Julie. *Do Glaciers Listen? Local Knowledge, Colonial Encounters, and Social Imagination*. Vancouver: UBC Press, 2005.

Cruikshank, Julie, in collaboration with Angela Sidney, Kitty Smith and Anny Ned. *Life Lived Like a Story: Life Stories of Three Yukon Native Elders*. Vancouver: UBC Press, 1991.

Daschuk, James. *Clearing the Plains: Disease, Politics of Starvation, and the Loss of Indigenous Life*. Regina: University of Regina Press, 2014.

Ferguson, Theresa A. "The 'Jarvis Proof': Management of Bison, Management of Bison Hunters and the Development of a Literary Tradition" In *Proceedings of the Fort Chipewyan / Fort Vermilion Bicentennial Conference*, edited by Patricia McCormack and R. Geoffrey Ironside, 299-304. Edmonton: University of Alberta Press, 1990.

———. "In Search of the Elusive: traditional native prescribed burning in the Northeastern Wood Buffalo Park Area." Discussion Paper. University of New Brunswick Fire Science Centre, 1989.

Ferguson, Teresa A. and Frank Laviolette. "A Note on Historical Mortality in a Northern Bison Population." *Arctic* 45 (March 1992), 47–50.

Fontaine, Theodore Niizhotay. *Broken Circle: The Dark Legacy of Indian Residential Schools — A Memoir*. Victoria, BC: Heritage House Publishing, 2010.

Fortna, Peter. *Cadotte Lake Métis: A Genealogical Narrative, 1850–2000*. Cochrane, AB: Willow Springs Strategic Solutions, 2021.

Foster, Janet. *Working for Wildlife: The Beginning of Preservation in Canada*. Toronto: UofT Press, 1978.

Fouillard, Camille, Mushuau Innu Band Council, and Naskapi Montagnais Innu Association. *Gathering Voices: Finding Strength to Help our Children*. Vancouver: Douglas and McIntyre, 1995.

Fumoleau, René. *As Long as this Land Shall Last: A History of Treaty 8 and Treaty 11, 1870–1939*. Calgary: University of Calgary Press, 2004.

Gaudry, Adam. "Researching the Resurgence: Insurgent Research and Community-Engaged Methodologies." In *Research as Resistance: Revisiting Critical, Indigenous, and Anti-Oppressive Approaches*, edited by Leslie Brown and Susan Strega, 243–265. 2nd edition. Toronto: Women's Press–Canadian Scholars Press, 2015.

Government of Canada. *Treaty No. 8. Made June 21, 1899 and Adhesions, Reports, Etc.* [1899]. Reprinted from file, the 1899 edition by Roger Duhamel, F.R.S.C. Ottawa: Queen's Printer and Controller of Stationary, 1966. https://www.rcaanc-cirnac.gc.ca/eng/1100100028813/1581293624572#chp4.

Graham, Maxwell. *Canada's Wild Buffalo: Observations in the Wood Buffalo Park, 1922*. Department of the Interior, Northwest Territories and Yukon Branch. Ottawa: F.A. Acland, 1923. https://babel.hathitrust.org/cgi/pt?id=mdp.39015006571528&view=1up&seq=1.

Greer, Alan. "Settler Colonialism and Beyond." *Journal of the Canadian Historical Association* 40, no. 1 (2019): 61–86.

Guha, Ramachandra. "The Authoritarian Biologist and the Arrogance of Anti-Humanism: Wildlife Conservation in the Third World." *The Ecologist* 27, no. 1 (January/February 1997): 14–20.

Hillman, Serena, Azadeh Forghani, Carolyn Pang and Carman Neustaedter. "Conducting Interviews with Remote Participants." In *Studying and Designing Technology for Domestic Life*, edited by Tejinder K. Judge and Carman Neustaedter, 11–32. Waltham, MA: Morgan Kaufman, Elsevier, 2015.

Himmerflab, David. "Moving People, Moving Boundaries: The Socio-economic Effects of Protectionist Conservation, Involuntary Resettlement and Tenure Insecurity on the Edge of Mt. Elgon National Park, Uganda." *World Agroforestry*, 2006. http://apps.worldagroforestry.org/programmes/african-highlands/pdfs/wps/ahiwp_24.pdf.

Huseman, Jennifer and Damien Short, "'A slow industrial genocide': tar sands and the indigenous peoples of northern Alberta." *International Journal of Human Rights* 16, no. 1 (2012): 216–237.

Johnston, Jason, W. and Courtney W. Mason. "The Paths to Realizing Reconciliation: Indigenous Consultation in Jasper National Park." *The International Indigenous Policy Journal* 11, no. 4 (2020): 1–27.

Joly, Tara. "Growing (with) Muskeg: Oil Sands Reclamation and Healing in Northern Alberta." *Anthropologica* 63, no. 1 (2021): 1–26.

———. "'Urban Buffalo': Human-Bison Relations in Northeastern Alberta. In *Extracting Home in the Oil Sands*, edited by Clinton Westman, Tara Joly, and Lena Gross, 139–159.

Justice, Daniel Heath. *Why Indigenous Literatures Matter.* Waterloo-Kitchener: Wilfrid Laurier University Press, 2018.

Keeling, Ann and John Sandlos, eds. *Mining and Communities in Northern Canada: History, Politics, and Memory.* Calgary: University of Calgary Press, 2015.

Keeling, Ann and John Sandlos. "Introduction: The Complex Legacy of Mining in Northern Canada" In *Mining and Communities in Northern Canada: History, Politics, and Memory*, edited by Ann Keeling and John Sandlos, 1–32. Calgary: University of Calgary Press, 2015.

Keller, Robert H. and Michael F. Turek. *American Indians and National Parks.* Tucson, AZ: University of Arizona Press, 1998.

Knickerbocker, Madeline Rose. "Making Matriarchs at Coqualeetza: Stó:lō Women's Politics and Histories across Generations." In *In Good Relation*, edited by Sarah Nickel and Amanda Fehr, 25–47.

Kovach, Margaret. *Indigenous Methodologies: Characteristics, Conversations and Contexts.* Toronto: University of Toronto Press, 2009.

Kwagu'ł Gix̱sa̱m Clan and Leslie Robertson. *Standing Up with G̱a'ax̱sta'las: Jane Constance Cook and the Politics of Memory, Church and Custom.* Vancouver: UBC Press, 2012.

Laforet, Andrea and Annie York. *Spuzzum: Fraser Canyon Histories, 1808–1939.* Vancouver: UBC Press, 1998.

Lewis, Henry T. "Maskuta: The Ecology of Indian Fires in Northern Alberta." *Western Canadian Journal of Anthropology* 7, 1 (1977): 15–52.

———. *Time for Burning: Traditional Indian Uses of Fire in Western Canadian Boreal Forest.* Edmonton: Boreal Institute for Northern Studies Occasional Publication no. 17 (1982).

Linabery, Jasmine R. and Stephanie A. Hamel. "Feminist Online Interviewing: Engaging Issues of Power, Resistance and Reflexivity in Practice." *Feminist Review* 115, no. 1 (2017): 97–113.

Longley, Hereward. "Uncertain Sovereignty: Treaty 8, Bitumen and Land Claims in the Athabasca Oil Sands Region." In *Extracting Home in the Oil Sands*, edited by Clinton Westman, Tara Joly, and Lena Gross, 23–47.

Loo, Tina. *States of Nature: Conserving Canada's Wildlife in the Twentieth Century.* Vancouver: UBC Press, 2006.

Lothian, William F. *A History of Canada's National Parks*, vol. 4. Ottawa: Parks Canada, 1981.

Mackenzie, John M. *The Empire of Nature: Hunting, Conservation and British Imperialism*. Manchester: Manchester University Press, 1988.

MacLaren, I.S., ed. *Culturing Wilderness in Jasper National Park: Studies in Two Centuries of Human History in the Upper Athabasca River Watershed*. Edmonton: University of Alberta Press, 2007.

MacLaren, I.S. "Introduction." In *Culturing Wilderness in Jasper National Park: Studies in Two Centuries of Human History in the Upper Athabasca River Watershed*, edited by I.S. MacLaren, xv–xliii.

Mason, Courtney. *Spirit of the Rockies: Reasserting an Indigenous Presence in Banff National Park*. Toronto: University of Toronto Press, 2014.

McCormack, Patricia. "Chipewyans Turn Cree: Governmental and Structural Factors in Ethnic Processes." In *For Purposes of Dominion: Essays in Honour of Morris Zaslow*, edited by K.S. Coates and W. R. Morrison, 125–138. North York, On.: Captus University Publications, 1989.

———. *Fort Chipewyan and the Shaping of Canadian History, 1788–1920s: "We like to be free in this country."* Vancouver: UBC Press, 2010.

———. "How the (North) West Was Won: Development and Underdevelopment in the Fort Chipewyan Region." Unpublished PhD diss., University of Alberta, 1984. https://era.library.ualberta.ca/items/e6fd4f8a-4c6d-4170-be46-8095429eca3b/view/6c34ae8d-d138-4daa-8856-7868184d60b3/NK67394.pdf.

———. "The Political Economy of Bison Management in Wood Buffalo National Park." *Arctic* 45, no. 4 (December 1992): 367–380.

———. *Research Report: An Ethnohistory of the Athabasca Chipewyan First Nation* (2 September 2012) .https://ceaa-acee.gc.ca/050/documents_staticpost/59540/82080/Appendix_D_-_Part_03.pdf.

———. "Studying the Social and Cultural Impacts of 'Extreme Extraction' in Northern Alberta." In *Extracting Home in the Oil Sand*, edited by Clinton Westman, Tara Joly, and Lena Gross, 180–198.

Meighen, Arthur. "Address of Welcome." In Commission of Conservation of Canada. *Proceedings of the National Conference on Conservation of Game, Fur-Bearing Animals and Other Wild Life*, 18–19 February 1919. Ottawa: King's Printer, 1919. https://www.canadiana.ca/view/oocihm.82935/16?r=0&s=1.

Merasty, Joseph Auguste, with David Carpenter. *The Education of Augie Merasty: A Residential School Memoir*. Regina: University of Regina Press, 2015.

Miller, J.R. *Shingwauk's Vision: A History of Native Residential Schools*. Toronto: UofT Press, 1996.

Milloy, J.S. *A National Crime: The Canadian Government and the Residential School System, 1879–1986*. Winnipeg: University of Manitoba Press, 1990.

Nakoochee, Roberta. "Reconnection with Asi Kéyi: Healing Broken Connections' Implications for Ecological Integrity in Canadian National Parks." MA Thesis. Guelph: University of Guelph, 2018. http://hdl.handle.net/10214/14187.

Neufeld, David. "Kluane National Park Reserve: 1923–1974: Modernity and Pluralism." In *A Century of Parks in Canada, 1911–2011*, edited by Claire Elizabeth Campbell, 235–272.

Neumann, Roderick P. *Imposing Wilderness: Struggles over Livelihood and Nature Preservation in Africa*. Berkeley: University of California Press, 1998.

Nickel, Sarah and Amanda Fehr, eds. *In Good Relation: History, Gender, and Kinship in Indigenous Feminisms*. Winnipeg: University of Manitoba Press, 2020.

Notzke, Claudia. *Aboriginal Peoples and Natural Resources in Canada*. Concord, ON: Captus University Press, 1994.

Paul, Elsie. In collaboration with Paige Raibmon and Harmony Johnson. *Written as I Remember It: Teachings (ʔems taʔaw) From the Life of a Sliammon Elder*. Vancouver: University of British Columbia Press, 2014.

Peterson, Laura. "Exploring the Egg Lake/ ?Eghés tu Landscape and the Lake One Trail: A Collaboration with Knowledge Holders in Wood Buffalo National Park." Unpublished MA thesis, University of Alberta, 2018. https://doi.org/10.7939/R3NZ81611.

Piper, Liza. *The Industrial Transformation of Subarctic Canada*. Vancouver: UBC Press, 2010.

Poirier, Robert. and David Ostergren. "Evicting People from Nature: Indigenous Land Rights and National Parks in Australia, Russia, and the United States." *Natural Resources Journal* 42, no. 2 (Spring 2002): 331–351.

Potyandi, Barry. *Wood Buffalo National Park: An Historical Overview and Source Study*. Parks Canada: Manuscript 345, 1979.

Price, Richard, ed. *The Spirit of the Alberta Treaties*. Edmonton: Pica Pica Press, 1987.

Qwul'sih'yah'maht (Robina Anne Thomas). "Honouring the Oral Traditions of the Ta't Mustimuxw (Ancestors)." In *Research as Resistance: Revisiting Critical, Indigenous, and Anti-Oppressive Approaches*, edited by Leslie Brown and Susan Strega, 177–198. 2nd edition. Toronto: Women's Press–Canadian Scholars Press, 2015.

Ramutsindela, Maano. "National Parks and (Neo)Colonialisms." In *The Cambridge Handbook of Environmental Sociology*, edited by Katharine Legun, Julie C. Keller, Michael Carolan and Michael M. Bell, 206–222. Vol. 1. Cambridge: Cambridge University Press: 2020.

Ridington, Robin and Jillian Ridington in Collaboration with Elders of the Dane-Zaa First Nations. *Where Happiness Dwells: A History of the Dane-Zaa First Nations*. Vancouver: UBC Press, 2013.

Robinson, Harry and Wendy Wickwire. *Write it on your Heart*. Vancouver: Talonbooks, 1992.

Rudin, Ronald. *Kouchibouguac: Removal, Resistance and Remembrance at a Canadian National Park*. Toronto: University of Toronto Press, 2016.

Sandlos, John. *Hunters at the Margin: Native People and Wildlife Conservation in the Northwest Territories.* Vancouver: UBC Press, 2007.

———. "Landscaping Desire: Poetics, Politics in the Early Biological Surveys of the Canadian North." *Space and Culture* 6, no. 4 (November 2003): 395–414.

———. "Not Wanted at the Boundary: The Expulsion of the Keeseekoowenin Ojibway Band from Riding Mountain National Park." *Canadian Historical Review* 89, no. 2 (June 2008): 189–221.

Scottie, Joan, Warren Bernauer, and Jack Hicks. *I Will Live for Both of Us: A History of Colonialism, Uranium Mining, and Inuit Resistance.* Winnipeg: University of Manitoba Press, 2022.

Seeland, Klaus. "National Park Policy and Wildlife Problems in Nepal and Bhutan." *Population and Environment* 22, no. 1 (September 2000): 43–62.

Sellars, B. *They Called Me Number One: Secrets and Survival at an Indian Residential School.* Vancouver: Talonbooks, 2013.

Smith, Keith Douglas. *Liberalism, Surveillance, and Resistance: Indigenous Communities in Western Canada, 1877–1927.* Edmonton: Athabasca University Press, 2009.

Smith, Linda Tuhiwai. *Decolonizing Methodologies: Research and Indigenous Peoples.* 2nd editions. London: Zed Books, 2012.

Smith, Linda Tuhiwai, Eve Tuck and K.W. Yang, eds. *Indigenous and Decolonizing Studies in Education: Mapping the Long View.* New York: Routledge, 2019.

Spence, Mark. *Dispossessing the Wilderness: Indigenous Removal and the Making of National Parks.* Oxford: Oxford University Press, 1999.

Todd, Zoe. "Foreword." In *Extracting Home in the Oil Sands*, edited by Clinton Westman, Tara Joly, and Lena Gross, viii–xiii.

Treaty 7 Elders and Tribal Council, with Walter Hildebrandt, Sarah Carter and Dorothy First Rider. *The True Spirit and Original Intent of Treaty 7.* Montreal and Kingston: McGill-Queens University Press, 1996.

Truth and Reconciliation Commission of Canada. *Honouring Truth, Reconciling for the Future: Summary of the Final Report of the Truth and Reconciliation Commission of Canada.* Ottawa, 2015.

UNESCO World Heritage Convention. Decision 39 COM 7B.18. Wood Buffalo National Park (Canada) (N256). 2015. https://whc.unesco.org/en/decisions/6275.

UNESCO World Heritage Centre and IUCN. 41 Com. Mission Report Wood Buffalo National Park (Canada) (N 256). *Report of the joint WHC/IUCN Reactive Monitoring mission to Wood Buffalo National Park, Canada, 24 September–4 October 2016.* Krakow, Poland: Convention Concerning the Protection of the World Cultural and Natural Heritage. Forty-first session. 2-12 July, 2017. https://whc.unesco.org/en/list/256/documents/.

UNESCO World Heritage Convention. Decision 44 COM 7B.190. Wood Buffalo National Park (Canada) (N256). 2021. https://whc.unesco.org/en/decisions/7906.

United Nations Educational, Scientific and Cultural Organization (UNESCO) World Heritage Convention. World Heritage Nomination: International Union for Conservation of Nature and Natural Resources (IUCN) Technical Review. 256 Wood Buffalo National Park. Nominated by the Government of Canada. 15 April 1983. https://whc.unesco.org/en/list/256/documents/.

Valadares, Desiree. "Dispossessing the Wilderness: Contesting Canada's National Park Narrative." In *Cultural Contestation: Heritage, Identity and the Role of Government*, edited by Rodenberg, J. and Pieter Wagenaar, 139–153. London: Springer International Publications, 2018.

Waiser, Bill. "'A Case of a Special Privilege and a Fancied Right': The Shack Tent Controversy in Prince Albert." In *A Century of Parks in Canada, 1911-2011*, edited by Claire Elizabeth Campbell, 103–132.

Webstad, Phyllis. *Beyond the Orange Shirt Story: A collection of stories from family and friends of Phyllis Webstad before, during, and after their Residential School experiences*. Unceded Sc'ianew, Lekwungen, and T'Sou-ke territory: Medicine Wheel Publishing, 2020.

Westman, Clinton, Tara Joly and Lena Gross. Eds. *Extracting Home in the Oil Sands: Settler Colonialism and Environmental Change in Subarctic Canada*. London and New York: Routledge, 2020.

Westman, Clinton, Tara Joly, and Lena Gross. "Introduction: At Home in the Oil Sands." In *Extracting Home in the Oil Sands*, edited by Clinton Westman, Tara Joly, and Lena Gross, 1–22.

Wheeler, Winona "Narrative Wisps of the Ochekiwi Sipi Past: A Journey in Recovering Collective Memories." In *The Canadian Oral History Reader,* edited by Llewellyn, K., Alexander Freund and Nolan Reilly, 285–296. Montreal/Toronto: McGill-Queen's University Press, 2015.

Wickwire, Wendy. "To See Ourselves as the Other's Other: Nlaka'pamux Contact Narratives." *Canadian Historical Review* 75, no. 1 (March 1994): 1–20.

Wildcat, Matthew. "Fearing social and cultural death: genocide and elimination in settler colonial Canada—an Indigenous perspective." *Journal of Genocide Research* 17, no. 4 (2015): 391–409.

Wilson, Shawn. *Research is Ceremony: Indigenous Research Methods*. Halifax: Fernwood Publishing, 2008.

Wolfe, Patrick. "Settler colonialism and the elimination of the native." *Journal of Genocide Research* 8, no. 4 (2006): 387–409.

Woolford, Andrew and Jeff Benvenuto. "Canada and colonial genocide." *Journal of Genocide Research* 17, no. 4 (2015): 373–390.

Youdelis, Megan. "'They Could Take You out for Coffee and Call it Consultation!': The Colonial Antipolitics of Indigenous Consultation in Jasper National Park." *Environment and Planning: Economy and Space* 48, no. 7 (2016): 1374–92.

Youdelis, Megan, Roberta Nakoochee, Colin O'Neil, Elizabeth Lunstrum, and Robin Roth. "'Wilderness' revisited: Is Canadian park management moving beyond the 'wilderness' ethic?" *The Canadian Geographer* (2019): 1–18.

Younging, Gregory. *Elements of Indigenous Style: A Guide for Writing by and about Indigenous Peoples*. Edmonton: Brush Education, 2018.

Index

1935 Order-in-Council, 25, 186–190, 194–97, 214–15, 239, 263
1944 membership transfer, 1, 8, 31, 39, 43–45, 49, 60, 116, 159, 209–11, 212-13, 217–18, 224–25, 254, 262, 267n12
 See also Chapter 4
27th Baseline, 83, 103, 125, 148, 187, 188, 194–97

A

ACFN Chief and Council, xii-xiii, 77, 248, 254–56
ACFN Elders Declaration of Rights to Land Use, xxi-xxii, 19–21, 68–69
ACFN Elders Council, xii, 248, 256
Adam, Allan, xi, xiii, xv–xvii, 2, 32-34, 113, 130, 132–34, 202, 214–15, 244, 245, 257
Adam, Cecilia, xiii, 67, 256
Adam, Horace, xxiii, 92, 113, 129, 140, 216, 259
Alberta Energy Regulator (AER), 287n34
Alberta oil sands. *See* resource extraction
Allen, D.J., 262, 264
assimilation, 14, 81, 223-24
 and national parks in Canada, 10–14
 See also residential schools
Athabasca River, 2–3, 4–5, 38–39, 45, 54, 58, 60, 67, 83, 103, 124–25, 135, 187, 216, 232, 261

B

Banff National Park, 9, 10, 13, 14–15, 94, 98, 111, 212–13
Big Point, 129, 133, 230
Bill C-31, 138, 281n9
Birch Mountains, 4, 5, 38, 45, 64, 120, 206
Birch River, 3, 38–39, 56, 64–65, 67, 83, 120, 141, 232, 261
Dene settlements at, xv, xix, 5, 15, 31, 39, 43, 47–48, 49–50, 54, 60–62, 107, 115, 127–29, 132, 134, 135, 136–37, 140, 140–42, 149, 155, 156, 169, 182–83, 194, 203, 206, 208, 212, 214, 216, 219–20, 222-23, 265n1
Boucher, Louis, 67–68, 113–14, 161
brucellosis, 101, 151, 166, 242
Bruno, Alec, xi, xv–xvi, xxiii, 30–31, 51–53, 73, 89, 111–12, 114–15, 132–34, 134–35, 161, 216, 248
Bruno, Francois, xxiv, 73
Bruno, Rene, xxiv, 25, 48, 51, 53, 68–69, 73–77, 162, 256

C

Canadian Parks and Wilderness Society (CPAWS), 2–3
Caribou Mountains, 4, 39, 45, 64–65, 92, 273n4
co-management (in national parks), 8–9, 33, 236–42, 244, 291n15
Committee for Cooperative Management [of WBNP] (CMC), 123–24, 237, 238–39
community steering committee, xi-xii, 25, 28
 See also Appendix 1
competition with white trappers, 106, 145, 151–54, 180, 185–88, 195–97, 204–5, 208
conservation (as justification for parks), 10, 12–13, 16, 97, 107, 121, 146–47, 174
 For conservation regulations in the Park, *see* Chapter 5
Conservation through Reconciliation Partnership (CRP), 241

303

controlled bison slaughter
  commercial, 122, 150, 170
  rations program, 118–19, 122, 149-50, 155, 166, 280n87
controlled burning practices, 42, 147, 151
Cory, W.W., 99, 103
Cumming, Austin L., 108–9, 180–81
cumulative impacts, 47, 102–3, 107, 108–9, 148, 158–59, 182–84, 262, 264

D

Dempsey, M.J., 47, 102–103, 107, 108-109, 148, 158–59, 182–84, 262, 264
Dene language, xiii, xix, 5, 23, 27, 38, 51, 53, 54–55, 190, 202, 203, 209–10, 211, 225, 228, 229–30, 254-55, 257, 266n2
Deranger, Fredoline Djeskelni, xxv, 47, 54, 77, 115
Deranger, Jim, xiii, xxv, 1–2, 4, 23–24, 24–25, 37, 40, 54–55, 68, 78, 98–99, 110, 115–17, 163–64, 216–17, 256
Deranger, Kristi, xiii, 256
Dominion Parks Act, 97–98

E

Egg Lake, 45
Eklund, R.I., 98
elimination, 2–3, 8–9, 10–13, 16, 17–22, 27, 31–33, 34, 72, 90–91, 93, 99, 146, 150–51, 159–60, 190–91, 201–206, 207–8, 211, 237, 249
Elk Island National Park, 98, 176
Embarras River, 39, 62, 83
epidemics, xv, 32, 48–49, 202, 222
  influenza, 22, 132, 202–4, 220, 231
  smallpox, 22, 132, 202–4
establishment of the Park, 1922, 1–4, 5–6, 9, 17, 30–31, 89–99, 123–24, 124–25
expansion of the Park, 1926, 2, 6–8, 30–31, 45, 83, 89, 91–92, 99–104, 105–6, 111–12, 113–26, 141, 150, 261, 263, 265n1
extreme extraction. *See* resource extraction

F

Finnie, O.S., 11, 92, 98, 99, 103–4, 106, 159, 182, 261
fisheries in the Park, 43, 149, 280n87
  McGinnis Fisheries, 195
Flett, Dora, xiii, xxv, 5–6, 45, 55–56, 112, 117, 217, 256

Flett (Piche), Eliza Marie, xxv, xxvii, 117, 140, 193, 219, 280n85
Flett, Elizabeth, xxvi, 43–45, 130, 138–39, 281n9
Flett, Garry, xiii, xxvi, 130, 138–39, 156, 164–65, 217–18, 256, 281n9
Flett, John, xxvii, 218–19
Flett, Leonard, xiii, xxvii, 117, 140, 192–93, 219, 256
Flett, Scott, xxvii, 39–40, 41, 56–57, 118, 140–41, 155, 165–66, 219–20, 259
Fort Chipewyan, xiii, xv, xix, 4, 17, 29, 30, 41, 43, 45, 56, 59, 64, 67–70, 77, 79–80, 86, 108, 140, 149–50, 174, 175, 181–82, 183, 184, 190, 196, 203, 204, 227–28, 232, 256, 265n2
Fort Fitzgerald, 62, 174, 230
Fort McMurray, 16, 19–22, 43, 45, 59, 63, 76, 187, 220, 229, 232, 275n10, 290n8
Fort Smith, 64–65, 164, 174, 200, 232, 238
Fraser, Fred (Jumbo), xxxvii–xxviii, 141, 166–67, 220, 259
Fung, Brian, xii, 248

G

genocide, 10-11, 18, 203–4, 208, 288n5
Gibot, Felix, 78–79, 118–119, 280n87
Gibson, R.A., 147–148
Graham, Maxwell, 6, 90–91, 92–95, 97–99, 235, 261
gravesites (in and near the Park), 5, 47–48, 50, 54–55, 56–57, 134–35, 203, 216, 222, 231
Grew, J.L., 152, 204, 262, 264
Group trapping areas (1949), 152, 217
Gull River, 3, 38–39, 45, 56, 57, 67, 83, 141, 232, 261

H

Harkin, James, 2, 6, 90–95, 96, 97, 99, 261
Head, P.W., 148, 153
History of Wood Buffalo National Park's Relations with the Dënesųłıné (the original report commissioned by ACFN), xi, 3–4, 250–251, 266n5
  See also Appendix 1
Hoffman, Lorraine, xiii, 256
Holden, Josh, xiii, 256
Holy Angels Residential School, xix, xxiv, xxvi, xxviii, xxxi, 63, 202, 203–204, 217, 265n2

homelands (of ACFN), xvi, xxi–xxii, 4–8, 18–22, 28–29, 206–10, 266n2, 266–267n8
Dene relations to, 28–29
See also Chapter 1
House Lake. *See* Birch River settlement
Hudson's Bay Company, 17, 41, 43, 59, 93, 172–173, 174, 204

I

IISAAK OLAM Foundation, 241
Imperial Oil tailings ponds leak (2022 & 2023), 190, 257, 287–88n34
Indian Affairs, 10–11, 14, 15, 30, 91, 93–95, 97–98, 99, 104, 110–11, 129–30, 137–38, 144, 149–50, 153–54, 172, 179, 186–87, 203, 219, 252
Indigenous consultation, xxi, 8–9, 30–31, 103–4, 110–12, 114, 121, 122, 129, 133–34, 143–44, 186, 291n15
Indigenous Leadership Initiative (ILI), 241
Indigenous Protected and Conserved Areas (IPCAs), 241, 290n12, 290n13
Indigenous sovereignty, 16, 17–18, 22, 49–50, 145–46, 150–51, 153–54, 179–84, 207–8, 212–13, 245
intergenerational impacts, xi, 3, 9, 20–22, 26, 27, 32–33, 89, 248, 254–55
See also Chapter 7
IR201 (ACFN reserves), 184–86, 186–87, 194–96, 214, 219, 288n35

J

Jackfish, 39, 57, 58, 61–62, 63, 64, 129, 133, 135, 140, 186–87, 219, 220–21, 227, 231, 233, 265n3
Jasper National Park, 9, 10, 12–13, 14, 15, 94–95, 98, 110–111

K

Keeseekoowenin Ojibway Nation, 12–13, 14–15, 208
Kitaskino Nuwënë Provincial Park, 280–81n88
Kitto, F.H., 92–93, 95–96, 99
Kluane Game Sanctuary/Kluane National Park, 12–13, 15, 146, 155–56

L

Ladouceur, Ray, 45, 57, 104, 119–20, 129, 141–42
Lake Athabasca, 5, 29, 54, 56, 68, 78, 115, 135, 141, 274–75n30
Lake Claire, 6, 38–40, 43, 45, 47–48, 56, 62, 64–65, 101, 118, 134, 136, 140–41, 149, 162, 232–33, 263
See also Birch River settlement
Lake Dene, 5, 45, 47, 54, 206
Lake Mamawi, 5, 38, 39, 45, 46, 64, 136, 206, 232
Laviolette, Alexandre, xxi, 25, 68, 73–74, 83, 84, 184–86, 194–95, 202, 215, 230, 239
Laviolette, Jonas, 71, 74, 107, 151, 167, 179–181, 184, 187, 194–97, 262, 263
Laviolette, Leslie, xxviii, 42, 47, 57, 120, 167, 206, 220–22
Lower Athabasca Regional Plan (LARP), xxii, 290n9

M

Marcel, Angela, xiii, 253
Marcel, Benjamin, 147, 194–195
Marcel, Big John, xxviii, 40, 58, 120, 142, 222
Marcel, Frank, xxviii, 120, 127
Marcel, John H., xxix, 194
Marcel, Margaret and Daniel, 79–80
Marcel, Pat, xi–xii, xxix, 25, 42, 71, 151, 167–68, 186–88, 194–97, 212, 239–41, 244, 247–48
McCall, F.A., 108, 155
McDougal, J.A., 99, 103, 154, 159, 264
medicines, 40–42, 59–60, 61–62, 229
Melling, John, 107–8, 110, 153, 262
Mercredi Shortman, Donna, xxxi, 3, 131, 143, 246
Mercredi, Charlie, xxix, 51–53, 142, 212, 222–223
Mercredi, Hazel, xiii, 256
Mercredi, Julie, xiii, 256
Mercredi, Marie Josephine, xxix, 49, 58–59, 80
Mercredi, Pierre, 69–71, 82
Mercredi, Victor, 84, 204
Mercredi, Victorine, xxx, 30, 59, 72, 80–81
Migratory Birds Convention Act 1916, 146, 175–76

Mikisew Cree First Nation (MCFN), 5–6, 39, 43, 68, 78, 106, 113, 114–17, 169, 212, 215, 217–18, 238, 242, 266n7
For the band membership transfer to MCFN, *see* 1944 membership transfer
Mission. *See* Holy Angels Residential School
Moose Island, 5, 45, 47–48, 63, 206

N

N22, xxvii, 195, 285n61
Northern Buffalo Management Board (1991), 236–37
northern fur trade, 17, 43, 49, 56, 62–63, 204, 205–206

O

Old Fort, 45, 57, 62, 79–80, 129, 133, 135, 142, 186, 197, 204, 221
one-hundredth anniversary of the WBNP, 2, 253
oral history (theory and importance), 2–4, 22–27, 28–33, 34–35, 245–46, 252–56, 271–72n75
oral promise to return the Park lands to Indigenous communities, 1, 28, 29–30, 89, 103, 111–12, 114–15, 115–19, 122–24, 125–26
Outstanding Universal Value. *See* UNESCO World Heritage Designation

P

Paul, Keltie, xiii, xxxii, 41, 59–60, 120–22, 168, 209, 223–24, 256
Peace Point settlement, 5, 38–39, 43–50, 64–65, 88, 97, 113–14, 127–28, 136, 138, 159, 173–74, 193, 206
Peace River, 3, 4–5, 6, 8, 38–39, 43–46, 57, 59, 63, 67, 83, 91, 93, 101–104, 105–6, 113–14, 120, 124, 125, 141–42, 205, 216, 226, 232, 289n31
Peace-Athabasca Delta, xix, 4–5, 22, 33–34, 38–39, 41, 50, 54, 56, 90–91, 95, 106, 124, 125–26, 135–36, 152–53, 162, 179, 186, 188, 195, 201–2, 205–6, 207–8, 211, 214, 219–20, 225–27, 231–32, 242, 282n10
permitting system (in the Park), 6–8, 15–16, 22, 31, 32, 63, 89, 91, 104–10, 112, 127–28, 132, 145, 147–49, 151, 153, 155, 159, 172–73, 173–75, 177, 180, 180–84, 188, 206–8, 210–11, 212–13, 262

Piche-Bruno, Helene, xi, xv–xvii, xxiv, 34–35, 130, 132–35, 214, 281n8
Piche, Ester, xi, xix, xxx, 40, 60-62, 134, 135–36, 194, 225
Piche, Johnny, 23–24
Point Brulé, 129, 221
Poplar Point, 62, 108, 117, 129–30, 135, 221, 240
preservation (as justification for parks), 10, 11–12, 16, 71–72, 89–91, 92–97, 121, 145

Q

Quatre Fourches, 48, 54, 155, 169

R

Ratfat, Ernie (Joe), xxx, 110, 122, 136–37, 169, 203, 210, 224–25
reconciliation, xix, 33, 237–39, 241, 243–45
Registered Fur Management Areas (RFMAs) [1942], 128, 151–54, 188, 196–97, 204–5
Registered Trapping Areas [1949], 152–54
residential schools, 17, 49, 221, 223–24, 225, 227–28, 288n5
See also Holy Angels Residential School
resource extraction, xvi, 9–10, 17–22, 31–33, 48–49, 56–57, 79–80, 188–89, 201, 205–6, 227, 240–41, 242–43, 287–88n34
Riding Mountain National Park, 12–13, 208
Rigney, Alice, xi, xiii, xix, xxxi, 27, 29, 32, 39–42, 49, 50, 60–62, 71, 81, 122, 130, 135–36, 145–46, 155, 169–70, 205, 213, 225–27, 245, 256–57
Rocky Mountains Park. *See* Banff National Park
Ronald Lake Bison Herd, 120, 240, 280–81n88, 290n9
Ross, Rose, xii, 248, 257
Royal Canadian Mounted Police (RCMP), 8, 15, 80, 109–10, 154–56, 165–66, 171–72, 172–73, 176–77, 181–82

S

Simpson, Isidore, 43–45, 138–39, 159, 217–18
Simpson, Mary "Cookie", 39, 122–23, 137–38, 171, 227–28
Site C Dam, 205, 243
Slave River, 3, 4–5, 38–39, 45, 54–55, 67, 83, 92, 101, 216, 232
Southern Tutchone, 12–13, 15, 146, 155–56

starvation (resulting from Park exclusions), 8, 83, 91-92, 94-95, 128, 159, 186, 179-80, 207-8, 262, 264
Stevens, Lori-Ann, xxxi, 39, 62-63, 210-11, 228-31
Stewart, Jack, 8, 127-128, 149-50, 156-57, 262

T

Teck Resources, Ltd., 240, 290n8&n9
Telegdi, Jay, xii, 248, 253
Tourangeau, Beverly, xxxi, 123-24, 231-32
tourism (in parks), 10-14, 15, 97
traplines, 58, 59, 120, 128-29, 140, 141, 151-54, 162, 196, 204, 207, 217, 223-24, 225-27, 264
  See also Registered Fur Management Areas and Registered Trapping Areas
Treaty 7, 107, 271n75, 280n78
Treaty 8, xxi-xxii, 2, 5-8, 30, 16, 23-26, 30, 38-39, 48-49, 89, 94-95, 104, 110-11, 112, 114-15, 123-24, 145, 156, 157-59, 175, 180, 182, 184-86, 192-93, 194-97, 202-3, 206, 213, 247-48, 261, 267n12
  See also Chapter 2
Treaty and Aboriginal Rights Research (TARR), 23-25, 67-68, 103, 110-11, 115-17, 153-54, 164, 184-85, 256, 272n80
Trippe de Roche, Edouard, xiii, xxxii, 32, 41-42, 63, 110, 112, 120-22, 137-38, 149-50, 151, 172-73, 197, 232, 256
Tssessaze, Lisa, xii, 248, 255, 257
tuberculosis (in bison), 101, 151, 242

U

UNESCO World Heritage Designation, 5, 33-34, 188, 237-37, 242-45
Unorganized Territories Preservation Act 1894, 92
Uranium City, 62

V

Vermilion, Basil, 163-64
Vermillion, Magloire, 81-83, 147, 156, 163-64, 173-75
Villebrun, Olivia, xii, 248, 254

W

W.A.C. Bennett Dam, 22, 48-49, 201, 205-6, 225-27, 233
Wainwright buffalo herd, importation to WBNP, 1, 6-8, 91, 99-104, 156, 170, 181-82, 261
  See also Oral Histories in Chapter 3
wardens, xv-xvi, 8, 14-15, 31-32, 47, 82, 83, 93-94, 107-10, 154-60, 164-67, 168-169, 171, 173-75, 176-77, 178, 181-83, 197-200, 232, 264
WBNP Management Plan (1984), 236-37
WBNP Management Plan (2010), 237
Wiltzen, Leslie, xii-xiii, xxxii, 64, 83, 124-25, 127, 129, 143-44, 175-77, 232-33, 237-39, 243-44, 248, 256
wolf culling, 93, 150-51, 161-62, 167-68, 170, 283n29

www.ingramcontent.com/pod-product-compliance
Lightning Source LLC
Chambersburg PA
CBHW042223250426
43661CB00081BA/2893